IN 1492, COLUMBUS SAILED THE OCEAN BLUE

More Cool Ways to Remember Stuff

Also published and available as
Miss Pell Never Misspells

Written by Steve Martin

Illustrated by Martin Remphry
and Michael Garton

Edited by Jen Wainwright
Designed by Barbara Ward

IN 1492, COLUMBUS SAILED THE OCEAN BLUE

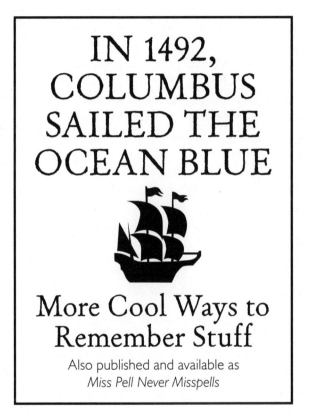

More Cool Ways to Remember Stuff

Also published and available as
Miss Pell Never Misspells

Library of Congress Cataloging-in-Publication data is available.

ISBN 978-0-545-56847-0

First published in Great Britain in 2012 by Buster Books, an imprint of Michael O'Mara Books Limited.

Also published and available as
Miss Pell Never Misspells

Text and illustrations copyright © Buster Books 2012

Cover design by Liz Herzog

All rights reserved.
Published by Scholastic Inc., 557 Broadway, New York, NY 10012, by arrangement with Buster Books.
SCHOLASTIC and associated logos are trademarks and/or registered trademarks of Scholastic Inc.

10 9 8 7 6 5 4 3 2 1   13 14 15 16 17
Printed in the U.S.A   23

First American edition, January 2013

CONTENTS

ALL ABOUT THIS BOOK

Do you sometimes sit in class wondering how the teachers expect you to remember all the information they're telling you? After all, there is just so much of it. You have to know math equations, stuff about yourself and other animals for science, and your geography teacher expects you to know all about everywhere!

Even when you are trying to relax at home, you're still being bombarded with information. Sports commentators will talk about the decathlon, expecting you to know which ten sports it includes. You may need to remember what currency you will need for your foreign vacation, or what you need to buy at the local store. Arrgh!

Well, the challenge of remembering all this information and much, much more is about to get easier, as you discover a whole range of tricks to help you remember anything at all.

This book will boost your brain power by showing you how to use *mnemonics* (pronounced ne – mon – ics), which is the fancy word for memory tricks. Here are some of the types of mnemonics you'll come across.

Rhymes

Inventing rhymes is a wonderful way of making learning and remembering both easy and fun. You can use them for anything – from learning the stages of the water cycle to the different army ranks, or from recalling the body's internal organs to how photosynthesis in plants works.

Acrostics

Acrostics are sentences that use
the first letter of each word to
help you remember information.
You might already know some
of these, such as "**ROY G. BIV**,"
which is used for the colors
of the rainbow (**R**ed, **O**range,
Yellow, **G**reen, **B**lue, **I**ndigo,
Violet). Later in this book, you
will come across more of these.
For example, you'll find out why
"**E**very **G**ood **B**oy **D**oes **F**ine."

Stories

Lists of information can be much easier to remember if they
are made into stories. Did you know that "George's Car
Trip" can help you learn the capital cities of South America?
All will become clear when you look at the section called "A
Capital Memory" on page 62.

Grouping

Grouping facts together tricks your brain into thinking it is
only learning one fact when it is really learning more. Use this
book to find out about the three **t**'s and how grouping will
help you remember those ten decathlon sports!

Linking

Many mnemonics link items together to help you to remember them. For example, you won't forget that an **oct**agon has eight sides if you link it to an **oct**opus, with its eight tentacles.

Pictures

You can either draw pictures or visualize them in your imagination to fix facts in your brain. You're unlikely to forget that the Spanish word for uncle is *tio* if you picture your uncle jumping out of his chair, yelling, "Oh!" after spilling a cup of tea on himself.

Acronyms

An acronym is a type of mnemonic that uses the letters of what you need to remember to make up words. For example, if you look at the Super Science section (pages 80–91), you will see how **COG** helps you to remember the three fossil fuels (**C**oal, **O**il, **G**as), or you can visit the Language Learner section (pages 10–35) to find out why **BAT SWAB** is such a useful acronym.

Wordplay

There are all sorts of plays on words you can use to remember things. You'll never struggle to spell *island* again once you know that an island **is land**.

The Memory Gym

This book will make it easy for you to remember hundreds of important facts. But there's no need to stop there. You can use the techniques to create your own mnemonics to remember absolutely anything you like. The Memory Gym section at the back of the book (pages 116–121) will help you to practice these techniques and build up your memory muscles.

Get ready to make your memory mighty!

LANGUAGE
LEARNER

HOW TO BE A SPELLING WIZ

Even though you try your best, there are probably certain words that trip you up when you try to write them down, and cause mistakes over and over again.

Don't panic! Use the memory tricks shown here, and your spelling will improve quicker than you can say—or spell—"Abracadabra!"

Acceptable

Acceptable can cause problems because you can't tell by the sound if it should end in –**able** or –**ible**. Remember the correct spelling by using the sentence:

I am **able** to **accept** that I can spell **acceptable**.

Arithmetic

With acrostics, the sillier the sentence, the more easily it will stick in your mind. Here's one to help you remember how to spell *arithmetic*. Remember:

A Robber **I**n **T**he **H**ouse **M**ight **E**at **T**he **I**ce **C**ream.

Believe

I do not bel**ie**ve your **lie**s.

Broccoli

My **BRO**ther **C**an't **C**hew **O**r **L**ick **I**t!

Calendar

People often forget that this word ends in **–ar**, not **–er**. Time for some visualization . . .

👁 *Imagine you are staring at a calendar, realizing that you have forgotten it is your mother's birthday, and screaming, "Aaaaar!"*

Now you'll never forget how to spell *calendar* . . . and hopefully you won't forget your mom's birthday, either!

Character

CHARlotte's **ACT**ing is t**ER**rible.

Forty

This play on words will help you to remember that the word *forty* drops the letter *u*:

> **U** may be four or fourteen, but not forty.

Friend

> I'll see my **friend** on **Fri**day, at the **end** of the week.

Gauge

People struggle to remember the order of the vowels in this little word.

> 👁 *Imagine walking into the cockpit of a plane and seeing someone messing with the instruments. You shout, "A U! (Hey, you!) Leave that **gauge** alone!"*

I Before E

> **I** before **E**, except after **C**,
> Or when it sounds like **A**,
> As in n**ei**ghbor and w**ei**gh.

So, you'll need *ie* in words such as *ach**ie**ve* but *ei* in words such as *dec**ei**ve, **cei**ling,* or *sl**ei**gh*.

Just to be tricky, there are some exceptions to this rule. These include words such as *spe**cie**s*. There's a *c* in *species*, but it is still spelled with an *ie*, because the *c* makes a *sh* sound. You will come across some other exceptions later.

Immediately

If you see a celebrity, call the **media** im**media**tely!

Island

This is easy to spell if you remember that an island **is land**.

Lose / Loose

The problem with the word *lose* is that it is easy to confuse with *loose*, which means untied. So, remember:

One of the **o**'s in l**oo**se is l**oo**se, so you might l**o**se it.

Mississippi

Mrs. **M** Mrs. **I** Mrs. **S S I** Mrs. **S S I** Mrs. **P P I**

Miniature

Miniature means really small. Spot the two really small words in the middle of it—*i* and *a*:

Min**ia**ture

Occur

The idea of crossing two seas (**c**'s) did not o**cc**ur to me.

Ocean

Old **C**amels **E**at **A**mazing **N**oodles.

Orangutan

To learn how to spell the word *orangutan* without any monkeying around, remember:

Be careful you don't turn **orang**e when **u tan**!

Pastime

Some words cause spelling problems because it's difficult to know if they have double letters or not. To remember that there are no double letters in this word, use the sentence:

Pa's time is spent on his **pastime**.

Questionnaire

His **question**s were **never aire**d.

Rehearsal

At the re**hearsal**, you'll **hear Sal**ly sing.

School

Students **C**an **H**ave **O**nly **O**ne **L**emon.

Subtle

If you want to **b** sub**t**le, you have to **b** silent!

16

Tomorrow

We might see **Tom or Row**ena **tomorrow.**

Tongue

Tiny **O**wls **N**est **G**rumpily **U**nder **E**lephants.

Weird

Weird does not follow the famous rule—*i* before **e**, except after **c**—so remember the spelling by the sentence:

We are so **we**ird!

Alternatively, just remember that the spelling of *weird* is weird because it doesn't obey the rule!

Withhold

It is really unusual to have a spelling with a double *hh* in the middle, which is why this spelling can look so strange. Use this sentence to help you remember it:

King **H**enry the **H**orrible wit**hh**olds his troops.

Yacht

Yellow **A**nts **C**an't **H**ave **T**oast.

SOUNDS THE SAME

Sometimes it's easy to get two or more words confused because, even though they are spelled differently, they sound the same. Words like this are called *homophones*. For example, if you had two pieces of a certain fruit, you might have a "pair of pears," but you would never have a "pear of pairs."

Confusing? Don't worry. Here are some memory tricks that will help you avoid any mix-ups.

Alter / Altar

To *alter* something means to change it, but an *altar* is found in a church. Remember:

A bride shouldn't be **tar**dy on her way to the al**tar**.

Beach / Beech

To tell these words apart, just remember:

You go to the b**ea**ch to swim in the **sea**,
but a b**ee**ch is a type of tr**ee**.

Berry / Bury

To sort out the difference between these two words, remember:

A be**r**ry is **r**ipe and **r**ed.
Sc**u**rvy pirates b**u**ry treasure!

Earn / Urn

People *earn* money by
working, while an *urn* is
another word for a vase:

He started **ear**ly to **ear**n
more money, so he could
afford that **u**gly **u**rn his
mother wanted.

Genes / Jeans

Your *genes* are the coding in your body. They cause you
to inherit certain character traits and make you who you are.
They influence things such as the color of your eyes or hair
and your height. Remember:

Generally, **gene**s make you look like your relatives.

The other spelling is used for denim pants:

Jeans are good for **j**umping around in.

Heal / Heel

A *heel* is part of a foot, while to *heal* something means
to make it well again. Use this sentence to remember
the difference:

I went to see **a** he**a**ler about my **two** he**e**ls.

Meet / Meat

Noticing the word hidden inside *meat* can help you make sure you don't confuse these two spellings:

I'll m**ee**t you in the restaurant, where you can **eat** some m**eat**.

Mousse / Moose

A *mousse* is a light, foamy substance. Remember:

Chocolate mou**ss**e is **s**uper **s**weet.

However, a *moose* is a large animal with antlers.

*Imagine a m**oose** on the l**oose** from a z**oo**.*

Piece / Peace

A *piece* of something is a part of it. So remember the sentence:

I'd love a **pie**ce of **pie**.

Peace means the opposite of war. This sentence will help you to remember the spelling of this word:

Please **E**nd **A**ll **C**onflict for **E**ver.

Prey / Pray

A **pre**dator eats **pre**y.
I **may** pray for a fine **day**.

Rap / Wrap

Rap means to beat or knock on something. With a silent *w* in front, it means to wrap something up. Use the following sentence to help you remember the difference:

The **rap**id **rap**ping at the door interrupted him as he **wrap**ped the **w**onderful present.

21

Reign / Rain

To *reign* means to be on the throne as a king or queen. The *rain* is the wet stuff that falls from the sky. Remember:

King Henry the **Eig**hth re**ig**ned for thirty-**eig**ht years.
But even for the king, getting wet in the r**ain** is a real p**ain**!

Stair / Stare

Even when he climbs into the **air** on the st**air**s,
you **are** not supposed to st**are** at him.

There / Their / They're

There is used for describing a place, as in "over there." You can remember this by noticing the word *here* hidden inside the word *there*:

Look **here** and t**here**.

Their means it belongs to them. An *heir* is somebody who inherits property or money. So, remember:

She will inherit t**heir** money because she is the **heir**.

Notice that *their* is another pesky word that doesn't follow the *i* before *e* rule (see page 13).

They're is short for "they are." The apostrophe is used to show that there are letters missing. In this word, the *a* is missing:

They're learning about apostrophes.

Too / Two / To

Too is used when we are talking about "too much" or "too many" of something. Its other meaning is when it is used to mean *also*.

$100 is t**oo** much money. $200 is t**oo** much money, t**oo**.

Two is the number 2.

👁 *Imagine **two** owls sitting in a tree.*

For other uses of the word, use *to*.

Wail / Whale

To *wail* means to cry or scream loudly. A *whale* is a huge mammal that swims in the ocean. Remember:

A w**h**ale has an *h* because it is **h**uge,
and if you heard a whale's **wail** it would be
Watery **A**nd **I**ncredibly **L**oud!

Week / Weak

I go to the gym **two e**venings a wee**k**,
but my **a**rms are still weak.

23

Which / Witch

Spelled with a *t*, a witch is someone who uses magic.

👁 *Imagine an old witch in a pointy black hat sitting by her cauldron drinking a nice cup of tea (***t***).*

In all other cases, use the spelling *which*.

Your / You're

Your shows possession, as does *our*.

That is y**our** house and this is **our** house.

You're is short for "you are."

You're using an apostrophe in this sentence.

THE GRAMMAR ZONE

Getting your grammar perfect will help you make sure that you're writing and speaking clearly and properly. Use these memory tricks to help you get a grip on some of English grammar's trickier parts.

 Nouns, Verbs, Adjectives, and Adverbs

Nouns, verbs, adjectives, and *adverbs* are all very important when speaking and writing, but what exactly are they? Use the following memory tricks to help you remember them:

A **n**oun is a **n**aming word,
like *ball* and *bag* and *bat* and *bird.*

Verbs are commonly called "doing words":

Vanishing, **E**ating, **R**unning, and **B**urping
are all examples of **VERB**s!

An adjective is a word that describes a noun. If you think something is *pretty, stinky, old,* or *scary,* you're using an adjective every time. Remember:

An **ad**jective **ad**ds description to something.

Adverbs are like adjectives, but they describe verbs. So, if you talk about someone vanishing *mysteriously,* eating *messily,* running *quickly,* or burping *loudly,* you're using adverbs.

An **adverb ad**ds description to a **verb**.

Sentences

Every sentence you say or write is built using different parts.

A sentence can be made of one word or many words, but it must make sense by itself.

It has to have a verb—a doing word—and most sentences also have a subject—the person or thing that is doing the doing! Many sentences have an object, too—the person or thing that the doing is being done to.

To make sure you don't forget which is which, remember:

The **subject** hit the **object**.

Clauses and Phrases

Some sentences include *clauses* and *phrases*. The following sentence will help you to remember the difference between the two:

He loved **clauses**, but not **phrases**.

"He loved clauses" is a clause, because it has a subject (*he*) and a verb (*loved*).

"But not phrases" is a phrase because it doesn't have a subject and a verb, and does not make sense by itself.

Conjunctions

Conjunctions join phrases, clauses, and sentences together, and there are three main types: coordinating, subordinate, and correlative.

1. Coordinating Conjunctions

These are the words we use for joining similar things (such as two sentences) together. There are seven of them and a mnemonic used to remember them is **FAN BOYS**.

For, **A**nd, **N**or, **B**ut, **O**r, **Y**et, **S**o.

2. Subordinate Conjunctions

Subordinate conjunctions join parts of a sentence that make sense on their own with parts that don't.

He tidied his room + **because** + he had to.

A mnemonic to remember common subordinate conjunctions is **BAT SWAB**.

Before, **A**fter, **T**hough, **S**o, **W**hile, **A**s, **B**ecause.

3. Correlative Conjunctions

These are always found in pairs. An example of a pair of correlative conjunctions at work can be found in the sentence:

She liked **both** pink **and** red roses.

A mnemonic for common correlative conjunctions is
BEN and **ANN:**

> **B**oth goes with *and*
> **E**ither goes with *or*
> **N**either goes with *nor*
>
> **A**s goes with *as*
> **N**ot only goes with *but also*
> **N**ot goes with *but*

Prefixes and Suffixes

Words sometimes change their meaning or use when letters
are added to the beginning (*prefixes*) or the end (*suffixes*).

Prefixes usually change a word's meaning. You can
remember the common prefixes below by using the
mnemonic **DREAM**.

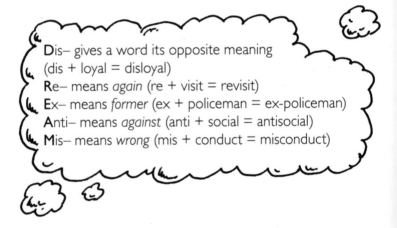

Dis– gives a word its opposite meaning
(dis + loyal = disloyal)
Re– means *again* (re + visit = revisit)
Ex– means *former* (ex + policeman = ex-policeman)
Anti– means *against* (anti + social = antisocial)
Mis– means *wrong* (mis + conduct = misconduct)

Suffixes can either change a word's meaning—for example, *use* + *less* equals *useless*—or how a word is used. For example, *quick* + *ly* changes the adjective *quick* (a word describing a noun) to the adverb *quickly* (a word describing a verb). Use the mnemonic **ICE TEA** to remember these common suffixes:

–**I**ze added to a noun creates a verb
(*symbol* + *ize* = *symbolize*)
–**C**y added to a verb, noun, or adjective makes a noun
(*urgent* + *cy* = *urgency*)
–**E**ry added to a verb, noun, or adjective makes a noun
(*bake* + *ery* = *bakery*)

–**T**ion added to a verb, noun, or adjective makes a noun
(*act* + *tion* = *action*)
–**E**nt added to a verb or noun makes an adjective
(*differ* + *ent* = *different*)
–**A**ble added to a verb or noun makes an adjective
(*drink* + *able* = *drinkable*)

Verbs in the First, Second, and Third Person

Verbs (doing words) can be written in the first, second, or third person.

First person is used when the writer or speaker carries out the action: I run, we run. Second person is used when referring to *you* in a sentence: you run. Third person is used when someone else is involved: he runs, she runs, it runs, they run.

👁 *Imagine you're waiting in line with a friend and his little brother to go on a theme-park ride. You say, "I will go* **first**, *you go* **second**, *and* **he** *can go* **third**."*

WORD POWER!

Did you know that an impudent philatelist is just a rude stamp collector? No? Well, here are ten words you can remember and use to wow your teachers and your friends.

Acquiesce

To *acquiesce* (pronounced ack–wee–ess) means to give in or to agree to something without complaining. Remember:

> I confess, I confess,
> I made the mess.
> So I'll clear it up.
> I **acquiesce**.

Chide

To *chide* means to tell off or to scold.

> A teacher may **chide** a **chi**ld.

Claustrophobia

Words ending in **–phobia** describe a fear of something. *Claustrophobia* means a fear of small, closed-in spaces.

> Santa **Claus** lives in the huge, open Arctic because he has **claus**trophobia.

Impudent

Impudent means rude or bold.

There's no creature so rude as an **imp**udent **imp**!

Myriad

Myriad means a very large number. Learn this short poem to help you remember the meaning.

Myriad friends will make you glad.
With so many friends you can't be sad!

Philatelist

A *philatelist* is the name for a person who collects stamps.

👁 *Imagine you are making a record of all the stamps in your collection and have to **fill out a list.*** *("Fill-out-a-list" sounds like philatelist.)*

Quash

Quash means to forcefully stop an activity. Look at the example below:

The army s**quash**ed the rebellion.

Remembering that "squashing a rebellion" and "quashing a rebellion" mean the same will help you remember the meaning of *quash*.

Serendipity

Serendipity is used to describe a lucky discovery. If you lose something and then find it when you aren't even looking for it, this is an example of serendipity.

> *Imagine that you are playing hide-and-seek with your friend. While hiding in the closet, you find a long-lost toy and excitedly leave the closet to show your friend. Your friend thinks you are giving up and says:*
> *"Do you **surrender**? **Pity**!"*
> *("Surr-en-der-pit-y" sounds like "ser-en-di-pit-y.")*

Superlative

Superlative means outstanding or brilliant, as in: The athlete made a superlative effort and won the gold medal. To help you with this word, remember that:

Superman is not just a superhero, he's a **super**lative hero.

Taciturn

A *taciturn* person is a person who is very quiet, and doesn't often join in conversations.

> I don't say much, I'm taciturn,
> So that's a word that I should learn.

GET JET SET!

A good memory is absolutely vital when learning a foreign language, as there are so many new words to remember. The visualization exercises shown here take Spanish and French as examples, but you can use this technique to help you learn new words in any language you wish in a quick and fun way.

Spanish Words

The Spanish word for *beach* is *playa*. To remember this, carry out the following exercise:

> 👁 *Close your eyes and relax. Imagine a game of beach volleyball where you are a **player**. After ten seconds, open your eyes.*

Yes, it really is that easy! To prove it works, write the word *beach* on a piece of paper and leave it somewhere. Later in the day, look at your piece of paper with the word *beach* written on it. The image you created should come back to you and remind you that the Spanish word for *beach* is *playa*.

Here's another example to
show how easy the visualization
technique is. The Spanish word
for *hand* is *mano.*

👁 *Close your eyes and imagine
a tiny man standing on your hand.
You are surprised to see him and
exclaim, "Oh!" in shock.*

Fixing this image in your mind will
guarantee that you never forget
that *mano* is the word for *hand.*

Here's one more example from Spanish, with a very silly
visualization to help you remember it. The Spanish word for
whale is *ballena.*

👁 *Imagine a huge whale dressed in a sparkly
pink tutu, just like a **balle**rina.*

For trickier words like this, choosing a funny or crazy image
to remember will help the word to stick in your mind more
easily. Your ballet-dancing whale will make sure you always
remember the Spanish word!

French Words

The French word for *father* is *père*. This is pronounced like the English word *pear*.

👁 *So, close your eyes and imagine your father eating a huge pear.*

The French word for *apple* is *pomme*.

👁 *This time imagine a cheerleader dancing at the side of a football field. However, instead of pom-poms she is holding a giant apple in each hand.*

The next time you go on vacation, or have language homework to do, try this technique and see how much easier it is to learn that vocabulary!

35

MATH MASTER

MAKING MATH ADD UP

Just the thought of math is enough to terrify some people, especially when they are faced with complicated calculations. But using memory tricks to help you will soon simplify your sums and make math less scary!

Tackling Tricky Sums

Using the acronym **PEMDAS** will help you remember the correct order of operations. Please Excuse My Dear Aunt Sally. Take this calculation, for example:

$$12 + 18 \div 6 \times (15 \div 5)^2 - 4$$

Order	Letter & Action	Calculation
1st	**P**arentheses – carry out the calculation inside the parentheses	$12 + 18 \div 6 \times (15 \div 5)^2 - 4$ becomes $12 + 18 \div 6 \times (3)^2 - 4$
2nd	**E**xponents – this means the power, in this case the ^{2} sign	$12 + 18 \div 6 \times (3)^2 - 4$ becomes $12 + 18 \div 6 \times 9 - 4$
3rd	**M**ultiplication and **D**ivision – multiply or divide from left to right	$12 + 18 \div 6 \times 9 - 4$ becomes $12 + 3 \times 9 - 4$ $12 + 3 \times 9 - 4$ becomes $12 + 27 - 4$
4th	**A**ddition and **S**ubtraction – add or subtract from left to right	$12 + 27 - 4$ becomes $39 - 4$ $39 - 4 = 35$

NUMBER SMART

Find factors, sort square numbers, and much more with these handy hints to help you become a true master of math. . . .

Prime Numbers

A *prime number* is a number that can only be divided by itself and the number 1. You can remember this using:

I am pr**1me** because I can only be divided by **1** and **me.**

An easy way to work out your prime numbers is by using the following rules:

- 0 and 1 are not prime numbers and, except for 2, no even numbers are prime.

- No numbers ending in 5 or 0 are prime, except for 5.

- If the sum of a number's digits is divisible by 3, it's not a prime number.

Cardinal and Ordinal Numbers

Cardinal numbers are used for **c**ounting, so they tell you how many of something there are, such as 1 or 5.

Ordinal numbers tell you the **ord**er of things, such as 1st, 2nd, or 3rd, for example.

Factors and Multiples

A whole number that divides into another whole number, with nothing left over, is known as a factor of that number. For example, 1, 2, 3, and 6 are all factors of 6.

A multiple of a number can be divided by that number, with no remainder. Some multiples of 6 include: 6, 12, 18, and 24.

Here's an easy way to remember them:

You **multipl**y to find a **multiple**, and it's a **fact** that some numbers can be divided by many **fact**ors.

Square Numbers and Cube Numbers

A *square number* is a number that's multiplied by itself. For example, 4^2, or 4 squared, means 4×4, which is 16. Remember this by picturing a square, which has two directions, and you'll remember that a square number has two numbers to multiply.

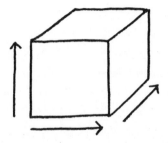

A cube has three directions, so a *cube number* has three numbers to multiply.

For example, 4^3, or 4 cubed, is $4 \times 4 \times 4$, which is 64.

Rounding Numbers

To round a decimal number to the nearest whole number, check the first number to the right of the decimal point. If it is five or more, round up. If it is less than five, round down. So, 4.7 would be rounded up to 5.

👁 *Imagine your math teacher giving you a high five for being a brainiac!*

Coordinates

When you are plotting a graph, you use numbers called coordinates—such as (2,4)—to tell you where to position the next point. But should you move along the X-axis or the Y-axis first? You can remember with these simple reminders:

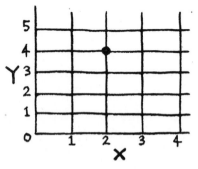

- The **X** coordinate is written first, and the **Y** coordinate second. Remember that **X** comes before **Y** in the alphabet to help you with this.

- On a graph, the X-axis is horizontal and the Y-axis is vertical. **X** is **a cross**, and it goes **across** the page.

- So, in the above example, (2,4) means two spaces across on the X-axis and four spaces up on the Y-axis.

Fabulous Fractions

A fraction represents part of a whole. Examples of common fractions you might come across are a half (½) or a quarter (¼).

Fractions are made up of two numbers. The *denominator* is the number on the bottom. This tells you how many parts the whole number has been split into. The *numerator* is the number on the top. This tells you how many parts of the number you're dealing with. For example, with ¼, the 4 lets you know that the whole has been divided into four pieces, and the 1 tells you that you have one of those four pieces.

To remember which is the numerator and which is the denominator in a fraction, use:

Numerator **u**p, **d**enominator **d**own.

Dividing with Fractions

A calculation that involves a fraction might look scary, but there's an easy way to simplify it.

Take, for example, the equation $10 \div ¼$. Use this little rhyme to help you:

Take the number you're dividing by,
Turn it upside down and multiply.

So, $10 \div ¼$ becomes $10 \times ⁴⁄₁$.
$10 \times ⁴⁄₁ = 40$, so $10 \div ¼ = 40$.

Averages

Do you know when to use the *mean*, *mode*, or *median?*
Each one means something different in mathematics.

MEDIAN IN THE MIDDLE
The median is the middle number when a series of
numbers is put in order. So, for example, in this series the
median is seven:

4, 6, **7**, 9, 9

MOSTLY THE MODE
The **mo**de is the number that occurs **mo**st often. So in this
series, the mode is nine:

7, **9**, 4, 6, **9**

AVERAGELY MEAN
The mean is the average number. To work this out, add the
numbers to find the total, and then divide the total by how
many numbers there are to get the average. For example:

7 + 9 + 4 + 6 + 9 = 35
There are five numbers, so 35 ÷ 5 = 7

Still not clear? This little rhyme will help you remember:

Middle median, mostly mode.
A **mean** old **add**er,
And a big green toad.

SHAPE UP

A two-dimensional shape (2-D), such as a square or a circle, is flat. It has two measurements: length and width. A three-dimensional shape (3-D), such as a cube or a sphere, has three measurements: length, width, and depth. But do you know your parallelograms from your pyramids?

2-D Shapes

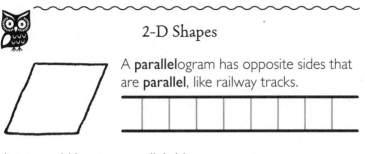

A **parallel**ogram has opposite sides that are **parallel**, like railway tracks.

A **trap**ezoid has two parallel sides and two that, if they kept on going, would eventually crash into one another and become **trap**ped.

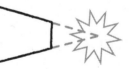

Penta comes from the Greek, meaning five. The word *penta* has five letters in it and a **penta**gon has five sides **on** it. A h**ex**agon has an **ex**tra one.

An **oct**agon has eight sides—just as an **oct**opus has eight tentacles.

43

3-D shapes

The Earth is a **sphere,** and so is the atmo**sphere** surrounding it.

A *cylinder* is a tube with two circles of the same size at either end. Picture a can of soup to remember this shape.

A **cone** has a round or oval base and narrows to a point, like an ice-cream **cone.**

A **pyramid** has four triangular sides that meet at a point. The base is usually square, like the **Pyramids** of Egypt.

A **cube** has six square sides. This means the length, width, and depth are all the same. To remember this shape, think of a sugar **cube.**

Easy as Pi

Pi, when spelled without an **e**, is a very important number in math, not a tasty thing to eat for dessert. Its symbol looks like this: **π**. It's especially useful when dealing with calculations to do with circles.

Usually, pi is shown as 3.14. But this is a number that has been rounded to two decimal places (see page 40 for more on rounding). In reality, the numbers after the decimal point go on infinitely. Why not impress your math teacher by remembering pi to 21 decimal places? Use this sentence:

How I wish I could calculate pi. People would buy giant presents—sparkling diamond offerings—for me. How terrific it'll always be!

How does this strange saying work? Count the letters in each word in the sentence and you will have the answer:

3.141592653589793238462

Circumference, Radius, and Diameter

Circle measurements may seem complicated, but they're easy to recall with these tips:

Diameter is a longer word than *radius*. This will help you to remember that the diameter is the longer distance.

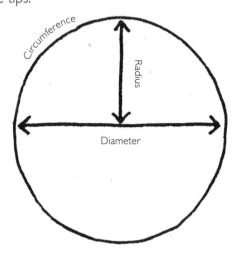

The *circumference* is the distance around the circle. Think of the **circ**umference as a **circ**uit around a **circ**le. You can work out the circumference using pi.

The circumference of a circle is pi multiplied by the diameter.

This simple sentence will help you to remember the formula:

I was **pied** (π**D**) at the **circu**s.

Access All Areas

Imagine a room. The *area* is the space occupied by a two-dimensional shape, such as the floor. Use this rhyme to help you find the area of a square, rectangle, triangle, or circle:

> For a rectangle or a square
> Use length times width and you are there.
> For a triangle it's base times height,
> Put ½ in front to get it right.
> Circles are tricky, but don't be scared
> It's just pi (π) times the radius, squared.

Va Va Volume

Imagine a room again. The *volume* is the space inside a three-dimensional shape, or the air inside the room.

If you know how to calculate the area of squares and circles, working out the volume of cubes and cylinders is easy.

Volume **E**quals (=) **A**rea × **D**epth

or

Violent **E**agles **A**re **D**angerous.

MARVELOUS MEASUREMENTS

Units of Measurement

The metric system has seven base units or *SI units* that measure different things:

Time is measured in seconds.
Temperature is measured in kelvins.
Length is measured in meters.
Current is measured in amperes.
Light is measured in candelas.
Amount is measured in moles.

You can remember these units using the following handy little story:

Mary the mole-catcher visited a **second** *time*. **Kelvin** waited in the *heat* at *length* to **meet her** (meter). There was no *current* for the **lamp** so he used **candle** *light* as he hunted the large *amount* of **moles**.

Quick Conversions

Most of the world uses the metric system (meters, kilometers) to measure length. The United States mainly uses the imperial system (feet, miles).

1 mile = 1.6093 kilometers (km), which can be rounded to 1.6 km. The easiest way to recall this is by remembering this little rhyme:

> Miles to kilometers, ain't it great,
> Just divide by 5 and times by 8.

1 inch = 2.54 centimeters (cm), which can be rounded to 2.5 cm. To remember this ratio, look at your school ruler.

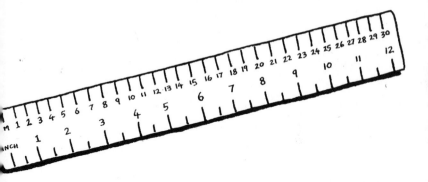

Most rulers are marked up to 12 inches on one side and 30 centimeters on the other.

$$12 \times 2.5 = 30$$

A GEOGRAPHICAL JOURNEY

PLANET POWER!

How much do you know about our amazing planet? This section will help you remember fascinating facts about Earth.

Inside the Planet

Planet Earth is divided into sections. If you were to dig deep down underground, you would pass through some very different layers.

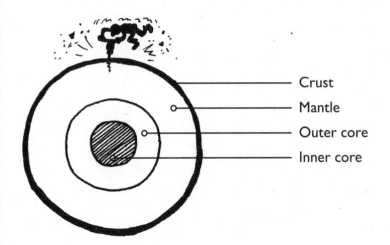

Crust
Mantle
Outer core
Inner core

Crust. You are standing on this layer right now. It's made of tectonic plates that move around, sometimes resulting in earthquakes. The crust is made of rock and it can be up to 43 miles thick.

Mantle. This layer is nearly 1,864 miles thick and is made of semi-molten rock. The closer to the center of the Earth, the hotter and softer the rock becomes.

Core. The Earth's core is split into two—the outer core and the inner core. The outer core is 1,429 miles thick and is made of liquid iron and nickel, while the inner core is mainly solid iron and about 746 miles thick. The inner core is incredibly hot, reaching temperatures of well over 9,032 degrees Fahrenheit.

You can remember the four layers as follows:

> There's the **inner** and the **outer core**
> Then the **mantle** and the **crust** make four.

Our Atmosphere

The layer of gases that surrounds Earth is called the *atmosphere*. All planets have an atmosphere, but the gases they contain vary greatly.

The common name for Earth's atmosphere is *air*, and it's made up of different gases. About 78% is made up of a gas called nitrogen, 21% is oxygen, and the remaining 1% is argon.

You can remember the three most common gases in air in order (nitrogen, oxygen, and argon) by using the sentence:

> Last **ni**ght, my smelly s**ox** (socks) caused an **arg**ument, and created a bad **atmosphere**.

Superb Spheres

The atmosphere changes as you move farther away from the surface of Earth. The higher you go, the thinner the atmosphere becomes, until it eventually merges with space.

Scientists have given different names to various parts of the atmosphere, which they call *spheres*. There are five of these:

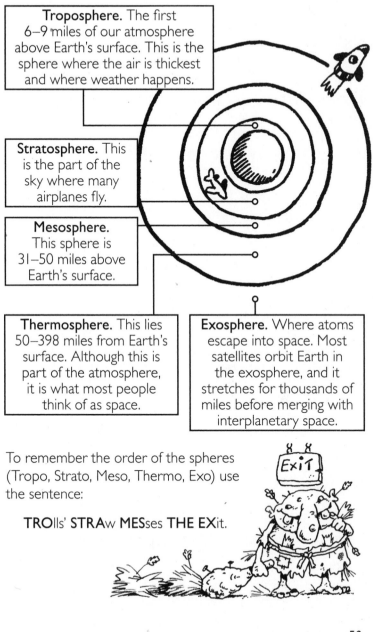

Troposphere. The first 6–9 miles of our atmosphere above Earth's surface. This is the sphere where the air is thickest and where weather happens.

Stratosphere. This is the part of the sky where many airplanes fly.

Mesosphere. This sphere is 31–50 miles above Earth's surface.

Thermosphere. This lies 50–398 miles from Earth's surface. Although this is part of the atmosphere, it is what most people think of as space.

Exosphere. Where atoms escape into space. Most satellites orbit Earth in the exosphere, and it stretches for thousands of miles before merging with interplanetary space.

To remember the order of the spheres (Tropo, Strato, Meso, Thermo, Exo) use the sentence:

TROlls' **STRA**w **MES**ses **THE EX**it.

Sunrise, Sunset

Every day, it looks as though the Sun is moving across the sky. In fact, it's you, here on the Earth, who are moving. The Earth turns toward the east, so it seems as though the Sun is rising in the east, as your part of the Earth turns toward it, and then setting in the west, as your part of the Earth turns away from it and night falls. To remember this, use the sentence:

> The Sun rises **ea**rly in the **ea**st and sets in
> the **we**st when it is **we**ary.

Arctic/Antarctic

The coldest places on Earth are the polar regions—huge ice-covered areas surrounding the North and South Poles.

The North Pole is found, as its name suggests, at the most northerly part of the planet, and the polar region there is called the Arctic. The South Pole lies at the most southerly part of Earth, and the polar region there is called the Antarctic.

To avoid confusing the two areas, notice that the only difference in the names is that one has the letters *Ant* in front of *Arctic*. To remember that the **Ant**arctic is in the south:

👁 *Imagine a little **ant** heading south for vacation.*

You probably already know that polar bears and penguins live at the poles. It might surprise you to learn that no polar bear has ever eaten a penguin. This is because polar bears live in the Arctic, and penguins live in the Antarctic. To remember that **pen**guins live in the **Ant**arctic:

👁 *Imagine your vacationing **ant** writing a postcard with a **pen**.*

Magma and Lava

Deep inside the Earth, the temperature is so hot that the rocks melt. This hot, liquid rock is called *magma*. Sometimes, this magma escapes to the surface when a volcano erupts. When the liquid rock is on the surface of the Earth, it is called *lava*. In other words, magma and lava are used to describe the same substance in different places. Many people confuse the two words but, remember:

Lava is on **la**nd.

Hurricanes, Typhoons, and Cyclones

The names of strong circular storms with very high winds that begin over warm seas vary depending on where they are found. When the storms occur in the Atlantic Ocean, they are called *hurricanes*, when they happen in the Pacific Ocean, they are called *typhoons*, and in the Indian Ocean, they are called *cyclones*.

So: Hurricane = Atlantic, Cyclone = Indian, Typhoon = Pacific.

This mnemonic will help you to remember what happens where:

> Mr **A. T. Lant**ic **hurr**ied as he **cycl**ed to **India**,
> but he grew **ti**red by the **pac**e.

Sorting Out Those Scales

Richter Scale. This scale is used to calculate the power of earthquakes. It is an unusual scale, as it increases by powers of ten. This means a quake measuring six on the scale is ten times more powerful than one measuring five! To remember the name of this scale:

👁 *Imagine a king losing all his **rich**es in an earthquake.*

Beaufort Scale. This is used to measure wind speed. 0 is calm weather, and the scale continues to 12, which means hurricane conditions with wind speeds above 73 mph.

👁 *Imagine someone trying to tie a **bow** to the top of a **fort**ress in the wind.*

Saffir/Simpson Scale. Once a wind becomes a hurricane, it moves beyond the Beaufort Scale and is measured by the Saffir/Simpson Scale. This goes from one to five. The most famous hurricane in recent history was Hurricane Katrina—a Category Four hurricane that caused terrible damage to the city of New Orleans in 2005.

 Imagine a ship called the **SS Hurricane** *on a stormy sea.*

Fujita Scale. This scale measures tornadoes, which can have wind speeds even faster than hurricanes! This scale goes from EF0 (up to 72 mph) to EF5 (over 260 mph). Visualizing something silly can help you remember this.

 Imagine a man being swept up in a tornado while eating **fudge**. *("Fudge-eater" sounds like "Fujita.")*

Tricky Temperatures

There are two different ways of measuring the temperature—in degrees Celsius, or in degrees Fahrenheit. The two scales are quite different, but you can use these two little rhymes to help you remember the difference between them:

Celsius
30 is hot,
20 is nice,
10 is chilly,
0 is ice!

Fahrenheit
32's freezing,
50 is not,
68's pleasant,
85's hot!

The Water Cycle

Water is vital for life on Earth. It doesn't run out because it is in constant motion—from the land, to the seas and rivers, to the sky and back to the land.

As it makes this journey, water changes from a liquid to a gas and back again (sometimes, it also becomes a solid when it turns to ice).

This continual movement of the Earth's water is called the *water cycle*. The stages of the cycle are shown in the diagram below.

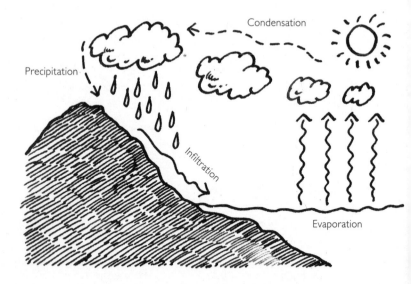

Don't worry if this diagram looks complicated—read on to find out more about each of the different stages of the water cycle and how you can remember them.

Evaporation.
Evaporation changes water into gas (this is why puddles disappear when the Sun comes out after rain).

Condensation.
Condensation changes a gas to a liquid. This process forms water droplets and creates clouds.

Precipitation.
Precipitation is a fancy word for any sort of water that falls from the sky, after it's been condensed. Rain, snow, hail, and even mist are all forms of precipitation.

Infiltration.
Infiltration happens when the rain hits the ground. Sometimes it soaks into it, and sometimes it runs off the surface and into rivers and lakes.

This poem will help you to remember the four stages and what happens in each:

Ev**ap**oration turns water into **vap**or, a gas floating on high,
Con**dens**ation makes it **dens**er, clouds appear in the sky,
Pre**cip**itation falls as rain that you can **sip**,
Then in**fil**tration **fil**ls up lakes and trickles drip by drip.

Cloudspotting

If you want to take up a new hobby, why don't you try cloudspotting? It's very easy, as all you have to do is find a comfortable patch of grass, lie down, and stare up at the sky. If anyone accuses you of being lazy, you can truthfully tell them that you are actually very busy cloudspotting. This picture shows the main types of cloud to look out for.

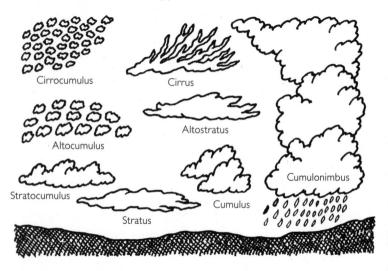

The names used to describe clouds can seem confusing at first, but there are clues to help you tell which is which. The first way of distinguishing clouds is by height. Use **CASE** to help you remember in *case* you see a cloud.

Cirrus is used for high clouds.
Alto describes clouds at middle height.
Stratus is used to describe low clouds.
Earth is where you're lying looking up at the clouds!

Other words to describe clouds are:

Cumulus. White, puffy clouds that looks like cotton balls:
CUMulus = **COM**fy cotton balls.

Stratus. Flat clouds spread out straight across the sky:
STRatus = **STR**aight.

Nimbus. Rain clouds:
You need to run **NIMB**ly to avoid rain from these
NIMBus clouds.

If you remember these terms, you will be able to decode
many different cloud types and impress people! For example:

Cirrocumulus = cirrus + cumulus = high, puffy cloud

Altostratus = alto + stratus = mid-height, flat cloud

Most Active Volcanoes

There are more than 1,500 volcanoes on land that have
erupted in the last 10,000 years. Some of the most active
volcanoes have been continuously erupting for hundreds
of years.

The three most active
volcanoes are: **M**ount **E**tna (in
Sicily), **S**tromboli (on the Aeolian
Islands off the coast of Italy), and
Yasur (on the island of Vanuatu
in the South Pacific). To recall
these three, remember:

Mom **E**ats **S**melly **Y**ogurts!

ALL AROUND THE WORLD

A Capital Memory

Turning a list of information into a story can really help your memory. You're about to read about George and his car trip, but you'll actually learn all the capital cities of South America! Start in Guyana and travel counterclockwise, then get ready to impress your friends with your slick city knowledge.

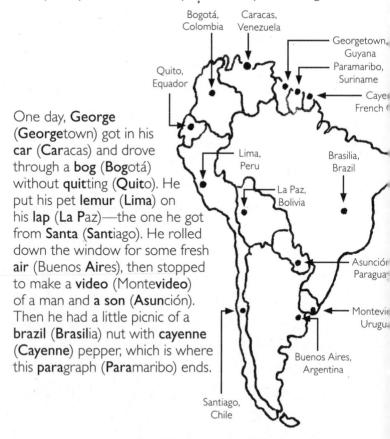

Bogotá, Colombia

Caracas, Venezuela

Georgetown, Guyana

Paramaribo, Suriname

Quito, Equador

Caye French (

One day, **George** (**George**town) got in his **car** (**Car**acas) and drove through a **bog** (**Bog**otá) without **quit**ting (**Quit**o). He put his pet **lemur** (**Lim**a) on his **lap** (**La P**az)—the one he got from **Santa** (**Sant**iago). He rolled down the window for some fresh **air** (Buenos **Air**es), then stopped to make a **video** (Monte**video**) of a man and **a son** (**A son**ción). Then he had a little picnic of a **brazil** (**Brasil**ia) nut with **cayenne** (**Cayenne**) pepper, which is where this **para**graph (**Para**maribo) ends.

Lima, Peru

Brasilia, Brazil

La Paz, Bolivia

Asunción Paragua

Montevi Urugu

Buenos Aires, Argentina

Santiago, Chile

62

Island Information

As well as its seven continents, the world is full of islands. Some of these are enormous—much bigger than many countries. With just a couple of silly sentences in your head, you'll be able to remember the five biggest islands in the world, as well as all the islands in the Mediterranean Sea.

The five biggest islands in the world each have a landmass of more than three thousand square miles. In size order, these are:

Greenland, **New Guinea**,
Borneo, Madaga**scar**,
and Ba**ffin**.

Have a look on a map of the world and see if you can spot them all. To remember these five supersized islands, think about this sentence:

My **green new guinea**-pig was **born** with a **scar** shaped like a pu**ffin**.

Now it's time for some Mediterranean sunshine. Here are the main islands of the Mediterranean Sea, in order from the west (near Spain) to the east (near Turkey): **Bal**earic Islands, **Sardin**ia, **Cors**ica, Si**cily**, **Crete**, **Cyp**rus.

Or:

Balloons in **sardin**es **cause silly crate**s of **soup**.

States and State Capitals

Trying to remember the 50 states and each of their capital cities might seem like an impossible task. But, by using a combination of memory tricks, your brilliant brain will tackle it in no time.

First, use the grouping technique to put the 50 states into five chunks of ten, in alphabetical order. Then, using some of those silly sentences, add in the information about each state capital.

Group One:

STATE	CAPITAL
Alabama	Montgomery
Alaska	Juneau
Arizona	Phoenix
Arkansas	Little Rock
California	Sacramento
Colorado	Denver
Connecticut	Hartford
Delaware	Dover
Florida	Tallahassee
Georgia	Atlanta

To remember these first ten state capitals, use the silly sentence:

My Jumping Pony Likes Shouting, "Delicious Hot Doughnuts!" Totally Amazing!

Group Two:

STATE	CAPITAL
Hawaii	Honolulu
Idaho	Boise
Illinois	Springfield
Indiana	Indianapolis
Iowa	Des Moines
Kansas	Topeka
Kentucky	Frankfort
Louisiana	Baton Rouge
Maine	Augusta
Maryland	Annapolis

Remember:

How Big Should I Decide To Finally Build An Ark?

Group Three:

STATE	CAPITAL
Massachusetts	Boston
Michigan	Lansing
Minnesota	St. Paul
Mississippi	Jackson
Missouri	Jefferson City
Montana	Helena
Nebraska	Lincoln
Nevada	Carson City
New Hampshire	Concord
New Jersey	Trenton

Remember:

Beautiful Ladies Slurp Juicy Jellies Happily, Looking Completely Cool, Too!

Group Four:

STATE	CAPITAL
New Mexico	Santa Fe
New York	Albany
North Carolina	Raleigh
North Dakota	Bismarck
Ohio	Columbus
Oklahoma	Oklahoma City
Oregon	Salem
Pennsylvania	Harrisburg
Rhode Island	Providence
South Carolina	Columbia

Remember:

Serious Animals Read
Books 'Cos Other Silly
Happy People Can't.

Group Five:

STATE	CAPITAL
South Dakota	Pierre
Tennessee	Nashville
Texas	Austin
Utah	Salt Lake City
Vermont	Montpelier
Virginia	Richmond
Washington	Olympia
West Virginia	Charleston
Wisconsin	Madison
Wyoming	Cheyenne

Remember:

Paul's Nephew Andrew Spilled Milk Right
On Charlie's Mom's Cat!

Money Money Money!

Money makes the world go 'round, but not every country uses the same sort of money, or *currency*. There are actually over 180 different currencies in existence throughout the world.

Don't get your pesos in a pickle or your dollars in a dilemma! Here's a quick mnemonic for the currencies of a dozen different countries:

> Just remember that a **CUP** of **chilly pesos** costs
> **JUST** a **dollar** or **A BIG euro**.

A

C (Colombia) ⎫
U (Uruguay)   ⎬ pesos
P (Philippines) ⎪
of
chilly (Chile) ⎭

costs ⎫
J (Jamaica) ⎪
U (USA)   ⎬ a dollar
S (Singapore) ⎪
T (Taiwan)   ⎭

or ⎫
A (Austria) ⎪
B (Belgium) ⎬ euro.
I (Italy)   ⎪
G (Germany) ⎭

THE LIVING WORLD

LIVING ORGANISMS

There are billions of living things crawling all over the planet. These are known as organisms. This section will help you to remember all sorts of cool stuff about animals and plants, as well as your fellow human beings.

Cool Characteristics

Living organisms can be as different as an elephant and a daffodil. However, there are seven characteristics shared by all living things. Look at the first letters of the list below, and you will see how **MRS. GREN** will help you remember these:

Movement. All living things move. Plants with roots move their leaves toward the Sun.

Respiration. This is the name given to the process where living organisms release energy from the food they consume.

Sensitivity. All living organisms can sense certain things in their environment that affect them (such as light) and respond to them.

Growth. All living things grow.

Reproduction. All living organisms reproduce in order to continue the species.

Excretion. Living things get rid of waste products. You do this by going to the bathroom.

Nutrition. Living organisms need to take in energy, usually by eating and drinking for animals, and photosynthesis for plants (see page 72).

WILD ABOUT PLANTS

Parts of a Flower

Flowers come in all sizes and colors, but did you know that all flowers are made up of different parts?

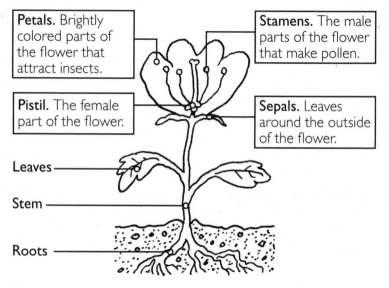

Petals. Brightly colored parts of the flower that attract insects.

Stamens. The male parts of the flower that make pollen.

Pistil. The female part of the flower.

Sepals. Leaves around the outside of the flower.

Leaves

Stem

Roots

Remember the parts of a flower using the sentence:

See (sepal) your **pet** (petal) **sta**nding (stamen) with a **pist**achio (pistil).

All flowers are plants, but not all plants are flowers. The three parts that all plants have are:

Stem. This structure helps the plant to grow and spread its leaves, and moves water and nutrients from the roots to the leaves.

Leaves. Green leaves capture energy from sunlight.

Roots. These absorb water and nutrients from the soil. They also hold the plant in place. Remember:

Starving **L**ions **R**oar!

Tree Types

There are two main types of trees:

Deciduous trees. These shed their leaves in the autumn and remain bare until the next growing season.

I **decide** to **leave** in the autumn.

Coniferous trees. These include pines and firs. Their leaves, which are like thin needles, are not shed. They are usually called *evergreen* trees or *conifers*.

It's a big **con** if **fir**s shed leaves because they're supposed to be evergreen.

Plant Growth

Plants need four things in order to grow. These are known as the **SWAN**:

Sunlight
Water
Air
Nutrients

71

Photosynthesis

The mnemonic **SWAN** on page 71 reminds you what plants need for *photosynthesis*, the process where green leaves convert sunlight, carbon dioxide, and water into sugar that helps the plant to grow. To remember this process, remember this rhyme:

> The plant takes carbon dioxide and water.
> And then the Sun shines just like it oughta!
> This turns them to sugar, the plant's favorite food
> And oxygen too, which it kicks out . . . how rude!

ANIMAL MAD

You Are What You Eat

Animals are divided into groups based on what they eat.

Herbivores. These animals only eat plants. Notice that the word **herb**ivore begins with *herb*. This will help you remember that these animals are plant-eaters.

Carnivores. *Carnivores* are meat-eaters. They get their meat by eating other animals. The Spanish word for meat is *carne*. If you eat the dish *chilli con carne*, you are eating chilli with meat. So **carn**ivore means meat-eater.

Omnivores. *Omnivores* eat plants and meat. Humans—unless they are vegetarians—are omnivores. So **om**nivores will happily eat a ham and spinach **om**elette.

Vertebrates and Invertebrates

Another way to classify animals is as either *vertebrates* or *invertebrates*.

Invertebrates. These animals do not have a backbone. You might think there are not many of these, but invertebrates make up the vast majority of the world's creatures—from octopuses and spiders to crabs and bees.

Vertebrates. These are animals that have a backbone or spine, like you.

Vertebrates are divided into five classes: **B**irds, **F**ish, **A**mphibians, **R**eptiles, and **M**ammals. Any animal that doesn't fit into one of these classes is an invertebrate.

You can remember the five classes of vertebrates by using the sentence:

Vertebrates must **Be** kept on a **FARM**.

Big Cats

There are lots of different species of wild cat, but only four of them are technically known as big cats. This classification actually has nothing to do with their size, but whether they can roar!

The true big cats are: leopards, lions, tigers, and jaguars. To remember them, use the sentence:

Leo Likes **To J**ump.

Marsupials

One group of mammals is known as marsupials. These animals give birth when their babies are not well-developed, so marsupials usually have pouches to keep their babies safe.

Many marsupials live in Australia. The most famous marsupials are **w**allabies, **k**angaroos, **w**ombats, and **k**oalas.

As these marsupials spend most of the day asleep, you can remember them by shouting, "**WaKey! WaKey!**"

Insects

Four out of every five species on the planet are insects. Some of the most common insects you'll find crawling and scuttling around are: **bee**tles, **bee**s, butter**flies**, **flies**, and **grass**hoppers.

This mnemonic will help you remember these five common groups:

Two **bee**s and two **flies** hopped on the **grass**.

THE AMAZING HUMAN BODY

The Truth About Teeth

Have you noticed that your teeth are different shapes and sizes?

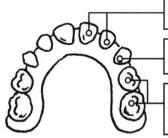

Incisors. These flat teeth help you bite into your food.

Canines. These are pointy teeth that help you tear food.

Molars. The thick teeth at the back of the mouth that are for grinding food.

To remember the three types of teeth, use the sentence:

My teeth bite **in**to (incisors) a **can** (canines)
of **mola**sses (molars).

Feel It in Your Bones

You might hear people talking about the *leg bone*, but did you know that actually there's no such thing? In fact, your leg is made of four separate bones. These are the *femur*, the *patella*, the *tibia*, and the *fibula*. To remember these, think about:

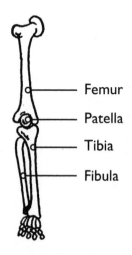

— Femur

— Patella

— Tibia

— Fibula

A **fem**ale (femur) called **Pat** (patella)
and her twins, **Tib** (tibia)
and **Fib** (fibula).

Veins, Arteries, and Capillaries

The heart pumps blood around the body. The blood travels through vessels called arteries, capillaries, and veins, which are like little pipes running through the body.

Arteries. These carry blood that has been pumped out of the heart and is full of oxygen.

Capillaries. These are very thin pipes, which allow the blood to release its oxygen through their walls into your body's tissue. Waste products are then sent back through the capillary wall and into the blood.

Veins. The veins take the blood back to the heart, ready for it to be refilled with oxygen.

So, **a**rteries send blood **a**way from the heart,
and **ve**ins re**ve**rse the direction.
Capillaries let oxygen es**cap**e through their walls.

Did you know?

If all the arteries, veins, and capillaries were taken out of your body and laid out in a single line, it would stretch at least twice around the planet!

77

Making Sense of Senses

You take in information about the world around you with your senses. There are five of these: sight, smell, touch, taste, and hearing.

To help you remember the five senses, just think of the five things on your face—eyes (sight), nose (smell), mouth (taste), ears (hearing), and skin (touch).

The Excellent Eyes

Your eyes are made up of several different parts, which all work together to help you see.

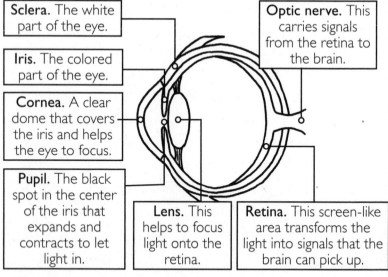

Sclera. The white part of the eye.

Iris. The colored part of the eye.

Cornea. A clear dome that covers the iris and helps the eye to focus.

Pupil. The black spot in the center of the iris that expands and contracts to let light in.

Optic nerve. This carries signals from the retina to the brain.

Lens. This helps to focus light onto the retina.

Retina. This screen-like area transforms the light into signals that the brain can pick up.

To remember the parts of your eye (**s**clera, **i**ris, **c**ornea, **p**upil, **l**ens, **r**etina, **o**ptic **n**erve), use the sentence:

SICk **P**enguins **L**ove i**RON**ing!

The Internal Organs

The human body is a very complex organism.

Inside your body, a lot of different things that are essential for life are happening all the time. There are specialized body parts that handle these tasks. We call these body parts organs.

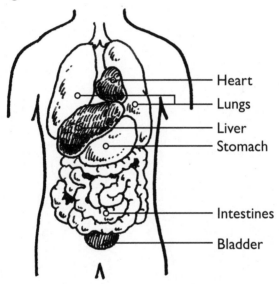

To help you remember what the internal organs do, learn this little rhyme:

Start with the **heart**, which pumps blood around inside,
Lungs take in oxygen and expel carbon dioxide.
The **liver** cares for the blood, removing the bad stuff,
The **stomach** digests your food for you, even when it's tough.
The **intestines** absorb food and get rid of the waste,
Then the **bladder** stores urine, so you don't pee in haste!

SUPER SCIENCE

GET SCIENCE STRAIGHT

Science is a fascinating subject to study, but there are lots of things to remember, which can sometimes make it tricky. This section will help you to conquer your chemistry and finesse your physics. Read on to become a science superstar!

Science VIPs

Science has advanced so much over the centuries because of the amazing work and discoveries of some of history's most brilliant minds, from Ancient Greece to modern times.

Use this little poem to remember some of the most famous scientists and their discoveries, and then read on to find out a bit more about them:

> The Greek **Archimedes** was a knowledge seeker,
> Thought up his Principle and yelled, "Eureka!"
> **Copernicus** told us Earth circles the Sun,
> While **Galileo**'s weights both fell as one.
> **Newton**'s law of gravity was more than a wish,
> And hydrogen was discovered by Mr. **Cavendish**.
> **Darwin** talked of evolution when no one dared,
> And **Einstein** taught us that $E = mc^2$.

ARCHIMEDES (AROUND 287–212 BC)

Archimedes came up with the Archimedes Principle. This states that when an object is put in water, it loses as much weight as an equal volume of the water. Legend says that he discovered this while sitting in the bath and was so excited by his discovery that he leapt out and ran naked through the streets, shouting, "Eureka!"

Nicolaus Copernicus (1473–1543)

Copernicus was an astronomer who stated that the Earth travels around the Sun and that the Sun remains in the same place. This was a very new idea because at the time, people thought that the Earth was at the center of the universe.

Galileo Galilei (1564–1642)

Galileo was an Italian scientist who made a number of important discoveries. He found out that all objects fall at the same speed. To prove this, he climbed to the top of the Leaning Tower of Pisa and dropped two balls. Although one of the balls was very heavy and one was light, they both reached the ground at the same time.

Isaac Newton (1642–1727)

Isaac Newton is most famous for his theory of gravity. This states that there is a force between objects and that the size of the force depends on their mass and the distance between them. In one of the most famous legends in science, it is said that his ideas about gravity struck him at the same time as he was struck on the head by a falling apple while sitting under an apple tree.

HENRY CAVENDISH (1731–1810)
Henry Cavendish was a British scientist who spent his life studying science and discovered the gas hydrogen.

CHARLES DARWIN (1809–1882)
Charles Darwin spent years sailing around the world studying the animals and plants he found. This provided him with much of the knowledge and information he needed for his book, *On the Origin of Species,* which explained his theories about how living organisms change over time to adapt to their environment.

ALBERT EINSTEIN (1879–1955)
Albert Einstein was the most famous scientist of the last century. He made huge contributions to physics, such as proving that atoms exist, but he is most famous for his theory of relativity. His ideas are very complicated, but this theory gave an explanation of light, distance, mass, and energy. One of the results of his theories was his discovery that the energy in an object can be calculated by multiplying the mass of the object by the speed of light squared. This is written as:

$$E = mc^2 \text{ (Energy} = \text{mass} \times \text{speed of light}^2)$$

What Makes a Metal?

Metals are very useful in all parts of our lives. They are used for making a wide range of objects—from enormous bridges and powerful machines to beautiful pieces of jewelry and the tiniest computer parts.

Most metals share the following characteristics:

- Shiny appearance
- Strength
- Solid at room temperature
- High melting point
- Good conductor of electricity and heat
- Malleable—this means it can be beaten into different shapes without breaking.

This short poem will help you remember the key properties of metals:

They're **shiny**, **strong**, and **solid**.
They **conduct** and they are **malleable**.
They do not **melt** easily,
That's why they are so valuable!

Marvelous Magnets

Magnetism is an invisible force that causes objects to attract each other. A magnet is an object that gives off a magnetic field. This means it applies a force over a distance that will attract anything made of iron.

Every magnet has two ends called the north pole (N) and the south pole (S). These are the magnetic poles.

If you put two magnets next to each other, they can either attract each other (where they snap together) or repel each other (where they push each other away). The rule is that:

Opposite poles attract and similar poles repel.

If you have two magnets, try this for yourself.

There is a saying that when it comes to romance, opposites attract. A loud person is likely to fall in love with a quiet person, for example.

Magnets may not be as romantic, but the rule of "opposites attract" can help you remember which poles attract and which repel.

ALL ABOUT ENERGY

Every time you turn on a light, run hot water, or travel in a car, you are using energy resources. Most of this energy comes from fossil fuels. However, as the world's energy demands grow, it has become important to find new sources of energy, especially renewable ones that will not run out.

Fossil Fuels

The fossil fuels are coal, oil, and gas. They are called fossil fuels because they have formed over millions of years from

 the remains of prehistoric plants and animals.

To remember these three fuels, think of fossil fuel energy being used to power the turning of a **COG**:

Coal **O**il **G**as.

There are two ways to use this fuel. Sometimes, the fuels are used directly when people burn coal for heat, or use gas for cooking and oil to power engines. However, most of our energy comes from power stations, where the fuels are burned to create electricity. This process goes like this:

Burn fuel to heat water and make steam.	→	The steam makes a turbine turn.	→	The turbine turns a generator.	→	The generator creates electricity.

To remember each **STaGE** in the process, remember:

Steam **T**urbine **a** **G**enerator **E**lectricity.

Renewable Energy

When we use fossil fuels, the source is used up forever. Renewable energy sources can be used again and again without running out. These include: wind farms, wave power stations, biofuel power stations (which burn solid waste instead of fossil fuels), geothermal energy (which uses the heat from inside the Earth), hydroelectric power stations (which use dams to channel water through tunnels), and solar energy from the Sun.

Remember these six renewable energy sources (**w**ind, **wa**ve, **b**iofuels, **g**eothermal, **h**ydroelectric, and **s**olar) by asking the question:

Why **Wa**ste **B**rilliantly **G**ood **H**eat **S**ources?

Kinetic and Potential Energy

Energy when it's in motion is called *kinetic energy*. For example, a big boulder rolling down a hill has lots of kinetic energy because it's on the move.

Energy that's stored or waiting to happen is called *potential energy*. When the boulder is sitting at the top of the hill, it's full of potential energy. Remember:

It's **ki**netic when it's **in** motion, and **p**otential when it's on **p**ause.

The Electromagnetic Spectrum

Energy often travels from one place to another in waves of charged particles. This is called electromagnetic radiation. Different types of waves have different wavelengths.

When the different electromagnetic wavelengths are positioned in order from the longest waves to the shortest waves, this is called the electromagnetic spectrum.

Visible light is part of this spectrum, and it's the only type of electromagnetic wave that your eyes can see. Visible light waves are split up into the colors of the rainbow, with red waves the longest and violet waves the shortest. When all the colored waves are seen together, they make bright white light.

The spectrum in full, going from the longest wave to the shortest wave, looks like this: **r**adio waves, **m**icrowaves, **inf**rared, **v**isible **l**ight (**r**ed, **o**range, **y**ellow, **g**reen, **b**lue, **i**ndigo, **v**iolet), **u**ltraviolet, **x**-rays, **g**amma radiation.

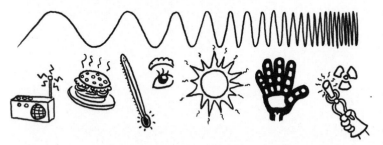

To remember the full spectrum, try using the silly sentence:

Rich **M**en **Inf**late **V**egetables **L**ovingly (**Re**ally **O**ld **Y**ucky **Gr**een **B**eans **I**ncite **Viole**nce) **U**sing **X**ylophones. **Gr**eat!

THE PERIODIC TABLE

Everything you can see around you, including yourself, is made of elements. These elements are the building blocks of the whole universe.

The elements are organized using the periodic table, which is shown below. This looks complicated at first glance, but is easy to follow once you know how it is arranged.

It's Elementary . . .

1 H																	2 He
3 Li	4 Be											5 B	6 C	7 N	8 O	9 F	10 Ne
11 Na	12 Mg											13 Al	14 Si	15 P	16 S	17 Cl	18 Ar
19 K	20 Ca	21 Sc	22 Ti	23 V	24 Cr	25 Mn	26 Fe	27 Co	28 Ni	29 Cu	30 Zn	31 Ga	32 Ge	33 As	34 Se	35 Br	36 Kr
37 Rb	38 Sr	39 Y	40 Zr	41 Nb	42 Mo	43 Tc	44 Ru	45 Rh	46 Pd	47 Ag	48 Cd	49 In	50 Sn	51 Sb	52 Te	53 I	54 Xe
55 Cs	56 Ba	57 - 71 La-Lu	72 Hf	73 Ta	74 W	75 Re	76 Os	77 Ir	78 Pt	79 Au	80 Hg	81 Tl	82 Pb	83 Bi	84 Po	85 At	86 Rn
87 Fr	88 Ra	89 - 103 Ac-Lr	104 Rf	105 Db	106 Sg	107 Bh	108 Hs	109 Mt	110 Uun	111 Uuu	112 Uub	113 Uut	114 Uuq	115 Uup	116 Uuh	117 Uus	118 Uuo

57 La	58 Ce	59 Pr	60 Nd	61 Pm	62 Sm	63 Eu	64 Gd	65 Tb	66 Dy	67 Ho	68 Er	69 Tm	70 Yb	71 Lu
89 Ac	90 Th	91 Pa	92 U	93 Np	94 Pu	95 Am	96 Cm	97 Bk	98 Cf	99 Es	100 Fm	101 Md	102 No	103 Lr

The periodic table is organized into periods and groups. The periods go across the periodic table in rows, and the groups go down the table in columns.

Each element is represented on the periodic table by a symbol. Sometimes, this is part of its name (**Li**thium is represented by **Li**, for example), but just to be tricky, some of the symbols represent the Latin name of the element. For example, potassium is represented by the letter **K**, because its Latin name is **K**alium.

Try not to let these confuse you. The periodic table is the perfect place to come up with some really silly sentences and get those elements memorized! Here's an example for Group One on the table, which is made up of hydrogen (**H**), lithium (**Li**), sodium (**Na**), potassium (**K**), rubidium (**Rb**), caesium (**Cs**), and francium (**Fr**).

Horrible **Li**ttle **Na**talie **K**eeps **R**obbing **C**atherine's **Fr**iends.

Now here's one for Group Two, which is made up of beryllium (**Be**), magnesium (**Mg**), calcium (**Ca**), strontium (**Sr**), barium (**Ba**), and radium (**Ra**).

Beginner **Mag**icians **Ca**n **Se**riously **Ba**ffle **Ra**bbits!

Try creating some silly sentences of your own for the other groups of the periodic table.

Chemical Compounds

A chemical compound is made from at least two different chemical elements found in the periodic table (see page 89).

A famous example of a chemical compound is water, which has the formula H_2O. It is made from hydrogen (H) and oxygen (O), with two hydrogen atoms bonded to every oxygen atom. Compounds are organized into the following categories:

Acids. These react with other chemicals. A well-known acid is citric acid, which is found in fruits such as lemons.

Bases. A base is the opposite of an acid. Acids are measured on the pH scale. A compound with a pH above seven is a base. One with a pH below seven is an acid.

Salts. Bases and acids can sometimes react to make a salt. The salt you put on your food is called sodium chloride and has the formula NaCl (Na is the symbol for sodium and Cl is chlorine).

Oxides. Oxides are compounds of elements with oxygen. When iron (Fe) forms a compound with oxygen (O), it creates iron oxide, which is better known as *rust* (Fe_2O_3).

Organic. An organic compound is one that contains carbon.

To remember these categories, it's time for a silly sentence:

Acidic **Base**balls **S**ave **Ox**en's **Organ**s.

HISTORY HELPER

REMEMBERING WHEN . . .

History is packed with important dates and events. Learning them all may seem tricky, but these tips will help you to keep track of what happened when.

BC or AD?

Sometimes dates have letters next to them—AD, meaning *Anno Domini* (Latin for "year of our Lord") or BC, meaning "Before Christ." These letters divide time before and after when people thought Jesus Christ was born. Remember:

BC comes **b**efore, **AD** follows **a**fter.

First Things First . . .

Early humans lived through three prehistoric ages: the **S**tone **A**ge, the **B**ronze **A**ge, and the **I**ron **A**ge. To remember these in the right order, use the sentence:

Sarah **A**lways **B**eats **A**nna **I**n **A**rithmetic.

The study of ancient civilizations is fascinating. To remember that the **A**ncient **E**gyptians came before the **A**ncient **G**reeks, who came before the **A**ncient **R**omans, use the sentence:

Alice **E**ats **A**pples, **G**rapes, **A**nd **R**aspberries.

93

Dinosaur Days

The dinosaurs roamed the Earth during three main geological periods—the Triassic, the Jurassic, and the Cretaceous.

TRIASSIC PERIOD (251–200 MILLION YEARS AGO)
During the Triassic Period, all the world's land formed one massive continent. The first dinosaurs evolved, along with pterosaurs—small flying reptiles.

In the **Tri**assic, a **tri**ckle of dinosaurs appear.

JURASSIC PERIOD (200–146 MILLION YEARS AGO)
In the Jurassic Period, the landmass began to break up into continents, and forests appeared. Larger dinosaurs, such as the diplodocus, stegosaurus, and brachiosaurus evolved.

The **J**urassic **P**eriod is **jam-p**acked with big dinosaurs.

CRETACEOUS PERIOD (146–66 MILLION YEARS AGO)
In the Cretaceous Period, the dinosaurs were at their peak. Tyrannosaurus Rex and Triceratops lived at this time. Near the end of this period, the dinosaurs became extinct.

In the **Cre**taceous Period, **cre**atures thrive, But by the end of it no dinos are alive!

To remember the order they come in, you could:

Try **j**uggling **cre**am cakes!

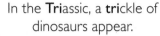

That's a Date!

Two-line rhymes can help you to remember important historical dates. You can even put them together for a whole series of events.

This poem will help you remember important events in the twentieth century and when they happened:

> In **1912**, in April,
> The ship **Titanic** was in peril.
> From **1914** for over four years,
> The **First World War** brought tears.
> In the year **1917**,
> **Russia's Revolution** was seen.
> From '**39** to '**45**,
> **World War Two** came alive.
> In space in **1969**,
> Neil Armstrong's **moon landing** was fine.

See if you can come up with some more rhymes for important dates in your life so far.

95

HISTORICAL WHO'S WHO

Ancient Greek Heroes

Ancient Greece was a world of gods, legends, and heroes. This phrase will help you remember six of the most famous Ancient Greek heroes:

Jason Or The Odd Achy Person.
Jason, **Or**pheus, **The**seus, **Od**ysseus, **Ach**illes, **Pers**eus.

Jason. Jason set sail with a team called the Argonauts, in search of the golden fleece.

Orpheus. This hero famously visited the Underworld to rescue his wife, Eurydice.

Theseus. He killed a beast called the Minotaur, who had been living in a maze and eating children.

Odysseus. He was the hero of Homer's poem, *The Odyssey*, which tells the story of his journey home after the Trojan war.

Achilles. This hero was an invincible warrior who died when an arrow struck his heel—his only weak spot.

Perseus. He killed Medusa, a hideous Gorgon, whose stare turned people to stone.

The Twelve Labors of Hercules

The most famous of all the Greek heroes was Hercules, who completed twelve impossible challenges, known as the Twelve Labors of Hercules. You can remember his tricky tasks with this little poem:

> **Lion**, **Hydra**, **Hind**, and **Boar**,
> Clean the **Stables** and off once more.
> **Birds**, **Bull**, and **Mares** to battle,
> Catch a **Belt** and then some **Cattle**.
> Golden **Apples** he had to steal,
> Then **Cerberus** to end the deal.

The twelve tasks Hercules had to tackle were: slaying the Nemean Lion and the nine-headed Hydra; capturing a deer that could run really fast, called the Cerynean Hind, and a wild boar; cleaning out some seriously stinky stables; taking care of some man-eating birds; capturing a giant bull; catching some fearsome horses, and stealing the belt of a warrior queen; bringing back a monster's cows, a god's apples; and, last but not least, capturing Cerberus, a three-headed dog at the entrance to the Underworld. And you thought your math homework was tricky!

Explorers and Their Discoveries

You probably already know about Christopher Columbus and his voyage of discovery to America. There's a famous mnemonic rhyme to help you remember when this took place. This begins:

> In fourteen-hundred-and-ninety-two,
> Columbus sailed the ocean blue.
> He had three ships and left from Spain;
> He sailed through sunshine, wind, and rain . . .

But what about other explorers who made important discoveries? This poem will help you remember them.

> So **Columbus** found the New World in **1492**,
> But five years later, **Vasco da Gama** set sail, too.
> He found a new sea route to the **Indian** land,
> Around Africa four ships took his brave band.
> In **1519, Cortez** conquered **Mexico**,
> While off to **Peru Pizarro** did go.
> But the longest voyage is yet to be told,
> **Magellan's round-world trip**, so daring and bold.
> Two hundred and fifty one brave men set sail,
> For three years they voyaged and did not fail,
> In **1522**, they reached home in their ship,
> Only 18 survivors from that long trip.

Inventors and Inventions

History has been changed by some amazing inventions. Where would we be without the wheel, or electric lighting? Make sure you're not in the dark about some of these famous folk:

ALEXANDER GRAHAM BELL (1847–1922)

A Scottish inventor who was fascinated by communication and whose studies led him to invent the first telephone in 1876. To remember who invented the telephone:

👁 *Picture a big **telephone** ringing like a **bell**.*

THOMAS EDISON (1847–1931)

Thomas Edison developed our modern lighting system with a bulb that burned brightly and for a long time. In 1882, he formed the Edison Electric Illuminating Company, and electric lighting began. To remember who invented modern lighting:

👁 *Imagine a man named Eddie congratulating his son Thomas for being so clever.*
("Eddie's-son" sounds like "Edison.")

The Wright Brothers

In 1903, Wilbur and Orville Wright made the first powered air flight for a historic, yet short, 12 seconds. Remember it using this sentence:

The first plane flew (**W**)**right** into the air.

John Logie Baird (1888–1946)

In 1924, Baird (pronounced bear – d) invented a machine that could transmit an image over a short distance. This was the birth of the television. To remember who invented TV:

👁 Imagine a **bear** dancing around on your **television** screen.

Alexander Fleming (1881–1955)

In 1928, Alexander Fleming accidentally discovered the antibiotic penicillin when some mold grew on a petri dish he had left uncovered. Remember:

Fleming didn't make a **pen**ny from his **pen**icillin invention, and yet he saved millions of lives.

BIG BUILDINGS

Castles

The Medieval Age was a violent, dangerous time to be alive. Kings and powerful lords were constantly waging war as they fought each other for land and wealth.

These kings and lords built huge castles to protect themselves from attack. Although each was different in its design, most were made up of the same parts. These are a **m**oat, a **d**rawbridge, a **p**ortcullis, a **g**atehouse, **b**attlements, an **o**uter **b**ailey, an **i**nner **b**ailey, and a **k**eep. Remember:

My Daughter **P**olly **G**oes **B**onkers **O**n **B**ananas **I**n **B**ubbly **K**etchup!

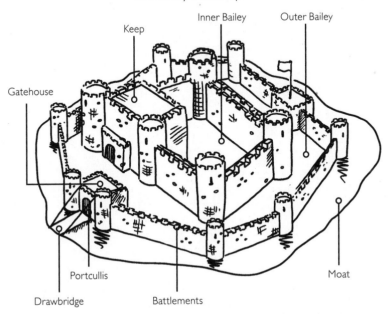

101

ART, MUSIC, AND LITERATURE

AWESOME ART

Art is all around you, in lots of different forms. Whether you like drawing, painting, or sculpting, or if you prefer to soak up the beautiful masterpieces of artists who've come before you, keep reading to impress your art teacher and make your life more colorful!

The Color Wheel

A color wheel will help you to remember how colors work, and how you can mix colors together to make different ones.

The three primary colors—red, blue, and yellow—are those that are not made by mixing other colors.

Each of the secondary colors—orange, green, and purple—is made by mixing the two primary colors on either side of it on the color wheel. To remember which are primary colors and which are secondary colors, use the rhyme:

First came **red** and **yellow** with their best friend **blue.**

Then came **green** and **orange**, and **purple** came, too.

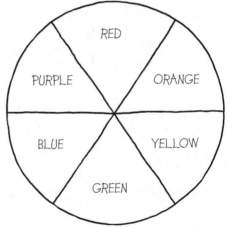

Art Through the Ages

If you study art, you will notice that there have been lots of different artistic styles used by painters and sculptors through the centuries. Use this simple sentence to help you to remember some of them, and then read on to find out a bit more about them:

Painting **A**rt **M**adly **R**eally **B**reaks
Rules = **I**nteresting **P**ictures!

Prehistoric. Prehistoric art dates from around 70,000 BC. Examples of art created by early people include the spectacular paintings in the Lascaux cave in France.

Ancient Art. Examples of ancient art include Roman frescoes and Greek vases.

Middle Ages. Art from the Middle Ages contains many religious scenes and objects.

Renaissance. This style includes works by Leonardo da Vinci, Botticelli, and Michelangelo.

Baroque. The Baroque period involved dramatic paintings and sculptures that were sometimes quite sinister.

Romanticism. Art in the Romantic period featured lots of sweeping landscapes.

Impressionism. The Impressionist artists focused on painting scenes as if they'd just caught a glimpse of them. One of the most famous Impressionist painters is Claude Monet.

Pop Art. Pop art uses bright colors and geometric shapes. Artists such as Andy Warhol and Roy Lichtenstein showed that anything from soup cans to comic strips could be art.

Six Famous Artworks

Read the poem below, and you'll learn about six of the most famous paintings in the world. If you have a favorite painting or work of art, why not make up a rhyme for it and add it to this poem?

Vincent Van Gogh's *Sunflowers,*
Show off the Dutchman's powers.
While **da Vinci**'s *Mona Lisa,*
Is certainly sure to please ya!
Michelangelo's *Sistine* ceiling,
Shows true artistic feeling,
And as for **Gustav Klimt**'s *Kiss,*
That's a painting not to miss.
The Scream by **Edvard Munch**,
Is the fifth painting in this bunch.
While **Andy Warhol**'s *Campbell's Soup,*
Finishes this famous group.

MARVELOUS MUSIC

Get ready to brush up your knowledge and impress people with your amazing musical memory.

Parts of an Orchestra

An orchestra usually contains four types of instruments. These are: **s**tring instruments, such as the violin; **p**ercussion, which are instruments that you can hit or shake; **w**oodwind instruments, such as the clarinet; and **b**rass instruments, such as the trumpet and the trombone.

Remember these types of instruments by using the phrase:

Symphonies **P**layed **W**ith **B**rilliance.

Music, Maestro!

These memory tricks will help you to remember more about the instruments that make beautiful music in an orchestra.

Strings And Things

To remember the most important string instruments in an orchestra, use the sentence:

Viola's **violin** said, "**Cello**" to the **double bass**.

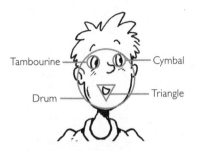

Tambourine

Cymbal

Drum

Triangle

Beat It!

To help you remember percussion instruments:

👁 *Picture a face, made from a drum, with a cymbal and a tambourine for eyes and a triangle for a mouth!*

Blow Your Own Trumpet

The following mnemonic will help you to remember four of the most important brass instruments:

The drinking **horn** held three teas (**t**'s)

The three **t**'s are the **t**uba, the **t**rumpet, and the **t**rombone.

Toot The Flute

Woodwind instruments may look very similar, but you can remember the names of some of them with this little rhyme:

Clarinet, **oboe**, and **bassoon**,
Piccolo, **flute**, and **saxophone**.

GET IT WRITE!

Get ready to beat even the biggest bookworm, as you learn how to remember some of the most famous works of literature.

Pottermania

Harry Potter and his wizarding adventures have entertained millions of readers. Use the following little story to help you remember all seven books in the right order.

Harry Potter was out walking when he tripped over a **stone** (*The Sorcerer's* **Stone**). He noticed a hidden trapdoor that led him to a **chamber** (*The* **Chamber** *of Secrets*), where there was a **prisoner** (*The* **Prisoner** *of Azkaban*) chained up inside. In the corner of the room was a roaring **fire** (*The Goblet of* **Fire**). Suddenly, a **phoenix** (*The Order of the* **Phoenix**) flew from the flames and transformed into a handsome **prince** (*The Half-Blood* **Prince**). Harry was so shocked that all he could say was, "**Hallo!**" (*The Deathly* **Hallo**ws).

Shakespeare's Plays

William Shakespeare wrote some of the most famous plays
of all time. This poem will help you to remember them.

Let's learn them *As You Like It*,
Without a *Comedy of Errors*,
From the *Merry Wives of Windsor*
To *Macbeth* and other terrors.
There's *Othello* and *King John*,
And there's *Hamlet* and *King Lear*,
Young *Romeo and Juliet*,
Who loved with a love so dear.
Henry IV Parts One and Two,
Henry V is another,
Henry VI One, Two, and Three
And *Henry VIII* the other.
Richard II and *Richard III*,
Are other kings from the bard's pen,
There's *Two Gentlemen of Verona*,
And even *Two Noble Kinsmen*.
He wrote of *Julius Caesar*,
Cymbeline, and *Pericles*, too,
He told of *Titus Andronicus*,
And of the *Taming of the Shrew*.
From a cool *Midsummer Night's Dream*,
To *The Tempest* and *A Winter's Tale*,
From *Timon of Athens* in Greece,
To *The Merchant of Venice* we sail.
There's the tale of *Love's Labour's Lost*,
And that of *Measure for Measure*,
There's *Much Ado About Nothing*,
And *Twelfth Night* is a real treasure.
Of *Troilus and Cressida*,
And *Coriolanus* I tell,
Of *Antony and Cleopatra*,
But *All's Well That Ends Well*.

OTHER STUFF

A LITTLE BIT OF EVERYTHING

The other sections in this book will help your massive memory to be the best in the classroom. This one will boost your general knowledge for when school's out, so you'll always be ready to impress your friends with your terrific trivia.

One for Sorrow

There are many superstitions that give meanings to everyday things. For example, you probably know that the number 13 is supposed to be unlucky. Some superstitions are more detailed, and need mnemonics to help people remember the meanings attached to them. Read the poem below to decode the meanings behind groups of magpies.

> One for sorrow, two for joy,
> Three for a girl, four for a boy,
> Five for silver, six for gold,
> Seven for a secret never to be told,
> Eight for a wish, nine for a kiss,
> Ten for a bird that's best to miss.

The Decathlon

The toughest athletic competition of all is the decathlon. Athletes have to compete in not just one, but ten track and field events! Here's a handy way to learn the sports that make up the contest, using the grouping technique.

Most athletics events involve running, jumping, or throwing, so group the events in this order:

Three runs (100 meters, 400 meters, 1,500 meters).
Three jumps (long jump, high jump, pole vault).
Three throws (discus, javelin, shotput).

You might have noticed that this only adds up to nine events but, as long as you remember these, you'll have no problem getting over the last **hurdle** (the tenth event is the 110-meter hurdles).

The Parts of a Ship

Sailors use different words to describe the front, back, left, and right of a ship. Use the following mnemonic—starting at the front of the ship and moving clockwise:

Bow to the **star**s (starboard),
turn (stern) to **port**.

Did You Know?
It is said that the word *posh* is an acronym for "**P**ort **O**ut, **S**tarboard **H**ome," and was used by wealthy passengers on long sea journeys to help them remember where to book the best cabins.

Types of Coffee

Coffee can be served with milk, with foam, even with chocolate! The different combinations of coffee and milk have different names. Read on to wow your friends with your sophisticated knowledge of coffee culture!

Espresso. This is a shot of pure black coffee, served in a tiny cup without milk.

Macchiato. This strong coffee drink is served in a small cup, with a shot of espresso and a small amount of steamed milk.

Americano. An Americano is a shot of espresso, served in a large mug and topped up with hot water.

Latte. If you order a latte, you'll be served a large cup filled with espresso and steamed milk, then topped with foamy milk.

Cappucino. This coffee is a shot of espresso, topped with lots of foaming milk and sometimes chocolate shavings.

Mocha. A decadent mocha contains espresso, chocolate, steamed milk, and sometimes a blob of whipped cream.

Remember the different coffees with the sentence:

Even **M**eerkats **A**re **L**ate **C**ounting **M**oney!

113

Signs of the Zodiac

Astrologists are people who believe people are influenced by the position of groups of stars at the time of their birth. The 12 constellations they use are called the Zodiac. Check out your star sign below and find out how to remember all 12.

Aries	The Ram	March 21–April 20
Taurus	The Bull	April 21–May 20
Gemini	The Twins	May 21– June 20
Cancer	The Crab	June 21–July 20
Leo	The Lion	July 21–August 22
Virgo	The Virgin	August 23–September 22
Libra	The Scales	September 23–October 22
Scorpio	The Scorpion	October 23–November 22
Sagittarius	The Archer	November 23–December 22
Capricorn	The Goat	December 23–January 20
Aquarius	The Water Carrier	January 21–February 19
Pisces	The Fish	February 20–March 20

You can use the first letter of each of the Zodiac signs to make a mega acrostic sentence, like this one:

All **T**he **G**reen **C**ats **L**ike **V**ery **L**arge **S**caly **S**almon **C**anned **A**nd **P**ickled.

Or, to remember the order with a picture

👁 *Imagine a clock face. Picture Aries (a ram) at number 12, and go around clockwise, replacing each number with a Zodiac sign.*

Ranks of the Army

The armed forces need to be very well organized indeed if they are to be effective. This is why having different ranks is so important. There are many ranks in the army, but there are nine main divisions. These, in order of importance, are: General, Brigadier, Colonel, Major, Captain, Lieutenant, Sergeant, Corporal, and Private.

The following poem will help you to remember them in the right order.

"In **general**," the **Brigadier** to the **Colonel** said,
"The **major** problem's the **Captain**, who stays in bed.
The **Lieutenant** is lazy, so the **Sergeant** taught us,
And the **Corporal**'s asleep in his **private** quarters."

Phases of the Moon

As the moon travels around the Earth, it seems to change. Night by night, the part of the moon you see grows (waxes) from a thin crescent shape to a full circle and then shrinks (wanes) back once more to a thin crescent before disappearing. The cycle then begins again. These changes are called the phases of the moon. To recognize the phases when the moon is in the night sky, use the word **DOC**.

Shape Of The Moon	Shaped Like A Letter	Phase
◗	D	Waxing
●	O	Full
☾	C	Waning

115

THE
MEMORY GYM

TERRIFIC TECHNIQUES

This book contains a whole range of mnemonic devices to help you remember information—poems, pictures, acrostics, numbers, patterns, phrases, sayings, puns, wordplay, stories, and journeys. Hopefully, you will be able to start using some of these tricks for other memory tasks you come across.

In this section of the book, you'll find some other techniques you can use and some games you can play to give your memory skills a good workout.

Chunking

Chunking is used to group items together to give you fewer *chunks* to remember. For example, if you had to remember the number 703861952, it is a much easier task if you try to remember it as:

703 – 861 – 952.

The reason it is easier is because you are tricking your brain into thinking it only has to remember three things instead of nine.

You can combine chunking with chants or rhymes to make it even more effective. Take, for example, the seven dwarfs from Disney's *Snow White*: **S**neezy, **S**leepy, **D**opey, **D**oc, **H**appy, **B**ashful, and **G**rumpy.

You can use chunking to remember them by using the chant:

Double **S**, Double **D**, and an **HBG**!

Number Rhyming

Number rhyming is really useful when you need to remember a list of items, such as when you go shopping.

To use number rhyming, you start by thinking of ten things that rhyme with the numbers from one to ten. Examples are given below, but making up your own rhymes is even better:

One rhymes with **sun**
Two rhymes with **glue**
Three rhymes with **tree**
Four rhymes with **door**
Five rhymes with **hive**
Six rhymes with **sticks**
Seven rhymes with **heaven**
Eight rhymes with **gate**
Nine rhymes with **sign**
Ten rhymes with **pen.**

Imagine your mother has sent you into your local supermarket and asked you to buy the following items: bananas, cake, lemonade, jelly, chocolate, spaghetti, burgers, bacon, and bread. She has told you that you can buy yourself a comic as well, while you are there.

Link up each of the items on your shopping list with a number from one to ten, and remember your number rhyme that goes with it. Then, picture the scene in your mind, and it's sure to stay there.

This may seem like even more things to remember, but you'll find it's a system that really works!

For example, bananas are first on your list, so they're number one. Remember that **one** rhymes with **sun**.

👁 *Imagine the **Sun**, with its rays made up of **bananas**!*

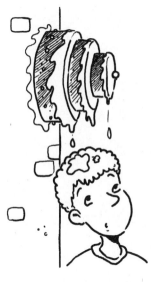

Cake is next on the shopping list, so that's number two. Remember that **two** rhymes with **glue**.

👁 *Picture a birthday **cake** **glued** to the wall!*

Keep on creating pictures in your head until you've completed the shopping list.

Once you have pictured all the scenes, see if you can remember all the objects. You should find you remember far more of the items on your list this way.

119

The Memory Palace

The memory palace helps you to remember items by wandering through a wonderful building that you have created in your imagination.

To practice the memory palace, read on to learn about the Seven Wonders of the Ancient World. These are: the Great Pyramid of Giza, the Hanging Gardens of Babylon, the Colossus of Rhodes, the Mausoleum of Halicarnassus, the Pharos of Alexandria, the Statue of Zeus, and the Temple of Artemis.

👁 *Imagine walking through the front door of your palace. You're standing in a huge hallway, where a* **great Egyptian** *Pharaoh greets you. (The Great Pyramid)*

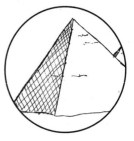

From the hall you walk up a wide staircase. At the top, a **baby** *in a stroller holds out a* **flower** *to you. (The Hanging Gardens of* **Baby***lon)*

You reach the top of the staircase and see two corridors disappearing off like long **roads***. (The Colossus of Rhodes)*

120

*You walk along a corridor to a big window looking out onto the grounds, where there is a large pond. You look out and see a **hali**but turning **cart**wheels. (The Mausoleum of **Halicar**nassus)*

*You turn a corner and enter a grand dining hall. A waitress named **Alexandria** offers you a tiny model of a **lighthouse** on a silver platter. (The Pharos of Alexandria)*

*Leaving the hall, you walk down three steps and into a busy kitchen, full of people running to and fro preparing a delicious meal fit for the god **Zeus**. (The Statue of Zeus)*

*The chef chases you away, and you run into a room, where the mistress of the palace is painting a work of art at an easel. She's an **arty miss**! (The Temple of Artemis)*

You have now completed your walk through the palace. Now, imagine going back to the front door and repeating your journey. See if you can see all the objects that help you remember each of the Seven Wonders of the World.

Once you get the hang of a memory palace, you can use it to remember absolutely anything.

121

THE GAME ROOM

Playing games can be a great way to give your memory a really good workout. The games below will help you to develop your memory muscles and have some fun, too.

Memory

To play "Memory," all you need is a pack of cards, a good memory, and an opponent.

Shuffle the cards and lay all of them facedown in four rows of 13. The object of the game is to find more matching pairs than your opponent. A matching pair is two cards of the same value and the same color. For example, the seven of clubs and the seven of spades would be a matching pair, as would the queen of diamonds and the queen of hearts.

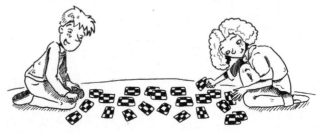

How to play: Player One picks a card and turns it over so both players can see it. He then turns over a second card. If they form a matching pair, he wins the cards, puts them in his pile, and has another turn. If they are not a matching pair, they are returned, facedown, to their place in the rows.

Player Two now turns over a card. If the card matches one of those turned over by Player One, she can turn that card over to make a pair. Otherwise, she turns over a different card.

As the game continues, it is important to remember the location and value of as many of the cards that have been turned over as possible. This will help you find more pairs than your opponent. Play continues until all the cards have been matched. The winner is the person with the most pairs.

I Went to the Store and Bought . . .

How to play: The first player thinks of an item to start the list. For example she might say: "I went to the store and bought a bucket."

The next player adds an item: "I went to the store and bought a bucket and a can of sardines."

Play continues with each person adding an item:

"I went to the store and bought a bucket, a can of sardines, a guitar . . ."

If someone forgets an item, they are out of the game. Play continues until there is only one person left.

I'm Sure There's Something Missing!

This game will help you develop your visual memory. Collect a dozen or so objects and lay them out on a tray. You can use anything you like—pens, paper clips, candy, rulers, pieces of paper, cups, and so on.

How to play: Show the tray to the other player and allow them twenty seconds to study it. Then ask them to turn around so they cannot see what you're doing.

Pick an object and remove it from the tray, then shuffle the objects and ask the person to turn around and tell you which item is missing.

The other player then chooses a group of items and it is your turn to try to remember which item is missing.

What's Happening?

"What's Happening?" is another game that helps develop your visual memory.

How to play: Find a picture that shows a lot of activity, such as the street scene opposite. Allow the other player to study it for a minute. Next, hold the picture so that your friend cannot see it, and ask ten questions to see how well he has remembered it. For example, in the scene on the next page, your questions could include:

1. How many people are wearing hats?
2. What is the name of the butcher's shop?
3. What is the dog doing?
4. Who is riding a bike?
5. What is the time?
6. What is the number of the bus?
7. What type of vacation is on the travel agent's poster?
8. What are the two men carrying?
9. Who is wearing a scarf?
10. How many birds are there?

INDEX

ALSO AVAILABLE . . .

The Boys' Book: How to Be
the Best at Everything
978-0-545-01628-5

The Girls' Book: How to Be
the Best at Everything
978-0-545-01629-2

The Girls' Book of Glamour:
A Guide to Being a Goddess
978-0-545-08537-3

The Boys' Book of Survival: How
to Survive Anything, Anywhere
978-0-545-08536-6

Thirty Days Has September:
Cool Ways to Remember Stuff
978-0-545-10740-2

THE ART OF LISTENING

THE ART
OF
LISTENING
Developing Musical Perception
FIFTH EDITION

Jeanne Shapiro Bamberger • **Howard Brofsky**
Massachusetts Institute of Technology   *Queens College,*
The City University of New York

with

Martin Brody • **Roland Vazquez**
Wellesley College   *Massachusetts Institute*
of Technology

WITH A FOREWORD BY ROGER SESSIONS

Harper & Row, Publishers, New York

Cambridge, Philadelphia, San Francisco, Washington, London, Mexico City, São Paulo, Singapore, Sydney

Illustration Acknowledgments can be found on page 465.

Sponsoring Editor: Barbara Cinquegrani
Project Editor: Ellen Meek Tweedy
Coordinating Editor: David Bain
Text Design: Robert Bull
Cover Design/Art: Miriam Brofsky
Photo Research: Mira Schachne
Production Manager: Willie Lane
Compositor: TAPSCO, Inc.
Printer and Binder: R. R. Donnelley & Sons Company
Cover Printer: New England Book Components

The Art of Listening: Developing Musical Perception, Fifth Edition

Copyright © 1988 by Jeanne Shapiro Bamberger and Howard Brofsky

Library of Congress Cataloging-in-Publication Data

Bamberger, Jeanne Shapiro.
    The art of listening: developing musical perception/Jeanne
Shapiro Bamberger, Howard Brofsky, with Martin Brody, Roland Vazquez;
with a foreword by Roger Sessions.—5th ed.
        p.   cm.
    Includes index.
    ISBN 0-06-360350-0
    1. Music appreciation.   2. Music—Instruction and study—Audio-
visual aids.   I. Brofsky, Howard.   II. Title.
MT150.B25 1988
780′.15—dc19   87-33473
                                                                      CIP

88 89 90 91 9 8 7 6 5 4 3 2 1

Dedicated to the memory
of Roger Sessions

Contents

PART ONE
Means and Possibilities

PART TWO
Process and Design

PART THREE
Structure: Form and Function

PART FOUR
Style and the Historical Context

Foreword *by Roger Sessions*

This book can be of great value to the student or layman who is attracted to music and who seeks to gain from it all that it has to offer him. To be sure, the reader will not be able to achieve his goal without effort; but it is not the authors of the book, but music itself, which demands this effort—an effort no greater and no less, after all, than that demanded by any of the other major arts.

The quotation from Stravinsky that begins the introduction should be pondered and kept constantly in mind as a kind of premise underlying all that the student can learn from the book. *The Art of Listening* is presented by its authors against a background of a general course in humanities at the University of Chicago; and the book's value derives from the authors' firm conviction that understanding of music, on any level whatever, is to be found only in music itself, and in a direct awareness of music rather than information about it. Much of the value of the book therefore stems to a large extent from its earlier portions, in which the reader is shown, through simple and effective steps, how such direct awareness can be cultivated. The authors have organized their material clearly and well, with a view to the reader's experience; they introduce each element first in its most immediately apprehensible form and follow this directly by illustrations of its application in a larger context. In doing so, material is drawn from a large variety of sources in such a manner, one would expect, as to stimulate the reader's curiosity and make him aware of the fact that the horizons of music are indeed very broad. The authors, by repeated emphasis, make clear the fact, often neglected, that these so-called elements of music must in no way be considered as independent of each other; they are facets of a whole that is indivisible by its very nature.

The authors also—without undue insistence but nevertheless very clearly—emphasize the importance of geniune involvement on the part of anyone who is drawn toward music, whatever the motive or the nature of this involvement may be. Such involvement is taken for granted by virtually everyone in literature and the visual arts, but is much less generally understood in music. No one could be very seriously regarded as a lover or connoisseur of poetry if his experience of poetry were limited to occasional cursory readings which did not include his lingering over the poem and savoring every detail to the full. The same quality of "savoring" is considered intrinsic to an appreciation of the visual arts. The problem with music, however, lies in the impermanence which constitutes its very nature. Far more than any art, its whole existence is in the realm of time, to which it gives shape and content. Like time, music passes, and its regulated flow is of the very essence. One cannot linger over music and enjoy its flavor to the full without, on the one hand, playing or singing it, or, on the other, listening to it attentively and repeatedly, and thus becoming aware of its movement in detail.

The authors (wisely, I believe) have left for the last chapters the section of the book whose function is solely to provide information of a historical nature. This information is provided in summary fashion, and ample indications are given as to where additional factual material can be found if desired. That such information should be offered is natural, if only to satisfy the curiosity of the reader. The reader will in the course of the book have become acquainted with a wide variety of music and may well have become curious as to the sources of and reasons for this variety. However, today probably as never before— and probably above all in colleges and universities—it needs to be tirelessly emphasized that music, like every other art, has existence and values of its own, quite distinct from its history, its ethnology, or its theory. It is these values which must be paramount if music is to be understood in any sense at all. The authors of *The Art of Listening* have, I believe, understood this point exceptionally well. Here too their aim is to stimulate the student's powers of observation and independent judgment. While starting with categorical distinctions of a conventional, and therefore convenient, nature, they quickly take pains to point out the looseness and inadequacy of these distinctions and the richness and variety and freedom of invention which lies beneath and ultimately remains quite independent of them.

Preface

To mark the fifth edition of *The Art of Listening* we have made significant additions: four new chapters, two new records, and nearly thirty new recorded examples devoted entirely to the study of style and music history. These additions have been stimulated by requests from colleagues around the country that we integrate into the text and recordings an approach to music history consistent with the integrity and spirit of the earlier chapters. The requests presented us with a serious challenge and to help meet it we enlisted the cooperation of two younger colleagues—Martin Brody, a theorist and composer, and Roland Vazquez, a music historian. Our commitment to make the new chapters grow naturally from the earlier ones has resulted, we believe, in an approach unique to texts on music history. In designing the new Part Four, we were able to build upon the listening skills students had already acquired in the earlier chapters while continuing our primary emphasis on learning through the direct experience of reflective listening.

Thus, the new history section is not just a chronology of pieces and facts about them as is so often the case in other texts, but rather a new set of musical experiences that encourages students to apply what they have already learned in new contexts. Subtle differences in rhythmic, textural, melodic, and harmonic relations that the students have learned to hear in the context of structural functions they now revisit as compositional means in the contexts of history, culture, and style.

In approaching music history, we have carried forward some of the central themes of the book. For example, the importance of context in giving meaning to musical events at all levels of structure: a small detail, a phrase, a whole passage. To this we now add the stylistic context, taking care to approach style also as a convergence of multiple factors at differing social, cultural, and musical levels: the more general musical and cultural assumptions of an era; those that emerge at a particular time or place (sometimes even on a particular occasion); the musical gestures that characterize a given composer's body of works; and, finally, those features that are unique to the single piece with which we may be concerned.

Our purposes, then, as in the rest of the book, are above all practical; our goal is to provide materials that will encourage students to experiment with new ways of listening, to question intelligently their own responses, and most of all to stimulate them to go on to other musical experiences beyond those they find in the book and on the records.

To do so, we have made a rather radical departure with respect to more traditional histories: We begin in Chapter 8 at the "beginning"—circa 800 with chant (but even here not only Western plainchant is represented)—move quickly on to listen closely to a work by Perotin (c. 1200), and then to a piece by Victoria (1572). We end Part Four with a tour through music composed between 1859 and 1913 in Chapter 12. But in the three middle chapters (9, 10, and 11) our procedure is not chronological. Instead, we focus on pairs of pieces that are strikingly contrasting in style while sharing some common human theme—love, religion, dance. In this way we give students the opportunity to practice hearing and experiencing for themselves the processes—the musical features and relations—that make one work so different stylistically from another. To help, we surround each piece with its cultural context and, again in a practical vein, try to give a sense of a composer's working life: his monetary and spiritual support systems, his audience, his colleagues and their music. Thus here, as elsewhere in the book, depth is more important than breadth; "learning how" is more important than "learning that." The paired examples, in all their particularity, do span a wide range historically: Machaut (c. 1350) and Schubert; Bach and Verdi; Chopin and Babbitt (1979). And in Chapter 12, we have included on the records many of the examples in our discussion (a revised version from earlier editions) of the period bounded by Wagner and Moussorgsky on one side and Schoenberg and Stravinsky on the other.

Finally, in Chapter 13 we have, as in other editions, put into chronological order all the examples from the entire book. Thus students have the opportunity to experience the effect of multiple views provided by multiple contexts as they reconsider the pieces they have come to know in other ways in juxtaposition with their historical neighbors.

The fifth edition also includes a number of other improvements:

> We have tried to make our writing clearer and more directly relevant to the listener's immediate experience. We also prepare students for material in Part Four by referring students frequently in the earlier chapters to the stylistic and historical implications of a work or a particular aspect of music which will become their focus later on.

We have significantly improved the recorded examples. We have added four complete record sides and upgraded the quality of many of the recordings—better performances and/or more modern recordings have been substituted wherever we thought necessary, and the electronically synthesized examples in the Lecture-Demonstration have been redone in the MIT Experimental Music Studio with much more modern equipment.

Revisions have been made within a number of chapters. We have made the chapter on rhythm, for example, more consistent internally and also rethought a number of basic concepts in the light of current theoretical and empirical research on rhythm and rhythm perception. In the chapter on melody we have expanded our discussion of motivic development and added several new examples in order to better prepare students for their later study of larger structures. The chapter on sonata form is now more complete since we include on the records a long excerpt from the Brahms *Symphony 3.*

Finally, the book has been given a whole new look: a hard cover for the first time; an improvement in the general design for easier readability; a number of interesting new pictures (especially in conjunction with the history section); and several newly developed historical time-lines—some relatively local in scope and specific to a group of works under concern; others more global, showing events as they converge across many areas of cultural history.

The Preface to the fifth edition would not be complete without a word about Roger Sessions, who died in 1985 at the age of 89. Sessions wrote the Foreward for the first edition of our book some 17 years ago. We have chosen to leave the Foreward as he wrote it out of respect and appreciation. Sessions's remarks also remain as a kind of trace of the book's history—with the addition of our expanded and rather unorthodox history section in this edition, we believe we have been responsive to his doubts concerning the role we have given to music history in the past: " . . . the function of the last chapter of the book . . . is solely to provide information of a historical nature." At the same time we have been sensitive to Sessions's admonition that "music, like every other art, has existence and value of its own quite distinct from its history, its ethnology, its theory." Thus, in redesigning these last chapters our emphasis has been not so much on providing "information" but rather on encouraging the student's direct experience and "genuine involvement" with a few exemplary works. Here, as elsewhere in the book, our aim, as Sessions puts it so well, has been "to stimulate the student's powers of observation and independent judgment."

Sessions has influenced this book in many ways, but one in particular comes to mind in rereading the Foreword: his belief in the importance of "savoring every detail" in music as in poetry. The importance Sessions gave to detail may account in part for our perhaps overly enthusiastic attention to detail in the book. But his remark also brings back the memory of a phrase he used once in an informal conversation not long before he died. In an effort to bring home his argument that every great piece and each of its details must be considered unique and never merely another version of some generalizable form, formula, or convention he said, referring to his own thinking and writing, "You know, I find it more and more difficult to use plurals." And it is revealing to notice that in the Foreward, Sessions speaks of potential readers and students as *individuals;* he always refers to *a* reader or *a* student (singular), never to readers or students (plural).

Sessions will be remembered as one of this century's greatest composers, and perhaps its greatest teacher of musicians. And for those of us who were his students, he will be remembered as one who inspired us to make music and to hear it with every detail related always to the "large line." But most of all we will remember him for believing in and nurturing our musical intuitions: What we learned to *do* as musicians was always more important than what we learned to say *about* music. This book is dedicated to Roger Sessions's memory.

Jeanne Shapiro Bamberger
Howard Brofsky

Introduction

. . . verbal dialectic is powerless to define musical dialectic in its totality.
—Stravinsky[1]

This book grew from our desire to teach introductory music from an entirely new and radically different point of view. When we first developed the materials for this new approach, we were both teaching the introductory humanities course at the University of Chicago. There were no prerequisites for the course. Neither an ability to read music nor any extensive familiarity with it was required. Through encouraging an exchange among students and between students and instructor, we tried to discover the paths through which students become actively involved with music. We concluded that the primary emphasis in our classes should be on experience itself rather than on facts about music, terminology, or techniques.

We have taken the same approach in this book. In every way possible, we have reinforced the principle of beginning with one's immediate response to a given piece of music rather than with "the acquisition of a vocabulary."

You, as a student using this book and its accompanying records, should first consider your own experience with a given example. Then try to determine what in the music has contributed to this experience. Having done so, you're ready to return once more to your own experience of the piece in the light of your more conscious awareness of what has stimulated it. The learning process must be an active one, one in which you are always personally involved, questioning, and critical.

Following the cue of our students, we begin with that aspect of music which seems most immediately accessible: its purely sensuous effect upon the listener. We examine a variety of possibilities for making and combining sounds in the works of different composers (Chapter 1). Having first isolated certain aspects of sound, we then show how these aspects are combined and interrelated in more complex fashions. Our analysis leads naturally into another aspect of music, rhythmic organization (Chapter 2).

---

[1] Igor Stravinsky, *Poetics of Music,* Cambridge: Harvard University Press, 1947, p. 123.

You will discover, for instance, the notion of measured time—the beat and the grouping of beats into larger units of time. You will also heighten your natural awareness of the grouping of musical events (tones) into musical gestures or figures and hear how these intersect with beats and beat groups. From here we go on to combine and interrelate other factors that contribute to a sense of organized time in music. You will consider relative duration and motion of larger musical gestures and then hear how changes and conflicts in rates of motion can affect your experience of specific passages.

At this point, you will step back from these broader considerations once again to isolate elements, this time to consider *pitch* and how it can be organized to form *melody* (Chapter 3).

Next you will consider aspects of music that contribute to its larger scale structure (*return* in Chapter 4; *harmony* in Chapter 5). Here you will naturally begin to move outward from the details of specific and rather isolated pitch and time relationships. Rhythmic, melodic, and harmonic aspects will eventually be heard not as isolated factors but as parts of an inseparable whole, combining and influencing one another to create the events, motion, and process of a unique work.

You will go on, then, to focus on the *functions* of passages within larger works (Chapter 6 and 7). In these chapters you will discover how the same melodic or rhythmic material can be dramatically transformed so as to create contrasts in the feelings they evoke (stability, instability, tension, repose) and also to create varying structural functions (statement, transition, development, ending) within a piece.

Having begun, then, with your response to an immediately perceptible aspect of music—its sound—our analysis becomes increasingly specific. Through a growing awareness of specific musical means we move toward more complete perception of, and response to, the total piece of music which those means generate. The excitement you feel in response to a significant detail in a small excerpt develops into the possibility for fuller participation in a complete work.

The process is paralleled in the recorded material itself. You will notice that the excerpts become longer as we move from isolated aspects of music toward the total experience of a work. For example, in the earlier portions of the chapters on texture, rhythmic relationships, or pitch relationships, you will find shorter excerpts chosen to focus your attention on one particular element. Later in these chapters (and especially when we deal with structure, function, or style), the excerpts will grow longer. Finally you are dealing with complete works.

This organization reflects in a practical fashion the process which we described above: the movement from the perception of *isolated* aspects toward the perception of these aspects as an inseparable *whole*—a specific work with its unique emotional impact.

With the goal of developing active and full perception, we ask you from the beginning to listen carefully to each example, always with the appropriate section of the book in hand. Without the book the musical examples will seem a strange and often meaningless hodgepodge. The short excerpts (particularly in the early chapters of the book) demand a special and probably new mode of listening to music. You cannot expect simply to put on a record and listen straight through an entire side. Instead you will need to concentrate on each individual example, sometimes listening to it more than once. In many instances you will be asked to listen for very specific details which may not be immediately apparent. If you cannot hear in the excerpt what is described in the text, go back and listen again, since it may be just these new dimensions of a composition that will give the piece quite a different meaning for you. Notice, also, that each of the records is banded at organizational division points. Bands will help you to locate a particular example or group of examples which you might want to hear again.

While some parts of the demonstrations may require repeated listening, others may seem overly simple, particularly to those of you who play an instrument. However, even these rudimentary concepts are fundamental to later concerns. They provide a base upon which to build by putting forth in as functional a manner as we are able, the underlying, often unconscious foundations on which your musical experience is based. For the less experienced listener the more rudimentary demonstrations can serve as initial steps. For the more experienced listener they provide an opportunity to become aware of knowledge and listening skills that may already have been acquired but in a less organized or conscious fashion. In either case it is important that you not only understand the concepts discussed and the specific descriptions of excerpts but that you also hear in the music what is being described.

You will notice, too, that the examples in any one demonstration are chosen from widely different periods (we've included all known dates of composition). Thus, in addition to the specifically stated reason for including an example, the wide variety will also gradually develop your awareness of and sensitivity to a broad range of musical styles. In fact, one purpose of the book is to broaden your taste. By first helping you to become aware of those aspects of music that you already hear and take for granted as "making sense," we will then go on to develop these givens until you are able to hear new aspects which contribute to less familiar musical styles. In this way pieces that you may initially feel are dull or even incomprehensible, you can come to enjoy—your musical taste will be expanded to include more and different kinds of music.

You will notice that we do group examples by historical periods at times (in Chapters 2, 5, and 7, for instance), but it is only in the last section of the book (Chapters 8 to 13) that we consider the historical context of music directly. We have put off specifically discussing the significance of the historical moment in which a work is written for two reasons: (1) To grasp fully the characteristics of the style of a particular composer or group of composers writing contemporaneously requires all the listening skill that you have been acquiring before reaching this section. (2) Historical significance can be understood only against the background of experience with music of all periods. By the time you reach the final section, your increased perception, your broader musical experience, and your growing sensitivity to stylistic differences will help you gain a deeper understanding of specific musical styles.

We do not attempt to provide a short history of music or even a summary of all the features of different styles. Rather, we ask you to consider how an awareness of tradition and style influences your perception of individual works. We are concerned, then, with historical context as only *one* of the aspects contributing to your total involvement with a piece of music. The primary goal of the last section of the book is to encourage you to listen to each piece of music *on its own terms.* This kind of listening requires an awareness of the terms—that is, of the style of the music. Remember, however, that the identification of a style, period, or composer ought not to be a substitute for actually listening to the unique events of each work.

At the end of most chapters you will find a section entitled Additional Materials. These sections should not be considered as "extra"; they are an integral part of the book. Sometimes they present various kinds of exercises which encourage you to "perform" actively; but most important, they recommend further listening through which you can extend your newly acquired musical perception beyond the excerpts in the demonstrations to longer musical examples—in many cases, to whole pieces. We have tried with these Additional Materials to show how various aspects of music actually function within the context of whole works. You are strongly urged to find recordings of the works recommended or refer back to the examples discussed if they have already been included in a demonstration. In some chapters there is also a supplementary section called Ancillary Reading, which provides a number of definitions and other relevant information.

One of the greatest problems we have faced in preparing this book is that of the inevitable distortion which occurs when some aspect of a total organism is isolated—whether that organism be a living thing or a piece of music. An examination of any one aspect of music immediately distorts your hearing of those works we have chosen as illustrations, since we are asking you to listen only to that one facet of the music and to leave out others which also contribute to the total effect.

This problem cannot be entirely avoided. Still, we have tried to overcome it in two ways: (1) by choosing examples in which the particular aspect of music under consideration is a significant factor in the total experience, and (2) by trying to keep in mind all the facets of a given moment in a piece—such as rhythm, harmony, and melodic shape—as they influence the particular aspect which may be our temporary concern.

The problem of distortion is complicated in that any excerpt is only a moment in the total time span of the work. When we analyze the music, we are slicing it not only horizontally, so to speak, into its component parts but also vertically, into bits of time. That music takes place in time and not statically in space is a constant problem in trying to describe its effect. As soon as we stop it to look or listen closely, we are distorting the work as a total organism.

We feel a certain discomfort in fracturing this continuous, often immediate, emotional experience which one wishes kept inviolable. But a degree of analysis and objective scrutiny, both of the music and of the listener himself, will contribute, in time, to even more intense, and equally inviolable experiences.

One more type of distortion inevitably plagues an analysis such as this—the distortion introduced by the words used to describe musical phenomena. Just as we urge you to consider your own responses to a given example first, so we urge you to search for words which will appropriately describe both your own response and the attributes of the music which have stimulated it. We have attempted to avoid all terminology which has been derived only from the vague, often inaccurate, assumptions of traditional usage. To describe what is a complex intellectual, emotional, and highly personal experience generated by an equally complex set of phenomena is difficult. We feel, however, that the effort can be a most important way of exploring the manifold dimensions of music itself.

During the long hours devoted to selecting examples and to the actual writing of the text, each of us used the others as sounding board, critic, and mentor; and thus no part of the book is the sole effort of any one of us. We hope that you, in using the book, will learn as much from it as we learned in preparing it.

Remember, however, that the book itself *tells* you very little. Its value lies in what you can discover yourself by actively studying the musical examples, using the book as a guide. The facts we give *about* music are only important when they are transformed into your live experience—and that you must have alone. "The really 'understanding' listener takes the music into his consciousness, and remakes it, actually or in his imagination, for his own uses."[2]

J.S.B.
H.B.

---

[2] Roger Sessions, *The Musical Experience of Composer, Performer, Listener,* Princeton: Princeton University Press, 1950, p. 97.

THE ART OF LISTENING

PART ONE

*Means
and
Possibilities*

CHAPTER 1

Triumph of Eternity, Chaumont tapestry panel, France, 1500–1510

Sound and Texture

Sound relationships and textures

THE IMMEDIATE SENSORY EXPERIENCE of sound itself is one of the most compelling dimensions of music. And music includes an enormous variety of sounds, limited only by the capabilities of the instruments (or voices) and by the imagination of the composer. The musical examples you will hear in this chapter present a broad range of sounds, yet they provide only a small sample of the many possibilities. Nevertheless, as you listen to these examples, you can begin to expand your sensitivity to the different ways in which sounds can be combined and interrelated.

DEMONSTRATION 1.1
The Variety of Sound
(Side 1)

Since music of some kind is a part of everyone's experience, these first examples are certainly not an introduction to music. Instead, they serve as an exploration of exactly *how* you listen to music and what you *hear* (and comprehend). These examples are chosen to begin the discussion—to raise questions rather than answer them. Later you may find it useful to turn back to this first set of examples to compare your initial responses with your more "educated" ones.

Example	Composer, title	Date
1.1	Stravinsky, *Le Sacre du printemps* ("The Rite of Spring"), "Dance of the Adolescents"	1913
1.2	Bach, *Concerto in D Minor for Harpsichord and Orchestra,* first movement	c. 1735–1740
1.3	*Viderunt Omnes* ("All Have Seen"), Gregorian chant	Middle Ages
1.4	*Music for the Rice Harvest* (West African)	

These four examples represent a wide range of music from very different times and places. As you listen, each excerpt will seem to create its own "sound world." It is unlikely that you would hear these four pieces one after the other except under the artificial circumstances of this book. But by listening to these unnatural neighbors in sequence, we can highlight the striking differences among them.

Finding words to express the differences you hear may be difficult, but certain aspects of each piece stand out right away. For example, the feeling of Example 1.1 is very different from the feeling of Example 1.2. But what in the music creates the differences? You may notice, for instance, that the sound of the orchestra is quite different in the two examples. This is due in part to the particular instruments that each composer has included in his score, as well as to what, and even how, the instruments are playing. For example, what are some of the differences in the kind of melody (or even lack of melody) that you hear, or the differences in rhythm, or the relationships among the various instruments? What other aspects of each piece do you think make the experience of listening to it unique?

Examples 1.3 and 1.4 are both music to accompany ceremonies. However, each creates a strikingly different ceremonial atmosphere. Notice that in the medieval chant, which is music for the Catholic service, all of the voices are singing the same tones at the same time. In contrast, the African ritual starts off slowly and spontaneously, seemingly out of a community gathering. First you hear one person singing, then more people join in, then drums, and finally a child's voice. Unlike those you heard singing the medieval chant, the participants here do not all sing and play the same tones together. Instead, as each person joins in, he sings or plays his own individual part. The particular sounds of each part and their complex interwoven relationships help to create the special quality of the piece.

Example	Composer, title	Date
1.5	Haydn, *Symphony 8,* first movement	c. 1761
1.6	Mahler, *Symphony 1,* fourth movement	1888
1.7	Debussy, *Rondes de printemps* ("Spring Rounds")	1905–1909

Examples 1.5 and 1.6 are both orchestral pieces and yet, again, each has a distinctive sound and feeling. This is partly because Haydn has written for a smaller *number* of instruments and also for fewer *kinds* of instruments than Mahler. A glance at the Haydn and Mahler scores on pages 7 and 8 will make this quite clear.

For example, look at the names of the participating instruments listed at the sides of the scores. Notice that the instruments are grouped (bracketed) according to families: from the top of the score there are woodwinds, brass, percussion (none in Haydn), and then strings. Haydn scores his piece for only three kinds of woodwinds: flute, oboe, and bassoon (the bassoon plays with the cellos and basses, so it is written out with them at the bottom of the score). Mahler includes more *kinds* of woodwinds (piccolo and clarinet in addition to those above) as well as more of each kind (for example, four oboes and four clarinets). Haydn uses only one kind of brass instrument, the French horn, while Mahler uses four different kinds of brass instruments, with more than one of each kind (and seven French horns!). Finally, Mahler has a large percussion section, while Haydn has none at all.

Listen to Example 1.5 again, this time trying to follow the score. Think of the score as a kind of map which shows the simultaneous paths of each participating instrument through time.[1] You may find it difficult to follow all the paths at once. Start by listening for the instrument that is playing the melody; then keep your eye and ear on just that part. (Notice that the score includes only the first portion of the recorded excerpt.) Mahler's much bigger orchestra makes it more difficult to follow his score, but it will be interesting to see how much of what you hear you can match with what is printed on the page. This is the last page of the Mahler score, and it is only the very end of the recorded excerpt. Because of Mahler's very large orchestra, a little musical time takes up a lot of space on a page.

A comparison of the Haydn excerpt with the Debussy (Example 1.7) will highlight another kind of difference in orchestral pieces, namely, each composer's *use* of the orchestra. Haydn uses his orchestra to underline or reinforce other aspects of the musical design. Debussy, however, uses his orchestra actually to create the design of the piece through the interplay of the various sounds of the instruments themselves.

Look at the Haydn score as you listen once more to the example. You can hear and see that the violins start off the melody, but the lower strings (violas, cellos, and basses) finish the first little phrase. Haydn changes instruments to underline the melodic structure; the switch from violins to lower strings helps to define the beginnings and endings of the melody. A little later on, Haydn introduces a new figure (♩. ♪♪♪ ♪) played by the violins, but also by the flute, which is a new instrument that adds a new sound to the piece. Try to shift your listening focus to the flute, noticing how and when Haydn uses its characteristic figure to liven up the melody which is usually played by the violins.

Although a score is often helpful in illustrating or clarifying exactly what you have heard, it is always a good idea to listen first and then to look. You will need to practice coordinating what you hear with what you see in musical notation. Remember that looking cannot

---

[1] For a discussion of music notation, see appendixes to Chapters 2 and 3. However, at this point it is better to use the score as a general map than as an exact note-to-note description.

Example 1.5 HAYDN, excerpt from *Symphony 8*

Example 1.6 MAHLER, excerpt from *Symphony 1*

Used by kind permission of European American Music Distributors Corp., sole U.S. agent for Ernst Eulenburg and Co. GmbH.

be a substitute for careful listening; you must believe first in what you hear.

Now listen to Example 1.7 again (no score is included here). Notice how Debussy uses the orchestra to create a kind of kaleidoscope of sounds, shifting your attention from one part of the orchestra to another, or sometimes combining instruments to create a unique sound. Unlike Haydn, Debussy uses contrasting sounds to shape the structure of the piece. He often repeats the same fragment of music several times using different instruments, one after the other. The change in tone color (**timbre**) gives a new impression to the same group of notes. The sensuous interplay of sounds might be compared with the patterns that are formed by color in a painting or by the play of light and shadow in nature. (You might refer to the Ancillary Reading at the end of this chapter for further discussion of the instruments of the orchestra. Also, you may want to listen to some of the many records available illustrating the instruments of the orchestra, as well as to Britten's *A Young Person's Guide to the Orchestra*.)

Changing Sound Environments

Example	Composer, title	Date
1.8	Sousa, *Semper Fidelis*	1888
1.9	Beethoven, *Symphony 9,* Op. 125, fourth movement	1824
1.10	Stravinsky, *Firebird Suite,* finale	1909–1910
1.11	Bach, *Suite in B Minor,* overture	c. 1740

You have already heard a variety of means that composers and performers use to create contrasting sound worlds. Examples 1.8 through 1.11 illustrate means that composers can use to create contrast in sound *within* a piece. In each of these examples, a single melody is *embedded* in an ever-changing sound environment. While the melody itself always remains much the same, it seems transformed as the sound environment around it changes. This process can be part of a composer's way of creating **variations on a theme.** In each such variation you hear the same melody but always with a slightly different effect.

For example, in the Sousa march (Example 1.8) each repetition of the melody defines a new section of the piece and a new variation on the theme. Since each includes one complete statement of the tune, all of the sections are of the same length. Notice also that the theme

In each example, a melody is embedded in an ever-changing sound environment.[2]

or principal melody is always played by the same instruments, the trumpets. But in each variation, other instruments playing new musical material are added to the basic sound environment.

Beethoven uses much the same general procedure (Example 1.9) as Sousa, but in a considerably more elaborate way. For instance, notice that each repetition of the theme is played by a new group of instruments. First we hear just the cellos and basses playing the theme in **unison.** Then, in the first variation, the violas and cellos play the theme, this time accompanied by the bassoon and double basses. Notice how different the melody sounds both as a result of the new instruments playing it and also because of the new sound environment in which it is embedded. In the next variation, Beethoven gives the theme to the violins. He surrounds the theme with more and still different instruments, creating another new environment for it. Interestingly, the theme moves higher and higher among the strings with each repetition. Finally, Beethoven gives the theme to the brass and woodwinds while the strings accompany it, weaving around the woodwinds and brass to disguise the repeated melody.

In the finale of the *Firebird Suite* (Example 1.10), Stravinsky also repeats a single melody and embeds it in changing sound environments, but the effect is rather different. This piece sounds more *continuous* than either the Sousa march or the Beethoven symphony excerpt. There are several reasons for this. The repetitions of the short theme (played first by the French horn) are not always literal, and therefore the lengths

---

[2] This illustration, and others like it throughout the book, is an artist's *graphic* expression of the *musical* relationships discussed. The sketch is not limited to one particular work, nor is it the only drawing possible. For example, the drawing could apply to this Beethoven piece or to any piece which follows a similar procedure. The illustration tells you nothing which the text has not already discussed, but it may help fix the idea in your mind by projecting some of its relationships visually. Try making your own sketches as you listen to examples or read the text. How do yours compare with those scattered throughout the book?

of the sections are not always the same. Also, there is a more gradual increase in the kind and number of instruments, which creates a continuous crescendo almost up to the end of the excerpt (and the piece). In addition, the piece sounds more continuous because the beginning and ending of the repeated melody is itself less clearly defined, which tends to blur the boundaries between each new variation. At the very end the orchestra suddenly plays much more softly in preparation for the grand climax (where's the theme?) with which the piece ends.

The excerpt from the Bach overture is also more continuous, but this time for still different reasons. You will notice that the participating

The texture grows increasingly more dense and more active.

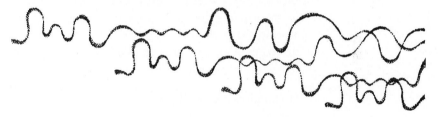

instruments enter this sound world one by one, each playing the *same* melody. Each instrument **imitates** the one preceding it. Once a player is in, he continues to play but always something other than the "constant" melody which he gives over to another player. Notice, too, that the instruments (flute and strings) enter in a regular progression from high to low—violin 1 (**doubled** by flute), violin 2 (playing lower), viola, cello (doubled by bass), and finally violin 1 once again. Each successive statement of the melody is heard in a new sound environment—one which grows more dense and more active as the instruments increasingly intertwine with one another.

Thus, while Examples 1.8 through 1.11 each have their own characteristic sound, all of them share a similar compositional procedure. In this sense, each of the examples illustrates the interplay of unity and variety which is so important to musical coherence. Each composer creates unity through the repetition of a single melody and variety by embedding this "constant" in new sound environments. And yet, each piece realizes this general procedure in a unique way. Learning to appreciate the interplay between unity and variety and between the defining limits of a procedure and its unique working out in a given composition is an important aspect of the art of listening.

In this demonstration you are asked to listen to an aspect of sound in music termed *texture*. The word *texture* is borrowed by analogy from another medium, as is often the case with technical musical terminology. Here, texture is borrowed from its more literal use in the description of woven fabric and its strands. In music the term refers to the particular way strands of *sound* intertwine and interweave with one another. Or, more specifically, the term refers to the way voices or instruments relate to one another. The word *voice* can refer to either instruments or singing voices as they weave together to form the particular texture of a composition. We can say, for example, that "the violin is the upper voice in the texture." We can describe the texture of a piece, or a particular moment in a piece, in terms of its *density* (how many parts are playing) or its *activity* (the relative degree of motion and contrasts in motion among the parts), or we can refer to the upper or lower strands, parts, or voices. Unlike its use in relation to fabric, however, texture, as used

Denim fabric (85X enlarged)

Texture: the particular way strands of sound intertwine and interweave with one another.

in music, does not refer to the sense of touch or to the atmosphere or mood of a piece, although particular textural relations may contribute to the feelings which a piece evokes in the listener.

Before you listen to the examples which illustrate various kinds of textural relations, a word about the uses of descriptive or technical terms may be helpful. Words about music, as used here, serve two purposes: (1) they direct your attention to some particular aspect of music which we want to illustrate by a given example, and (2) they help you to grasp and make explicit what you can hear but what may be still quite elusive to you. Translating your perception into a verbal description helps to single out just what is contributing to your experience. Both uses are part of what is essentially an intermediary process between your initial impression of a work and your later more complete experience of it. The process is one of learning how to find, in your immediate sensory experience, that set of features or relations to which a given term or verbal description applies or to search for a way of expressing this in words.

Keep in mind, then, that language about music can only be a guide or momentary pointer; it cannot substitute for careful listening. For example, no one term can capture the interplay of relations in various dimensions of a piece as it moves through time. Further, remember that the recorded examples are often short excerpts from larger works. Each excerpt has been carefully chosen to focus your listening on some particular aspect of the piece—for instance, the variety of possible sound relationships. But any large work will include many varieties of sound and texture within it; the particular moment we have chosen is just one part which contributes to the organization and *effect* of the whole. Listed at the end of the chapter are several short but complete works that will encourage you to listen to the variety of sound and texture within the framework of an entire piece.

Remember, then, that it is your increased ability to *hear*—to distinguish and interrelate—the various dimensions of the music itself which must teach you, and not merely the words about it.

Solo Playing

Example	Composer, title	Date
1.12	Varèse, *Density 21.5*	1936
1.13	Bach, *Partita 2 for Unaccompanied Violin,* gigue	c. 1720

Examples 1.12 and 1.13 can both be described as having a one-stranded texture since each is a solo played by one instrument alone. However, neither piece may strike you as being a melody in the sense of a popular tune or folk song. An important question, to which we will return in Chapter 3, is just how each melody differs from your intuitive idea of what a tune is. However, it should be clear that the character of the melody is influenced by the fact that both Varèse and Bach, each in his own way, have skillfully "pushed the limits" of their respective instruments, giving each of the performers full opportunity to display virtuoso skill as a soloist. Varèse's focus on the instrument and its possibilities is reflected in the title of the piece, which alludes to the platinum flute of Georges Barrère, the flutist who commissioned Varèse to write the piece for him. The approximate density of platinum is 21.5 (21.37 grams per cubic centimeter).

Unison Playing or Singing

Example	Composer, title	Date
1.14	*Singing Game* (West African)	
1.15	Bach, *Concerto in D Minor for Harpsichord and Orchestra,* first movement	c. 1735–1740

In the next two examples (Examples 1.14 and 1.15), there is again just one melody line, but now more than one instrument or voice is playing it. This is called singing or playing in unison, as in the medieval chant heard earlier (Example 1.3). The African *Singing Game* demonstrates in lively, playful fashion the contrast between solo and unison singing. You first hear one melody line with one person singing and then, in contrast, one melody line with several people singing. The piece sounds like a game of musical catch. The soloist is free to invent, since he is all alone, while the chorus, sometimes interrupting, always picks up and repeats the same beginning fragment of the soloist's tune—the opening motive.

Instruments rather than voices play in unison in the Bach excerpt (heard earlier as Example 1.2). Notice that unlike the African song, the melody line in this excerpt is played in different **pitch** areas; that is, all the instruments play the same pitches, but in different octaves—some higher (violins), some in the middle (violas), and some lower (cellos and basses).

Example	Composer, title	Date
1.16	Moussorgsky, *Pictures at an Exhibition*, "Promenade"	1874
1.17	*The Bird Has Come* (Bulgarian folk song)	

Examples 1.16 and 1.17 illustrate unison of a very different kind. Notice that in the excerpt from the Moussorgsky work, the trumpet first plays alone and then is joined by the other instruments. Trumpet and orchestra alternate throughout the excerpt. As the others join in, they all play nearly the same *rhythm* as the trumpet but not the same *pitches*. This we call playing in *rhythmic unison*.

Similarly, the Bulgarian folk song begins with all the women singing in unison, but then the group breaks up into two and then several parts. As in the Moussorgsky piece, all the women continue to sing the same rhythm, but not always the same set of pitches. So if the women, instead of *singing* the pitches of their respective parts, just *clapped* the rhythm, you would not hear any differences among them. Only pitch differentiates the various strands of sound.

Interestingly, the example also serves to demonstrate the two basic components of a **tone** and of a succession of tones (a melody), namely, pitch and duration. That is, while the *durations* of the notes are the same for all the performers throughout the excerpt, their pitches are sometimes the same (unison) and sometimes different (rhythmic unison). As a result of these changes from unison singing to rhythmic unison, you hear contrasts in sound and in the relations among the parts as the piece goes along. These contrasts create a sense of widening or deepening (as the pitches vary) and then again narrowing of the sound universe (as the pitches converge into unison). All the parts move along together, yet sometimes the top voice is reinforced and enriched as it becomes part of a deeper sound space.

Example	Composer, title	Date
1.18	Bach, *St. Matthew Passion*, chorale	1729

In the Bach example (Example 1.18), all the voices generally move together in rhythmic unison. However, upon close listening you will hear that the lower parts sometimes move independently of the top part, creating a contrast with the prevailing rhythmic unison texture. At these moments both pitch and duration contribute to a somewhat more active texture. While Bach started with a preexistent melody (a **chorale,** or Lutheran hymn) which he gives to the sopranos at the top of the texture, he sets this melody off so that the three other voices (altos, tenors, basses) have a certain rhythmic and melodic independence. Note that in the Bulgarian folk song the lower voices at times diverge from the upper voice, but only in pitch, not rhythm. In the Bach example, however, the lower voices of the texture begin at times to take on a life of their own as they diverge in rhythm as well as pitch.

Melody and Accompaniment

Example	Composer, title	Date
1.19	*Sourwood Mountain* (American folk song)	
1.20	Verdi, *La Traviata,* aria	1853
1.21	Haydn, *Concerto for Trumpet and Orchestra,* third movement	1796
1.22	Babbitt, *Philomel*	1964

In the previous three examples you heard a melody reinforced, but by an accompaniment that had little distinguishable character of its own. The next four examples (Examples 1.19 to 1.22) illustrate melody with a clearly subordinate accompaniment and yet one which has its own distinctive character. While the examples are clearly different from one another in feeling and in the kind of sound world they create,

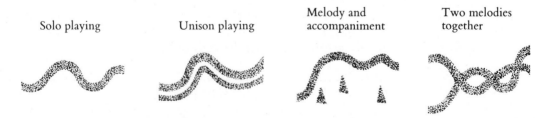

Solo playing   Unison playing   Melody and accompaniment   Two melodies together

they are all similar in texture—they all present a foreground melody with a background accompaniment. In the American folk song *Sourwood Mountain* (Example 1.19), notice that the accompaniment creates a steady beat and also hardly moves from its one sound (a single chord), while the melody line moves freely above it. *Sourwood Mountain* was recorded in Thomasville, North Carolina, in 1945; I. G. Greer, a native of Thomasville, is accompanied on the dulcimer by his wife.

The Verdi **aria** (Example 1.20) seems to epitomize the notion of melody with accompaniment. You hear the singer (sometimes joined by the violins) soaring over the "oom-pah-pah" accompaniment that is clearly subordinate and yet consistently and solidly present. The Haydn *Concerto for Trumpet and Orchestra* (Example 1.21) similarly sets off soloist from background accompaniment, the soloist displaying his virtuosity while the orchestra provides a discrete sound setting for him. Compare this accompanied virtuoso solo with the unaccompanied solos of Examples 1.12 and 1.13.

Babbitt's accompaniment in *Philomel* (Example 1.22) is electronically synthesized and is "played" in performance by a tape recorder while Bethany Beardslee (for whom the piece was written) sings, live. Notice that as in Examples 1.19 and 1.20 the singer's voice clearly dominates this portion of the piece, while the accompaniment always remains in the background.

Two Melodies Played or Sung Together

Example	Composer, title	Date
1.23	Gibbons, *Fantasia a 2*	c. 1608
1.24	Mozart, *Duo for Violin and Viola*, K. 424,[3] second movement	1783
1.25	Gordon, Roberts, and Kaufman, *Me, Myself and I* (sung by Billie Holiday)	1938

Examples 1.19 through 1.22 involved pieces with more than one instrument or voice, but in each excerpt the upper part tended to predominate. There was a clear foreground-background relationship. Examples 1.23 through 1.25 illustrate music in which two instruments are of equal importance. This equality of the parts results in a more complex sound fabric with a more *active* texture. We call the texture active because, in listening, you must follow not just one predominant part but rather shift your attention from one part to the other, or sometimes attend to both as the two individual parts vie with one another for the foreground role.

---

[3] K.424 means the 424th work in a chronological arrangement of Mozart's music made by Ludwig von Köchel in the nineteenth century.

In the Gibbons *Fantasia* (Example 1.23) you hear two recorders playing in close *imitation*. (Compare this with Bach, Example 1.11.) That is, one instrument starts and the other follows right after with a melody that always begins in the same way as the first but then goes its own way. The result is a texture of much greater activity than you heard in the examples of melody with accompaniment. Each of the two instruments is playing a related but distinct melody which can stand on its own, has its own integrity. The ear, in a sense, must jump around to follow each part.

The Mozart *Duo* (Example 1.24) is particularly interesting because you hear, even in this short excerpt and with only two instruments, a variety of textural relations. First you hear an active texture with each instrument playing the same melody but "out of phase" with one another. That is, the violin begins and then the viola follows, imitating almost exactly what the violin started. Notice that while each part is thus self-sufficient, the melody is composed so that it "fits" when played against itself.[4] Then, as the piece progresses, one has a sense of decreasing activity and intensity as the texture moves from an active, imitative one to rhythmic unison, and finally to a melody played by the violin with an accompaniment played by the viola. This is a good example of how textural contrast can contribute to changes in the feelings evoked—in this case from the sense of intensity resulting from the complex, active texture to relative calm resulting from the more homogeneous rhythmic unison, and finally melody with accompaniment.

On first listening to *Me, Myself, and I* (Example 1.25), it may seem to you that the singer Billie Holiday occupies the foreground role exclusively. But if you listen again more closely you can hear that Lester Young, playing tenor saxophone, is vying with her for the foreground role as he plays a different but equally important melody. This kind of perceptual "surfacing" of inner lines is the sort of experience that can change your appreciation of a piece. The rest of the group plays a rhythmic accompaniment which is subordinate to the voice and saxophone. Compare the texture of this piece with the previous examples, noticing that it includes two voices (specifically voice and tenor saxophone) of equal importance, as well as a subsidiary accom-

---

[4] You are probably familiar with this kind of procedure, called a *canon* or *round*, as in *Three Blind Mice* or *Row, Row, Row Your Boat*.

paniment. The two foreground parts are each playing a different melody, not the same melody in imitation.

Several Melodies Played Together

Example	Composer, title	Date
1.26	Gabrieli, *Ricercare*	c. 1580
1.27	*African Drums* (West African)	
1.28	Bach, *St. John Passion,* chorus	c. 1723

Examples 1.26 to 1.28 all involve several independent lines and a consistently active texture. This kind of activity among the parts—the opposite extreme from rhythmic unison—is often referred to as **polyphony** ("many voices"). But notice what differences there can be! In the Gabrieli *Ricercare* (Example 1.26), for instance, the same short melodic fragment is tossed about among the brass instruments. In the African piece (Example 1.27), on the other hand, each of the percussion instruments plays a different rhythmic figure, but not really a melody, which perhaps emphasizes the importance of rhythm in generating polyphony. While there are many differences between the two examples (instrumentation, kinds of rhythm, imitation and no imitation), the result in both is a highly complex and active texture.

Rhythmic unison   Active texture

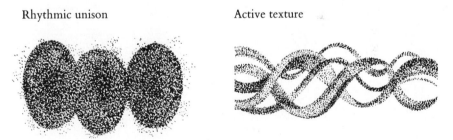

Following the score of the Gabrieli *Ricercare* may help you to shift your focus from one instrument to another as each picks up the same short melodic fragment. Notice that you need to shift your *visual* focus rapidly about within the "sound space." Now listen again without the score to hear how the voices interweave to create an active, complex texture.

You can also compare the Gabrieli *Ricercare* with the West African *Singing Game* (Example 1.14), which we described as a game of musical

Example 1.26 GABRIELI, *Ricercare*

catch. Notice that in *Singing Game* the melody, sung by a single child, is picked up by the group, but the soloist and the group sing *one after the other* (in succession, not simultaneously) to create a single-stranded, inactive texture. In the *Ricercare,* on the other hand, you hear a single motive at first played against itself (as in the two-voiced Mozart *Duo* and Gibbons *Fantasia*), then in all of the parts to form a many-layered, active texture. The *Ricercare* again illustrates what is technically called *imitation.* That is, a melody or melodic fragment (motive) is played in different strands of the texture but out of phase with itself. The motive moves about within the texture—you might say, *embedded in itself*—to generate this active, complex sound. *Singing Game,* in contrast, illustrates *successive* repetition—a single-line restatement of a melody or motive.

The chorus from Bach's *St. John Passion* (Example 1.28), which occurs at a climactic moment in this monumental musical setting of the Crucifixion, shows you the dramatic effect of voices combining to create many actively moving lines.

Putting It All Together

Example	Composer, title	Date
1.29	Haydn, *Symphony 99,* minuet (first section)	1793
1.30	Stravinsky, *Four Études for Orchestra,* no. 2	1914–1918
1.31	Handel, *Concerto Grosso,* Op. 6, no. 2, fourth movement	c. 1739

So far you have listened to various aspects of sound, but generally only in short, isolated excerpts. To conclude the demonstration, listen now to complete movements by Stravinsky and Handel and a complete section of a movement by Haydn. One of the goals in developing musical perception is the ability to appreciate the larger structure of a work. The composer's use of contrast in sound and texture often plays an important role in generating this overall design. Learning to hear and respond to these varieties of sound relations can thus help you to participate more fully and with more understanding in the process of a given work. These examples will give you the opportunity to use your increased perception to hear how each composer uses varying sound relationships within a work to create contrast which helps to shape the structure of the whole.

Listen first to the Haydn minuet (Example 1.29). Your increased sensitivity to changes in sound should help you to hear how rapidly the sound changes within this section. For example, the piece begins in unison, followed quickly by rhythmic unison which fills out the sound and reinforces the initial statement. Haydn then repeats this same contrast. Next he increases the *rate* of contrast by alternating between unison and rhythmic unison more quickly (in fact, twice as fast). At the same time Haydn also creates a thinner sound—fewer instruments are playing. This then leads into a more active texture with imitation between the upper and lower parts. This is followed by a more relaxed section of clear melody and accompaniment, with which a significant section of the piece comes to a close. This entire section is then repeated literally.

Example 1.29 HAYDN, *Symphony 99,* minuet[5]

The various contrasts in sound are striking, but you must listen actively in order to hear them. Once these changes in sound and texture become part of your listening experience, you will also become aware of the role they play in articulating or shaping the musical process. Specifically, you can appreciate the role of instrumentation and texture in defining the structure. Haydn uses the orchestra to reinforce events in other dimensions of the music, such as melody, rhythm, and harmony, much as he does in *Symphony 8* (Example 1.5). All these dimensions work together to create a dynamic movement between moments of relative stability and moments of relative tension, or what we will later describe as differing *structural functions.* Contrast in sound is an immediate way of approaching the perception of larger structural design. Others will emerge and become part of your listening experience as you move through the various demonstrations, culminating in their necessary integration when we examine the organization of large-scale works in the latter part of the book.

Stravinsky, in this *Étude* no. 2 (Example 1.30), displays a far wider variety of sounds in a relatively short period of time. When one compares this piece with Haydn's minuet, it becomes abundantly clear that sound is a primary building material for Stravinsky and thus necessarily

---

[5] The symbol ‖: :‖ indicates that the music between the signs is to be played again.

of your listening focus. In this respect Stravinsky is much like Debussy (see discussion of Example 1.7). In the Stravinsky *Étude* you first hear the various instruments playing primarily in unison or in rhythmic unison. They are interrupted by the brass and piano, which, along with the strings and woodwinds, play an important role. This more active passage in turn quickly dissolves into a short oboe solo and another unison passage. Next you hear what seems like an accompaniment looking for a melody, and the melody finally materializes in the flute and piccolo solos. The *Étude* ends with a return to the opening material, now truncated and fragmented.

But to speak only of kinds of texture in describing this work clearly does it an injustice. The play of instrumental colors—sometimes particular combinations of instruments, sometimes the characteristic sound of one alone—appeals to that direct sensuous aspect of listening which is a large part of what this chapter is all about.

Finally, in the finale from the Handel *Concerto Grosso* (Example 1.31) you can hear two clearly opposed textures, each associated with its own melody. In the first, we have a melody presented in imitation. (How many statements of this melody do you hear moving throughout the string section?) That texture is followed abruptly by a softer, more lyrical passage in which you hear a slower melody with a faster-moving accompaniment. As the piece progresses, these two "characters" in the drama (the faster-moving, more actively textured first section and the slower-moving melody with accompaniment) move closer and closer together. Contrast thus occurs more rapidly until finally you hear the melodies superimposed. The slower, more lyrical melody is sometimes heard below and sometimes above the more vigorous opening melody. Thus Handel creates rich varieties of sound and texture and also new embeddings for two persistently recurring melodic ideas. Near the end of the piece the opening melody is played in closer imitation as instruments enter virtually tumbling over one another, as if each cannot wait for the other to finish the tune.

You might like to go back and listen to the first four examples again. Do you hear more than you did initially? Can you now find just what aspects of each excerpt characterize its particular sound world?

EXERCISE 1.1
Sound and Texture
(Side 2)

The exercises in this book provide you with additional experience in listening within a particular framework. But they also have another purpose: to present self-correcting material through which you can discover how well you have learned to make distinctions. The exercises are a test only in the sense that they can help you to test your own perception.

Means and Possibilities

At the beginning of each exercise you will find a description of the problem and a blank chart for answering the questions. In the chart following the examples you will find the correct answers (p. 26). We suggest the following procedure for each exercise:

1. Study the problem and the specific questions.
2. Do the first three questions and check the answers against the answer chart to see if you are doing better than guessing. If not, go back and do the three questions again.
3. Finish the exercise and check your answers. You many want to listen to the whole exercise again while checking. This procedure will give you a chance not only to correct yourself but to hear again a "demonstration" within the framework of the particular problem described.

Exercise 1.1 explores further the various kinds of sound relationships you have been hearing. In Examples 1.32 to 1.37 the instruments or voices play different roles in relation to one another. Match each excerpt with the correct statement below.

A. The texture is relatively *inactive.* For example, one instrument or voice plays a dominant role (melody and accompaniment), or the parts play in unison, or in rhythmic unison.
B. The texture is relatively *active.* The instruments or voices move independently of one another; all are of equal importance.

Example	A Inactive	B Active
1.32		
1.33		
1.34		
1.35		
1.36		
1.37		

In each example of the next group (1.38 to 1.43) you will hear a change in the relative degree of textural activity. Match each excerpt with the correct statement below.

A. This excerpt changes (abruptly or gradually) from a relatively inactive texture to a more active texture.

B. This excerpt changes (abruptly or gradually) from a relatively active texture to a less active texture.

Example	A Inactive → Active	B Active → Inactive
1.38		
1.39		
1.40		
1.41		
1.42		
1.43		

CORRECT ANSWERS

Example	A Inactive	B Active
1.32 Vivaldi, *Concerto,* Op. 3, no. 11, c. 1712	X	
1.33 Beethoven, *Quartet,* Op. 59, no. 3, fourth movement, 1806		X
1.34 Hindemith, *Mathis der Maler,* 1934	X	
1.35 Hindemith, *Mathis der Maler,* 1934		X
1.36 Morley, *Ho! Who Comes Here?* 1594		X
1.37 Milhaud, *La Création du monde,* 1923	X	

Example	A Inactive → Active	B Active → Inactive
1.38 Bach, *Cantata 31,* 1715[a]	X	
1.39 Bizet, *L'Arlésienne Suite 2,* 1872[b]	X	
1.40 Mozart, *Quartet in G,* K. 387, fourth movement, 1782		X
1.41 Bach, *St. John Passion,* c. 1723	X	
1.42 Haydn, *The Seasons,* "Summer," 1801		X
1.43 Beethoven, *Symphony 3,* Op. 55, second movement, 1803[c]		X

[a] The piece begins with only one melody line played in unison by all the instruments of the group.
[b] This piece begins in rhythmic unison, and then goes into imitation.
[c] This excerpt has been included because it is such an extraordinary example of the dramatic effect of textural change. More "lifelike" than some of the earlier examples, it moves through several phases—from an active, complex texture generating tremendous tension to a gradual lessening of this tension through clarification and simplification of the texture.

ADDITIONAL MATERIALS

The examples suggested here[6] illustrate additional aspects of sound relationships not included in the previous demonstrations and in some cases reemphasize the crucial role sound can play in creating musical structure.

[6] Pieces discussed under the head "Additional Materials" are primarily for outside listening and are not necessarily included in the accompanying recordings.

I   Haydn, *Symphony 8,* first movement, c. 1761 (Example 1.5)
Debussy, *La Mer,* 1903–1905
Lully, *Armide,* overture, 1686
Gibbons, *Fantasia a 4,* c. 1608
Mahler, *Symphony 1,* first movement, 1888

Listen to the Haydn symphony and Debussy's *La Mer,* noting the striking difference in sound which results from different instrumental combinations and uses of these combinations. Notice that Debussy uses a much larger orchestra and a greater variety of instruments than Haydn (see the discussion of musical instruments in the Ancillary Reading section, p. 31).

Haydn (as in Example 1.29) uses his orchestra to reinforce the musical design. His contrasts in instrumentation, for example, tend to coincide with and help to articulate such musical events as the advent of a new phrase or section. Debussy (like Stravinsky), on the other hand, uses his orchestra as an end in itself. In his sensuous *La Mer,* we hear how contrasting instrumental colors, contrasts in density of texture, and the extramusical associations of particular qualities of sound generate the events of the piece. Which of these works would lose the most if transcribed for the piano?

The Lully and Gibbons pieces are both written for a group of strings, but Lully's orchestra, suited for a public performance, is large, while the Gibbons piece, scored for only four solo viols, sounds small and intimate. (Unfortunately, sometimes recordings distort this kind of difference since the decibel level tends to be equalized for all records by sound engineers. Thus, the enormous difference between a live performance by 50 musicians and one by 4 musicians is often lost in a recording.)

The last example of the group demonstrates how, with a large, varied orchestra, Mahler achieves an effect quite different from Debussy's, although the actual instruments present on the stage are nearly the same as those used in *La Mer.* In what ways is Mahler's use of the orchestra unlike Debussy's? In what ways is it similar to Haydn's?

II   Stravinsky, *Firebird Suite,* finale, 1909–1910 (Example 1.10)
Moussorgsky, *Khovantchina,* prelude, 1872–1880
Stravinsky, *Le Sacre du printemps,* "Rondes printanières," 1913
Beethoven, *Symphony 3,* Op. 55, fourth movement, 1803
Beethoven, *Trio,* Op. 11, third movement, 1798

These pieces, like Examples 1.29 through 1.31, illustrate the crucial role of texture and sonority in creating structure. In the finale of the *Firebird Suite,* notice how the effect is cumulative and climactic. We move from the opening solo horn statement to the full orchestra playing fortissimo at the conclusion. The Moussorgsky piece is similar to the *Firebird* in that the composer maneuvers the orchestra in relation to a melodic constant.

The excerpt from *Le Sacre du printemps,* however, is more complex. Listen carefully, noting the changes that occur in (1) timbre, (2) the range of instruments (high and low), (3) activity and density of texture, and (4) foreground-background relationships. These changes contribute significantly to the articulation of the four basic sections of the excerpt.

The Beethoven symphony movement is radically different from the preceding pieces, for it has fundamentally different goals. While in the first three examples the course of events depends on the manipulation of sound (as in Debussy's *La Mer*), in the Beethoven example sound tends rather to *reinforce* the course of events (as in Haydn's *Symphony 8*). Some of the dramatic changes in texture and sonority in this symphony were illustrated in Exercise 1.1. Listen to these and other striking changes in texture and sonority, now within the context of the whole movement.

The final movement of Beethoven's *Trio,* Op. 11, is less immediately striking in its sound contrasts because the composer uses a smaller and less varied group of instruments. However, close listening will reveal a remarkable variety of sounds within the small ensemble of clarinet, cello, and piano. You will notice that a particular sonority or texture remains constant for relatively long periods, and this constancy helps to articulate the *larger* divisions of the structure.

For example, following a section in which all three instruments participate (the **theme**), there is a section for piano alone (variation 1), which is followed by a section for cello and clarinet alone (variation 2). Notice that there is also a change in the activity of the texture from the theme to variation 2; the single line with accompaniment in the theme changes to two equal parts played in imitation in variation 2. In variation 3 the piano plays an accompaniment, first to the clarinet and then to the cello. Then in variation 4 the piano sound alternates with the clarinet-cello sound.

Listen to the whole movement, noting as carefully as possible the characteristics of each change in texture and sonority. Then listen to it again just for the pure pleasure of savoring the marvelous play of sounds.

ANCILLARY READING

Acoustics[7]

Acoustics is the science of sound. Sound, in music, consists of the impact on the ear of air vibrations set in motion by (1) the vibration of some elastic material, (2) the vibration of an air column in a pipe, or (3) vibrations electrically produced or transmitted. The elastic material may be: (*a*) a gut string or wire set in motion by a bow (violin), or plucked with the fingers (harp) or a plectrum (mandolin) or a quill (harpsichord), or hit with a metal tongue (clavichord) or a hammer (piano); (*b*) a reed or reeds set in motion by air pressure (oboe, clarinet); (*c*) a membrane set in motion by air pressure, such as the vocal cords (human voice) or the lips (brass instruments), or struck with a beater (drums); (*d*) a solid body set in motion by striking (bells, triangle, xylophone).

The *intensity* of a note is determined by the amplitude of the vibration. Hence force is needed to produce a loud note.

The *pitch* of a note is determined by the frequency of the vibration. A low note vibrates slowly, a high one quickly. The frequency of the vibration may depend (1) on the length, thickness, tension, and density of the vibrating material, (2) on the length and density of the air column and the nature of the tube enclosing it, or (3) may be directly produced by electrical processes. Thus, other things being equal, a short string will produce a higher note than a long one, a taut string a higher note than one less taut. A short air column will produce a higher note than a long one: the piccolo is shorter than the flute and so higher in pitch. On the other hand, the clarinet, though approximately the same length as the flute and oboe, is much lower in pitch than either. This is because it has a cylindrical tube stopped at one end (the mouthpiece), whereas the flute, though cylindrical, is open at both ends and the tube of the oboe, though stopped at one end, is conical or expanding. String and wind instruments are differently affected by temperature. A rise in temperature causes strings to expand, so that their tension is relaxed and they drop in pitch; but the expansion of air decreases its density, so that the pitch of wind instruments rises, the expansion of their material not being sufficient to counteract this.

The *resonance* of a note depends on the presence of some auxiliary

---

[7] This entire section on acoustics is reprinted, with permission, from *New College Encyclopedia of Music,* ed. J. A. Westrup and F. L. Harrison (New York: Norton, 1960).

material or an air column that will vibrate either in sympathy or by direct contact with the original vibrations. Thus the violin owes its resonance to its belly, the oboe to the air column contained in its tube. There is, however, an important difference. In the violin the belly has to vibrate as the strings dictate. In the oboe (as in other wind instruments) the vibrating air column, being of a definite length, controls the vibrations of the reed, so that in this case the resonator determines the pitch.

The *quality* of a note depends on the complex character of the vibrations. A stretched string does not merely vibrate as a whole. It also vibrates simultaneously in sections, which are in an exact mathematical relationship to the length of the string. These sections are the halves, thirds, quarters, fifths, and so on. The halves produce a note an octave higher than the note sounded by the whole string, the thirds a note a twelfth higher, the quarters a note two octaves higher, and so on. The "overtones" sounded by the respective sections fall into a series known as the *harmonic series*. If the principal note or "fundamental" is

the series will run as follows:

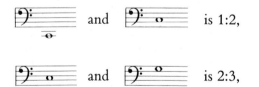

1 2 3 4   5 6 7 8 9 10 11 12 13 14 15 16

(The notes marked *x* are not in tune with our ordinary scale.)

The numbers of the series indicate exactly the mathematical relationship between the frequencies of the notes. Thus the ratio between:

and   is 1:2,

and   is 2:3,

and so on. The sound of the overtones is very much fainter than that of the note produced by the whole string, but without them the note heard by the listener would lose its luster. The air column of a wind instrument or an organ pipe also vibrates in sections. If it is stopped at one end, as in some organ pipes, only alternate sections vibrate, so that a stopped pipe produces only Nos. 1, 3, 5, 7, etc. of the harmonic series. Much the same thing happens with the clarinet, with its cylindrical tube stopped at one end. The characteristic tone-quality of instruments is thus due to the extent to which the "upper partials" (the overtones of the harmonic series) are present or absent and to their relative intensity. This makes it possible, in electronic instruments like the Hammond organ, to imitate closely the sound of orchestral instruments by presenting an artificial selection of the appropriate upper partials and giving to each the necessary intensity. In some instruments the overtones do not fall into the harmonic series and are therefore "inharmonic." The result may be a confused but recognizable sound, as in a bell, or one of indeterminate pitch, as in most percussion instruments.

By touching a string lightly at a point halfway from the end, the player can prevent the whole string from vibrating while leaving the two halves free to vibrate. A similar result can be achieved by touching the string at other sectional points. The notes so produced are known, for obvious reasons, as *harmonics.* In the same way a wind-player, by increased lip-tension (known technically as "overblowing"), can split the air column in the instrument into one of its component parts, so that instead of sounding No. 1 of the harmonic series it produces one of the upper partials as its principal note. This is done to a limited degree on woodwind instruments and extensively on brass instruments. The horn, for example, has a choice of upper partials from the 2nd to the 16th harmonic. This explains why horn-players sometimes seem uncertain about their notes. The higher harmonics lie very close together, so that the selection of the right one by lip tension calls for considerable skill. The extent to which members of the harmonic series are available on brass instruments depends on the relation between the diameter of the tube and its length. Neither the horn nor the trumpet, being narrow-bored instruments, can sound No. 1 of the series.

Musical Instruments

As we maintain throughout this book, it is your *experience* of music that is primary. Thus, in learning about musical instruments, it is essential that you hear various instruments to find out what they sound like and what kinds of things they can do, separately and in combination. At this point, therefore, you should listen to a recording of the instruments of the orchestra. What follows is a list and brief discussion of musical instruments.

Look again at the final page of the score of *Symphony 1* (1881) by Gustav Mahler, which we have reproduced on page 8. Compare the Mahler score with the page from the score of Franz Josef Haydn's *Symphony 8* (c. 1761) on page 7.

The changes that occurred in the orchestra in little over a century are apparent at a glance. The Haydn example illustrates the so-called classical orchestra, with its nucleus of strings and a few added winds. During the nineteenth century, more and different winds and percussion were added, and many more players were added on each part in the string section.

In the Mahler score the 29 staves of music are played by approximately 100 players constituting an orchestra similar in makeup, if not in sound, to that in Debussy's *La Mer* (see the Additional Materials section of this chapter). At the left of the page the names of the instruments are given, and braces divide the staves into four groupings. The traditional divisions of the symphony orchestra are *woodwinds, brass, percussion,* and *strings.*[8]

Woodwinds

If we read down from the top of the Mahler score, we find the woodwinds listed as follows: first and second *piccolos;* first and second *flutes;* four *oboes;* three *clarinets* in C, the fourth in E-flat; and three *bassoons.* According to the method of sound production and other factors, we can divide the woodwinds into three families, arranged from high to low within each family, as follows:

> *Flute:* Piccolo; flute, alto flute, bass flute (rare).
> *Clarinet:* E-flat, B-flat, bass clarinet, double bass clarinet (rare);
>   saxophones: soprano, alto, tenor, baritone, bass.
> *Oboe:* Oboe; English horn; bassoon; contrabassoon.

The *flute,* though classed among the woodwinds, is today usually constructed of metal. The player blows across a hole near the end of the instrument, causing a column of air to vibrate inside the tube. (See Example 1.12.)

The *piccolo* (Italian for "small") is literally a small flute; it is approximately one-half the size of the flute and consequently one octave higher in pitch.

---

[8] An all-encompassing scientific classification of instruments is as follows: *idiophones* (made of naturally sonorous material, such as cymbals and chimes), *membranophones* (made of stretched membrane, such as drums), *aerophones* (wind instruments), *chordophones* (strings), and *electrophones* (electronic instruments, such as the theremin and the electronic organ, or the great variety of music synthesizers).

The Heath Brothers in concert (left to right: electric piano, tenor sax, bass, drums, guitar)

The *clarinet* has a single reed which the player causes to vibrate against a slot in the pipe. Clarinets are known as "transposing instruments"; except when they are in C, they do not sound as written. (See Examples 1.37 and 2.26.) In the Mahler score, the first three clarinets are in C and, like most other instruments, sound as written. The fourth clarinet, in E-flat, however, sounds a minor third higher than written.

The *saxophone* is a single-reed instrument and of much later invention (nineteenth century) than the other woodwinds. (See, for the alto sax, Examples 3.17 and 5.44; for the tenor, Examples 1.25 and 3.16).

The *oboe* is a double-reed instrument. The reeds are made of cane. The player, inserting them into his mouth, makes them vibrate against each other by blowing. (See Examples 2.8 and 3.21.)

The *English horn* (not used in the Mahler score) is in effect an alto oboe, pitched a fifth below the oboe.

The *bassoon,* pitched approximately two octaves below the oboe, is also a double-reed instrument. (See Examples 1.9 and 2.8.) The Mahler score shows bassoon parts written in the tenor clef (see the Ancillary Reading section in Chapter 3).

Brass

The brass instruments in the Mahler symphony are seven (French) *horns,* five *trumpets,* four *trombones,* and *tuba* (set unusually in the score). All these instruments are played by the players' lips vibrating in a

Tuba

mouthpiece inserted into the end of a folded metal tube of some length. All except the trombone vary their pitch by means of a combination of valves and "overblowing" (increased tension of the lips). The trombone uses a slide rather than valves. (For trumpet, see Examples 1.16 and 1.21; horn, Examples 2.8 and 4.1; all the brass together, Example 1.26.)

Percussion

The percussion instruments shown in the Mahler score are two *kettledrums* or *timpani* (here played by two musicians), *triangle, cymbals,* and *bass drum.* These are only some of a wide variety of percussion instruments. Others are drums of various sizes and kinds, gongs, castanets, wood block, chimes, glockenspiel, tambourine, xylophone, and many more instruments.

Strings

The four principal strings are the *violin* (usually, as in the Mahler score, divided into first and second violins), *viola, cello* (full name, *violoncello*), and *double bass* (so named because it frequently "doubled" the cello an octave lower; also called the *contrabass, bass fiddle,* or simply *bass*). These instruments all have four strings and are most often played with a bow (**arco**) but are occasionally plucked (**pizzicato**). (For the violin, see Example 1.11; for viola, contrasted with the violin, Example 1.24; cello, Examples 2.26 and 3.1; cellos and basses together, Example 1.9.)

As we noted, the orchestra playing the Mahler symphony would be composed of about 100 players—the 32 winds and 5 percussionists called for in the score, plus about 66 strings divided as follows: 18 first violins, 16 second violins, 12 violas, 10 cellos, and 10 basses. In short, the strings constitute two-thirds of the orchestra, although they require only 5 of the 29 lines in this particular score.

You may be thinking that we have overlooked some very important instruments. The organ, piano, harp, guitar, celesta, saxophone, and vibraphone are not traditionally included among the regular components of the symphony orchestra, yet they are being utilized by composers more and more frequently today. In addition, there are the so-called ancient instruments, those which became obsolete at some point but which, either as originals or modern reconstructions, have

Full symphony orchestra

been revived in the twentieth century. Among these you may have heard the viols, recorder, harpsichord, clavichord, lute, cornetto, and shawm.

Finally, various smaller combinations of instruments, as they occur in *chamber music,* may be mentioned here:

> *Trio:* Usually *string* (violin, viola, cello) or *piano* (piano, violin, cello).
>
> *String quartet:* Two violins, viola, cello.
>
> *Quintet: String* (two violins, two violas, cello; or two violins, viola, and two cellos), *piano* (piano and string quartet), or *woodwind* (flute, oboe, clarinet, bassoon, and horn).

Dynamics and Expression

Dynamics

Dynamics[9] refers to the relative loudness or softness (intensity) of musical tones. Markings derived from Italian are used to indicate dynamics. The basic signs are:

p	*piano,* soft
f	*forte,* loud

Modifications of these serve as very rough dynamic indications for the performer:

pp	*pianissimo,* very soft
ppp	even softer
pppp	still softer
ff	*fortissimo,* very loud
fff	even louder
ffff	still louder
mp	*mezzo piano,* "half soft" (less soft than *piano*)
mf	*mezzo forte,* not as loud as *forte*
<	*crescendo,* gradual increase in loudness
>	*decrescendo, diminuendo,* gradual decrease in loudness

---

[9] In medieval and Renaissance music there are no indications of dynamics and expression, but from the seventeenth to the nineteenth centuries they proliferate. It is in the "romantic" music of the nineteenth century and especially in contemporary music that we find the most detailed markings by composers.

Expression

Italian terms serve as indications to the performer of expressive shadings and character. Some of the more frequently encountered terms are:

animato	animated
appassionato	passionate
cantabile	in a singing style
con brio	with spirit
con fuoco	with fire
con moto	with movement (moving along)
dolce	sweet (soft)
espressivo	expressive
grazioso	graceful
legato	bound together, smoothly connected
maestoso	majestic
marcato	marked, emphatic
pesante	heavy
sforzando (sf)	forcing, that is, a single note strongly accented
sostenuto	sustained
staccato	detached, short
tenuto	held (the full value of the note)

Obviously these indications of dynamics and expression are vague and subjective enough to allow for interpretation by the performer. For example, the term *appassionato* (to be played in a "passionate" manner) may have meant something specific to the composer, but it will mean different things to different performers. In a sense, the whole area of the interpretation and performance of music arises out of this terminological imprecision. And it is this imprecision, among other factors, which has led some composers recently to take their music into their own hands (and out of those of the performer) by electronically synthesizing their work.

CHAPTER 2

Stroboscopically lighted exposure of a single stroke by a squash player

Time and Movement: Rhythm

Marcel Duchamp, *Nude Descending a Staircase, No. 2*

WHILE OUR FOCUS IN CHAPTER 1 was primarily on sound and texture, it was necessary throughout the chapter to include time and movement in our discussion. This is not surprising, since sound, in music or in the world around us, cannot exist without its extension in time. Discussing texture, for example, we noted than an active texture is created when the voices move *rhythmically* independently of one another. In contrast, a relatively inactive texture is created when the voices move more or less together. We also talked about the *rate of change* from one texture to another within a piece. For example, the Haydn *Symphony 99* excerpt (Example 1.29) changed rapidly from unison texture to rhythmic unison and then later to an active texture, ending with melody and accompaniment, all within a very short period of time. And in the discussion of the Bulgarian folk song (Example 1.17), we needed to separate the pitches in each voice from their durations in order to describe the changes from unison texture to rhythmic unison. That is, the women sang the same rhythm (same set of durations) throughout, but not always the same pitches.

DEMONSTRATION 2.1
Fundamentals of Rhythm
(Sides 2–3)

In this chapter we ask you to focus your attention on the ways in which composers (or composer-performers) organize time. Actually the organization of time often accounts for your most immediate, almost visceral, experience of excitement in music.

Beat and Nonbeat

Example	Composer, title	Date
2.1	Haydn, *Symphony 88,* minuet	1787
2.2	Ravel, *Daphnis and Chloé*	1909–1912
2.3	*Bhimpalasī* (sitar played by Ravi Shankar)	

We begin with a broad comparison: three excerpts that are strikingly different in style and sound. As you listen to Examples 2.1 to 2.3, pay attention to the specific differences in your experience of time and how it is organized. For example, try to clap or tap your foot as you listen to each excerpt. You will notice that it is easy and quite natural to "keep time" as you listen to the Haydn excerpt. Haydn, in composing the *Minuet,* has created a clear beat that is easy to follow. Each beat— each tap of your foot—is experienced as marking off time into equal units. But in the Ravel excerpt it is difficult to find an underlying pulse—an underlying constant unit of time that you can tap out. Rather, Ravel seems to create a kind of suspended or floating motion, not marked off or measured by an internal clock created by the music itself.

Beat   Nonbeat

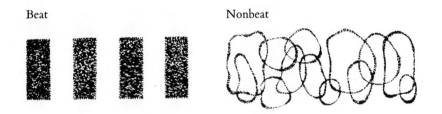

Notice, too, how differently you experience the *passing* of time in the two excerpts. Actually, both examples last slightly less than a minute as measured by ordinary clock time. But the clock's measure is an external one, different from and not relevant to your experienced time in either piece. Each piece generates its own internal temporal organization. Why, for example, does the same measured minute seem so different? Whether you experience it as longer or shorter, the reason is probably much the same. As in everyday life, your sense of how much time has elapsed depends on what you are doing—on what kinds of things are happening and how you feel about them. In the Haydn piece there is a lot going on in just one minute. In fact, the rate of events is so fast that a whole section of the movement is played and even repeated in this one minute. But the Ravel piece barely begins in the same minute of clock time; the rate of events and of change is extremely slow.

In listening to a piece of music, the presence or absence of an audible beat also contributes to your experience of time passing. With a strong beat (as in the Haydn minuet), you have a sense of clearly marked-off time and movement—like traveling on a highway watching regularly spaced telephone poles passing by. Without a strong beat (as in the Ravel), time seems to linger, marked off only by changing sound-shapes—like watching a gradually changing landscape.

You can experience a similar contrast in time and motion by making a simple experiment in paper-space. Follow the dots that appear below across the page by using your finger to "step" from one dot to the next, keeping a regular pulse as you go.

.   .   .   .

Ravi Shankar playing the sitar, accompanied by a tabla player

Now move your finger continuously along at about the same pace, following the continuous line that is just below the dots. The total time (and the total distance) from the beginning to the end of your "trip" across the page is more or less equal whether you "step" across the dots or slide continuously along the line, but the experience of time passing is quite different. In "stepping" across the dots you mark off time into separate, equidistant (in time and space) events—more like the Haydn. In sliding along the line, you move continuously through the same time-space—more like the Ravel. The two experiences of movement in time and space are quite different from one another but similar to the two musical experiences in time and sound.[1]

In Example 2.3 you hear both beat and nonbeat passages. The Indian piece begins with Ravi Shankar playing the **sitar** accompanied

---

[1] You can compare this experiment in space-time more directly with a sound-time experience through the examples in the Lecture-Demonstration (p. 49). There we juxtapose two examples that are the same in their total time but again quite different in how that time is experienced. The first is a series of clearly separate drum sounds marking off events that are "equidistant" in time (a steady beat), while the second is a single continuous tone.

by a **tamboura** which plays a drone in the background. Later these two instruments are joined by the **tabla,** an Indian drum (see p. 42). Listen for this change in sonority when the tabla enters and, along with it, a change from music without any underlying pulse to music with a very strong beat. Also notice the striking change in your experience of time and movement as this change in the temporal organization of the music occurs.

Beat Groups: Meter

Example	Composer, title	Date
2.4	*Power in the Blood* (hymn; adapted by M. Paich, sung by Mahalia Jackson)	
2.5	*Veni Creator Spiritus* ("Come, Holy Spirit"), Gregorian chant	Middle Ages
2.6	Stravinsky, *Octet for Wind Instruments,* first movement	1922–1923
2.7	Sousa, *Stars and Stripes Forever*	1897

With these examples we raise the following question: Given that a piece creates an underlying beat or pulse, can you also find and clap a slower but equally regular beat? For example, when you listen to Mahalia Jackson singing *Power in the Blood* (Example 2.4), you can easily keep time. In fact, some of the power of the music and of the performance comes from the clearly marked beat played in the bass and drums and emphasized by the singer. But you can also find a slower beat which, in this excerpt, is doubly marked—the first syllable of "power," for instance. Notice that there is a regular relation between the slower and faster beats. You can count two (or perhaps four) faster beats for each slower beat. (We will return to this relation between slower and faster beats in a moment.)

Listen now to the Gregorian chant *Veni Creator Spiritus* (Example 2.5). You can probably find and clap an underlying pulse as you listen, but it is much less compelling than in the preceding example. Actually, each note (or each syllable) is of equal duration, and thus the singers create a regular but rather gentle beat. But can you clap a slower pulse without forcing it on the movement of the melody? Probably not. The beats you feel—those the monks create as they sing each note—do not naturally group together to form a slower but equally regular beat.

The next two examples (2.6 and 2.7) illustrate a somewhat similar contrast. The Sousa march, like *Power in the Blood,* creates a clearly audible faster beat and these beats, in turn, are clearly marked off or grouped by an equally regular slower beat. When two sets of beats coincide—that is, when fast and slower beats meet—they create an accent. An *accented event* is one that is somehow marked for attention. Try clapping faster and slower beats. What is their relation to one another?

In the Sousa march accented events occur just as regularly as the underlying beat itself. But in the excerpt (Example 2.6) from the Stravinsky *Octet* (a piece for eight instruments) Stravinsky plays with these expectations of regularity. First, he lets you settle into a regular relationship between slower and faster beats. Then, having set you up, he delightfully toys with your expectations for continuation by speeding up and slowing down the rate of the slower beat. In doing so, he keeps you off balance by shifting the occurrence of accented events—that is, the moments when faster and slower beats coincide. Listen carefully to this excerpt because the shifts in accent are quite subtle. Try clapping the slower beat and notice how Stravinsky seems to "take it away from you."

You have heard examples with and without a clear beat (Examples 2.1 to 2.3) and examples with and without a regular grouping of the beats (Examples 2.4 to 2.7). But notice that music must first generate an underlying beat before it can create a regular *grouping* of that underlying beat. If there is a regularly recurring accent which groups the underlying beat, we describe the piece as *metric.* If there is no regular grouping of the underlying beat, we describe the piece as *ametric.* Thus, there can be beat without meter but not meter without beat. Before going on, you may want to go back and listen to the first four examples in Chapter 1, paying specific attention to the presence or absence of a beat and/or meter. This new awareness may give you some more insight into the differences in style and in character among those widely diverse examples. We will return to issues of style and rhythmic organization in Part Four.

Rhythm and Structure

Example	Composer, title	Date
2.8	Hindemith, *Kleine Kammermusik,* Op. 24, no. 2, fourth movement	1922

In the fourth movement of the Hindemith *Kleine Kammermusik* ("Little Chamber Music"), change in rhythmic organization coincides with change in instrumentation and texture. In fact, the movement (recorded in its entirety here, Example 2.8) is organized around this contrast. Rhythmic-unison texture along with a clear beat alternate with solo passages that do not create a clear beat. The spontaneous, improvisatory feeling of the solo passages results in part from this absence of, or freedom from, an underlying pulse. Notice, however, that each time the unison passage returns, the group plays much the same music, while each solo section is performed by a different instrument playing a new melody that seems designed for just that particular instrument. Think of the unison passages as a kind of refrain which keeps recurring, while the solo passages give each instrumentalist a chance to come forward and play his or her own part in his or her own way. Below is a diagram of the whole movement:

refrain	flute solo	refrain	bassoon solo	refrain	clarinet solo	refrain	oboe solo	refrain	horn solo	coda

This piece is a good one for learning more about how to follow a score, since the contrasts between the refrains (always played by four instruments in rhythmic unison) and the solo sections are quite visible. Look at the score reproduced on pages 46–47 and try to see each of the contrasting sections that are shown in the diagram. Notice that the score is much more detailed than the diagram. While the smallest "element" shown in the diagram is just a box which stands for a whole section of the piece, the smallest element in the score is a symbol standing for a single note. Notes follow one another on separate *staffs*, one staff (of five lines) for each of the five participating instruments. The five staffs are in turn grouped together by a *brace* at the left side of the page. As you listen, your eye must follow all five instruments along together from left to right and then shift down to the next brace of five staffs as the music continues.

Despite all this necessary detail, the contrasts between refrain and solo sections are still quite visible. The movement begins with the first refrain, which is played by all the instruments together with the exception of the flute. You can see that in this opening refrain the notes of the four lower instruments all go along together, while the flute staff is occupied only with rests. Next the flute plays alone, creating the contrast in sound and texture. The staffs of the other instruments are now occupied only with rests. Notice, too, that the vertical lines (**bar lines**) do not coincide with or mark off the beginnings and endings of these contrasting sections. This is an important point which we will return to in the discussion of metric in contrast to "figural" grouping.

Example 2.8 HINDEMITH, *Kleine Kammermusik*

New York Woodwind Quintet (front: clarinet; back, left to right: french horn, flute, bassoon, oboe)

Notice that Hindemith has indicated (above the flute part) that the flutist should play freely (*frei*), which accounts for the sense of freedom from a beat. He also blurs the sense of regular pulse by telling the flutist to get faster at the end of the solo (*accel.,* for **accelerando**), thus quickening the pace of whatever internal clock the flutist was following.

When the refrain returns, Hindemith tells the performers to re-turn to the original pace, or to play "in time" (*a tempo*), and we also once again hear a clear beat. The flute joins in for this second refrain, but the bassoon drops out in preparation for its upcoming solo. Hin-demith indicates that the bassoon solo should start out slowly (*langsam*) and then, like the flute solo, speed up (*accelerando*).

Notice that if you follow the score along with your finger as you listen, you must change your rate of motion to coincide with the performers' changes in rate of motion, that is, their changes in **tempo.** So the same amount of "paper-space" may not stand for the same amount of "time-space." Finally, you will see and hear that the total time—the time proportions—of the **refrains** and the solo sections is not always the same. Thus, the rate at which contrast occurs also varies. For example, the third and fourth refrains are shorter, quickening the rate of change in the middle of the movement.

Now listen to the whole movement again, following the recurring refrain and the various solos as they occur in the score. The movement ends with a brief **coda** which is similar to the refrain but varied both in instrumentation and in rhythm so as to make a fitting ending.

LECTURE-DEMONSTRATION
(Side 3)

The next band on the record moves into a Lecture-Demonstration as we take a closer look at the temporal relations in both a Sousa march and a dance by Lanner. For this purpose we have used electronically generated sounds[2] which intentionally do not sound like the instruments you heard playing the march. Although artificial, this method should help you to isolate the various elements that contribute to your experience of beat and groupings of beats as well as to your experience of larger but equally regular time units.

To simplify the demonstration, the discussion is included directly on the recording (hence the term *lecture-demonstration*). Certain fundamental concepts which are illustrated on the record are defined in the following text. A graphic description of the examples is also included in the text to help you *see* the distinctions which you *hear* in the music. For further explanation of the graphic description and for a discussion of standard rhythm notation, see the Additional Materials and the Ancillary Reading sections at the end of this chapter.

Beat. The underlying pulse which marks off the passing of time into more or less equal units. It is generated by the pattern of varied durations that is actually played or sung, together with the pitches of a melody and sometimes also by percussion instruments or bass in an accompaniment. It also functions as a unit of time for measuring these varied durations.

---

[2] The electronic sounds used in the lecture-demonstration were generated in the Experimental Music Studio at the Massachusetts Institute of Technology.

Elevation of the nave of Amiens Cathedral

The metric hierarchy reflected in architecture ("frozen music").

Meter. The organization of the beat into groups which form longer but equally regular units of time. When the groups include two or four beats (Examples 2.4 and 2.7), the meter is duple, that is, beats are grouped in twos or a multiple of two. When the groups include three beats (Example 2.1), the meter is triple. When the groups include more than four beats, they are usually perceived as multiples of 2 or 3 (for example, a group of six beats as 2×3 or 3×2, or eight beats as 4×2 or 2×4) or as asymmetrical (and comparatively rare) groups such as 5 or 7.

Downbeat. The beats within the underlying pulse which are regularly marked for attention, that is, accented. Thus, it is the regular recurrence of downbeats which generates beat groups. The downbeat is labelled "1" to mark it as the first in each beat group. Note, however, that accent is not necessarily generated by *stress.* That is, the accented note need not be played louder. Its function as the downbeat derives from a number of sources, including the particular pattern of varied durations as well as pitch and dynamic relations.

Upbeat. The unaccented beat preceding the downbeat, that is, the last note or notes of each beat group. The term *upbeat* reflects the active, onward movement and thus the "tension" often associated with upbeat events. The name also reflects the conductor's upward motion on upbeats in contrast to his downward motion on accented beats, or downbeats. For example, *Stars and Stripes Forever* begins with an upbeat. However, the terms *up*beat and *down*beat should not be confused with up or down in pitch (see Chapter 3).

Metric Grid. The regularly ordered relations among the various levels of time units. The metric grid, as a whole, forms a hierarchy which can be described in terms of the proportional relations among the units of time, or beats, at each level of the hierarchy; for example, the relations between the beat, the lower level *division* of the beat, and the higher level *grouping* of the beats. This grid forms the underpinnings of the temporal structure; it is the organized framework in relation to which we hear the more dynamic ebb and flow of time in much of Western music.

Tempo. The rate of the underlying beat and thus (proportionally) the rate of all the other levels of the metric grid. (See Ancillary Reading for more details.)

Duration. The time from the onset or attack of an event (note, chord) to the onset or attack of the next event. (See Ancillary Reading for the notation of durations.)

SOUSA, *Stars and Stripes Forever*

(a) Melody alone

| | | ||| |||　　　||| ||| ||| 　 | melody

(b) Melody and beat

| | | ||| |||　　　||| ||| ||| 　 | melody

| | | | | | | | | | | | | | | | | beats

(continued)

(c) Melody, beat, and meter

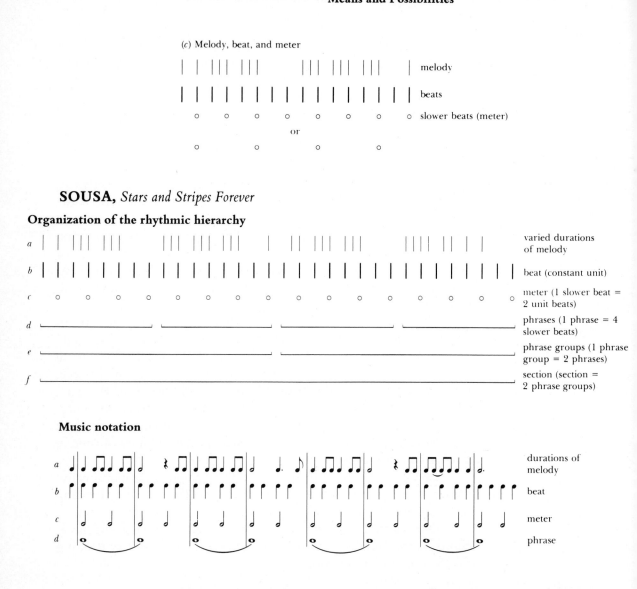

SOUSA, *Stars and Stripes Forever*

Organization of the rhythmic hierarchy

Music notation

Notice when you listen to the melody that the tones are *sustained,* thus "filling out" the full duration of each note. In contrast, when you hear only the rhythm played on the synthesized drum, there is "space" (silence) between the short sound of the drum hit itself and the next attack point. However, in both cases the rhythm created by the successive attacks—that is, the duration of the events—is the same. The *duration* of an event, then, is taken to include both sound and silence between attack points.

The metric grid: duple meter

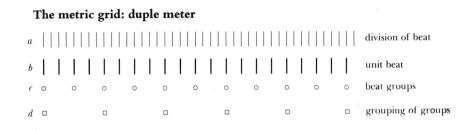

Notice that at any one level the ratio is 2:1 between it and the levels above or below it—a:b = 2:1; b:c = 2:1; c:d = 2:1.

LANNER, *Styrian Dances*

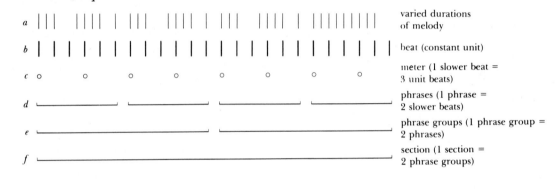

Music notation

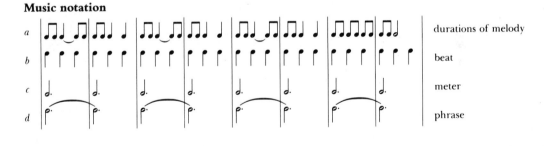

The metric grid: triple meter

Notice that the ratios between levels are not symmetrical—a:b = 2:1; b:c = 3:1.

The metric grid: compound duple meter

a ||||||||||||||||||||||||||||||||||||||||||||||||| division of beat

b | | | | | | | | | | | | | | | | | unit beat

c o   o   o   o   o   o   o   o beat groups

The ratios among levels are again asymmetrical but in the reverse order as compared with the triple meter grid—a:b = 3:1; b:c = 2:1.

Notice that standard rhythm notation includes bar lines which indicate the higher level metric units, or **measures.** The bar lines look as if they *contain* these beat groups, like boxes containing time. But they should not be interpreted as interrupting the flow of events. Unlike the notes themselves, which are symbols telling the performer to *do* something (how long to play each tone), the bar lines tell the performer *about* the music. They show the performer where events lie in relation to the metric grid.

It is particularly important to notice that bar lines do not show you the boundaries of motives or phrases. These rhythmic *figures*—the "gestures" formed by relations among events in a given melody— often overlap the measured time units indicated by the bar lines. While the listener can usually readily perceive these figural groups, they are not evident in standard rhythm notation since it is concerned entirely with measuring events in relation to some unit time.

For example, the first figural group in *Stars and Stripes* starts before the bar line and is bounded by the longer note which occurs at the *beginning* of the second measure. Thus, the figural group *ends* where the metric group *begins.* So if we count beats consecutively from the

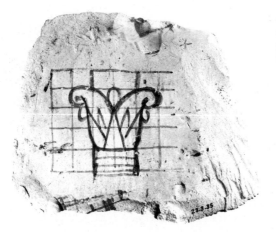

An ancient Egyptian artist's design superimposed upon a grid—one a gesture ("figure"), the other a measure ("metric")

beginning to the end of this figural group, we can count eight beats in all. But if we count beats according to the metric grid, we begin with 4 (the upbeat) and start over again with 1 at the beginning of each beat group:

Notice that the rhythm of the second group is slightly varied. It also begins before the bar line (with an upbeat) but extends past the accented downbeat ending on the third beat of the measure.

In the Lanner dance the relation between beat groups and figural groups is somewhat different—figural groups begin and end *within bar lines*. That is, the first figural group includes the first two measures; it begins on the downbeat—on 1—and ends on the last beat of the second measure. Thus, the Sousa march can be characterized as having figures which go *to* an accent, while the Lanner dance can be characterized as having figures which begin on a downbeat, that is, proceed *from* an accent.

It is also interesting to observe that in the Lanner dance above, the pattern of durations is the same within each figural group, with the exception of the last one. Indeed, this repetition is one factor which creates these figural groupings.

Looking back at the Hindemith piece, you will see (and hear) that sections always end at the *beginning* of beat groups; that is, each section ends on a downbeat. It is for this reason, as we noted earlier, that the boundaries of sections do not coincide with the boundaries of metric groups indicated by the bar lines.

EXERCISE 2.1
Meter
(Side 3)

These examples will give you practice in finding the meter of a piece. Remember, however, that knowing the meter is in no sense a primary goal of listening to music. Once you can recognize differences in metric organization, though, this can serve as a basis for hearing other, more interesting aspects of temporal organization. If you have any difficulty in determining the meter of a piece, you may:

1. Clap the underlying beat.
2. Clap only the slower beat (sometimes, as we have noted, called the accented beat, or downbeat).
3. Clap all the beats, calling the accented beat "1." See how far you can count before you must say "1" again. If you can count to 2 or a multiple of 2, the meter is duple. If you can count to 3, the meter is triple.

Duple meter   Triple meter

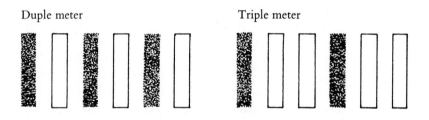

Listen to the examples, decide whether they are in duple or in triple meter, and mark the appropriate column. The answers are given on pages 58–59.

Example	Duple	Triple
2.9		
2.10		
2.11		
2.12		
2.13		
2.14		
2.15		

It will be useful in checking your answers to listen to the examples once more while reading the following additional comments.

DEMONSTRATION 2.2
Rhythmic Complexity
(Sides 3–4)

The preceding examples and Lecture-Demonstration illustrated some of the basic means through which time is organized in music. These include the metric grid, which is organized into beats, the grouping of these beats, the various divisions of the beat, and the relations among these levels of the metric hierarchy. In turn, music is organized by its figures—especially in terms of the position of accents within figures, for example, beginning-accented or end-accented figures. Now that you are familiar with these "givens," which are shared by much of the music in Western culture, we will go on to see how composers have played with these givens to create interest, variety, and in many instances a special kind of almost visceral excitement.

The examples that follow (2.16 through 2.31, beginning after the Correct Answers section) are grouped according to their date of composition. While we have alluded casually to musical *style* and seen how it is associated with the particular historical period in which a composer lived, we have been more concerned with juxtaposing examples because they are similar in their compositional *means* (texture, instrumentation, beat, nonbeat), though they may be rather different in style and date of composition. In this final section examples in each group roughly share their dates of composition and thus their musical

Charlie Chaplin in *Modern Times*
Rhythmic complexity: ". . . each instrument plays its own individual and rhythmically independent line."

CORRECT ANSWERS

Example	Composer, title, date	Duple	Triple
2.9	J. Strauss, *Emperor Waltz*, 1889		X
2.10	Tchaikovsky, *Marche slave*, 1876	X	

Waltzes (Example 2.9) are by definition in triple meter; as the old song goes, "Two hearts [beat together] in three-quarter time." The Tchaikovsky march (Example 2.10) is clearly in duple meter. But notice that while the trumpets always mark the strong beats (1 and 3 in the four-beat group), the rest of the orchestra consistently plays accents on the "off-beats"—that is, on 2 and 4, which are weak beats. The rhythmic conflict created when accents occur on events which are normally unaccented in the metric grid is called **syncopation.** Notice that these off-beat accents are created by stress—by playing louder—in contrast to normal metric accents which result naturally from a particular pattern of durations and pitches. Notice, too, that in the second part of the excerpt the conflicting accents stop, which leads to a lessening of tension.

Example	Composer, title	Duple	Triple
2.11	*Move Members Move* (spiritual; sung by Rosie Hibler and Family)	X	

The compelling character of this spiritual (Example 2.11) is created in part by the traditional clapping on off-beats; it seems almost to epitomize the notion of syncopation.

Example	Composer, title, date	Duple	Triple
2.12	S. Rollins, *Valse Hot*, 1956		X

Jazz waltzes were very rare before the mid-fifties; the music of jazz had always been in duple meter from its origins. Notice the syncopation in this "hot" waltz (Example 2.12) created primarily by off-beat drums and piano chords, but also by several striking stresses in the melody on weak beats. (In Chapter 11, you will encounter a piece by the contemporary composer Milton Babbitt that pushes to the very limits the intuitive idea of a waltz.)

Example	Composer, title, date	Duple	Triple
2.13	Sousa, *Semper Fidelis,* 1888	X	(X)

Like all **marches,** this one too (Example 2.13) is duple in meter (think what would happen to your two feet if you had to march to a piece in triple meter). However, in this march the two strong beats are subdivided into three rather than the usual two, as in *Stars and Stripes Forever.* When a basically duple meter is subdivided into threes, the meter is described as compound duple meter—that is, both twos and threes. Notice that there are six faster notes in each measure rather than the usual eight or four of simple duple meter. This presents interesting possibilities for composers to play with the relations between compound duple meter and triple meter which also includes six faster beats in a measure. (See the diagram of the metric grid for compound duple meter and triple meter on pages 53–54.)

Example	Composer, title, date	Duple	Triple
2.14	*America the Beautiful* (played by the Al Cohn Quartet), 1976	X	

Here is a "jazzed-up" version of a very familiar melody (Example 2.14). Bass, drums, and piano provide an accompaniment with the rhythmic character of the Brazilian bossa nova; in conflict with the basic beat in the drums and bass, the piano plays chords that often do not coincide with the strong beats and are thus syncopated. In the foreground, the tenor saxophone plays a relatively straightforward version of *America the Beautiful* in the first **chorus,** and then **improvises** for a second chorus.

Example	Composer, title, date	Duple	Triple
2.15	Rossini, *William Tell,* overture, 1829	X	

style. In addition, they all illustrate some kind of interesting rhythmic complexity. Some of these means of creating rhythmic interest will be found in all periods (and thus will be found in all of the following groups of examples), and yet the particular effect may be quite different within differing styles of composition. In listening to these examples, then, we are asking you to pay attention to particular means for creating rhythmic complexity. At the same time, we ask you to notice characteristics shared by music written during a given historical period, as

Rhythmic complexity

well as the differences which result from changes in style across historical periods.

Renaissance and Baroque

Example	Composer, title	Date
2.16	Anonymous, *Bransle de Poitou*	Renaissance
2.17	Jacchini, *Sonata with Two Trumpets,* third movement	1690
2.18	Telemann, *Trio Sonata in D Minor,* second movement	1740
2.19	Bach, *Cantata 31*	c. 1715

The first of these examples (Example 2.16) is a French dance, the **bransle**, composed during the Renaissance; the rest belong to the Baroque period.[3] In the *Bransle*, syncopation creates a certain metrical ambiguity; for example, what is the meter? Actually it is a triple-meter dance, beginning here with an upbeat. But in the third and seventh measures a stress on the second beat (syncopation) upsets the regular flow.

In the *Sonata with Two Trumpets* by Jacchini (Example 2.17) we have another example of syncopation in which the stressed accents occur on a normally unaccented beat, as in the bransle, the Tchaikovsky *Marche slave,* and the spiritual *Move Members Move.* That is, there is a stress on the second beat of the triple meter which conflicts with the underlying accent on the first beat of the triple meter. Thus there is a kind of tension between the regularly recurring accent set up by the

---

[3] For approximate dates of each historical period, see Chapter 13.

rhythm and pitch patterns and the stressed second beat which, so to speak, attacks this given metric accent. The word *syncopation* is given to all situations in which one hears simultaneously the framework of a well-formed metric grid and events which go against the norms of that framework.

If you focus your listening on the accompaniment (organ, basses, and tympani), you will hear that they sometimes play only on the downbeats

```
 /     /     /     /
|  _ |  _ _ |  _ _ |  _ _
1 2 3 1 2 3 1 2 3 1 2 3
```

but sometimes go on to play two notes in a row, giving an extra stress to the second

```
  /      /      /      /
| | _ | | _ | | _ | | _
1 2 3 1 2 3 1 2 3 1 2 3
```

It is this displacement of the normal accent that we call syncopation.

Drummer (German print, 1562)

Recorder players with singer (Italian print, 1535)

In Example 2.18, a trio for flute, oboe, and basso continuo (that is, the background accompaniment played by the harpsichord and cello together), the accompanying instruments generally play a regular duple meter while first the oboe and then the flute play *between* the beats, creating syncopation. However, this piece also differs from the preceding examples in that the flute and/or oboe *anticipate* the beat rather than follow it.

In the excerpt from the Bach *Cantata* (Example 2.19) we hear rhythmic *contrast* rather than rhythmic *conflict.* The excerpt begins with all the instruments playing in unison and also playing notes of relatively long duration. Then at the end of the unison passage the melody gets faster—there are more notes per beat. This leads to a section in which this more active rhythmic movement continues, but the texture also becomes more active. We hear many parts playing rhythmically independently of one another. So the excerpt includes an increase in both rhythmic activity and textural activity without any change in *tempo*— that is, without any change in the rate of the underlying beat.

The piece begins in unison, followed by a more active texture.

Classical

Example	Composer, title	Date
2.20	Mozart, *String Quartet in G Major,* K. 387, fourth movement	1782
2.21	Beethoven, *Variations on "God Save the King"*	1803
2.22	Beethoven, *Sonata for Cello and Piano,* Op. 69, scherzo	1808
2.23	Haydn, *String Quartet,* Op. 76, no. 5, minuet	1797

These four examples are from the so-called **Classical** period, and they include works by the three greatest composers of that era—Haydn, Mozart, and Beethoven. Example 2.20, from one of Mozart's string quartets (two violins, viola, and cello), again includes contrast in rhythmic and textural activity. Like the Bach example, this one begins with notes of longer duration and changes in the second section to much faster rhythmic motion. Also like the Bach, there is no change in the rate of the underlying beat (that is, no change in *tempo*) or in the prevailing meter (duple here, triple in the Bach). However, in this excerpt *slower* rhythmic motion (fewer notes per beat) goes together with *greater* textural activity, while *faster* rhythmic motion (more notes per beat) goes together with *less* textural activity.

In the first section, then, you hear imitation—the instruments enter one by one, each playing the same slow five-note motive. And once in, each instrument goes on to play its own individual and rhythmically independent line. Notice too that the rhythmic independence

The Coull String Quartet (left to right: first and second violins, cello, viola)

of the lines is created in large part as a result of syncopation. That is, the instruments that play against the slow-moving melody are also playing against the underlying beat (in between the beats). In the second section syncopation disappears, and textural activity lessens. We hear one clear melody with an accompaniment, but the running melody is made up of many very fast notes. Thus when the rhythm grows more active, the texture becomes less active.

A theme followed by a set of variations on it was a favorite way of organizing music in the Classical period, often through improvisation. You heard another example of a theme and variations in Chapter 1—the theme and some of the variations from the fourth movement of Beethoven's *Symphony 9* (Example 1.9). Composers sometimes also borrowed themes from elsewhere, and in Example 2.21 we have Beethoven composing variations on the British national anthem, *God Save the King* (which we in turn borrowed and know as *America*). Listening to Beethoven's setting of the familiar tune followed by one of the variations, it should be quite clear that Beethoven had a good time varying the straightforward theme by introducing syncopation. Of course, that was not all he did; in fact, you may have a little trouble at first finding the familiar tune in the variation. It may help if you sing the tune along with the variation. You will see that it fits perfectly, except you will be *on* the beat while the melody line of the variation is often between the beats. In addition, the downbeats are sometimes not sounded in the melody, leaving a silence just where we expect to hear an extra emphasis. In this way Beethoven shifts the accent to the second beat of the triple meter, most noticeably at the end of each section of the piece. Compare the effect of this shift of accent to the weak second beat with the same sort of syncopation in the Jacchini *Sonata* (Example 2.17). This is a good example of the way a composer can toy with givens—in this case the givens of the theme itself as well as the givens established by the underlying metric grid.

In Example 2.22 we again hear Beethoven making use of syncopation but this time in a rather different way and with different effect. On first hearing you may find it hard to tell which is the beat and which is the off-beat. For example, when the cello joins in, is it that instrument or the piano playing on the beat? In fact, the cello *anticipates* the beat at the beginnings of phrases and then plays on the beat and with the piano accompaniment at the ends of phrases. Notice particularly that at the end of the cello's first phrase, and again with its repetition, both cello and piano arrive together on the downbeat, but they seem to plummet into that abrupt stop as if arriving too soon. In the second part of the excerpt, the cello's syncopated notes seem to

Example 2.23 HAYDN, *String Quartet,* Op. 76, no. 5, minuet

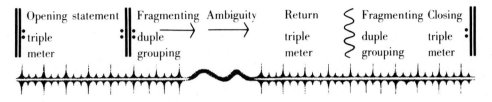

drive the piece forward to the climax, which then suddenly subsides as the syncopation ceases, giving way to a much more lyrical passage.

Finally, in the Haydn string quartet (Example 2.23) we have a beautiful example of shift in meter. In this minuet (the third movement of four in the quartet), Haydn first creates a clear triple meter. But after the repetition of this first section, there is an abrupt shift to duple meter. Haydn creates this shift in meter by simply shortening or fragmenting the figure with which the first section ends. The ending figure ♩ | ♫ ♩ is abbreviated to become ♫ ♩ . He gives this fragmented figure to the violin, which plays a number of them (♫ ♩ ♫ ♩ ♫ ♩ ♫ ♩). And since the abbreviated figure is now only two beats long (instead of three), the repetitions cause the beats to group in twos instead of the initial threes. Haydn then fragments the figure still further by chopping off the last note, leaving a series of notes of equal duration (♫ ♫ ♫ ♫) . For a moment the meter becomes ambiguous; we hear simply an ungrouped series of beats. With the return of the opening material, the meter is once again triple; the tension and resulting intensity subside almost as if nothing at all had happened. The fragmenting process occurs once again, this time with the cello playing the abbreviated two-beat figure. The minuet ends with a new transformation of the motive. We hear repeated statements of the original figure in its clear triple-meter form (♩ | ♫ ♩), which brings the movement to a solid and stable close. Notice that the second part of the minuet is also repeated.

Romantic

Example	Composer, title	Date
2.24	Schubert, *String Quintet in C,* Op. 163, scherzo	1828
2.25	Chopin, *Mazurka,* Op. 17, no. 4	1832–1833
2.26	Brahms, *Trio for Piano, Cello, and Clarinet,* Op. 114	1891

In the first of these Romantic period examples, Schubert adds another cello to the string quartet. You will hear in this excerpt (Example 2.24) a change from straightforward rhythmic stability at the beginning, to conflict and tension in the middle, to a return to rhythmic stability at the end. As in several of the earlier examples (the Telemann trio and the Beethoven cello and piano sonata), conflict is created here by an accent which precedes, or *anticipates,* the normally accented downbeat (thus syncopation). But in this excerpt the syncopation grows out of a transformation of an earlier rhythmic figure. The movement itself begins with a quick upbeat which adds power to the longer, stressed downbeat that follows. At the beginning of the excerpt you hear hints of that opening figure in the passage just preceding the syncopation. Then, at the climax (created in part by the excitement of rhythmic conflict), Schubert reminds us of the upbeat in the upper strings, but this time he withholds the downbeat! Only the cellos play the downbeat, as if teasing the upper strings to try and join them. Finally, all five strings do come together to play the original upbeat-downbeat figure with which the movement begins. It is a marvelous example of building anticipation and drive in preparation for return and stability—a subject to which we shall return in Chapters 4 and 6.

In the Chopin *Mazurka* (Example 2.25) we hear a kind of rhythmic complexity that is particularly associated with the Romantic period of music. Not surprisingly, it is highly dependent on a "living" interaction between composer and performer. Indeed, during the nineteenth century the individuality of the instrumental performer—as virtuoso, as "star," as unique personality—comes much more to the fore. We find composers like Chopin (as well as Liszt, Paganini, and others) writing works which are in part a showcase for the performer's technical and expressive skills. One aspect of this presence of the performer as an individual is his or her use of **rubato.** The term comes from the Italian word for "robbed." It refers to the performer's freedom to slow down or speed up the tempo—to extend or shorten the time of an event or group of events. Thus it is like "robbing" time from one event or from a moment in the flow of the piece (speeding up slightly) and "paying it back" a little later (slowing down proportionally). This should not be understood, of course, as a process of actually measuring, but rather as a kind of subtle give-and-take or flexibility with which the performer treats the underlying pulse. While the purpose is one of achieving greater expressiveness, it requires a deep interaction between the structural relations of the piece itself and the performer's understanding of these structural relations, especially in their potential for expressiveness.

Figural grouping plays an important role, for it is particularly in terms of figures—that is, phrases, motivic groups, gestures of the music—that the performer makes decisions (certainly not always conscious or explicit) concerning the use of *rubato*. In fact, a performer who might be described as using *rubato* tastefully is one who robs and pays back in response to such figural structure, while the performer who uses *rubato* in bad taste is often one who robs and pays back without sufficient attention to these structural relations or in violation of them. Besides the use of *rubato* to project figural groupings, there is its use by performers to emphasize or even prolong a climactic moment (slowing down), to reinforce a passage which is restless or driving forward (speeding up), and so forth.

Listen again to the Chopin *Mazurka* and notice particularly how the pianist "bends" the underlying beat which is always present in his left hand—that is, in the bass. Chopin encourages the pianist to let the right hand move more freely by sometimes composing a melodic line which is unmeasured with respect to the beat. For example, he writes the following:

This means, essentially, "fit those 15 notes into the time of the three underlying beats in a free and expressive way." So, while it would not be quite appropriate to speak of rhythmic conflict here between the melody and the accompaniment, it does seem appropriate to note the rhythmic complexity and the expressiveness which results from the relations between the notated underlying pulse and the performer's liberties with that pulse, as well as the relations between the fairly regular bass and the relatively freer melody.

Finally, while the use of *rubato* is perhaps more pronounced in the performances of romantic music, it is not limited to this music. In fact, all performers include some give-and-take with the notated time in projecting structural relations and for purposes of expressiveness. This is very clear if you compare the computer "performance" with the live performance of the Lanner dance in the Lecture-

Demonstration. Indeed, it is precisely the lack of give-and-take—the exact and rigid marking of the beat and measuring of each event—which often makes computer music sound so inhuman and mechanical.

But bear in mind that the liberties performers (including conductors) take with the rhythm of a piece as notated by the composer are very small and tasteful in the ways described above. Such liberties should not be confused with "arrangements" of a tune, as is common with popular music, and certainly not with improvisation, such as we will discuss in the next group of examples. The performance of a composed and written-out work must be faithful to the printed score. The composer notates all the pitches and their durations as well as the instrumentation (in an orchestral score) just as he or she wants them, and they are played essentially as the composer wrote them. The question of "interpretation" is precisely one of coming to understand—to "hear" the work as much as possible in terms of the composer's musical intentions—and then to find the appropriate means for projecting this understanding in performance. In a very profound sense the performer, as he or she studies a score, is also practicing the "art of listening."

The first movement of the Brahms *Trio for Piano, Cello, and Clarinet* (Example 2.26) includes in it nearly all the varieties of rhythmic complexity we have illustrated thus far—shifts in meter, syncopation (accent shifted to weak beats or between beats), changes in the division of the beats, changes in the degree of rhythmic and textural activity, as well as *rubato* playing by the performers. And yet the effect is not one of continuous conflict and tension as we might expect, but rather one of metric ambiguity or perhaps metric fluidity. Most of all Brahms creates a different relationship between metric and figural groupings. He asks you to focus more on the gesture—on the figural groups formed by motives and phrases which are in a dynamic, changing, almost fluid relationship to the underlying metric grid. The listener rarely loses a sense of beat but at times loses the sense of regularly recurring accents altogether, though still following the flow of the gesture from one goal or boundary to the next. Brahms writes motives that create their own inner accents which may or may not coincide with those of the initially established duple meter: downbeats are often silent or held over from the preceding upbeat; the four-beat measure is divided into three beats, obscuring the normal pulse; motives played by two instruments overlap in their grouping, placing their accents ambiguously in relation to the metric grid; a motive begins with an accent, apparently a downbeat, which turns out to have been a metric weak beat and not the metric accent at all. The result of all this is a temporal organization which is highly pliable and still tightly structured. Brahms causes time seemingly to expand and contract, ebb and flow, as it constantly frees itself from and then reaffirms an underlying pulse and meter.

With the next group of examples we move into our own century. Paradoxically, the works written most recently may sound the most strange. This is partly, as you will hear, because of the new ways some twentieth-century composers have found to organize time as well as pitch (we will return to the issue of pitch in Chapters 3 and 5). And yet we also find contemporary composers using some of the same means for creating rhythmic complexity as earlier composers but now within a musical style that gives them a rather different effect.

Twentieth Century

Example	Composer, title	Date
2.27	Stravinsky, *Petrouchka,* scene 3, waltz	1910–1911
2.28	Bartok, *Sonata for Two Pianos and Percussion,* first movement	1937
2.29	Webern, *Five Pieces for Orchestra,* Op. 10, no. 2	1913
2.30	S. Joplin, *Maple Leaf Rag* (played by S. Joplin in 1916)	1899
2.31	S. Joplin, *Maple Leaf Rag* (played by Jelly Roll Morton)	1938

In the excerpt from *Petrouchka* (Example 2.27) you hear a new kind of rhythmic conflict, namely, two different meters superimposed on one another. Stravinsky creates this playful conflict in an ingenious way: He takes the same triple-meter dance by Lanner that you heard in the Lecture-Demonstration (borrowing a tune like Beethoven did) and superimposes it on his own accompaniment composed so that it generates compound duple meter. As a result you hear two meters simultaneously pitted against one another.

The excerpt begins with the bassoon playing alone in notes of equal duration but the pitch relations cause this "melody" to group into two groups of three notes each, thus compound duple meter:

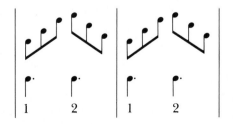

This bassoon "melody" becomes an accompaniment as Lanner's melody enters played by trumpet and flute. Recall that Lanner's accompaniment to this same melody was the simple "oom-pah-pah" bass that is so characteristic of triple meter. But Stravinsky creates a delightful new effect by superimposing this triple-meter melody on his own compound-duple-meter accompaniment.

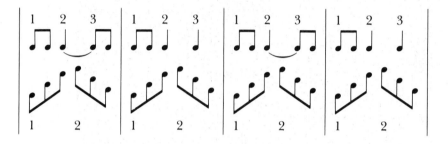

The excerpt from Bartok's *Sonata for Two Pianos and Percussion* (Example 2.28) gives us an example of a real change in tempo. Unlike the Mozart quartet or the Bach cantata excerpts, where there was an increase in rhythmic motion but no change in the rate of the underlying beat, in this example the rate of the beat does actually increase. This, you may recall, is known as an *accelerando.* You saw the word in the score and heard its effect on a small scale in the Hindemith *Kleine Kammermusik* movement. Notice the difference between getting faster with no change in tempo or meter—that is, within the framework of an unchanging metric grid (as in Examples 2.19 and 2.20)—and getting faster when the framework itself gives way. In the earlier examples we heard, on one hand, more notes per beat, but the beat remained as the fixed reference. In this example, on the other hand, there is a continuous acceleration: the beat slowly speeds up rather than changing from, say, two notes per beat (eighth notes) to four notes per beat (sixteenth notes).

Example 2.29 is a complete little piece, one of five that Webern wrote to be played as a group. This piece, as well as the others in the group, differ from any of the other examples you have heard thus far in that an underlying metric grid is almost entirely absent. In its place the structure of figural groups formed by motives and their resulting gestures becomes the basis for organizing time. With the loss of even a sense of underlying pulse, and with it, of course, the loss of meter, you may indeed feel as if the music has lost all rhythmic coherence. In fact, the piece is highly organized rhythmically, but Webern's means of organization and thus his means of generating coherence—even comprehensibility—derives from a different notion of structuring time. He asks you to attend to the unique structure formed by the movement from one figural boundary to another and by the repetition of rhythmic patterns within figures, rather than have you search for the accustomed metric grid. Can you find rhythmic structure without the security of reference to a grid? It is a challenge which has been described as follows:

> Through the power of an ever new, internal logic, each work will rouse the listener from his state of passivity and make him share in its impulse, so that there will no longer be a difference of kind, but only of degree, between inventing music and listening to it.[4]

Perhaps the challenge of discovering the "ever new, internal logic" demanded by this music is also appropriate to more familiar music. Listening to music that is very familiar we tend too easily to fall into a "state of passivity." Simply following the norms of a regular beat and meter, we fail to listen actively enough to the unique rhythmic complexities found even in the more traditional music of earlier times.

We end this section on rhythmic complexity and the chapter on rhythm with two interestingly different performances of the "same" piece. Scott Joplin (Example 2.30) plays his own rag in a straightforward way, unembellished with rhythmic complexity. Jelly Roll Morton (Example 2.31), some 20 years later, turns Joplin's piece into a sparkling, elaborate, and virtuoso performance. He does so in part by playing with the rhythm of the original melody so it conflicts through syncopation with the solid beat and meter which is nevertheless always clearly present. You might compare these two performances with Beethoven's variations on *God Save the King.* In Beethoven's work we hear one composer in one piece toying with a set of givens. In the two performances of the *Maple Leaf Rag,* we hear one performer "commenting" on the composition and performance of another.

But there is an important difference here. The transformations which Beethoven creates are composed and written out, and they are played essentially the same today as they were in Beethoven's own time. Jelly Roll Morton's transformations are, at least in part, the result of stylistic change; that is, they are the result of history. Within the

---

[4] C. Levi-Strauss, *The Raw and the Cooked* (New York: Harper & Row, 1969), p. 26.

jazz culture one person's tune (the given) becomes the very material of change. The same tune is reborn through another individual's art of improvisation. One composer's tune is another performer's point of departure. And within Morton's own performance, just as in Al Cohn's *America the Beautiful,* we also hear several variations on this performer's own version of the given tune. Comparing the Beethoven work with the performances of Joplin and Morton, we have a rich example of the possibilities of structuring and restructuring time (as well as pitch): Transformation takes place within the "history" of a single composed piece (Beethoven), through the years of history (Joplin to Morton), and within the live "history" of a single, unique, improvised performance (Morton).

Having traveled through 400 years of music history, what can we say about the changes in musical style? In order to answer this question meaningfully, we would need to consider all the dimensions of musical composition—instrumentation and texture, rhythm, pitch relations, harmony, aspects of structure and form, and the interactions among all these dimensions. It is exactly for this reason that we have left issues of stylistic analysis until the end of the book. In Part Four we focus explicitly on style and stylistic change. There we ask you to listen to and compare several groups of two or three works that are distinctly different in style, and also in the social and cultural contexts within which each was composed. At the same time, all the pieces in a given group share something essential—and historically revealing—in common: dance music (the waltz), a traditional theme (romantic love), or religion.

Part Four is many weeks of listening away, but you will be able to recognize and place a composition with respect to its historical period long before you will be able to say explicitly how the style of one composer differs from another. So as you go on to study the various dimensions of musical structure, you might ask yourself what is it in the music itself that makes Bach and Telemann, for example, sound more alike than Bach and Brahms? Like other aspects of music, we would like you first to *perceive* similarities and differences: later you will be able to account for them. In the meantime, practice your ability to listen stylistically along with learning to differentiate and coordinate within and among the various dimensions of music. As you develop these listening skills, you may like to return to the short trip through music history in the preceding pages and consider these stylistic questions again.

ADDITIONAL MATERIALS

I   While we have carefully chosen examples in each chapter to illustrate a particular aspect of music, it will often be useful to revisit earlier examples in the light of issues taken up in later portions of the book. For example, now that you have some experience with the fundamentals of rhythmic organization, you can listen again to the following examples from Chapter 1, paying attention now to their rhythmic complexity.

> Stravinsky, *Le Sacre du printemps,* "Dance of the Adolescents"
> (Example 1.1)

As in much of Stravinsky's music, rhythm and rhythmic complexity play a central role. In this excerpt you hear a marked and steady beat throughout, but accents occur quite irregularly and thus unexpectedly. Of course, accents would not be unexpected if Stravinsky did not first set up some initial expectations—that is, some initial regularity. The excerpt begins in a clear duple meter, but with the entrance of the repeated chords we hear accents (created by stress) which confound the initial duple meter. Stravinsky notates the piece in duple meter throughout, so in these terms we might describe these accents as syncopation—they occur on weak beats or off-beats in the notated duple metric grid. However, the perceived effect seems more like shifting meter or even ambiguity of meter; we lose all sense of regularly recurring accents at times. But it is this contrast between moments of regularity of meter and moments which are ametric or ambiguous in meter, but heard in relation to the strong reiteration of an underlying pulse, which helps give the piece its wild, even savage power.

> Bach, *Concerto in D Minor for Harpsichord and Orchestra*
> (Example 1.2)

This example also includes syncopation but in such a different stylistic environment that it seems almost inappropriate to use the same word for describing both the Bach and Stravinsky excerpts. Notice that in the harpsichord concerto we never lose a sense of the duple meter. However, you may be fooled at the outset concerning just where the downbeat comes. The movement begins with the figure ♫ ♩ ♩ , which seems to place the accent on the longer quarter note following the two shorter notes. In fact, the piece begins on the downbeat, which becomes quickly clear as the piece moves on. Syncopation occurs as the excerpt continues; the downbeat accent is anticipated (in a fashion similar to the excerpt from the Telemann *Trio* in Example 2.18) and then tied over the bar line, repressing the expected accent on the downbeat.

Moussorgsky, *Pictures at an Exhibition,* "Promenade"
  (Example 1.16)

In this example you hear again a clear and marked beat, but the meter seems to be elusive. Unlike the Stravinsky example, however, where our sense of meter is thrown off by unexpected accents, in the "Promenade" each beat is of equal weight with little sense of a higher-level grouping of these beats. Try counting as you listen; it seems quite possible to count in twos, in threes, or in fours. But notice that the result is not one of unrest or conflict; quite the contrary, we simply move along, step by step, with the even beat. With no strong expectations for the regular occurrence of accents, we are not bothered by their absence. The steady, ungrouped beat contributes to the "promenade" aspect of the piece. (You might compare this with the Gregorian chant, Example 2.5, which is somewhat similar in its rhythmic organization.)

Beethoven, *Symphony 9,* Op. 125, fourth movement
  (Example 1.9)

Here we have an example of syncopation used to help articulate the structure of a melody. Notice that the theme includes an opening section, a contrasting middle section, and then a return (see Chapter 3 for a further analysis of the melody). The return is signaled, or set off, by syncopation. That is, the first note of the return comes "too soon"; it occurs on the fourth beat of the measure instead of on the expected downbeat which follows. This displaced accent is the result not only of stress but also of the melodic leap which stands out in this otherwise stepwise melody.

II   We suggest now a more active participation in the musical process which should help you to listen more responsively. For example, several students might get together to form a "rhythm band," either with toy or actual percussion instruments or simply with clapping or rapping. One player can establish the beat, another the meter by "playing" only the downbeats; then one or two others can beat various patterns, introducing syncopation or even changes of meter. Three possible rhythmic combinations are given as practice problems.

Practice Problem 1

Practice Problem 2

Practice Problem 3

ANCILLARY READING AND PROJECTS

Rhythm Notation

Rhythm notation is based on a set of symbols that stand for the duration of an event as measured against a given unit time or meter. The ability to read standard rhythm notation assumes the ability to hear a set of durations (in a melody, for example) in relation to this unvarying beat. The beat functions, then, as a constant unit of time against which the varied durations of a melody can be measured.

The Basic Symbols

The symbols used in standard notation relate to one another by multiples of two, or, to put it conversely, by division into halves.

Notes   *Rests (meaning silence, which is also measured)*

𝅝 = whole note   ▬

♩ = half note   ▬

♩ = quarter note   𝄽

♪ = eighth note   𝄾

♪ = sixteenth note   𝄿

To express these relationships in notational equations we have:

𝅝 = ♩ ♩

♩ = ♩ ♩

♩ = ♪ ♪ or ♫

♪ = ♪ ♪ or ♬

The notation may be confusing at first, because the whole note, from which the other symbols derive their names and values, is rarely used as the symbol for the unit time. The most common notation for the underlying beat is probably the quarter note. Thus if you are keeping time to a piece (as in the exercise on meter), the beat that you are clapping is most often (but certainly not always) written as a quarter note, with the particular durations of a melody written as multiples or divisions of that basic quarter-note beat.

Meter

While the entire hierarchy of beats forms the overall meter of a piece, the term **meter** conventionally refers only to the higher level metric unit formed by the regular grouping of unit beats. Bar lines are used to indicate this higher level or slower metric unit which is conventionally called a *measure*. The first beat in each measure is called the *downbeat*.

The four levels of the metric hierarchy when there are four beats in a measure (duple meter) would look like this in standard notation (see also p. 53):

Three levels of the metric hierarchy when there are three beats in a measure (triple meter) would look like this (see also p. 53):

Notice that horizontal beams connecting notes together (♫ or ♬) and vertical bar lines (| | | |) "enclosing" notes serve a similar function but at different levels of the metric hierarchy: A beam connecting notes together indicates that these notes, as a group, equal a beat at the next higher level. For example, in the diagram for triple meter, above, each group of two beamed eighth notes (♫) equals the beat at the next level of the hierarchy which is, itself, represented as a quarter note (♩). In turn, each group of three quarter notes enclosed by bar lines (| ♩♩♩ |) equals a beat at the still next higher level or what is conventionally called the measure.

The *time signature* placed at the beginning of the piece indicates (1) the meter (the number of beats in a measure) and (2) the notational symbol which will represent the unit time or the beat. Thus in the time signature $\frac{4}{4}$, the upper number means that the beats are grouped in fours. This grouping is reflected in the division of the written music into measures, each including the equivalent of four beats, or four beats in total duration. The lower number means that the basic beat or unit time will be represented by a quarter note (♩). For example:

The most common time signatures are $\frac{2}{4}$, $\frac{3}{4}$, $\frac{4}{4}$ (or c), where the unit time is notated as ♩; $\frac{3}{8}$, $\frac{6}{8}$, $\frac{9}{8}$, $\frac{12}{8}$, where the unit time is notated as ♪; and $\frac{2}{2}$, $\frac{3}{2}$ where the unit is notated as ♩.

Other Conventions

A dot after a note is used to extend its duration by half again its notated value. Thus ♩. means ♩ + ♪, while ♪ means ♪ + ♪. The same values can be notated using a *tie:* ♩♪. The tie means "these notes are tied together; do not make another attack on the second one; the duration of the event is the sum of both." For example: ♩ = ♩♪ or ♪ = ♪♪.

An indication of a triplet ($\overset{3}{\text{♩♩♩}}$) is a direction to the performer to play three notes in the time usually taken by two notes of the same value.

Thus $\overset{3}{\text{♩♩♩}}$ = ♫ = ♩, that is, three notes are to be played in the time taken by one quarter note. In addition, the basic 2:1 ratio among notational symbols can be circumvented as follows:

Tempo Designation

Tempo, or the rate of the underlying beat, cannot be indicated by the symbols of music notation alone, since these symbols are entirely relative. That is, any one symbol tells you the time value of a note only in proportional relation to the value of the other symbols. In order to specify the tempo of a piece in the score, then, composers must use a fixed time reference to set the absolute value for one symbol, usually that representing the perceived unit beat. A device called a **metronome** is used for this purpose. An adjustable weight on the pendulum of the metronome makes it possible to specify tempo in terms of the exact number of beats per minute. For example, if the quarter note represents the perceived unit beat, a metronome marking of $\quarternote$ = 120 means that, in playing the piece, there should be 120 quarter notes or 120 beats per minute. In practical terms, a performer seeing a tempo marking of $\quarternote$ = 120 would set the metronome to 120 and then, letting the metronome keep time, match playing of the beat with the resulting ticks of the metronome. While performers use the metronome marking to establish a basic tempo, no performer plays or measures time in this precise way throughout a whole piece; his or her performance is always responsive to the context, which results in a certain give-and-take with respect to the precisely measured beat (see the discussion of *rubato* on p. 66).

Pieces are often preceded by more general indications of tempo, and here Italian terms predominate.

adagio	slow
largo	very slow ("broad")
andante	moderately slow ("walking")
moderato	moderate
allegretto	moderately fast
allegro	fast ("cheerful")
vivace	fast ("lively")
presto	very fast
prestissimo	as fast as possible

Learning to Notate Rhythms

In the discussion of beat and meter, and especially in the discussion of the Sousa march and the Lanner dance (pp. 54–55), we made a distinction between *beat groups* and *figural groups*. We pointed out that only beat groups are captured by standard rhythm notation; that is, rhythm notation is intended to tell the performer how to measure the time of each event. However, figural groups, which are often readily perceived by the listener, are not shown by the symbols of rhythm notation; indeed, these symbols often *look* as if they go against the grouping of events into gestures, motives, or figures.

In order to help you see the difference between these two aspects of rhythmic structure, and at the same time see how they can be coordinated with one another, we have suggested a kind of spatial notation. Our experience suggests that this spatial notation can work as an intermediary between your immediate sense experience of rhythm and the measured descriptions of rhythm found in standard notation.

Means and Possibilities

The following exercises will take you through the process of moving from clapping to spatial notation to standard rhythm notation.

Clap the rhythm of *Happy Birthday*. Now, with pencil in hand, "play" this rhythm on a piece of paper by tapping out the melody, making a dot for each event as you move along a piece of paper from left to right at a regular pace. You should leave a trace that looks something like this:

. . .   .

Notice that the *space* between dots (claps) corresponds to the *time* between claps; that is, larger spaces will correspond to longer times. Notice too that the trace falls into two identical figures separated by a longer space-of-time. You can see quite clearly, then, the figural grouping of the tune.

Next, turn the dots into lines, keeping the spatial relations the same:

| | | | | | | | | | | | |

Now clap just the underlying, regular pulse as you sing the tune. Or, if you find this difficult, get a friend to clap the rhythm of the tune while you clap the beat, and then change parts. As you play together, pay attention to how and where the beat coincides with the events of the piece—that is, try to find the beat in the piece. Now try to draw this regular beat, the underlying unit time, so that it "fits" with the tune just as your duet did:

| | | | | | | | | | | | |

| | | | | | | | | | | |

The upper row of lines shows you the rhythm of the melody. The lower row of lines (all equidistant from one another) shows you the underlying beat and where it coincides with events in the melody. You have here a sort of spelled-out version of standard notation showing both the rhythm of the tune and the constant unit time (the beat) with which you can measure the varied durations of the tune. Now you can transform the spatial notation into standard notation. Simply follow these rules:

1. If a tune event equals the unit time, leave it alone.

2. If the tune includes more than one event per unit time (beat), join these lines together just *up to* the next beat mark.
3. If there is more than one beat for a single tune event, use a symbol ("head") for that event equal to the number of beats that go by. Now put "heads" on all the lines.

If you follow these instructions, the two-layered spatial notation will be transformed into standard notation as follows:

Notice that in the process the first three taps which previously seemed to form a little figural group are now broken up visually into 2 + 1. This is a good example of the differences between metric and figural groupings. The first two notes together equal one beat, which is exactly what the "beam" joining them indicates. Thus beams are used to indicate a group of notes that together equal one unit time, or beat. The figural group, however, includes the longer quarter note; in fact, the longer duration (♩) following the two faster notes (♫) *functions* as the goal of this small figure, though neither this function nor the group itself is represented by the graphics. In much the same way the longer half note (♩) functions to delimit or mark the boundary of the two larger figures.

To put in the bar lines, follow these instructions:

1. Clap the rhythm of the tune again.
2. Sing the tune (or get someone else to sing it) while you clap a slower, but equally regular, pulse.
3. Add a third row of lines showing where this slower pulse coincides with the tune and the beat:

4. Put in a bar line *before* each occurrence of this slower beat:

Notice that the bar lines again interrupt, or break up, the figural groups. The bar lines show you where the downbeat occurs, and because the figural groups go *to* the accented downbeats (the figures begin with an upbeat) they are interrupted each time by a bar line.

Sometimes composers (or, later, editors) add marks which indicate figural groups or phrasing, as follows:

rit.

However, the problem of finding the figural groups is often left up to the performer. Indeed, many performers would agree that "interpretation" depends in large part on how the performer translates the notated durations into musical gestures, giving the piece both a sense of beat and meter and a sense of motion to goals. Such understandings are reflected in the performer's decisions concerning fingering, bowing (on stringed instruments), breathing (on wind instruments and in singing), dynamics, and the subtle give-and-take of the underlying pulse.

Following the same steps, now try notating *America.*

1. "Playing" the rhythm on the paper:

2. Spatial notation:

3. Two-level notation—piece and beat:

4. Three-level notation—piece, beat, and meter:

| | | | | | | | | | | | | | | | | | | | |

| | | | | | | | | | | | | | | | | | | | |

| | | | | | |

Before making the transformation to standard notation, notice that the events on the syllables "tis" and "lib" each include one beat plus half of the next beat, or 1½ beats in all. Looking back at page 78 you will see that this can be notated either with a tie (♩♪) or by adding a dot to the quarter note (♩.).

5. Now you are ready to put heads on the notes and put in the bar lines:

Now that you have learned how to notate rhythms that you can *clap*, go back and see if you can *read* the notation in the "rhythm band" examples on page 75.

CHAPTER 3

Hokusai, *Fisherman with Cormorants* (Woodcut, 1823–1829)

Pitch and Movement: Melody

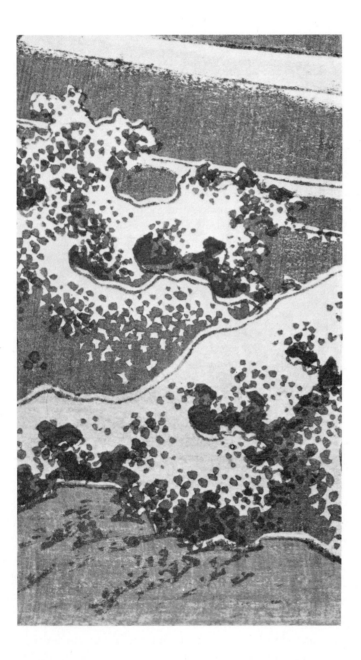

WHEN COMPOSERS COMBINE pitch and movement (time) they create, among other things, a *melody;* and it is to melody that we turn our attention in this chapter. This is hardly your first introduction to pitch and melody. In Chapter 1, for example, we spoke of high and low "sounds"; these can be described more precisely as being made up of high or low "pitches." Again, in the discussion of texture we spoke, for instance, of "many actively moving lines" (see page 21). "Line" is, of course, a metaphor for a succession of tones—that is, a melody. We could say more literally (and more awkwardly) that you heard several different instruments each playing a different succession of pitches and a different rhythm. In considering rhythm in Chapter 2, you were also necessarily concerned with pitch. In fact, it is usually a succession of tones which articulates or defines time and generates your experience of a particular rhythmic structure.

We would like you to focus now on the specific relations of pitch and time as they interact to form melody. Along with rhythm, melody seems to be the most immediately tangible aspect of music—that which is often remembered, later to be hummed or whistled. But as you have seen, melody is seldom the sole component in a piece of music. Indeed, there are many compositions in which you hardly find a melody at all; you are drawn instead to action in other dimensions of the music, such as texture and rhythm. One could even dispute what is or is not "a melody." For example, some of the excerpts in Chapter 1—Varèse's *Density 21.5* and the African *Singing Game*—may not correspond to your idea of a melody. But this idea of melody—a kind of intuitive model of what a tune is—varies among cultures and even within cultures such as ours with its diversity of musical styles.

DEMONSTRATION 3.1
Melodic Coherence
(Sides 4–5)

Listen now to Examples 3.1 through 3.6. All these melodies belong to our own Western culture, yet probably only two or three match what we think of as the prototypical tune. What contributes to the differences, and how can we account for them? Notice that the examples span more than 200 years in their dates of composition, that one is a folk song and anonymous (Example 3.4), and that another (Example 3.6), while composed, comes out of the popular culture rather than the concert-hall culture. Notice, too, that some are vocal melodies and some instrumental, and that even the instrumental melodies differ in their instrumental medium—solo piano, violin and orchestra, full orchestra. Finally, the vocal melodies are associated with a text and are about something specific, as indeed is the excerpt from the Liszt *Faust Symphony,* which

Example	Composer, title	Date
3.1	Vivaldi, *Concerto Grosso,* Op. 3, no. 6, second movement	c. 1712
3.2	Liszt, *Faust Symphony,* first movement	1854–1857
3.3	Berg, *Wozzeck,* "Lullaby"	1917–1922
3.4	*Did You Ever See a Lassie?*	
3.5	Mozart, *Sonata for Piano in A,* K. 331, first movement	1781–1783
3.6	Gershwin, *I Got Rhythm* (sung by Ethel Waters)	1930

is intended to convey a mood inspired by Faust's encounter with the devil. Thus the date of composition and the musical style current to the time, along with the particular subculture from which the piece comes and to which it is addressed influence the kinds of melodies we can expect. Then, too, the medium suggests particular melodic possibilities as well as constraints, as do the composer's expressive intentions.

Let us look more closely at the specific musical differences among the melodies and consider how each in its own way develops a particular sense of what a melody is or can be. Then we can go on to compare these characteristics with the simple tune *Lassie.*

We can ask, for example, what makes for coherence in the Vivaldi and Liszt excerpts (Examples 3.1 and 3.2). The Vivaldi excerpt is from a concerto for solo violin accompanied by the orchestra. The violin occupies the foreground role, and our listening attention is clearly focused on it. The melody has an almost serpentine quality. While it includes brief pauses which allow the listener to "frame" its movement through time, these pauses are not *predictable* in their moments of occurrence. We hear first two segments, and then time seems to be stretched. We go on and on with the unwinding melody as it slowly descends, finally coming to a close just where it began. How different from our typical folk song, in which each musical phrase or gesture is

The melody has an almost serpentine quality.

predictable in its time span! But if you listen again to the Vivaldi melody, you may hear that the descent is marked by repetitions of a brief musical figure, each repetition starting lower than the preceding one, and with the final one breaking the pattern. This process of repeating a figure starting on successively higher or lower pitches is called a **sequence,** and it accounts for one of the primary means of coherence in such continuously unwinding melodies.

Now, listening to the Liszt melody, you will notice again this sense of going on and on: here too in descending steps, but marked by

The melody seems to creep down, while within each small gesture it goes up.

the repetition of a three-note figure, or **motive.** (See p. 94 for more on motives.) The melody seems to creep down, while within each small gesture it goes up. Notice, too, that while the "pitch-shape" remains the same within each gesture, the rhythm varies, helping to create a further sense of slippery elusiveness—variety within unity. As for *meter,* it is hard to find a regularly recurring accent. The *rhythmic structure* of the melody surely differs from the regular metric structure associated with our intuitive model of a sensible tune. The organization of time seems more dependent on the recurring sequential motive. Finally, notice how the melody, having descended in slow steps, then suddenly expands its range, or its scope in pitch-space. The melody, still based on the same three-note motive, covers two octaves in the same time that it covered but half an octave previously, giving the illusion of getting faster as it covers more space in less time. This extension of range, together with the stretching and compressing of time, distinguishes the Liszt melody from both the Vivaldi example and the folk tune. Of course, the particular *choice of pitches* is very important, and we will have more to say about that in Chapter 5, on harmony.

The "Lullaby" from Berg's opera *Wozzeck* (Example 3.3), although written almost 70 years after the *Faust Symphony,* has important similarities to it. What musical means have the composers used to convey the dramatic situation?

Did you e-ver see a las-sie go this way and that?

or

Did you e-ver see a las-sie go this way and that?

(Even without playing or singing the above examples, you can get the effect by, for example, singing the same pitch on "that" as you sing on "this" in the first case, or singing the same pitch on "that" as you sing on "and" in the second.)

Notice that it is not a matter of the substituted pitch being higher or lower than the original ending pitch. Rather it is that the phrase must stop specifically on a particular pitch if the phrase is to sound conclusively ended. This pitch is called the **tonic.** The definition of *tonic* is a functional one and highly dependent on the context. That is, *tonic* can be defined as that pitch which, in a given context of pitches, sounds most stable. Thus, as a result of the particular selection of pitches included in the tune so far, together with the particular order in which they occur, this one pitch gains special significance as an "ender." Think of it for now as that pitch toward which all the other pitches in the piece gravitate. But remember that this central pitch (F in this situation) can be played in any octave, and it still maintains its *functional* significance as being most stable. Or, putting it another way, any particular F is a member of the **pitch-class** F, whose members are all the other pitches named F. If we ended this second phrase in *Lassie* on an F an octave higher or lower, it would certainly make a difference to the tune—it would not sound right. And yet on the more general level of functional stability, any F, in this context of pitches, would maintain its identity as tonic. (We will return to this subject later in the chapter.)

Many aspects of a tone contribute to its particular effect: Its position in the *metric grid,* its *pitch class,* and the function which that pitch class has gained contextually, as well as the particular *instance* of that pitch class—a higher or lower F, for instance. While all of these aspects of an event are merged or fused together in our actual experience of an event, the capacity to differentiate them perceptually can often heighten our appreciation of the subtle ways in which composers play with their various combinations.

Looking at even smaller dimensions of this simple tune, consider the following: We can further segment the first phrase into (1) "Did you ever see a lassie":

and (2) "a lassie, a lassie":

Each of these subphrases uses different melodic-rhythmic material, or different *motives*. A motive is a small melodic-rhythmic pattern—a few notes which have some distinctive shape that is somehow bounded or self-contained to form a recognizable figure. All melodies are made up of motives. After the single tone, a motive is the smallest link in the melodic chain, and perhaps the smallest *structural* unit which the listener focuses on as a significant element in the tune.

Even in such a simple tune as *Lassie,* the relationship among motives exemplifies the basic aesthetic principle of *unity and variety,* to which we have already referred. For example, through the repetition of motives, unity is achieved. Variety comes about through the use of *contrasting* motives, as well as through the modification, manipulation, or new juxtapositions of previously stated motives. The sequential repetitions heard in the Vivaldi concerto, the Liszt excerpt, and even the Berg "Lullaby" are examples of this kind of variety within unity.

In *Lassie* we have at first an example of contrasting motives. The initial motive ("Did you ever see a lassie") has a pitch shape or contour that could be described as ⌒. And notice that it makes use of different note values (♪, ♩., ♩). The second motive ("Go this way and that way") contrasts with this initial one in its pitch-shape (⌒⌒) as well as in its rhythmic pattern—it makes use of only quarter notes. Moving up one level in the structural hierarchy from the smaller motive to the larger phrase, we see that the second phrase (a')—the *consequent* phrase—is exactly the same as the first phrase—the *antecedent* phrase—except for the last two notes—again an instance of variety within unity.

Going further into the tune, you may be surprised to realize that the third phrase in the melody—"Go this way and that way, and this way and that way"—is simply the second motive of *a* stated twice.

b. Go this way and that way, and this way and that way,

That is, the pitches and durations for "go this way and that way" are identical to those for "a lassie, a lassie." Why do they sound so different? Here is an example of the influence of context or situation. Consider the differences in the situations in which we encounter this motive. At first we hear the motive ("A lassie, a lassie") functioning as the *ending* of a phrase. This later statement ("Go this way and that way") functions as the *beginning* of a phrase and also the beginning of a new part of the piece—that is, it comes after a big point of arrival and after a "gap" in the regular flow of events (the rest). Further, this motive is followed by itself—the same motive serves to begin and end this third phrase. The principle of unity and variety is again realized. We hear the same motive (unity) but with new effect as a result of its being embedded in a new context and with a different function (variety). One even might question what we mean by "the same." You can

The same motive may sound quite different when embedded in a new context

One guitar looks bigger than the other, the rear edge of the carpet looks shorter than its front-to-back dimension, the front edge of the carpet looks shorter than the bottom edge of the back wall.

compare this effect of the situational embedding of a motive with the examples of *textural* embedding discussed in Chapter 1.

This third phrase, then, is different from the first two but related to them in important ways. We call it *b* to point to its contrasting function within the structure of the tune as a whole. Finally, there is a *return* to phrase *a',* the consequent:

a'. Did you e-ver see a las-sie go this way and that?

We thus have *a, a', b, a',* and each of these letters stands for a phrase which is exactly four measures long. (See the brief discussion of phrase rhythm in the Lecture-Demonstration in Chapter 2 in connection with *Stars and Stripes Forever* and the Lanner waltz.)

a   *a'*

1   2   1   3

Did you e-ver see a las-sie, a las-sie, a las-sie, Did you e-ver see a las-sie go this way and that?

b   *a'*

2   2   1   3

Go this way and that way, and this way and that way, Did you e-ver see a las-sie go this way and that?

This equality in phrase length we call *balanced* phrase structure by analogy, perhaps unfortunately, with weight—two phrases equal in duration are compared with two objects equal in weight. The whole tune is, in fact, balanced: The first period (*a* + *a'*) is equal in length to the second period (*b* + *a'*), and the melody can be diagramed as follows:

Motive:	1	2	1	3	2	2	1	3
Phrase:	antecedent		consequent		contrast		return	
Period:	*a*	+	*a'*		*b*	+	*a'*	

A Mozart Melody

Let us now consider a carefully composed melody which is in many ways similar to *Lassie* in its general structure and yet seems much more complex and sophisticated—Example 3.5, from the Mozart *Sonata for Piano in A*. The excerpt is the theme for a series of variations. In writing a series of variations, the composer usually keeps important aspects of the *whole theme* intact during the course of each variation. For example, the whole melody may be repeated, only being varied by the sounds or textures in which it is embedded (as in the excerpt from the Beethoven symphony in Example 1.9). Thus each variation becomes a separate little whole and the entire movement a set of small pieces, each maintaining the proportions and general structure of the original theme. But as you heard in *Lassie* and in some of the other melodies, variation can also be used on a level of greater detail to transform or develop through different means the initial motive—in a sense, the melody grows out of the motive. Indeed, it is the subtlety of motivic development that perhaps more than anything else distinguishes the Mozart melody from the much simpler *Lassie*.

The overall structure of the melody, like *Lassie,* can be diagramed as follows:

antecedent		consequent	contrast		return	extension
a	+	*a'*	*b*	+	*a'*	*(a + b)*

As in *Lassie, a* and *a'* are balanced phrases and they complement one another. Together they constitute a musical sentence (or period) which presents the basic motivic material. The term **antecedent-consequent phrase relationship** refers to this sense of complementarity—two phrases which begin much the same but in which the first ends less conclusively than the second. The relationship is somewhat analogous to a rhymed couplet in poetry:

> In poets as true genius is but rare,
> True taste as seldom is the critic's share.
> A. POPE

That is, there is a comma, or half cadence, at the end of the first line (phrase), and a period, or full cadence at the end of the second line (phrase). Together they make up a sentence, or what is called in music a period. The first two phrases of *Lassie* were described in much the same way.

Example 3.5 MOZART, *Sonata for Piano in A, K. 331*

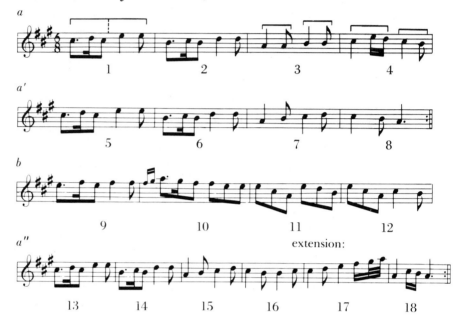

The *b* section is a contrasting segment in which the initial motivic material is elaborated or developed in a more far-reaching way. It leads back to a restatement of the consequent phrase, *a',* followed by an extension.

Let us consider more closely now the means Mozart uses to develop his initial motivic material—to explore and reveal the implications of the opening motive. Listen to just the first phrase, *a.* The germinal motive, from which the whole melody quite literally grows, is presented in the first five notes of this phrase: ♫♩♪. Clap the rhythm of this motive to become more immediately familiar with it.

Notice that Mozart continues the phrase by simply repeating this motive sequentially, somewhat as in the beginning of the *b* section of the Berg "Lullaby." Indeed, the rhythmic pattern of the two motives is quite similar. But next Mozart fragments this motive; he picks up just the last two repeated notes: ♩♪. Interestingly, the repetitions of this fragment, one after the other moving up the scale, cause the tiny motive to regroup, even though the pitch relations and the durations remain essentially the same. You hear the grouping indicated by the lower brackets:

Moreover, the third statement of this fragment is embellished so that the last two statements seem to merge. These repetitions of the fragmented motive bring the phrase to an inconclusive close; the phrase ends on a weak beat and on a pitch which is not the tonic.

The consequent phrase, *a'*, is itself a variant of the antecedent phrase. It begins just as *a* did, but then ascends more quickly (with a variant of the fragmented motive); it then descends to end conclusively on a *strong beat*, with a note of *long duration* and on the *tonic.* Once again the sense of arrival at a conclusive goal results from several converging factors.

As we go on to the *b* section of the melody, variation of the motivic material becomes faster and more elaborate. We call this section *b* not because it introduces different material, but because the original material is more extensively transformed, creating more contrast and also a sense of instability or tension. For example, while the *a* section stays entirely within the pitch area defined by the first five pitches of the A-major scale,[4] the *b* section immediately moves off into the upper part of that scale, where we again hear the opening motive.

The melody ascends to its highest point, with rhythmic or melodic variants of the germinal motive. The rhythmic movement then becomes more continuous ($\flat\flat\flat$ $\flat\flat\flat$ $\flat\flat\flat$) but a single pitch (e), the middle pitch of the range, stands out in the midst of this continuous motion (measure 11):

---

[4] For a discussion of scales, see pages 131–132.

The germinal motive, almost lost in this wealth of variation, still remains present, however, as the primary unifying factor.

The return (*a″*) seems to be a literal repetition of the consequent phrase up to the moment of expected ending (m. 16) where Mozart leads us on once more, spilling over the moment of anticipated resolution. There follows the brief extension, where the melody again rises to its highest point (covering nearly the whole range of the melody thus far) and, finally, dropping a whole octave, comes to rest on the tonic.

Looking back on this process of melodic invention, it seems now that the melody can hardly be described as "the same" in overall structure as *Lassie*. Once again we need to emphasize that any general description (such as *a* + *a′*, *b* + *a′*) must take into account the particularities with which that general structure is realized. And yet it is just such common procedures which underlie our intuitive sense of the prototypical melody. Some of the characteristics which we found common to both *Lassie* and the Mozart melody account for our intuitive model of what a tune is: Clearly metric, balanced and unambiguous phrase structure, the sense of a tonic or central pitch to which we can relate the others, and often an overall structure described as statement-digression-return. But it is important to remember that the familiar may sometimes make it too easy to miss what is unique and special in a melody, just as the unfamiliar may lead us to dismiss a melody simply because its means of organization are different from those which we have come to take for granted—our tacit model of a sensible melody.

The song *I Got Rhythm* (Example 3.6), composed by George Gershwin in 1930 for the Broadway musical *Girl Crazy,* was a great success and remains with us in various manifestations. The title is immediately reflected in the syncopated motive which recurs throughout the song: | ♪ ♩ ♩ | ♩ ♩ ♪ | . Characteristically in popular music, the singer freely interprets the rhythm, singing it somewhat differently each time. Gershwin states this rhythm three times, extending it the third time to end the phrase. The repertory of pitches derives from what we call a **pentatonic** scale (one with only five tones related to each other as the black keys on the piano); the melody moves up and down the scale, coming to rest on the tonic in the eighth bar.

As to overall structure, what do we find but *a a b a′*, the same as *Lassie* and the Mozart melody. It further resembles the Mozart in that there is a little "tag" at the end of the song, adding two more measures to the standard 32-bar popular song structure and featuring the tune's melodic climax. In what ways does the *b* section differ from *a*? The *b* section, known as the "bridge" (or, less frequently, "channel"), while retaining the rhythmic figure ⎸ ♩ ♩. ♩ ⎸ ♩. ♩. ♩ ⎸ , moves away from "home" by beginning higher in the scale, as well as through the use of different chords (see Chapter 5) underneath the melody.

Motivic Development

In talking about all these melodies, we have found it useful (even necessary) to point to specific *motives*—particular melodic shapes. By pointing to motives, we were able to describe to you, the listener, the

Leonardo da Vinci, Studies for *The Battle of Anghiari* (1503–1504)

Motivic transformation: subtle transformations of a basic shape through which a whole composition may evolve.

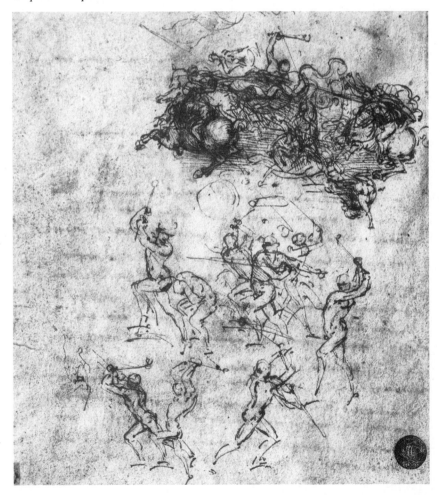

means by which each melody evolved and gained its unique coherence. You could hear the motive as a vehicle which carried the melody, in a particular way, through time and through its pitch-space.

The motive often functions as a kind of *germinal idea* from which a whole melody can evolve. We have seen how composers, through subtle manipulations of its various features, can use a basic shape to build unity and at the same time create new melodic ideas and new structural functions. For example, the composers may subtly transform pitch-time relations, fragment the melody, or regroup its initial motivic "chunks" to create a new musical effect. Arnold Schoenberg says of this fundamental compositional process:

> Even the writing of simple phrases involves the invention and use of motives, though perhaps unconsciously. . . . The motive generally appears in a characteristic and impressive manner at the beginning of a piece. . . . Inasmuch as almost every figure within a piece reveals some relationship to it, the basic motive is often considered the "germ" of the idea. . . . However, everything depends upon its use . . . everything depends on its treatment and development.[5]

We have seen examples of this process, but to make Schoenberg's point clear, consider for a moment a very simple phrase—the first one in *Mary Had a Little Lamb*. Notice that the last two "chunks" of the phrase (T_1 and T_2) are fragments of the longer first chunk. In this sense they are both variants of the longer first chunk—a development of it. (Similarly, Mozart, in the previous example, split his germinal motive into two parts, working with both fragments to extend the melody in time.)

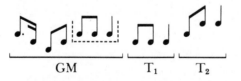

GM T_1 T_2

But notice that the degree of variation, or the degree of transformation, increases even within this short phrase: T_1 is a transformation of GM (the germinal motive) not only because T_1 is a fragment but also because it makes use of a *new set of pitches*. However, T_1 and

---

[5] Arnold Schoenberg, *Fundamentals of Musical Composition* (New York: St. Martin's Press, 1970), p. 9.

the "tail" of GM are the same in their *set of durations* and in their *pitch-shape*—in each a single pitch is repeated. But with T_2 only the set of durations remains the same; both the set of pitches and the pitch-shape are varied. Indeed, the sense of tiny climax at the end of the phrase results in part from this increase in the degree of transformation. Also, T_2 moves out of the previous, very limited *range* of the tune, reaching the high point of this miniscule world. And this too can be thought of as a structural transformation.

A few further examples of motivic transformation and development will be cited now—you will become more and more aware of this fundamental musical process as you listen. Schubert's hauntingly beautiful song *Frühlingstraum* ("Spring Dream") begins with a piano introduction which foreshadows the vocal melody (Example 3.7).

Example	Composer, title	Date
3.7	Schubert, *Frühlingstraum* ("Spring Dream")	1827

Note the resemblance to the Mozart motive rhythm:

♪ | ♩.♪♪♩ ♩ ♪ | ♩ ♪

Here, however, the germinal motive (*a*) spans two measures. In the second statement (*b*), Schubert moves into a higher pitch range, modifies

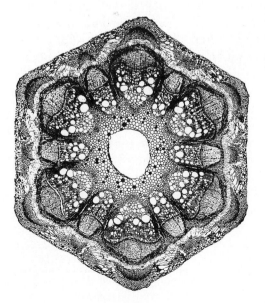

Cross section of a twig

Through subtle manipulations of a basic shape composers build unity and also new structural functions

Example 3.7 SCHUBERT, *Frühlingstraum,* ("Spring Dream")

Ich traum - te von bun - ten Blu - men, so wie sie wohl blü - hen im Mai, Ich
I dreamed of col - or - ful flow - ers, such as bloom in May, I

traum - te von grü - nen Wie - sen, von lu - sti - gem vö - gel - ge - schrei,____ von____
dreamed of green fields, of the hap - py cries of birds, of the

lu - sti - gem Vö - gel - ge - schrei.
hap - py cries of birds.

the trochaic ending "Blumen" (♩♪) to a slightly more conclusive "Mai"
(♩), and further intensifies the movement by repeating the ♩♫ rhythm
in the second half of the measure. In the third statement (*c*), Schubert
changes the pitch contour as well as the rhythms, while in (*d*) he
deflects the expected point of arrival in measure 8 by extending the
phrase with a more florid "Vögelgeschrei" ("bird cries"). Without
going into much more detail, note the prominence in the next section
(B), of the motive ♩♪ (from the second half of measure 1) as well as
references to ♩♫. Of course, Schubert uses a variety of means to reflect
the dramatic changes of mood, scene, and season of the text. (In Chapter
9 we will focus in great detail on Schubert's mastery of these means.)
The overall structure of the song, A B C, might be thought of as a
kind of thesis (A)—antithesis (B)—synthesis (C); in C Schubert
smooths over the rhythms of the germinal motive.

The motives of opening themes have crucial implications for the
entire piece, as can be seen in the next two examples.

Example	Composer, title	Date
3.8	Haydn, *Symphony 104,* first movement	1795
3.9	Beethoven, *Symphony 5*	1808

The opening theme of the first-movement "Allegro" of Haydn's *Symphony 104* (Example 3.8) is rich in motivic possibilities, all of which Haydn explores in the course of the movement. Here is the theme with some of the leading motives bracketed:

Note how these motives recur in various guises throughout the movement. For example, immediately after the opening statement of the antecedent-consequent melody, the entire orchestra enters *forte* with motive *a,* played twice. Later on, Haydn works with motive *c,* the character of which he gradually transforms from a *staccato* melody to a *legato* songlike theme incorporating motive *a*

Finally, Beethoven, in his *Symphony 5* (Example 3.9), works almost obsessively with his opening motive[6]

some of the transformations of which are presented on the record.

In later chapters the concepts of **development,** the extension of a piece in time, and the overall structure will all become the focus of your listening attention. Motivic transformation, that is, the development of germinal motives, is of utmost significance in those procedures: "The child is father of the man."

<table>
<tr><td>

DEMONSTRATION 3.2
Pitch, Scale, Tonic, Range
(Side 5)
</td><td>

Throughout our discussion of melody, especially in trying to account for the contrasts among cadences—conclusive and inconclusive, full and half—as well as when pointing to the listener's expectation of a certain melodic outcome, we have spoken of the "tonic" or "central pitch," and of
</td></tr>
</table>

---

[6] Because this motive represents the letter *V* in Morse code—three shorts and a long—Beethoven's symphony came to symbolize *V* for Victory during World War II. Of course its heroic uplifting character goes beyond just the letter symbolism of the opening motive.

What you can do with a line

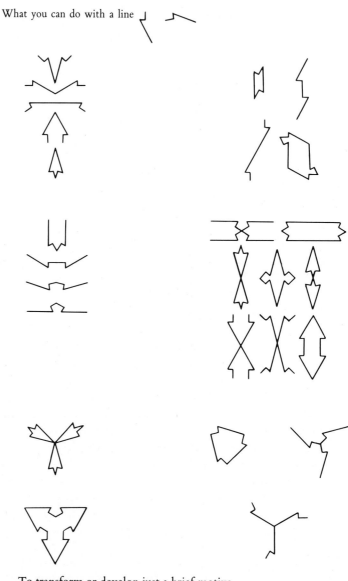

... To transform or develop just a brief motive
The small "motives" at the top form the entire material for all of these designs.

scales or parts of scales, and so forth. In this section we will focus specifically on these issues, setting forth in a more systematic way some of the fundamental organizing principles of pitch relations.

Probably the most obvious aspect of pitch—the one we notice

and make use of even in everyday life—is simply that of *high* and *low.* We even describe the sounds of the city or of nature as "high" or "low." Actually, these everyday sounds are often made up of a pitch *continuum,* like a siren or a motor revving up. By contrast, most of the music you know is made up of discrete, or separate, pitches—a particular selection from the possible pitch continuum. The result of this process of selection is a series, or ladder (Italian *scala*), of discrete pitches. Moving upward from any one pitch, and playing all the tones in order, we find that after 12 different pitches (the **chromatic scale**) have been played, the pitches are repeated in a higher register. We call this repetition of the pitches in different registers the phenomenon of the *octave.* In the discussion of unison playing in Chapter 1, we pointed out that instruments or voices can play or sing in unison but in different octaves, as in Example 1.2, in which a group of instruments play the same melody together, the violins playing an octave higher than the violas, which play an octave higher than the cellos and basses.

Putting it another way, this particular selection of 12 pitches from the pitch continuum divides the octave into 12 equidistant tones. These tones constitute all the different pitches generally found in Western music; they are separated from one another by the interval of a *half step,* or *semitone.* An **interval** is the distance between any two tones; the half step is the smallest interval. (See the Ancillary Reading, page 132, for further discussion of intervals.) The next largest interval is the whole step. The octave can also be divided into six equidistant pitches separated by whole steps. (This is the *whole-tone scale*—note the striking difference in effect between this scale and the chromatic scale.)

In addition to equidistant pitches, the octave can also be divided into seven different pitches separated by various whole and half steps. The particular ordering of whole and half steps creates a number of different **modes.** Two of these, the **major** and **minor** modes, are the principal modes used by composers in Western music from the seventeenth to the twentieth century. Indeed, some composers still think in terms of them.[7]

It should be emphasized that a scale or mode is not in itself a melody, but rather an abstraction derived from the pitch material of actual melodies. Thus, instead of presenting the major scale as an

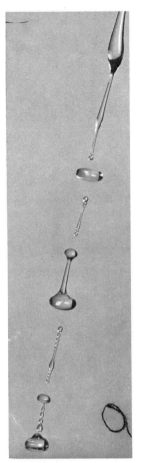

Water drops: discrete pitches

A pitch continuum

---

[7] Before the seventeenth century other modes were described by theorists and given names derived from ancient Greek music—for example, Dorian, Phrygian, and Lydian (see p. 131).

entity, we will demonstrate how it can be derived from the melody *America:*[8]

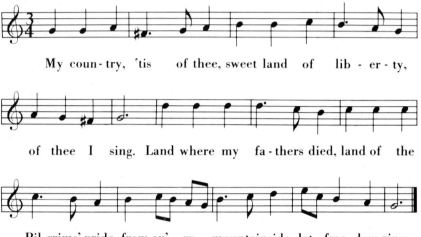

My coun-try, 'tis   of thee, sweet land   of   lib - er - ty,

of thee I   sing. Land where my   fa - thers died, land of   the

Pil-grims' pride, from ev' - ry   mountainside let free - dom ring.

Now if we reorder the pitches which occur in this melody, moving from the lowest to the highest, the result is as shown here:

This, then, is the complete pitch material of the melody. Now sing the tune and determine which pitch sounds the most stable, the most at rest. Then sing or play the pitches as arranged from lowest to highest again, determining the most stable.

In both cases you probably found that the note G, the tone with which the melody both begins and ends, sounds most final.[9] Indeed, the sense of completeness, of finality, at the end of *America* is generated to a large extent by the function which the note G has acquired through its contact with the specific collection of pitches and their particular arrangement in this melody. Remember that the stability or instability—that is, the function—of a particular pitch derives from its relation

---

[8] The rhythm of this melody was illustrated in the Additional Materials at the end of Chapter 2; for information on pitch notation, see page 129 of the Ancillary Reading.

[9] Of course, not all melodies begin or even end with this stable tone; for example, try *Happy Birthday.*

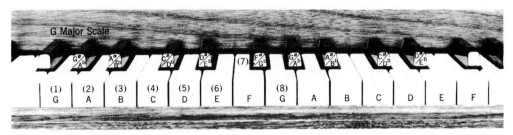

Piano keyboard
(Courtesy of Steinway & Sons)

to the other pitches which surround it. Within a different collection of pitches this same G might sound very unstable. The function, or "meaning," of a pitch, then, is always *relative* in that it depends on the context of pitches in which it is found (see Demonstration 5.2).

In a given context of pitches, the one that sounds most stable assumes a special position as the central tone in relation to which we hear all the others; the others seem to gravitate toward it.[10] This central tone is called the *tonic*. The generating of a tonic, or tonal center, has been a crucial factor in the organization and comprehensibility of music since about 1650, if not longer. (See Chapter 13.)

Let us now reorder the pitch material of *America,* beginning with the tonic G:

(Notice that we have used the rule of "octave equivalence" to fill out the scale—that is, the low F-sharp has been moved up an octave and the low G has been repeated an octave higher.) We have now derived a particular scale—the G-major scale. Using it as a structural model, we can discover exactly what combination of whole and half steps generates the major mode and can then build a major scale starting on any pitch. The simplest way to see the whole-step–half-step arrangement is by looking at the piano keyboard (although the best way would be to *hear* the difference between whole and half steps). Looking at the diagram of the piano keyboard, you can observe the following:

---

[10] Music theorists have discussed at length the question of whether this phenomenon is inherent in the natural properties of sound or whether it is the result of musical conditioning.

Between any two adjacent keys (even white keys) the distance is a half step. Thus, G to A is a whole step, because there is a pitch (black key) between; but B to C is a half step, because there is no pitch (no black key) between. So the G-major scale has the following arrangement of whole and half steps:

DEGREE:	1	2	3	4	5	6	7	8
PITCH:	G	A	B	C	D	E	F#	G
INTERVAL:		1	1	½	1	1	1	½

An important characteristic of this model is its division into two symmetrical parts—degrees 1–4 and degrees 5–8—the two parts being separated by a whole step. (The term **degree** refers to the numbers assigned to elements of the scale. Starting on the tonic as 1, elements are numbered from low to high, consecutively. But notice that while numbers proceed consecutively suggesting an equal relationship between elements, the consecutive pitches are not related by equal intervals.)

Using this model we then can build a major scale starting on, for example, F:

Looking back at *Lassie,* you can perform the same exercise. That is, order the pitches in the tune, as written, from low to high:

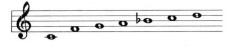

Rearranging these pitches, starting from the one that sounds most stable (F) and using the rule of octave equivalence, we have all the pitches of the F-major scale except for E. It is important to note that

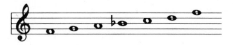

if we had chosen to write out *Lassie* starting one whole step higher (G), keeping all the pitch *relations* (that is, all the intervals) the same, we would have all the pitches of the G-major scale except for F-sharp, and G would become the tonic pitch. Thus, any traditional melody can be played or sung starting on any pitch, but depending on which pitch you choose, a different set of pitches and a different tonic will be generated. This process of moving a tune from one set of pitches to another or from one **key** (tonal center) to another is called **transposition.** For example, here we transposed *Lassie* from the initial key of F to the key of G:[11]

Try building scales starting on other pitches, using the model and the piano keyboard.

A model for the minor scale (below) is useful only for the first five degrees, since the upper part may take several different forms (see the Ancillary Reading, p. 132.)

Notice that the distinguishing difference in the minor mode is the half step between the second and third degrees (instead of the whole step at the same point in the major mode). In the case of G minor, then, we have B-flat at this point rather than B-natural. (Try playing *America* on p. 108 substituting B-flat for B-natural wherever it occurs.)

If you now once again play or sing *America* as it is written, you will hear that the melody is organized in two parts, the first ending with "of thee I sing." This first part is organized around the tonic— it begins there; moves below, above, and through it; and finally returns to it. The second part of the melody moves to the fifth degree of the scale and minimizes the first degree until it returns to it at the end.

---

[11] For more on transposition, see page 183.

Note that the setting of "land of the Pilgrims' pride," in relation to that of "Land where my fathers died," is an example of sequence (see p. 88). This organization of the melody, as in the Mozart theme, reflects somewhat the organization of the scale into two halves and points up the significance of the fifth degree (the starting point of the second half) as the second "pillar" of the tonal structure. The fifth degree is called (misleadingly) the **dominant.** We shall explore its significance further in Chapter 5.

To summarize, then, we have moved from the most general aspect of pitch (high and low) to a selection from this continuum (the 12 pitches forming the pitch material of most Western music) to a still more specific selection (the seven different pitches of the major and minor modes, which can be built from specific sets of whole and half steps). The most significant aspect of this selection is its creation of a hierarchy of stability-instability among the resulting pitches.

Having considered to some extent the pitch relationships in *America,* let us consider now how the melody moves through time. From what rhythmic patterns is the melody made, and how do these patterns contribute to its unity and variety? Tap the rhythm of the melody. As mentioned in Chapter 2, there is a rhythmic pattern (*motive*) repeated, with slight variations, a number of times: ♩ ♩ ♩ | ♩ ♪ ♩ |. This underlying figure helps to unify the melody. In the third statement of the motive ("of thee I sing"), the last two notes are dropped and the fourth note is extended: ♩ ♩ ♩ | ♩. |. The rhythmic activity of the phrase, not its length, is lessened as it comes to rest on the longer note. This dotted half note is also the tonic and marks off a section of the song both rhythmically and tonally. The second and concluding section contains four statements of the rhythmic pattern. The first two statements present the pattern in its original form. These are followed by two statements which give variety to the song by manipulating the basic pattern and which, at the same time, reach a climax both in pitch and in rhythmic activity. The first: ♩ ♫ ♫ | ♩ ♪ ♩ | is followed by: ♫ ♩ ♩ | ♩. |.

Range

In discussing the Liszt and Berg melodies (Examples 3.2 and 3.3) we noted that both had a large *range.* That is, the pitch distance from the lowest to the highest point of the melodies was relatively large. This was one of the aspects of the two melodies that seemed to distinguish them from more traditional tunes. In that discussion we also observed

Horn section of an orchestra

that the large range of the Berg "Lullaby" helped to enrich its expressive quality.

Generally, vocal melodies have a smaller range than instrumental melodies; the human voice has a smaller range than most instruments, and furthermore, folk songs or popular songs are written to be sung by numbers of people with untrained voices. The range of a melody and the way the melody moves within this range are important factors in creating its particular effect.

America, for example, is very easy to sing, and this is because it moves in small steps and avoids leaps or large intervals. (We say it is a **conjunct** melody.) The most noticeable leap occurs at a crucial point, that is, between the two halves of the melody (from "sing" to "land").

Example	Composer, title	Date
3.10	Tamil folk song (Indian)	
3.11	R. Strauss, *Ein Heldenleben* ("A Hero's Life")	1898
3.12	Stravinsky, *Octet for Wind Instruments,* second movement	1922–1923

Examples 3.10 through 3.12 illustrate the importance of the range of a melody and the way it moves through that range in creating its particular effect. For example, the Indian melody (Example 3.10), a Tamil folk song, has a very small range; that is, it moves within a very limited pitch-space[12] from its highest to its lowest points. The consecutive tones are very close to one another in this conjunct melody, and there are no leaps. Not being part of the Western tradition, it uses "odd-sounding" tones, that is, pitches other than the 12 of the chromatic scale. (If you try to play this example on the piano you will observe that the tones don't exactly match—you would have to play "between the cracks," that is, between the keys.) Try to sing it in the Indian fashion!

In striking contrast to the Tamil folk song, the aggressive Strauss melody (Example 3.11), difficult if not impossible to sing, moves predominantly by leaps (**disjunct**) through a very wide range. Yet another instrumental melody, from the Stravinsky *Octet* (Example 3.12), maintains a very small range, as in the Tamil folk song. But at the end the top boundary seems to give way as the range expands upward. Interestingly, the Stravinsky melody up to this point of expansion has exactly the same range as the Tamil song, but it somehow sounds less restricted. Perhaps the range sounds greater in part because the melody is played on the clarinet and "doubled" two octaves higher by the flute—another way of talking about playing in unison. Rhythmic factors (tempo, for instance) and the particular order in which the pitches occur also contribute to this difference in effect. If you listen very closely to the two examples, you will notice that each pitch in the Tamil song is as close as possible to the one preceding and following it, while in the Stravinsky piece there are tiny skips which, within this very small pitch world, create a significant difference in effect.

---

[12] Of course, talking about pitch-space is again a metaphor, since pitch doesn't occupy space at all. For a description of the physical properties of pitch (frequency), see the section on acoustics in the Ancillary Reading of Chapter 1.

Example	Composer, title	Date
3.13	Mozart, *The Magic Flute,* aria	1791
3.14	Schoenberg, *Herzegewächse* ("Foliage of the Heart")	1911

The next two excerpts, like the Berg example, are vocal melodies which span a large range. While they were composed in different centuries and represent quite different ways of relating pitch and time, they still bear a striking similarity. If you try to imagine singing either one of them yourself, for instance, you will immediately realize the incredible demands each composer makes on the singer's pitch and breath control. Not only is the range relatively large in the Queen of the Night's aria in Mozart's *The Magic Flute* (Example 3.13), but much of it lies near the very top of the singer's upper register. In addition, the soprano must control the large leaps with which she moves through this range. Then, too, she must often sing *staccato* (leaving a little space between each attack) as she performs this jagged melody; this is particularly noticeable on the repeated pitches which precede each leap in the latter portion of the aria.

Schoenberg (Example 3.14) has a different idea about arranging pitches—a different notion of "comprehensibility"—but he also asks his performer to control an enormously large range. (She spans three octaves!) Moving in large leaps at the beginning, she quickly (in a slow tempo) moves from low to high. Settling in this high register momentarily, she then expands the range still further upward, gradually moving once more down again as the tension of "highness" gives way. In this piece the soprano sings **legato** (joining pitches to one another in a single breath), in contrast to the **staccato** of the Mozart aria.

Once again, the dramatic intent of the composer is important here. Mozart is trying to express in music the "blind passion of the direful Queen," and he does so by asking her to sing at the extremes of her range and to leap about dramatically within it. You might compare this Mozart melody with the theme from his *Sonata for Piano in A* (Example 3.5). Interestingly, the instrumental melody is much more constrained in its range and in its movements through that range than is the vocal melody you have just heard. The comparison should make quite clear the importance of the composer's intentions in writing a melody—just where and how he or she wants to use it. Can you imagine a set of variations based on the Queen of the Night's aria?

Music occupies time; you have already experienced this not only on lower levels of temporal organization—pulse, meter, durations, or rhythmic patterns—but also through larger gestures such as the movement of a melody to its goals. These goals are moments of arrested motion, or *caesuras.*

The manner in which they are reached—the motion of a melody from one goal to another—creates an organic rhythm, crucial to the effect of each piece, which involves the unique relationship of all the dimensions of that piece (such as melodic direction, range, motive, grouping, and texture). We are really talking about how a melody "breathes."

Referring back to the Vivaldi and Liszt excerpts, we noted that each differed from our prototypical tune in that it seemed "serpentine"—to go on and on as if continuously unwinding. While there were brief pauses in the melodies which allowed the listener to "frame" its movement through time, these pauses were not predictable in their moments of occurrence. We can now contrast these characteristics with the clear and balanced phrase structure of *Lassie,* with its predictable moments of arrival—an aspect of melody which seemed central to our model of a sensible tune. Melodies of the first sort we describe as being more *continuous;* melodies of the second sort we call *sectional.*

Having analyzed carefully two sectional melodies (*Lassie* and the Mozart sonata theme), listen now to another example of a continuous melody (heard earlier as Example 1.13).

Example	Composer, title	Date
3.15	Bach, *Partita 2 for Unaccompanied Violin,* gigue	c. 1720

Notice that the questions we posed on pages 90–91 as an introduction to our study of *Lassie* are almost irrelevant to this continuous piece. Where does the melody breathe? Where are the caesuras that mark off phrases? Where are the boundaries of groups, and how can you relate these goals to one another? After the opening complementary motives, the melody seems to unwind in a seemingly never-ending series of runs. It simply does not lend itself to the kind of schematic description (*a a' b a'*) which seemed quite appropriate for *Lassie* or the Mozart piano sonata theme. What, then, constitutes its means of coherence—particularly its ways of organizing time? As in the Vivaldi and Liszt pieces, the melody is highly dependent on the use of sequences. Listening closely, you will hear chains made up of a repeated motive, the whole chain forming a sequential module—a larger structural element in the flow of the melody. The length of the larger module together with the length of the motivic units within that module create the structural rhythm of the piece. That is, time is marked off by the length of each unit of a sequential chain and, on a larger scale, by the total time of each linked module. One never knows just when a sequential chain will break, moving into a more freely structured passage, or when the more free moments will subside into the more regular pulse created by sequential repetition. It is this ebb and flow of clearly marked repetition—its interruptions and the resumption of a different sequentially repeated motive—that helps to create the underlying coherence of the melody.

In listening to the melodies that follow, we will need to ask the following: Are all melodies either sectional or continuous—one or the other? Perhaps it is best to think in terms of a continuum, with "continuous" at one end and "sectional" at the other. Most melodies will actually fall somewhere along that line—usually closer to one end or the other. *Lassie* and the Mozart piano sonata theme are of course way at the sectional end, and the Bach gigue (Example 3.15) at the continuous end. It will be helpful to think of this continuum in approaching the melodies which follow.

Nautilus shell
Sequentially repeated motive

Example	Composer, title	Date
3.16	Gershwin, *I Got Rhythm* (performed by Don Byas and Slam Stewart)	1945
3.17	C. Parker, *Steeplechase* (performed by Charlie Parker and Miles Davis)	1948

Example 3.16 is an instrumental version of *I Got Rhythm*. In the almost 60 years since its composition, the Gershwin tune has served as the basis for countless jazz renditions, in which at the beginning either the original melody is retained or a new melody is composed above the harmonic substructure. The original tune and its *a a b a* structure are readily apparent here, even without the words. We have, in effect, a theme and five variations on *I Got Rhythm*. The theme (without the two-bar tag) is stated clearly at the beginning by the tenor saxophone with *pizzicato* bass accompaniment. The saxophonist then improvises four consecutive **"choruses"**; that is, new melodies above the 32-bar *a a b a* harmonic pattern repeated four times. Then the bassist takes one chorus, beginning with a restatement of the original melody.

In Example 3.17 Charlie Parker has written a new melody based on what jazz musicians call "Rhythm changes"—the chord progression (harmonic substructure) of Gershwin's *I Got Rhythm*. After a four-bar piano introduction, trumpet and alto saxophone state this theme in unison for *a* and *a* again (that is, the first sixteen bars). Parker then improvises on *b* after which the *a* melody returns. Then follow the improvised solos: one chorus by Parker (alto saxophone), one chorus by Davis (trumpet), sixteen bars piano (*a* + *a*), eight bars Parker (*b*), then a unison statement of the last *a*. Listen closely and try to follow this; you can even sing the *I Got Rhythm* melody along with the unison and the solos.

Example	Composer, title	Date
3.18	*Cowboy's Lament* (American folk song, sung by Burl Ives)	
3.19	*Bonnie Wee Lass* (Scottish folk song, sung by Burl Ives)	

Balanced phrase structure is readily apparent in these two folk songs. In *Cowboy's Lament* (Example 3.18) there are four lines of text in each stanza (or verse) and, correspondingly, four four-bar phrases, only the last of which ends on the tonic:

I
> As Í walked oút in the stréets of Larédo,
> As Í walked oút in Larédo one dáy.

II
> I spíed a young cówboy all wrápped in white línen,
> Wrápped in white línen as cóld as the cláy.

(Notice that lines 1 and 3 each end on a weak beat; 2 and 4 end on a strong beat.)

Bonnie Wee Lass (Example 3.19) has an equally clear pattern until the ending of the fourth line, which you expect to be the final phrase. What happens at that point?

I
> A bónnie wee lássie whose náme it was Néll,
> Líved in a hoúse where her grándmother dwéll,

II
> The hoúse it was smáll and the wíndows no léss,
> Háving four pánes one néeded a gláss . . .
> That níce little wíndow, that cúte little wíndow,
> Swéet little wíndow where grándmother dwéll.

The fourth phrase slides right through the moment of expected rest, momentarily upsetting the regularity of the structural rhythm. Having heard two complementary phrases ("A bonnie wee lassie whose name it was Nell,/Lived in a house where her grandmother dwell,"), we are led to expect another pair of complementary phrases. Instead, the melody continues on through the expected stopping place into the next two lines of text. These last two phrases, then, are an *extension*. The song finally comes to a close at the end of the *sixth* phrase, just as we had expected it to at the end of the fourth phrase. While all the phrases are, in fact, equal in length (four bars) and thus balanced, the regularity of phrase rhythm is upset—first by the run-on through the expected downbeat and then by stretching or extending the anticipated 2 + 2 phrase symmetry to make 2 + 4.

This may seem like a very complicated description of a perfectly obvious tune, but it is perhaps just in such small deviations from the norm that music gains its expressiveness. Notice, however, that without the culturally acquired, and thus seemingly intuitive, sense of "norm," the whole effect would be lost.

Example	Composer, title	Date
3.20	Mozart, *Don Giovanni*, duet	1787
3.21	Moussorgsky, *Khovantchina*, prelude	1872–1880

Mozart also plays around with phrase rhythm in the duet from *Don Giovanni* (Example 3.20) in which the aristocrat Don Giovanni (Don Juan) plays around with the peasant girl Zerlina. We hear first two short melodic motives sung by Don Giovanni. Together they constitute the *antecedent phrase* which ends—inconclusively—on the *dominant*. Don Giovanni's next two melodic motives constitute the *consequent phrase*, which ends—now conclusively—on the *tonic*. When Zerlina takes up the melody, we expect a continuation of this balanced phrase structure, since she begins with an almost literal repetition of Don Giovanni's antecedent phrase. The consequent phrase proceeds much as before, but then the last short melodic motive is unexpectedly extended, which beautifully upsets the previously established symmetry. The regularity of the structural rhythm, which the listener has come to take for granted and almost to depend on, is disrupted as Zerlina's melody continues on past the moment of expected rest—almost as if Zerlina wants to make the moment last a little longer.

Example 3.21 by Moussorgsky differs from the Mozart melody in that a normative phrase length is never established—the listener cannot predict arrival at a goal, when the melodic motion will come to rest. The effect of this melody, particularly in its sense of freedom,

Example 3.20 MOZART, excerpt from *Don Giovanni*

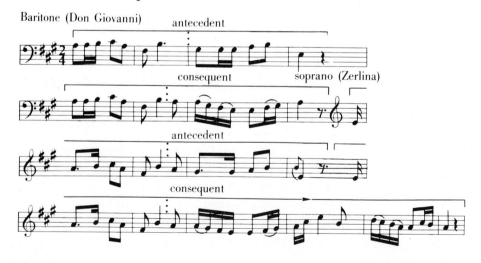

The last short melodic unit is unexpectedly extended.

is quite different from the preceding examples in which a regular structural rhythm is first established and then varied.

The mobility of phrase rhythm in the Moussorgsky prelude goes together with a lack of definition in the metric structure. In spite of the clear division of the beat into twos, there is no clear sense of a regularly recurring higher-level accent. In addition, there is an elusiveness about the melody line itself. Specifically, the melody is ambiguous in generating a tonic—almost as if there were a floating pitch center. As a result, the listener cannot tell whether the melody has reached a full stop—a point of rest—or will continue on.

Listen, for example, to the first two phrases in the opening statement. While the first phrase is, in number of beats, actually longer than the second, the asymmetry is not particularly evident or even important—especially when compared to the noticeable asymmetry of phrase rhythm at the end of the Mozart duet.

With the next pair of phrases another aspect of the melody emerges. While the first of these phrases is actually a variation of the initial phrase, you cannot quite be sure whether or not it is a literal repetition. In fact, this phrase is a compressed version: Three measures of the original are compressed into two here. While the pitches, except for the first, are identical, the durations of the notes are quickened to shorten the total time span of the phrase.

In the second phrase of this pair, however, the variation is clear. Moussorgsky initially varies the pitch shape somewhat but arrives in the same time span at the pitch which we expect to provide a breathing space. But the break never materializes. Instead, the melody goes on to elaborate and expand both the range and the motivic material—as if time were stretched.

While the last six examples differed in degree and kind of symmetry or balance, they are all fundamentally similar in that phrases and motives are clearly articulated. Their melodic motion can be characterized as a succession of bounded, melodic gestures which sometimes vary in their moments of arrival, but the listener can still follow the movement from one goal to the next, comparing the goals as the melody goes along. All these melodies, then, lie toward the sectional end of the continuum, with the Moussorgsky excerpt tending a bit toward the continuous end as the listener gives in to the freedom with which gestures begin and end.

Example	Composer, title	Date
3.22	*Offertory* (Gregorian chant from the Christmastide Midnight Mass)	Middle Ages

Where does Example 3.22 lie on the continuum of sectional-continuous melodic organization? In this Gregorian chant (known also as plainchant) you certainly hear melodic motion delimited by caesuras—the melody stops and the singers breathe. You can easily follow the motion from one "breath" to the next, although, as in Example 3.21, the lengths of these units are not predictable.

What, then, is the difference between the melodies in Examples 3.21 and 3.22? While the Moussorgsky melody did not generate a strong sense of meter, the plainchant melody is even less defined in its higher-level grouping of beats. Like the *Khovantchina* prelude, too, the chant does not create a sense of compelling motion directed toward points of rest. What is its tonic?

But the significant difference between the two melodies lies in the role played by motivic repetition and transformation. In fact, in the chant motivic patterns are neither repeated nor even structurally varied. The chant melody seems tied to—motivated by—the text and contained by the upper and lower pitch limits of each phrase. The result is a melody which, despite its "breathing spaces," seems more continuous than sectional.

Example	Composer, title	Date
3.23	Bach, *St. Matthew Passion*, aria	1729
3.24	Wagner, *Tristan and Isolde*, "Love-Death"	1857–1859

Examples 3.23 and 3.24 are even more continuous, or cumulative, in their effect than the plainchant. In the Bach aria, for example, the tenor seems hardly to have an opportunity to breathe. After the instrumental introduction, with one brief vocal interpolation, the melody moves continuously forward, growing out of itself. There is no periodic phrase structure established by a series of related, regularly recurring

The melody moves continuously forward, growing out of itself.

goals. The effect is one of organic growth—a constant process of becoming.

Example 3.24, from Wagner's *Tristan and Isolde,* illustrates what the composer termed "endless melody," which, in a sense, has features of both cumulative and periodic melodic processes. The melody is shared jointly by soprano and orchestra. The soprano breathes, but the orchestra continues. Through sequential development and extreme harmonic instability (where do you settle on a tonic?), the motion is continuous in a series of increasingly intense climaxes.

Now that you have listened carefully to a wide variety of melodies and gained some understanding of the more formal properties and relations that characterize them, it will be helpful to listen again to Examples 3.1 through 3.6. In the light of your experience with the material in the remaining parts of the chapter, how would you now answer our initial question: What contributes to the differences among these first six melodies, and how can you account for these differences? In turn, what can you say now about the characteristics of the proto-typical tune—our cultural model of a melody that makes sense?

Several aspects seem to be basic to such an intuitive model: Meter, sectional organization with balanced phrase structure, and a clear sense of tonal center. Yet as you have seen and heard in the analysis of *Lassie* and the theme from the Mozart piano sonata movement, as well as in the discussion of continuous melodies, other factors can also play an important role in creating a sense of organized movement and musical coherence. Factors such as repetition of a rhythmic pattern, sequential repetition of a melodic fragment, and manipulation, even transformation, of a germinal musical idea all contribute to creating a meaningful whole.

As you become more sensitive to these aspects of even the most familiar tunes, you may also discover these same aspects in melodies that previously seemed strange, even incoherent. Thus, a more fully developed perception and understanding of what you know and can do already is the touchstone to learning how to appreciate music that may at first seem incomprehensible. But the virtuosity of composers (and performers) in finding new modes of expression and particular ways of building coherence demands a certain virtuosity from the listener—an expanded awareness or expanded consciousness that frees him or her to listen to a piece on its own terms. Your study up to this point, and as it continues, should help you to achieve this new and greater awareness.

ADDITIONAL MATERIALS

I   Practice Problems 1 through 4 give you only the pitches of five familiar tunes; neither their varied durations nor meter (that is, bar lines) are indicated. Play the notes on the piano or some other instrument. For each example, identify the melody and write it out with the correct rhythm and meter.

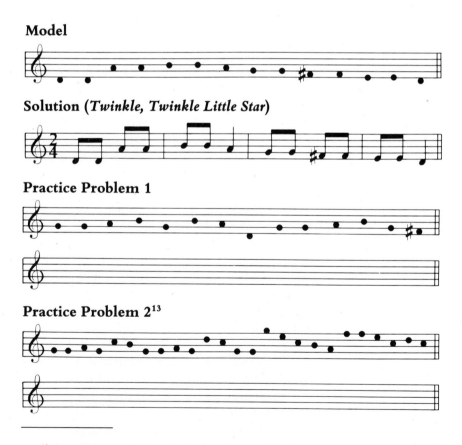

Model

Solution (*Twinkle, Twinkle Little Star*)

Practice Problem 1

Practice Problem 2[13]

Practice Problem 3

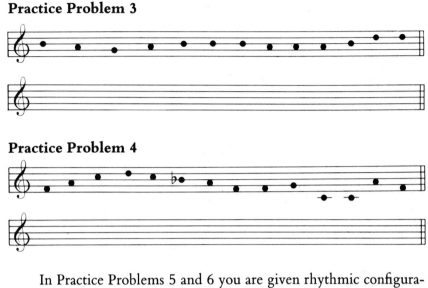

Practice Problem 4

In Practice Problems 5 and 6 you are given rhythmic configurations. Provide each rhythmic configuration with appropriate pitches.

Model

Solution

Practice Problem 5

Practice Problem 6

In Practice Problems 7 and 8 you are given pitches (this time not taken from familiar tunes) without durations. Provide each pitch shape with an appropriate rhythmic shape.

Model

Solution

Practice Problem 7

Practice Problem 8

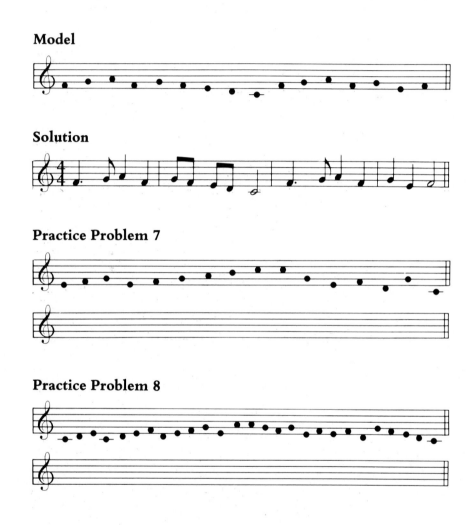

In Practice Problems 9 through 13 you are given a set of pitches which were generated randomly by a computer. Using Problems 9 and 10 as your model, modify the remaining sets to form a "sensible tune" by deleting and/or adding pitches and by varying the durations. As you work, try to observe the bases for your decisions; from them you may be able to derive your model of a "sensible tune."

Practice Problem 9

Practice Problem 10

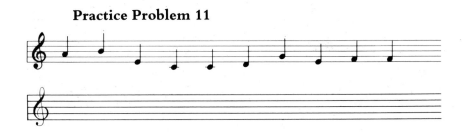

Practice Problem 11

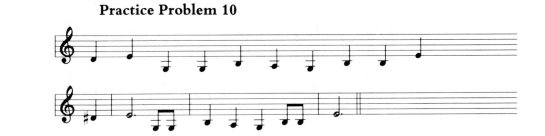

Practice Problem 12

Practice Problem 13

II   Study in detail some well-known tunes, trying to discover the fundamentals of their organization. Look, for example, for motives and their manipulation, melodic shape, and phrases and the relationships among them (length, kind of cadence, and so on). Try the following three tunes.

> *Silent Night*
> *Twinkle, Twinkle Little Star*
> *Early One Morning*

III   Listen carefully to and study (as with the familiar tunes above) some more complex melodies.

> Mozart, *Eine Kleine Nachtmusik,* K. 525, minuet 1787 (Example 4.10)
> Schubert, songs from *Die Schöne Müllerin* ("The Beautiful Maid of the Mill"), 1823: "Der Jäger," ("The Hunter"), "Des Müllers Blumen" ("The Miller's Flowers"), "Ungeduld" ("Impatience"), and "Morgengruss" ("Morning Greeting"). Note, among other things, the readily apparent rhythmic patterns of the first three songs, compared with the almost speechlike quality and the much more subtle patterns of "Morgengruss."

IV   Contrast, as examples of sectional and continuous melodic organization, the opening melodies that you hear in the following pieces:

> Haydn, *Symphony 99,* third movement, 1793 (Example 1.29)
> Handel, *Concerto Grosso,* Op. 6, no. 2, finale, c. 1739 (Example 1.31)
> Mozart, *Symphony 39,* K. 543, fourth movement, 1788
> Bach, *Brandenburg Concerto 5,* first movement, c. 1721

V   Listen to the composer's manipulation of motives, on a larger scale, in the course of an entire movement such as those listed below.

Beethoven, *Quartet,* Op. 131, first movement, 1826
Schoenberg, *Pierrot Lunaire,* "Mondestrunken," 1912
Bach, *Well-Tempered Clavier,* Book I, C-minor fugue, 1722
Stravinsky, *Three Pieces for Clarinet Solo,* 1920

ANCILLARY READING

Pitch Notation

As an oddity of the history of music, only seven letters came to represent the twelve tones employed in Western music. The letters A through G, with the aid of *accidentals* [*sharps* (♯) and *flats* (♭)], provide names for these twelve tones. In addition to being named by letter (which does not indicate the octave), pitches are notated on a five-line *staff* ≣ . A *clef* (Latin *clavis,* "key") provides the key to the staff, as follows:

𝄞 is a G, or treble, clef. It fixes the G above middle C.

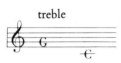
treble

𝄽 is a C, or alto or tenor, clef. It fixes middle C. The alto clef is used principally by the viola; the tenor clef by the bassoon, cello, and trombone.

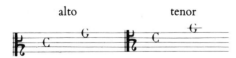
alto   tenor

𝄢 is an F, or bass, clef. It fixes the F below middle C.

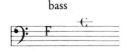
bass

Here are the twelve tones on the piano keyboard (see p. 109):

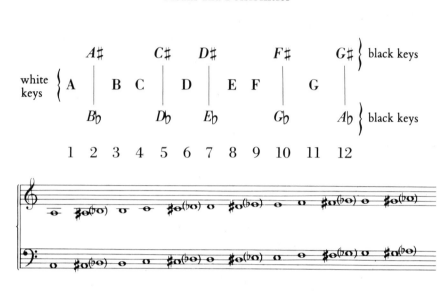

Oddly enough, A-sharp and B-flat, for example, are played by the same key; they are called *enharmonic* equivalents.[14]

Key Signatures

In tonal music (music written in a particular key), the key is indicated at the beginning of a piece by means of accidentals (flats or sharps) which constitute the key *signature.* Thus 🎼♭ means that all the B's in the piece are flatted, and the piece is in either F major or D minor; while 🎼♯ indicates G major or E minor. A so-called "circle of fifths" illustrates the 24 major and minor keys. Starting from C major or A minor, the keys with no sharps or flats, each sharp added to the key signature raises the key by the interval of a fifth, and each flat added lowers it by a fifth. In the circle of fifths on page 131, capital letters indicate the major keys, and small letters represent the minor keys.

---

[14] These equivalents derive from a system of tuning called "equal temperament," which became standardized during the eighteenth century. While it is imposed on the piano by its construction, and thus on instruments playing together with it, string instruments playing together in small groups (a string quartet, for example) may make fine adjustments in pitch so that B-flat in a certain context may be slightly lower than A-sharp.

Circle of fifths

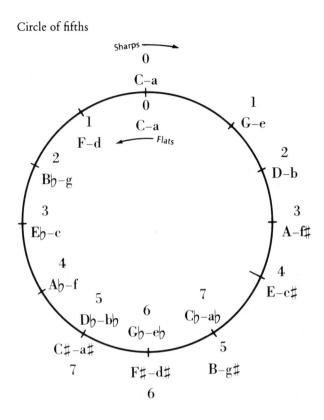

Modes and Scales

The division of the octave into seven tones with varying intervals between them creates the diatonic modes shown in the following table.

Name	Starting note	Interval pattern[a]
Dorian	D	1 $\frac{1}{2}$ 1 1 1 $\frac{1}{2}$ 1
Phrygian	E	$\frac{1}{2}$ 1 1 1 $\frac{1}{2}$ 1 1
Lydian	F	1 1 1 $\frac{1}{2}$ 1 1 $\frac{1}{2}$
Mixolydian	G	1 1 $\frac{1}{2}$ 1 1 $\frac{1}{2}$ 1
Aeolian (minor)	A	1 $\frac{1}{2}$ 1 1 $\frac{1}{2}$ 1 1
Locrian	B	$\frac{1}{2}$ 1 1 $\frac{1}{2}$ 1 1 1
Ionian (major)	C	1 1 $\frac{1}{2}$ 1 1 1 $\frac{1}{2}$

[a] Thus playing all the white keys on the piano beginning on D would give you the Dorian mode, playing all the white keys beginning on E would give the Phrygian mode, and so forth. The interval pattern may be transposed to begin on any of the eleven other tones.

The degrees of the scale in major and minor are named as follows:

1. Tonic
2. Supertonic
3. Mediant
4. Subdominant
5. Dominant
6. Submediant
7. Leading tone

There are three different forms of the minor scale. Note that these differences involve only the sixth and seventh degrees of the scale.

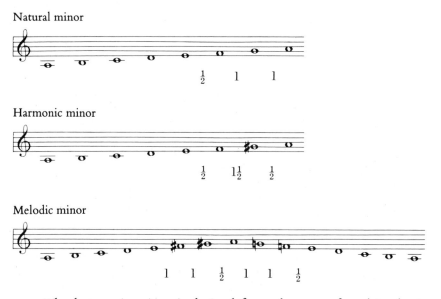

Natural minor

Harmonic minor

Melodic minor

The harmonic minor is derived from the notes found in the I, IV, and V chords in their most common form (see the Ancillary Reading for Chapter 5). The melodic minor is derived from ascending or descending melodies in the minor mode.

The term *pentatonic* is used to describe various possible divisions of the octave into *five tones* (for example, the black keys on the piano).

Intervals

The distance between any two tones is called an *interval*. In discussing scales and modes, we spoke of a half step or a whole step; these may be more properly described as a *minor second* or a *major second*. The principal intervals within the octave are indicated below.

Rules for Naming Intervals

The *perfect* intervals are the *prime* (the same note; for example, two people singing in unison), *fourth* ($2\frac{1}{2}$ steps), *fifth* ($3\frac{1}{2}$ steps), and *octave.* Lowering a perfect or a minor interval by a half step creates a *diminished* interval; lowering a major interval by a half step creates a *minor* interval. Raising a major or a perfect interval by a half step creates an *augmented* interval; raising a minor interval by a half step creates a *major* interval.

PART TWO

Process and Design

CHAPTER 4

Rice terraces
A particular way of building up the world . . .

Means of Organization

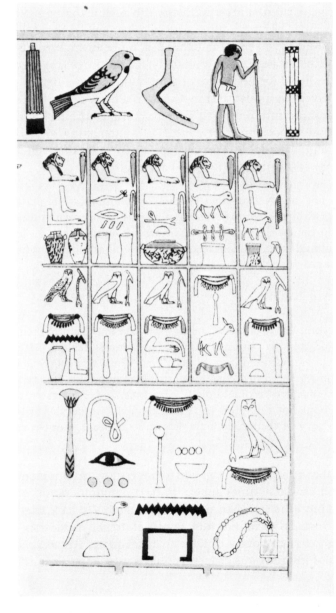

Egyptian hieroglyphics
. . . as in the creation of language.

WHAT HAS HAPPENED SO FAR in your perception of music? Try rereading the Introduction and listening again to the first seven examples in Chapter 1. Do you find that you are beginning to expand your focus? Those factors which, of necessity, have been temporarily isolated can now begin to merge. Analysis and terminology can assume their proper roles as means toward direct and immediate involvement in the total process of a work. And as you enjoy an expanded, more aware involvement, you may find justification, at least partially, for the use of language which may at times have seemed more of a hindrance than a help.

Naming an object or a relationship—such as a beat, tonic, triple meter—often appears to interfere with your response to the feelings, character, and mood which music generates. It is interesting to read what Kurt Goldstein, a biological psychologist, has said concerning the connection between language (naming) and feeling:

> [Language] is not merely a superficial means of communication, not a simple naming of objects through words; it represents a particular way of building up the world—namely, by means of abstractions. . . . In none of his cultural creations does man reveal himself as fully as in the creation of language, itself.[1]

But a problem arises, because:

> If we try to become aware of them [feelings] we have to transform them into objects, and then their original character of attitudes, feelings, etc., is lost, and they are distorted into "things." . . . Thus, a phenomenon which is not experienced in a conscious form [feelings, attitudes, etc.] can never subsequently become directly conscious; and, conversely, a conscious phenomenon can never work directly upon attitudes or feelings. Only by way of the whole, by a detour, so to speak, can either influence, arouse, or disturb the other.[2]

These general comments may help you to understand this moment in a process which can sometimes appear to be a conglomeration of analytical bits and pieces rather than a total experience. We have tried to emphasize, however, that an atomistic approach to the musical experience is, except as a temporary expedient, inadequate. Remember how the concerns of the previous chapters could not be kept separate?

---

[1] Kurt Goldstein, *Human Nature* (New York: Schocken Books, 1963), p. 83.
[2] Ibid., pp. 152, 154.

Just as our discussion of sound led to rhythmic organization, which merged into melodic organization, so our discussion of melodic organization turned to rhythmic considerations.

From now on we will pursue a broader approach. First, in Exercise 4.1, we ask you to pay attention to specific means through which composers create a sense of unity and variety in building whole structures. Then we move to a consideration of two fundamentally different approaches to creating these structures (Demonstration 4.1). Next we introduce the subject of harmony, which "more than any other musical element, brings to music the possibility of extension, or larger design."[3] And finally, incorporating all that has gone before, we move to a consideration of these "larger designs," concentrating on their varying effects.

EXERCISE 4.1
Return
(Side 6)

Exercise 4.1 asks you to discriminate between those pieces which include a return to the opening musical material and those which do not. To hear the difference between these structural procedures, you will have to focus on musical events on a larger scale (in less detail, but for longer time spans than in the preceding chapters), and you will need to remember these events throughout the excerpt.

Note that Examples 4.2, 4.4, and 4.8 are each complete pieces; in these examples you will hear how contrasting procedures can influence the effect of a whole design.

Remembering a musical event (or any event, for that matter) becomes easier if you can "identify" with its expressive character— becoming actively involved in it, instead of trying to remember its smaller details, such as a melodic or rhythmic configuration. A precise awareness of such specifics is extremely important when you are delving into a work, but here you can pause in your examination of details to consider larger design in one of its most general aspects. Listen to the difference between pieces in which you have the experience of returning after some kind of digression, and those in which your experience is one of continuing onward. (Note that in a number of the examples in Exercise 4.1 the composer has helped you to "fix" the initial events by repeating the opening section.)

---

[3] Roger Sessions, "The Composer and His Message," in *The Intent of the Artist,* ed. Augusto Centeno (Princeton: Princeton University Press, 1941), p. 111.

Pause in your examination of details . . . to consider larger design

As you listen, think not only about this fundamental difference in organization, but also, in those examples which include a return, about the differences in the way this return occurs. Is the return "announced"—are you told musically that it is approaching? Or does it simply happen without any preparation? Notice, too, that in a number of instances the return is somewhat varied, although it still clearly projects the feeling of coming back after a contrasting middle section.

We have chosen to introduce an exercise rather than a demonstration at this point to encourage you to begin your own discovery of larger design. In a general sense, this exercise also functions as an introduction to the subject of *harmony,* which plays a crucial role in determining structure. You will hear how a digression—a contrasting middle section—can lead you away from home (to a new key[4] and its tonic), while a return to a previously heard theme usually coincides with a return to the home key and its tonic. Harmony is playing a role in your perception of structure on some level, even though you cannot yet *say* how.

Even with a simple melody like *Cowboy's Lament,* harmonic implications play a significant role in your sense of intelligibility: for instance, the feeling of incompleteness at the end of the first three phrases, contrasted with the conclusiveness of the fourth phrase. Har-

---

[4] While the meaning of *tonic* or *tonal center* was discussed in Chapter 3, the possibility of *changing* the tonal center (and thus the key) was only hinted at in that discussion. How this change is made and its various effects will be discussed further in Chapter 5.

mony functions in a similar way in these longer examples. You might think of it as a set of ground rules which you have learned quite naturally, much as when you were a child you naturally learned the rules of grammar that made spoken language intelligible to you.

Remember, however, that harmonic frameworks differ from one culture to another and even within cultures from one historical period to another. You will meet these issues directly in the next chapter and then again in Part Four. For now do the exercise, keeping in mind that your sense of coherence, including contrast and return, is being generated in part by your built-in awareness of harmonic relations.

Please do not consider this exercise as a test. After you have completed the examples, look at the answers below. You will also find additional comments on some of the examples. Try listening to the examples again while reading these comments instead of simply checking to see if your answers are right or wrong. First listen carefully to Examples 4.1 and 4.2 (for which answers are given); these can serve as models in doing the rest of the exercise.

Example	No return	Return
4.1		X
4.2	X	
4.3		
4.4		
4.5		
4.6		
4.7		
4.8		
4.9		

CORRECT ANSWERS AND COMMENTS

Example	Composer, title, date	No return	Return
4.1	Mozart, *Concerto for Horn and Orchestra*, no. 2, K. 417, third movement, 1783		X
4.2	Bach, *Well-Tempered Clavier*, Book I, Prelude no. 2 in C minor, 1722	X	

The first two examples demonstrate how fundamentally different structures can create strikingly different effects. In Example 4.1, the feeling of coming back is clearly prepared for by the pause of the horn together with the rest of the orchestra, as well as by harmonic means. (Can you tell what happens to the harmony? Listen, for example, to the bass alone just before the return.)

Contrast the feeling of the return in Example 4.1 with the tension created by the continuously unfolding motion in Example 4.2, though the forward movement is disrupted by changes of tempo at the end.

Example	Composer, title, date	No return	Return
4.3	Bach, *Concerto in E Major for Violin and Orchestra*, third movement, c. 1720		X

The contrasts between the full orchestra (called the ***tutti,*** meaning "all") and the solo violin with accompaniment define the sections in Example 4.3. After the solo there is a return to the *tutti* playing the opening theme. Here are two works by the same composer (Examples 4.2 and 4.3) which exemplify the different structural procedures under discussion.

Example	Composer, title, date	No return	Return
4.4	Chopin, *Prelude*, Op. 28, no. 18, 1838	X	

Compare the sense of ongoing movement in the Chopin prelude (Example 4.4) with that in the Bach prelude. How do they differ?

Example	Composer, title, date	No return	Return
4.5	Haydn, *Symphony 96,* fourth movement, 1791		X

Here Haydn (Example 4.5) has a good time playing around with your anticipation of a return before he actually presents it.

Example	Composer, title, date	No return	Return
4.6	Vivaldi, *Concerto Grosso,* Op. 3, no. 7, first movement, c. 1712	X	

This excerpt from the Vivaldi *Concerto Grosso* (Example 4.6) includes repetition but not return. The work proceeds sequentially. It progresses by what we might call "rhythmic stepping stones" formed by the repetition of a motive at successively higher or lower pitch levels within the same strand of the texture. In this excerpt there are two sequential passages, each with its own motive.

Example	Composer, title, date	No return	Return
4.7	Stravinsky, *Petrouchka,* 1910–1911		X

Did you hear the harmonic joke in Example 4.7, an excerpt from the ballet *Petrouchka?* Just before the contrasting section begins, Stravinsky brings things to a stop, but not to an end. The harmony at this point is directed toward a tonic which, in fact, does not materialize. The melody of the next section begins in a different key from the one intuitively anticipated by the listener. Only later, with the varied return, does Stravinsky come back harmonically to where he left off at the end of the first section. (We will return to these questions of harmony in Chapter 5.)

Example	Composer, title, date	No return	Return
4.8	Webern, *Five Pieces for Orchestra,* Op. 10, no. 2, 1913	X	
4.9	Bizet, *Symphony in C,* third movement, 1855	X	

Egyptian vase: sectional organization

American Indian pot: continuous organization

The continuous motivic development (over a very brief time span) in the Webern piece (Example 4.8) may make it difficult for you to orient yourself to the piece after only one or two hearings. Why does such continuous development make return inappropriate?

Notice that in Example 4.9 you are led to expect a return. As in many of the examples in which there were returns, Bizet repeats the opening part before going on to the contrasting section. In addition, he presents a long preparation which seems to anticipate return. Instead of returning, however, the composer goes on to introduce new material.

DEMONSTRATION 4.1
Sectional and Continuous Organization
(Sides 6–7)

Demonstration 4.1 introduces you to the study of large-scale structure in music. While some aspects of structure have been discussed previously,[5] we have not yet focused on overall musical design. You will hear in this demonstration mostly short pieces or complete movements which illustrate two fundamentally different approaches to larger musical design: (1) pieces which one hears immediately as divided into parts, whether or not they include return (*sectional*), and (2) pieces which one cannot easily divide into parts (*continuous*).

This fundamental distinction was discussed in Chapter 3 where

---

[5] See Chapter 1, sonority and texture as organizing factors; Chapter 2, rhythm (beat, meter, phrase) as an organizing factor; Chapter 3, motivic development; and here in Chapter 4, return.

continuous melodies were contrasted to those "with clear and balanced phrase structure and predictable moments of arrival." But now when we refer to dividing a piece into "parts," we mean not smaller units (such as phrases defined by *caesuras*) but rather those larger structural units that stand out as the significant sections of a piece—those units which lend themselves to schematic representation and can, for example, be meaningfully designated A, B, C, and so forth.

Of course, these larger sections are, in turn, composed of smaller units (phrases), and the relations among these phrases generate the particular character of the section. In a whole piece you can hear a kind of hierarchy of structural relations: phrases combined to make up sections, sections combined to make up still larger parts, and these larger parts combined to make up the whole.

Example	Composer, title	Date
4.10	Mozart, *Eine kleine Nachtmusik* ("A Little Night Music") K. 525, minuet	1787
4.11	Chopin, *Prelude,* Op. 28, no. 18	1838

Examples 4.10 and 4.11 should make the fundamental distinction between sectional and continuous organization clear. Example 4.10, by Mozart, is a late eighteenth-century stylized dance movement, the third movement of a four-movement instrumental work. It is clearly divided into three large parts, the first and last being identical (except for the absence of repeats in the last part). Its overall structure may be diagramed as follows:

$$A \qquad\qquad\qquad B \qquad\qquad\qquad A'$$
$$\|:a:\|:b + a':\| \qquad \|:c:\|:d + c:\| \qquad a\ b + a'$$

Note that each of the three sections is "closed out," or relatively complete in itself; in addition, within each of the larger sections, A, B, and A', one hears a somewhat similar inner structure: $\|:a:\|:b + a':\|$. Notice, that unlike the clear delineation between B and A', *b* and *a'* flow into one another; thus they are designated *b + a'* rather than *b a'*.

In addition, note that section *b* is made up of the same motivic material as *a* (and *d* bears a similar relationship to *c*). In fact, its function is to create something new out of the old by developing the motives

Mozart minuet

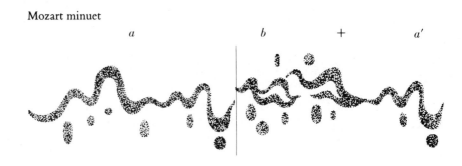

already present in section *a*. By contrast, B presents entirely new material not drawn from A in any obvious way at all. The comparison demonstrates nicely the hierarchical relations mentioned above: sections *a* and *b* are separated from one another and are clearly different, but both the separation and the degree of difference are significantly less than that between A and B in the larger design of the piece. A and B are therefore not only *longer* than *a* and *b*; they also present a higher degree of contrast and distinctness.

With these basic distinctions in mind, what other differences do you hear between the ABA′ structure and the *a b + a′* structure, and what specific differences do you hear among the smaller parts—*a*, *b*, and *a′*?

In contrast to the Mozart minuet, the Chopin prelude (Example 4.11) cannot be divided into parts—it moves continuously forward in

The Chopin prelude cannot be divided into parts.

spite of the caesuras, or "breathing" pauses, which are not moments of rest, not stable points of arrival. It would also not be possible to make a schematic representation of the structure of this piece, such as ABA, for example. We will return to Examples 4.10 and 4.11 in Chapters 6 and 7, respectively.

Sectional Pieces

Example	Composer, title	Date
4.12	Schubert, *Ländler,* Op. 171, no. 4	1823
4.13	Mozart, *Variations on "Ah, vous dirai-je, maman,"* K. 265	1781–1782
4.14	M. Reynolds, *Little Boxes* (sung by Pete Seeger)	1962

The next three examples, like Example 4.10, are sectional, yet each is organized differently. The Schubert dance (Example 4.12) is in two clear sections: A B. Each part is repeated, ‖:A:‖:B:‖, but there is no return (see the Additional Materials for further discussion of this dance).

The theme of Example 4.13 will certainly be familiar to you, though under a different name. Included here are the theme and two of the twelve variations that Mozart wrote on this theme. In Mozart's time it was common for composer-pianists to improvise in public on well-known melodies. Mozart's composed piece gives us some idea of what such a performance might have been like.

A theme and variations

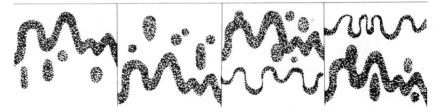

The theme may be diagrammed as follows: ‖:*a*:‖:*b* + *a*:‖. Each of the two variations included in Example 4.13 follows this same large design. In addition, each variation also follows the underlying structure of the theme. For example, in the theme and in each variation you will hear:

> The same phrase structure and the same relations between phrases (like antecedent-consequent)
> The same basic pitch-shape for each phrase (although this skeletal shape is "dressed" differently each time)

> The same set of harmonic relations (like full and half cadences, which occur in each variation just as they did in the theme)

Try to follow the structure of the theme as it is realized anew in each variation. At the same time you will discover that each variation has its own character. What means does Mozart use to give each of these larger sections its individuality? Finally, even though not all the variations are included in this excerpt, you can sense the additive quality of the piece. Each large section (variation) is added on to the previous one, and all of them together make up a particular kind of whole.

Another kind of additive piece is the simple verse form of the ballad. In the song *Little Boxes* (Example 4.14), as in most ballads, it is the words that hold your interest, and it is only the words that change. You take for granted the exact repetition of the music (melody and harmony) that marks off each section of the song. In contrast, each of the variations of Mozart (Example 4.13) repeats the general structure of the theme, but each time the structure appears in a new guise— sometimes more in a disguise.

The differences between the song and the variations have much to do with the social function of the two pieces. One listens to the words of the ballad to agree (or disagree?) with its message. The music is only a medium—a vehicle that exists perhaps to strengthen the verbal message or, occasionally, as with *Little Boxes,* even to create a musical picture of it. With the Mozart variations, however, one listens to the medium itself—the medium *is* the message!

Continuous Pieces

Example	Composer, title	Date
4.15	Victoria, *Missa O Magnum Mysterium,* Sanctus	1592
4.16	Bach, *Two-Part Invention in F Major,* no. 8	1723

Examples 4.15 and 4.16 are organized so as to create a continuous structure, but one listens to each of them rather differently. The Renaissance piece by Victoria (Example 4.15), a movement from a setting of the text of the Catholic **Mass,** is active in texture; the parts enter in imitation and are rhythmically independent. The piece creates an effect of unceasing movement characterized by melodic homogeneity. There

is, however, changing tone color and an increase in textural density as the parts pile up on top of one another.

The piece is continuous, with only one break in the musical flow. Close listening reveals "sections" marked off by carefully concealed points of arrival; the "Hosanna" stands by itself. In this polyphonic piece the text is a significant structural determinant, for a new series of imitative entries occurs with each line of text, plus at "gloriatua":

Sanctus, Sanctus, Sanctus,	Holy, Holy, Holy,
Dominus Deus Sabaoth,	Lord God of Hosts,
Pleni sunt caeli et terra gloria tua,	Heaven and earth are full of thy glory,
Hosanna in excelsis!	Hosanna in the highest!

What musical elements create the "section" boundaries? How are these points concealed?

The Bach invention (Example 4.16) is also active in texture, but this time, since there are only two "voices," the texture is thinner throughout. As in the Victoria, the piece begins with imitation. However, the Bach piece has a clear point of arrival one-third of the way through (see also the Additional Materials at the end of this chapter).

An eighteenth-century harpsichord with two keyboards

Rondos

Example	Composer, title	Date
4.17	Rameau, *Suite in E,* gigue no. 2	1724
4.18	Haydn, *Trio in G,* "Rondo all' Ongarese"	1790
4.19	S. Reese, *Which Side Are You On?* (sung by Pete Seeger)	1932

Examples 4.17 through 4.19 are again sectional. Unlike Examples 4.15 and 4.16, they can be meaningfully diagramed—a diagram will represent the progress of the piece and the perceived relationships among the parts. Rameau's piece (Example 4.17) can be thought of as having a refrain (A), the entire gigue proceeding as follows: ‖:A:‖ BACADA. (How do the various sections differ? Are they each in themselves relatively sectional or continuous?)

The Haydn trio[6] (Example 4.18) proceeds similarly, although it is much more extended in each of its parts, and consequently much longer. It may be diagramed as ABA'CA" Coda. Unlike Rameau, however, Haydn further subdivides each section into two or more smaller parts. A, for example, may be diagramed as ‖a + a'‖:b + a':‖. The type of structural procedure illustrated by Examples 4.17 and 4.18 is called a **rondo.**

A rondo

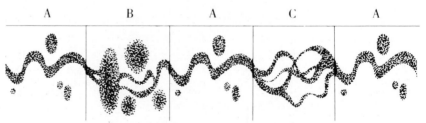

| A | B | A | C | A |

You are probably more familiar with the rondo procedure as it appears in a ballad, such as Example 4.19 with its refrain (A) sung to the words "Which side are you on?" But as in the previous ballad, *Little Boxes,* it is the words more than the music that make for change in the contrasting sections of the song. Considering *only* the words,

---

[6] The title "Rondo all'Ongarese" means "Rondo in the Hungarian Style," which refers to certain characteristics of Hungarian gypsy violin music (especially rhythmic figures) that Haydn makes use of in this movement.

Frank Lloyd Wright, "Fallingwater" House, 1936
Sectional or continuous?

we might diagram this ballad the same way we diagramed the Rameau gigue: ABACADA. The impact of the returns to A, sung by the whole audience after each word-contrasting section, demonstrates the powerful political and social function return can have in songs such as this one, written during a bitter coal strike in Kentucky. Furthermore, the effect of return in this verbal context points up the function of returns in a nonverbal context, where the contrast is purely musical—as in the rondos of Rameau and Haydn.

Continuous or Sectional?

Example	Composer, title	Date
4.20	Schubert, *Impromptu,* Op. 90, no. 2	1827
4.21	Schoenberg, *Six Little Piano Pieces,* Op. 19, no. 4	1911
4.22	J. Lewis, *Django* (played by the Modern Jazz Quartet)	1960
4.23	Stravinsky, *Le Sacre du printemps,* introduction	1913

In categorizing a piece as sectional or continuous, it might be best (as with melodies) to think in terms of a continuum with "sectional" and "continuous" at opposite ends; most pieces will lie somewhere on that continuum, closer to one end or the other. The Schubert *Impromptu* (Example 4.20) may at first appear to be continuous because the melody is a series of rapidly flowing notes that seem never to stop—there is no caesura in this upper part of the texture. But would the piece be accurately described as continuous? No, but why not? The answer lies in the very clear balanced phrase structure generated by the chords in

M. C. Escher, *Metamorphose*
(Escher Foundation, Collection Haags Gemeentemuseum, The Hague)

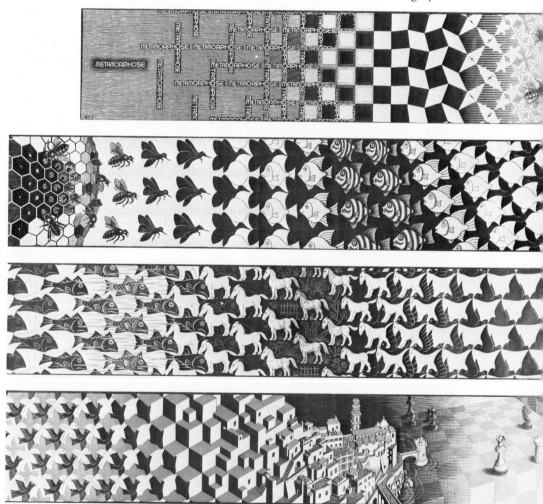

the left-hand accompaniment. You must direct your attention beneath the flowing notes in the right hand to the chords in the left hand.

In comparison, the Chopin prelude heard earlier (Example 4.11) seems, on the most immediate level, very discontinuous, proceeding in fits and starts. Yet the overall impression, created primarily by the restless unstable harmony, is that the music never really stops at the breaks—that it synaptically flows onward until the final cadence.

You can also compare the Chopin prelude with the stylistically different Schoenberg piece (Example 4.21). Both have a continuously onward impulse despite clear caesuras. Both have a rhythmic and me-

The whole evolves dramatically and organically out of its initial fragment.

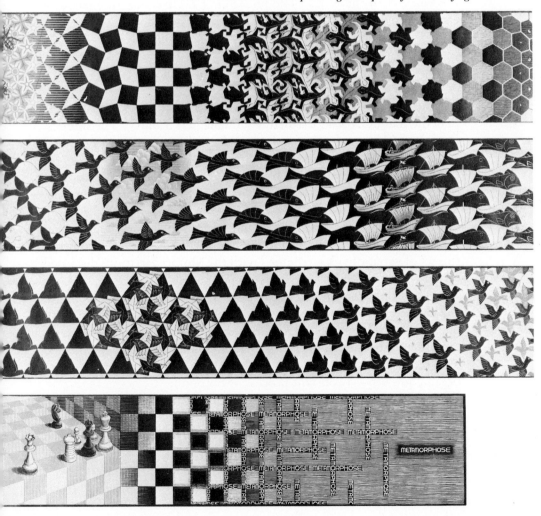

lodic freedom which gives them an improvisatory air; yet both grow unceasingly out of the initial motivic material, which undergoes almost magical transformation. Continuous pieces like these (see also the Webern piece, Example 4.8) often gain their unique coherence through just such continuous development of a germinal motive.

John Lewis's piece *Django* (Example 4.22) has at least one point of similarity with the Schubert *Impromptu,* that is, a seemingly continuous surface above a less immediately apparent sectional substructure. The piece begins with the shared statement of a melody by vibraphone ("vibes"), piano, and bass—slow and without a steady beat at first, then gradually picking up the tempo. With the entrance of the drums (played with brushes), we proceed to a series of improvised "choruses" by first the vibes, then the piano. The underlying substructure (the basis for each improvised chorus) might be diagramed as follows:

$$a \quad a \quad b \quad a' \quad c \quad \text{sections}$$
$$6 \quad 6 \quad 8 \quad 4 \quad 8 \quad \text{number of bars (measures)}$$

Though 32 bars in length, this is more complex and harder to hear than the traditional *a a b a* structure (cf. Chapters 3 and 5). The signpost for *b* is the repeated note in the bass (called a "pedal"); that for *c* a "bluesy" theme in the bass.

There are three choruses by the vibes followed by a brief **codetta** (Italian, *coda + etta,* "little tail") leading into two choruses by the piano. The group slows down in the *c* section of the last piano chorus, leading into the restatement of the opening theme and conclusion. (The excerpt includes only the three choruses by the vibes.) You might compare this set of variations on a "theme" with the Mozart variations discussed earlier (Example 4.13).

Listen now to the Bach aria heard previously as Example 3.20, and characterized as follows: "After the instrumental introduction, with one brief vocal interpolation, the melody moves continuously forward, growing out of itself. There is no periodic phrase structure established by a series of related, regularly recurring goals. The effect is one of organic growth—a constant process of becoming."

While we were speaking there of only one aspect of organization, *melody,* you can now hear how a continuous melody tends to generate a continuous structure, which is further reinforced by homogeneity of texture and singleness of theme.

Example 4.23, the beginning of Stravinsky's *Le Sacre du printemps,* has no caesuras. Paradoxically static and in motion at the same time, its feeling might be characterized as one of dynamic stasis. There is a gradual build-up to a climax: Beginning with a solo bassoon in its upper register, Stravinsky gradually adds more and more instruments (predominantly winds) until the loud muted trumpets bring us to the peak. The solo bassoon then ends the excerpt as it began. Changes in sonority and texture create a sense of kaleidoscopic motion, yet the motion is inhibited by the persistence of a few melodic and rhythmic fragments.

You might go back now and listen again to two pieces heard earlier in the chapter (Examples 4.2 and 4.8). They are both relatively continuous pieces without a return. The Bach prelude is a kind of perpetual motion piece until the freer, more improvisatory closing; there are, furthermore, no caesuras marked off by conclusive cadences.

In the Webern piece one hears, in contrast, a filigree of sounds so tightly interrelated that, as in the Schoenberg piano piece (Example 4.21), the whole evolves dramatically and organically out of its initial fragment. If you listen to this brief composition several times, you will gradually come to hear more details, more events, and more contrast. At the same time the piece may appear to get longer and even less continuous as your perception of contrast leads you to hear the momentary articulation of structural divisions. Perhaps we will find that *sectional* and *continuous,* like many other terms used to describe music, do not define discrete and unvarying characteristics of an entire work but rather *tendencies* toward which a work or moments of a work seem to lean.

ADDITIONAL MATERIALS

The examples in Demonstration 4.1 were chosen primarily as illustrations of the difference between sectional and continuous structure. We can now consider some of these examples and several additional ones more deeply in order to perceive the individual aspects of works and at the same time become aware of further general aspects of musical design. Consider the following questions carefully in relation to all the works in this section.

1. Does the piece divide into larger sections which are readily perceived?
2. Within these larger sections, is the structure basically sectional or continuous?
3. Does a schematic representation of the piece, such as ABA, come readily to mind?
4. If there are no clearly defined sections, what creates structure?

5. What defines or marks off sections?
6. What is the relationship among sections?
7. What are the sources of contrast? Of unity?

I   Listen again to the following two pieces, both of which were included
in Demonstration 4.1:

> Schubert, *Ländler,* Op. 171, no. 4, 1823 (Example 4.12)
> Bach, *Two-Part Invention in F Major,* no. 8, 1723 (Example 4.16)

In Demonstration 4.1 Schubert's work illustrated a sectional piece;
Bach's illustrated a continuous one. The two pieces are superficially
similar in that each has a point of arrival—a caesura—dividing it into
two parts. Nevertheless, they operate on fundamentally different structural principles. Schubert's piece has a melody-and-accompaniment
texture; it proceeds in clear, four-measure phrases—two phrases in Part
A, two in Part B—creating two equal halves. The relationship between
the first two phrases is rather different from the relationship between
the second two phrases. The first two are essentially antecedent and
consequent phrases. What generates the sense of tension in the third
phrase, and why do we have almost a sense of return—at least return
to stability—in the concluding phrase?

Bach's invention, on the other hand, is a *polyphonic* piece which
begins imitatively and continues with an active texture in which the
two parts, though similar melodically, retain their rhythmic independence throughout. This rhythmic independence does not allow for the
kind of clear, balanced phrase structure heard in the Schubert *Ländler*
(which, in fact, defined it as sectional). Why? When one part momentarily pauses, the other, pursuing its own path, continues on to *its*
goal. Each part overrides the caesura of the other, creating an unceasing
onward flow.

The continuous flow is finally interrupted with a caesura (not,
however, exactly at the midpoint, where it came in Schubert's piece,
but only one-third of the way through). Following the caesura, the
opening imitation reappears, but not in the tonic key of the piece and
without a strong sense of return to the opening—it is merely another
phase in the continuous development of the initial figure. (Can you
hear how Bach exploits motives from that figure throughout the piece?)

The last portion of the invention is exactly the same (except in
a different key) as the part before the caesura, yet we do not hear this
repetition as a return. Why? Primarily because the "return" does not
begin with a clear statement of the theme. As the passage continues,
however, it emerges as a restatement of the opening portion of the

piece up to the caesura—but *without* the characteristic theme with which the movement began. Bach creates a return of *becoming* rather than an abrupt, announced one. It is, in short, a return consistent with the continuous nature of the piece as a whole.

II   Listen to and compare the following two pieces. You heard the Haydn minuet as Example 1.29; however, now we ask you to consider its organization on a larger scale.

> Mozart, *German Dance,* K. 605, no. 1, 1791
> Haydn, *Symphony 99,* minuet, 1793 (Example 1.29)

The *German Dance,* like the Mozart minuet in Example 4.10, illustrates a clear ABA′ structure. A and B in turn are divided into ‖:*a*:‖:*b* + *a*′:‖, while A′ is the same as A without repeats. The Haydn minuet could be schematically diagramed in exactly the same way, yet it is a much larger, more imposing work. What happens within A and B to sustain the greatly expanded proportions? Notice, for example, that while the *a* section of the *German Dance* is a simple two-phrase, antecedent-consequent statement, the *a* section of the Haydn minuet is only one-third complete at the end of its opening antecedent-consequent statement. (Example 1.29 comprises only this *a* section.) It continues on to a section which generates more tension and ends with a closing passage which is more stable. What causes these differences in effect? How does *b* differ from *a*, how is the return to *a*′ effected, and what surprising events occur in this return? A careful study of the Haydn minuet should give you an appreciation of its composer's genius in generating out of very simple musical material a work filled with contrasts. It is a stylized dance, but it also has suspense, humor, and climax—all making a tightly packed, eminently satisfying whole. (This minuet is discussed again in Chapter 6.)

III   The following are large complex pieces, a detailed discussion of which would require many pages. Listen to them on your own, for they will provide invaluable experience in coming to grips with extended works. Ask the seven questions listed at the beginning of the Additional Materials as you listen to each piece.

> Purcell, *Dido and Aeneas,* "Dido's Lament," 1689
> Wagner, *Tristan and Isolde,* prelude, 1857–1859
> Handel, *Concerto Grosso,* Op. 6, no. 2, c. 1734 (Example 1.31)
> Mozart, *Sonata for Piano in F,* K. 332, first movement, 1781–1783

CHAPTER 5

Victor Vasarely, *Oeta*, 1959

Harmony

Constantin Brancusi, *The Kiss,* 1908

THE SUBJECT OF HARMONY has come up several times in previous chapters, but we have reserved the detailed discussion of it until now. Of course, you already have gained a general sense of the important role of harmony as it articulates or even sometimes blurs structural relations. For example, you heard in the Liszt and Wagner excerpts (Examples 3.2 and 3.24) and the Chopin prelude (Example 4.11) how harmony can create a restless mood and consequently a more continuous organization. By contrast, in the discussion of the Mozart sonata theme in Chapter 3 you heard how harmony functions to create phrase boundaries—both complete and incomplete cadences. In that chapter we also discussed scales and their relation to a tonal center which, as you will see, is a fundamental aspect of harmony. Likewise, in Chapter 4 you heard the role that harmony can play in creating return. All these earlier experiences with sound, time, and pitch should help you to understand this crucial aspect of music, one which is, paradoxically, both intuitively familiar but at the same time elusive in its explanation.

DEMONSTRATION 5.1
Harmonic Frameworks
(Sides 7–8)

Harmony is often defined as "the relationship among chords," a *chord* being the sounding together of two or more pitches. We will broaden the meaning to consider harmony as the *basic pitch framework* of a given piece or even a particular kind of music. Indeed, when we speak of sound—the sound of African music or the sound of Renaissance music (as in Chapter 1)—often we are referring to the particular harmonic framework of the style. In addition, when you single out a special moment in some composition and exclaim, "Listen to that sound!" you probably have been attracted by an unusual combination of pitches—a chord—which is somehow unexpected in the context of that piece. Thus harmony has both broad and very detailed, specific implications. It is this dual aspect that often makes harmony difficult to talk about: The context defines the particulars, and the particulars generate the context.

For example, the study of harmony traditionally means the study of *tonal,* or *functional,* harmony—the framework within which most Western composers have worked from about 1650 on into the twentieth century. Most of the music with which you are familiar takes this framework as an assumption, and you tacitly absorb this assumption as a basic means of comprehension. In order to help you become aware of this assumed framework, we begin with some examples in which functional harmony is *not* the underlying basis for coherence—where, in fact, it is not operative.

Possibilities Other Than Functional Harmony

Example	Composer, title	Date
5.1	*Dodoitsu* (Japanese)	18th century
5.2	*Citombe* (East African)	
5.3	*The Moon Shines* (Bulgarian)	

Examples 5.1 and 5.2 are both from non-European cultures. Example 5.1 is a Japanese love song with accompaniment on the **shamisen;** Example 5.2, an East African dance tune played on the **mbira,** or thumb piano, and recorded in Southern Rhodesia. Example 5.3, while from European Bulgaria, does not operate within the pitch framework of functional harmony either. For the people of these areas, this music

Japanese shamisen

African mbira

is as natural, coherent, and meaningful as tonal music is to us. Indeed, Japanese, Africans, or Bulgarians who have grown up singing, playing (often by ear), and listening to music with different assumptions from ours are likely to find our music as incomprehensible as we find theirs. Those who study music of other cultures (*ethnomusicologists*) are able to isolate and describe the various bases of pitch organization which give the music of each culture its particular coherence. In doing so, they reveal a framework that is both systematic and complex. What may appear chaotic to us in the music of other cultures seems so only because we are unaware of another order.

Notice that we are speaking of harmony not so much in terms of chords but in terms of a framework of pitch material and pitch relationships: The selection of pitches from the continuum (see Chapter 3) and the various ways in which these pitches characteristically are combined, either simultaneously or in succession. In this sense a melody like the Japanese song, where there are no chords even in the accompaniment, also establishes and works within a harmonic framework.

While tonality and functional harmony provide the framework

for the music with which we are most familiar in our own Western culture, music before the mid-seventeenth century and after the early twentieth century operates within different harmonic frameworks. The next two examples illustrate music written before and after the central tradition of tonal music in our own culture—a tradition which we usually tend to take for granted.

Example	Composer, title	Date
5.4	Gesualdo, *Dolcissima mia vita*	1611
5.5	Boulez, *Le Marteau sans maître*, "Après l'artisant furieux"	1952–1954

In the Gesualdo example, for instance, you hear chords and chord progressions which sound familiar, but there are moments of unexpected sound or an "odd" progression from one chord to the next (Example 5.4). You sometimes expect certain chords but they don't arrive. This sense of expectation derives exactly from our habitual ways of listening and understanding within a tonal framework. You will also notice an uneasy, slippery quality to the pitch motion—it sometimes seems to lose its direction. In fact, it is precisely this sense of *directed* pitch motion that is most characteristic of tonal harmony. Once this framework has been learned, simply through persistent contact with the music that is most often around us, we take it as a norm—a given. But, as you can hear in this example, it is not always an appropriate set of assumptions; it has not always been the underlying principle of harmonic organization. (We will return in Chapter 8 to the question of what are appropriate assumptions in listening to music composed around the time of Gesualdo.) Notice, too, that Gesualdo at times uses harmony for what is called "word painting." That is, he uses a particular chord as an expressive means to help convey the feelings intended by the words. For example, on the word *morire* (die), you hear a harmony that sounds particularly poignant. You will discover other instances of "word painting" as you listen again to the Gesualdo example and follow the text:

Dolcissima mia vita,	Sweetest love,
A che tardate la bramata aita?	Why do you hold back the desired aid?
Credete forse che'l bel foco ond'ardo	Do you think perhaps my ardor

Sia per finir perchè torcete'l guardo?	Will come to an end, because you avert your face?
Ahi, non fia mai ché brama il mio desire	Alas, this will never be, for I must
O d'amarti o morire.	Either love you or die.

Leaving this pretonal world and skipping over the seventeenth through nineteenth centuries (the age of tonality in the West), listen to Example 5.5, the short movement from Boulez's *Le Marteau sans maître* ("The Hammer Without a Master"). Much of its strangeness in sound results from Boulez's abandonment of the previous tonal framework and his development of other ways of relating pitches to one another. On first or second hearing the piece may seem to be simply without organization—random or chaotic. In fact, it is a highly organized, tightly composed piece, and given sufficient experience you can come to perceive it as such. For the moment, however, the piece can serve to raise questions concerning not only its particular means for creating structure, order, and changing effect, but also those means for creating structure that we take for granted in more familiar music. These examples, together with the ones from other cultures, should make clear, then, that music which depends on functional harmony for its underlying coherence actually belongs to a limited culture and to a limited historical tradition.

In Part Four you will get a more complete sense of the position this tradition occupies in music history. There you will listen to music that was composed during the long period preceding the age of functional harmony as well as to music of more recent times where you will hear signs of a gradual dissolution of functional harmony as the fundamental basis of comprehensibility.

Functional Harmony

With the next examples we ask you to narrow your focus to music that *does* operate within the framework of functional harmony. We will deal first with the contrasts between harmonic stability and instability. Then later in the chapter, when you have had some experience discriminating among these general harmonic functions, we will concentrate on the detailed and specific means that generate them.

Examples 5.6 through 5.12 illustrate three kinds of structural functions that tonal harmony can create: statement, stasis, and waiting. They are grouped together here because each of them depends for its effect on there being a single tonal center in relation to which all the events are heard. That is, each of the excerpts remains in one key. In this broader sense they are all harmonically stable. This broader sense of harmonic stability is reflected in your perception of clear and ordered direction in the music. You have the feeling of knowing where you are and what to expect. With this sense of orientation goes an intuitive awareness of tension and repose—harmonic movement away from the tonic, associated with tension, and harmonic rest when the tonic returns. That is, you can spontaneously recognize when a passage arrives at a point of rest or when it is still moving toward such a point.

Statement Passages

Example	Composer, title	Date
5.6	*Old Blue* (sung by Burl Ives)	
5.7	Weber, *Invitation to the Dance*	1819

In Chapter 3, we described the tonic as the pitch which gives a melody a sense of arrival. The chord which is built on this tonic note—the one which harmonizes, elaborates, or reinforces it—is called the tonic **triad.** We will return to a further discussion of triads in Demonstration 5.2. In Examples 5.6 and 5.7 you will hear only two chords: the tonic chord and, in contrast to it, the dominant chord built on the fifth degree of the scale. As you listen, notice that it is the movement from one to the other—the interaction between them—which creates both movement and rest within the framework of a single tonal center. The tonic always sounds relatively stable; the dominant, by contrast, provides movement away and the expectation of return once again to the tonic and rest. Examples 5.6 and 5.7 then, are straightforward, unambiguous *statements* created by the two basic *harmonic functions,* tonic and dominant, to which the term *functional harmony* most explicitly refers. Listen for the change from one chord to the other—tonic (at rest) and dominant (in motion).

Harmonic Stasis

Example	Composer, title	Date
5.8	Wagner, *Das Rheingold,* prelude	1854
5.9	Beethoven, *Symphony 3,* Op. 55, fourth movement	1803

While Examples 5.6 and 5.7 might be described as *statements* setting forth the stable and complementary relations between tonic and dominant chords, Examples 5.8 and 5.9 can be described as *static*. Both include simply an elaboration of the tonic harmony. But the *harmonic stasis* created by the use of one central chord functions rather differently in each piece. The Wagner example (Example 5.8) is the *beginning* of a dramatic work, and it sets the scene and mood as well as the central tonality. The Beethoven excerpt (Example 5.9) is the *ending* of a whole symphony; it brings the intense, rhythmically active final movement to an extended and solid conclusion.

Waiting Passages

Example	Composer, title	Date
5.10	Bach, *Brandenburg Concerto 5*, first movement	c. 1721
5.11	Tchaikovsky, *Nutcracker Suite*, "Waltz of the Flowers"	1892

Examples 5.10 and 5.11 also make use of only one chord, but the difference between these two examples and Examples 5.8 and 5.9 is crucial, the effect almost opposite. Both Examples 5.10 and 5.11 are built on the dominant harmony in contrast to the tonic chord of Examples 5.8 and 5.9. The result is a sense of tension, but a tension that is clearly directed. You know where you are going tonally, and you sense a continuous build-up as you move unswervingly toward the inevitable goal—the tonic. Such passages, generating *directed tension,* function within the structure of the piece as **waiting passages.**

In the Bach excerpt (Example 5.10) the dominant tone is sounded by the cellos (and bass of the harpsichord) on the first beat of every measure (the first of every eight cello tones). Above this underlying dominant, the chords change every measure. Notice the fast-moving, right-hand harpsichord figures and, especially, the trills in the flute and violin. And experience the resolution of tension with the return of the theme and the long awaited tonic.[1]

Example 5.11, from Tchaikovsky's music for the ballet *Nutcracker,* is almost the essence of a waiting passage. The harpist, playing as a soloist, extends the pitches of the dominant triad with its added seventh

---

[1] This is not the tonic of the piece, but of just this part of the piece.

(called a dominant seventh chord) through time and through the whole range of the instrument. Starting slowly, the passage becomes faster and faster to reach a climax in a sweeping flourish. Slowing down to the "grand pause," it builds expectation as the strings enter playing the tonic triad in the characteristic "oom-pah-pah" waltz accompaniment. As the harpist plays, one can imagine the dancers poised in a gesture of expectation. And as the strings enter with their waltz accompaniment resolving the dominant harmony to the tonic, the dancers also relax into the movements of the waltz that follows.

Despite their differences, Examples 5.6 through 5.11 are similar in that each remains solidly centered in one key. They differ, however, in the particular ways that they do so—that is, in the ways they relate to or even define their respective tonal centers. For instance, in Examples 5.6 and 5.7 the tonic is clearly established through the regular movement between the tonic and its dominant, while in Examples 5.8 and 5.9 the tonal center is affirmed simply by lack of movement—a single chord, which we take to be the *tonic,* stretched out through time- and pitch-space. By contrast, in Examples 5.10 and 5.11 the tonic is affirmed more by its absence than by its presence. Here, the *dominant* harmony is extended through time- and pitch-space, establishing the tonic not by stating it but rather by strongly directing our attention to its imminent arrival.

Of particular importance is your intuitive ability to hear and to feel the differences among these examples even though you may not be able to recognize by their formal names the specific elements and relations that account for these differences. Tonality is, then, a commonly shared, experienced reality—a context for comprehensibility that you know how to work with without "knowing it" in words.

Changing Tonal Centers

Turning now to the next group of examples, your intuitive familiarity with the potential of the tonal context is broadened to include music that moves out of one key into another. Consistent reference to a single tonal center gives way to a broader sense of movement and instability when composers shift the tonal frame of reference itself. Just as you can hear the movement from tonic to dominant chords creating contrast between motion and rest *within* the boundaries of one key, you will hear how the movement *across* tonal boundaries—from the frame of one whole key area to the frame of another whole key area—creates a sense of motion and subsequent rest as tonal movement encompasses a broader scope.

Indeed, we can speak of levels of harmonic movement: *Within* one key, where all chords are heard in relation to a single tonic; and *among* keys, where chords are heard first in relation to one tonal center and then, by a usually significant shift, in relation to another tonal center. Within the larger framework of key relationships, these shifts create contrast, sometimes ambiguity, and often greater intensity. Notice, however, that as with your response to rhythmic conflict (syncopation or shift of meter), your response to these moments of change or ambiguity is predicated on your perceived sense of a norm—in this case a normative "key feeling."

Example	Composer, title	Date
5.12	Schubert, *Quintet in C,* Op. 163, second movement	1828
5.13	Mahler, *Symphony 1,* second movement	1888
5.14	Johann Strauss, *Voices of Spring*	1883
5.15	Tchaikovsky, *Symphony 4,* second movement	1877–1878

Example 5.12, an excerpt from the Schubert *Quintet* (written for string quartet with an added cello) will serve as a transition from the earlier examples that remain clearly centered in one key to this group of tonally shifting examples. As in the passages of directed tension, the harmony in the Schubert quintet creates an effect of searching; but here the search seems endless, and one loses all sense of time. Although the harmony at times wanders, obscuring the tonal frame of reference, it repeatedly approaches a tonic cadence (directed tension), only to go on without reaching resolution. Finally the process is halted, not by arrival but by the appearance of a new element which is equally unstable. We have the feeling of being lost and searching for rest within a world of unending motion.

Vortexes in a stream of water

. . . repeatedly approaches a tonic cadence only to go on without reaching resolution

In Examples 5.13 through 5.15 the composers generate a clear tonal center (a harmonic norm), then move away from it to establish a new tonal center. Such compositional means can create their desired effect only because of your intuitive sense of a tonality as a fundamental framework. Again, you may not be able to point to or label the means each composer uses to create these moments of ambiguity or change, but hopefully you will be able to hear and to sense an appropriate feeling of momentary disorientation as one reference frame (one key) yields to another. While Examples 5.13 through 5.15 all move from one key to another, they do so in different ways. Mahler (Example 5.13) states his motive in one key, then immediately begins again with the same motive but in a new key. There is no transition, only juxtaposition.

In contrast, Example 5.14, an excerpt from Strauss's *Voices of Spring,* has a short but decisive transition which shifts the tonal center. The first two phrases (the second is somewhat extended) are clearly in one key, ending with a cadence on the tonic. This same chord which forms a tonic ending to the first portion is then transformed, through the addition of a pitch "foreign" to the initial key, so that the tonic becomes the dominant in the new key. The extension of this transformed chord—now functioning as a dominant—becomes the harmonic basis for a brief waiting passage that leads to the new melody and to the new tonic.

Putting this process another way, we might say that when the chord that functioned as the chief tonic chord (I) in the first part of the excerpt is dethroned by a "foreign" pitch (belonging, as it does, to a different tribe of pitches), it becomes second in rank (I becomes V) in the new collection of pitches, or new key. This single chord transformed by its "foreign" pitch plays the role of "pivot" between the two tonalities, serving as the central chord of the first tonality and then, when transformed, as the dominant, foreshadowing chord of the second. After a short transition, the excerpt continues with a new melody in the new key. Can you hear the moment of change in this excerpt? Go back and try to sing the tonic during the first two phrases. Then try to sing the new tonic as the excerpt goes into the new melody, which ends (here) on the new tonic chord.

Example 5.15 resembles Example 5.14 in that you hear first one melody, then a transition where the tonal center shifts, and then a waiting passage which functions as a preparation for a new melody in a new key. But in the Tchaikovsky excerpt the transition takes longer. Where Strauss used a relatively abrupt pivot chord, Tchaikovsky moves

Paris, Etoile

A single tonal center . . . clear and ordered direction . . . you have the feeling of knowing where you are.

Boston, downtown area

Tonal ambiguity . . . you lose your sense of orientation and direction.

more gradually from the first tonal area toward another. This process, called a **modulation,** creates a momentary tonal no-man's-land.

Notice that the first melody is heard twice: first played by bassoon and violas, then repeated an octave higher by the strings with added figuration in the winds. This shift in register should not be confused with modulation. In modulation the crucial factor is not a change in register but rather a change in both the fundamental set of pitches being used and the pitch that sounds most stable or central.

If you listen carefully to the excerpt, you will hear the modulation occurring during a sequential passage where each statement of the melodic fragment (♫ ♫ ♩ ♩ ♩) serves to shift and confound your sense of tonal direction. The modulation settles into a waiting passage where you hear the new dominant harmony extended through repetitions of a short melodic figure that again shifts only in register. The motive is played first by the flutes in a high register; then (descending in register) by the clarinet, the horn, and, in an abbreviated version, the violas; and finally by the cellos. The transition to the new key and new melody is very smooth. Your musical vantage point is gently eased from one view of the pitch universe to another.

Chromaticism

Example	Composer, title	Date
5.16	Bach, *Well-Tempered Clavier,* Book I, fugue no. 24 in B minor	1722
5.17	Beethoven, *String Quartet,* Op. 133 (*Grosse Fuge*)	1825–1826
5.18	Liszt, *Faust Symphony,* first movement	1854–1857
5.19	W. Shorter, *Pinocchio* (played by the Miles Davis Quintet)	1967

In Examples 5.16 through 5.19, the tonal no-man's-land which characterized the transition between the two tonally stable statements in Example 5.15 becomes much more extensive—nearly all-pervasive. You hear long passages of tonal ambiguity. You lose the sense of orientation and direction created by the relation of all the pitches and chords to a single, central one—the tonic. Such dramatic moments are generated by the composer's extensive use of pitches that belong to more than one "family" of pitches.

You will remember from Chapter 3 that major or minor scales (sometimes called *diatonic* scales) include a particular subset of the twelve possible pitches. Each of these collections of seven pitches constitutes what we can call a *family,* each family of pitches centering around one particular pitch. There are twelve such families, each centering around one of the twelve possible pitches. Thus the key of C major has C as its tonal center and includes the family of pitches found in the C-major scale. The key of B major has B as its center and includes the family of pitches found in the B-major scale. In these passages of tonal ambiguity composers include pitches from more than one family, sometimes introducing all 12 possible pitches in close succession. In this way they upset your tonal equilibrium but also create a feeling of greater expressiveness as harmonic relationships take on new meaning and are enriched by new, sometimes not yet realized, possibilities. Such passages are described as **chromatic** (from the Greek *chroma,* or "color") because of their use of all or most of the twelve pitches of the chromatic scale in contrast to the seven pitches of a diatonic scale.

Listen, for example, to the Bach excerpt (Example 5.16) which is the first part of a fugue (see Example 1.11 and Chapter 7). It begins with a single unaccompanied melody, called the fugue **subject.** Try to sing the melody. You will probably find it difficult because while it begins with the pitches of the tonic triad, the subject quickly introduces all twelve tones of the chromatic scale and also modulates from the initial B minor to the key of F-sharp minor.

Example 5.16 BACH, *Well-Tempered Clavier,* Book I, fugue no. 24

A second part then enters with essentially the same melody (though starting on a different tone), then a third, and finally a fourth part at the top of the texture. The very active texture complements the harmonically unstable (though periodically resolving) harmony.

Example 5.17, by Beethoven, sounds almost chaotic on first hearing. Harmonically, the excerpt is an example of intense and brilliantly composed chromaticism. At moments you can hear rapidly shifting tonal centers, but at times tonality seems to be nearly obliterated. Listen to the example several times. As you listen pay attention to the repetition of rhythmic and melodic motives. These repetitions, even though embedded in an intensely active texture, will provide an initial basis through which to grasp the unique coherence of this remarkable passage.

The beginning of Liszt's *Faust Symphony* (Example 5.18) was discussed in Chapter 3 in the context of melodies different from those we are used to. There we commented on the continuousness of the opening created in part by its ambiguous rhythmic structure and also by the particular relationships among the pitches of the melody. We can now make these relationships more explicit. The three-note motive itself confounds your sense of tonal center. The pitches in the three-note motive are equidistant from one another, each separated by two whole steps. Together the three pitches of the motive form an **augmented triad**—a triad that does not exist within the family of pitches belonging to any one major scale (see Ancillary Reading for this chapter). In turn, each new statement of the motive begins one half step lower than the previous one, the four statements together forming a *chromatically* descending sequence which includes all twelve pitches of the chromatic scale.

Example 5.18 LISZT, *Faust Symphony,* opening theme

The transformations of this germinal motive form the fundamental material for the rest of the passage. Note the elusiveness of the beat and meter, the large range, the big melodic leaps (often contrasted with half-step motion), and the limpid sound of solo woodwinds or of strings playing in unison. The diabolical character of the piece (Faust makes a pact with the devil) can be directly related to these rhythmic, melodic, and sound relationships as well as to the continuously moving and shifting tonal framework.

Jazz, like "classical" music in the nineteenth century, became increasingly chromatic through the sixties, as can be seen in Example 5.19. Here, in a piece by the tenor saxophonist Wayne Shorter, Miles Davis on trumpet and Shorter play a highly chromatic theme in unison. While its phrase structure is still somewhat regular (8 + 10 bars), note that the melody is not easy to sing; listen also to the "dissonant" chords in the piano. Where is the tonic? The place of rest? Yet how different it is from the previous three chromatic examples (and from the other

Miles Davis playing the trumpet

jazz pieces later on in the chapter). Why? Obviously instrumentation and rhythm are crucial factors in this difference.

While Examples 5.16 through 5.19 are all highly chromatic, each composer in his own way pushing the limits of tonality, they still depend on the broad framework of tonal functions for their intense dramatic effect. But in retrospect, the Liszt *Faust Symphony* and other works by Liszt's contemporaries in the mid-nineteenth century can be seen as making initial moves towards the total chromaticism that composers embraced in the early twentieth century. Through this extension of chromaticism, tonality as a fundamental frame of reference essentially disappears. The excerpt you heard from Boulez's *Le Marteau sans maître,* Example 5.5 written in the early 1950s, almost exactly 100 years after the *Faust Symphony,* is an example of music composed after the dissolution of tonality. In this music tonality is no longer taken to be a norm, a "given" for constructing coherent harmonic relations. We will return to the practical implications of these issues in Part Four: In particular, to the gradual change in stylistic norms that occurred during the 100-year period between the mid-nineteenth century and the mid-twentieth century.

Structural Functions of Harmony

Example	Composer, title	Date
5.20	Chopin, *Étude,* Op. 10, no. 3	1832

In the Chopin *Étude* (*étude* means "study," and this is one of many Chopin wrote for the piano) we hear a piece with the familiar ABA′ structure—statement, contrasting middle section, and return. But in this piece (Example 5.20) Chopin creates contrast by dramatically introducing chromatic harmony into an initially straightforward tonal setting. The piece begins with two statements of the opening melody accompanied in the lower part (played by the pianist's left hand) by a somewhat syncopated repeated rhythmic figure. The second statement reaches a brief climax and then subsides into a cadence on the tonic.

The middle section begins slightly faster as the piece becomes somewhat more agitated. This increase in intensity is created also by movement away from the stable tonality. Chopin passes through several new key areas repeating the same musical material in each one. This is followed by a slow build-up to the climax of the whole *Étude.* In the process we lose all sense of clear melody as the pianist plays only chords; at the same time we lose all sense of tonal center as the harmony becomes highly chromatic. The chords are themselves ambiguous; neither major nor minor, they seem to defy direction or specific implications for resolution.[2] In addition, Chopin repeats the same ambiguous chord in continuously ascending and descending chromatic steps, up and down the piano keyboard.

The grand climax subsides as the tempo again slows down, and we hear hints of the initial melodic material. The harmonic motion once more becomes clear and directed as Chopin arrives at and extends the dominant harmony to create a waiting passage—a preparation for

---

[2] Like the successive pitches in the Liszt melody, these chords are made up of simultaneously sounding pitches separated by equal intervals. They are called *diminished seventh chords* (see Ancillary Reading), where each pitch of the chord is a minor third away from each other pitch. Interestingly, this is the chord often used in the past in movies when the situation gets frightening or dangerous—most typically when the "bad guy" enters the scene.

return. Harmonic tension is finally resolved as we return to the opening melodic material harmonized by the tonic chord calmly alternating with its dominant, each reaffirming the other. The *Étude* concludes with a quiet cadence on the tonic chord which is briefly extended as the melody also descends to the tonic note.

This *Étude* is a beautiful example of the use of harmony to create *structural* functions—statement, ambiguity and climax, waiting, and return. Each of these structural functions is largely dependent for its effect on the *harmonic* functions defined by the network of relations we call tonality. While its workings may seem complex when analyzed and spelled out in words, it is a kind of "grammar" that everyone in our culture seems to learn and respond to as spontaneously (and remarkably) as the grammar of our own spoken language. We will return to the structural functions of harmony in Demonstration 5.3.

DEMONSTRATION 5.2
Fundamentals of
Tonal Harmony

Now that you have had some experience listening to relations within (and without) tonal harmony, we ask you to consider in greater detail factors that generate these tonal relationships. Unfortunately, constraints on recording space-time limit us to discussion only here. It is important therefore that you go back and listen to the examples in Demonstration 5.1 again as well as those which follow in order to bring to life the theoretical discussion in this Demonstration.

The basic building block of tonal harmony is the **triad.** A triad is a chord made up of three tones (*tri*-ad). Strictly speaking, a triad is a chord built up in a particular way from its lowest tone called the **root.** The term *root* derives from the notion of a root-tone from which the triad grows. More exactly, the root of a triad is the note which the triad elaborates, reinforces, or extends. A triad can be built on any degree of the scale, each triad elaborating that particular degree:

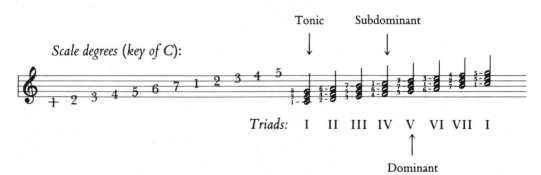

The triad is built by adding to its root the pitches which lie a third and fifth above it in the scale. For example, the tonic triad, or I, is built on the scale degree 1. Its root is the tonic note and above it are added the third and fifth degrees of the scale. The dominant triad, or V, is built on the scale degree 5. Its root is the fifth degree and above it are added the seventh and second (or ninth) degrees of the scale. (Notice that scale degrees are represented by arabic numerals while triads are represented by roman numerals.) The notated triad when in root position (that is, with the root pitch as its lowest tone) forms a pattern of notes all of which are either on lines or in spaces.

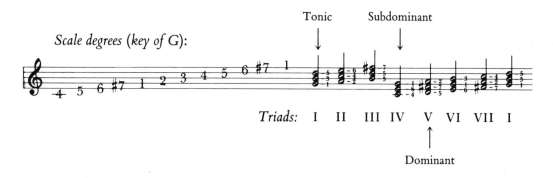

As you have heard (Examples 5.6 and 5.7), the tonic and dominant triads, along with the subdominant triad built on the scale degree 4, form the pillars of tonality. Notice that the root of the V chord is an interval of a fifth *above* the I chord while the root of the IV chord is an interval of a fifth *below* the I chord (giving it the name **subdominant,** meaning *under-*dominant). It is the relationships among chords as they progress from one to the next that establishes our sense of tonal center. Any triad by itself is ambiguous in its tonal function or meaning. Only when we hear two or more triads can we be sure which one is the most stable—the one to which we will give the name *tonic.* It is these relationships, then, which establish a particular tonal context, the *key.*

Throughout the book we have emphasized the importance of context in giving meaning to an event. In discussing sound and texture we heard how the same melody can sound quite different when embedded in a new sound context (Examples 1.8 through 1.11, for instance). In discussing melody we noticed that the same motive or figure could sound quite different when it occurred at a different place in a tune and with a different function. For example, the same motive which *ends* the first phrase of *Lassie* ("... a lassie, a lassie") sounds different when it functions as the *beginning* of the *b* section ("Go this way and that way"). In similar fashion the same chord will sound quite different when embedded in different tonal environments. The name given to a triad—tonic, dominant—names its harmonic function. However, the same triad can assume different functions when embedded in different harmonic (tonal) contexts. For example, the C triad will be called the tonic when it functions as the most stable chord in the key of C. But it will function as the dominant, and be labeled as such, when heard in the key of F, and as the subdominant when it is heard in relation to G as tonic:

Key of C:				I	2	3	IV	V	6	7	1		I	= Tonic
Key of G:	1	2	3	IV	V	6	7	I					IV	= Subdominant
Key of F:	1	2	3	IV	V	6	7	I					V	= Dominant

In listening to music we respond most readily to these tonal functions—for example, the sense of waiting and its associated tension in Examples 5.10 to 5.12, where we hear predominantly dominant-function chords, in contrast to Examples 5.8 and 5.9, where we hear predominantly tonic-function chords. In fact, two triads that have the same function but different pitches (two tonics) may sound more similar than two triads that have exactly the same pitches but different functions. It is precisely this chameleon-like quality of chords to take on meaning according to their harmonic environment that makes it possible for composers to shift or slide so smoothly from one key to another. For example, in the Strauss *Voices of Spring* (Example 5.14), a single triad functions at one moment as the tonic and in the next moment as the dominant.

The word *function* is used in several different but interrelated ways in this chapter and in music theory generally. To help prevent understandable confusion about the use of this word, two distinct uses of it should be clarified. In Demonstration 5.1 we used the word *function* to refer to the *structural functions* of certain passages (statement, stasis, waiting). The structural function of a passage, then, can be described as the particular role the passage plays in a whole piece. (We will return to this sense of structural function in Chapter 6.) In this Demonstration we are speaking of the *harmonic function* of a particular chord within the framework of a given tonality. The interaction between two chords, the movement from one to the other, usually defines the function of each. For example, hearing one chord (perhaps a C chord) in juxtaposition with another chord (a G chord) allows us to label one (C) as tonic and the other (G) as dominant. It is a reciprocal relation, like friendship or an argument—you need a two-way interaction to define each member.

There is an important connection between structural functions and harmonic functions. A passage which functions as a statement within a piece will often include only tonic and dominant harmonic functions. Thus, the two uses of the word are related like means and ends: The use of only tonic and dominant harmonic functions is a means toward the end of creating a passage which has a stable structural function within the piece as a whole. This relation of means and ends will be developed at greater length in Demonstration 5.3 (see also the discussion of the Chopin étude on p. 175).

Returning now to the fundamentals of tonal harmony, notice that the interval of a fifth plays a special role within this framework. Its importance can be seen on the smallest and the largest levels of musical structure. For example, the triad, the basic element of the harmonic framework, is outlined or bounded by the interval of a fifth. Chords whose roots are related by fifths (IV-I-V) are pillars within a tonality, they establish the *key* of a piece (in many ways, the key *to* the piece). Fifths also define the harmonic "distance" *among* keys. For instance, keys related by the interval of a fifth (C-G-D, and so forth) are most closely related because their pitch collections differ only by one pitch. The so-called circle of fifths shows the harmonic distance among all the keys (see p. 131 for a picture of the circle of fifths). Any two keys next to one another around the circle are most closely related; they share six pitches and four triads in common.

This relationship among the most closely related keys can be seen quite clearly when you notice, first, that the sequence of intervals for any major scale is identical in both its top and bottom halves.

Scale degrees: 1 2 3 4 5 6 7 8

Intervals: 1 1 ½   1 1 ½

As a result, the top half of a scale in one key can also serve as the bottom half of a scale in another key. For example, the top half of the C-major scale (G A B C) is also the bottom half of the G-major scale. In turn, the bottom half of the C-major scale (C D E F) is the top half of the F-major scale. The diagram below shows the network of over-lapping scales. Notice that each scale overlaps with two other scales related to it by the omnipotent fifth.

Bb   C   D

Eb F G Ab Bb C D Eb F G A Bb C D E F G A B C D E F♯ G A B C♯ D E F♯ G♯ A

Eb   F   G   A

Interestingly, a major scale can also be described in terms of fifth relationships. Starting on any pitch and proceeding up by fifths, you will accumulate all the pitches of the major scale that is the second element in this series:

C Ⓖ D A E B F♯   or   G A B C D E F♯ G

F Ⓒ G D A E B   or   C D E F G A B C

G Ⓓ A E B F♯ C♯   or   D E F♯ G A B C♯ D

In terms of harmonic functions, this description is actually more re-vealing than the usual "layout" of the scale where pitches are simply arranged from lowest to highest. That is, when pitches are ordered by fifths, the spatial ordering also reflects closeness of harmonic relations. For example, in the key of G, the pitches, C, G, and D are the most central and the triads built up from them are the most closely related harmonically. Described in this way, the pitch collection within any one key can be seen as a kind of microcosm of the larger intersecting network of key relations.

Composers make use of closely related keys to create both unity and variety in larger pieces. For example, at the end of the *a* section of a minuet (see Chapter 6) there is often a *modulation* to the closely related key of the dominant—that is, from C to G or from A to E and so forth. The change in tonal center creates variety while still maintaining unity through the shared pitches and triads among these closely related keys. Similarly, the second group in the exposition of a sonata form movement is usually in the key of the dominant (see Chapter 6); the second entrance of the subject in a fugal exposition is also in the dominant (see Chapter 7). Finally, most folk songs and much of jazz and rock use primarily I, IV, and V chords to harmonize their melodies. In Demonstration 5.4 you will hear a number of twelve-bar blues. A particular sequence of I, IV, and V chords forms the harmonic skeleton for all of them.

Having set forth some of the general aspects of the tonal framework, we list below further components and possibilities composers and performers use to flesh out or expand these basic tonal relationships.

Inversion: A rearrangement of the pitches of a triad so that the root is no longer the lowest tone:

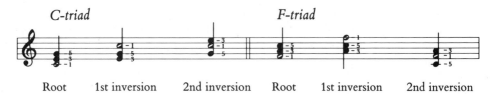

C-triad   *F-triad*

Root   1st inversion   2nd inversion   Root   1st inversion   2nd inversion

Rameau, an eighteenth-century composer and theorist, was the first to observe systematically that even when the pitches of a given root position triad are rearranged (as in an inversion), the resulting chord can still be considered "the same" as when it is in root position. That is, it was Rameau who developed a theoretical framework in which this rearrangement of the same pitches could be considered an inversion of a single, fundamental chord. Along with this came Rameau's systematic description of triads in terms of their root functions— that is, the use of roman numerals to represent the harmonic function of a chord in terms of its root. The illustration above shows you the three possible positions or rearrangements of a triad. Notice that inversions allow composers to create contrast even *within* a single triad or harmonic function. For example, a I chord in first inversion will be somewhat less stable, less solidly I than the same chord in root position. In the Haydn minuet from the *Symphony 100,* for instance (see the score on p. 190), only root position chords are used in the opening statement section (except for one inversion in measure 7). Later, in the *b* section where Haydn begins to develop his material, we find him also using more inversions—in measure 18, for example, where we hear an inversion on a strongly accented event.

Arpeggio, *or* **Broken Chord:** The notes of a triad played one after the other rather than played simultaneously:

A triad can be animated or stretched out through time and pitch-space in this fashion. A good example of this stretching out of a triad is the opening of Wagner's opera, *Das Rheingold* (Example 5.8). You hear first simply a single, long sustained tone played by the string basses, and then gradually the other pitches of the triad emerge over this initial root tone. The whole passage is an extension of that root tone through its triad. In the next example (Example 5.9) you hear Beethoven stretching out the closing tonic triad over several octaves and considerable time to bring the movement to a resounding close. On a much more detailed level, broken chords are often used as the basis for common accompaniment figures. For example, in the minuet from Haydn's *Symphony 100* again, the second violins and cellos play a broken chord figure in measures 9 and 10. In this way Haydn creates a more animated version of the opening passage found in measures 1 and 2 where the same tonic triad is played as a simple chord, a group of simultaneously sounding tones.

Full Cadence: The progression from the dominant chord to the tonic chord at the end of a phrase.

Half Cadence: The use of the dominant chord at the end of a phrase. For example, in the song *Old Blue* (Example 5.6) the first phrase ends with a half cadence ("... and his name was Blue"). The word *Blue* is harmonized by a V chord. The second phrase ("And I betcha five dollars he's a good one, too") ends with a full cadence. The entire second phrase is harmonized by the V chord followed by the I chord on the last word, *too*. The contrast between full and half cadences is usually quite obvious since the full cadence sounds more complete and more stable than the half cadence which sounds incomplete and less stable. See also the discussion of phrase structure and cadences in Chapter 3, especially the discussion of the Mozart piano sonata theme. The exercise on full and half cadences (pp. 186–189) will give you practice in hearing the difference between the two kinds of cadences, and perhaps more importantly, give you some good, clear examples of what the terms refer to.

Consonance *and* **Dissonance:** The terms *consonance* and *dissonance* refer most specifically to the relationships between two pitches—the interval formed by the two pitches. In traditional tonal theory intervals are classified as either consonant or dissonant (although the classification has changed through the course of history, along with changing musical styles). For example, intervals of a third, fifth, sixth, and octave are usually considered consonant, while intervals of a second, fourth, and seventh are usually considered dissonant. (For further discussion of intervals see the Ancillary Reading for Chapters 3 and 5.)

However, the terms also refer more generally to harmonic movement within the context of a particular piece or even a particular style. This usage of the terms is much more difficult to define. A description of its meaning (rather than a definition) must include the notion that consonances tend to be stable, even conclusive, while dissonances tend to be dynamic, in need of resolution. This more general sense of consonant and dissonant is related to another use of the terms which is widespread but often misapplied. With this usage the term consonant tends to be associated with "pleasing," while dissonant is associated with "disagreeable," "harsh," or even "incoherent." For example, to describe a whole piece as sounding dissonant or sometimes "unharmonious," is to refer, most likely, to its general harmonic framework when that framework is something other than a tonal one. You might be tempted, for instance, to call the Boulez piece (Example 5.5) dissonant. In terms of tonal harmony it does, in fact, make use of traditionally dissonant intervals and few simple triads. But, as we have pointed out, the means Boulez uses for creating contrasts in stability and instability are not based on the assumptions of tonal or functional harmony. Thus, to describe the whole piece as dissonant is to describe it in terms of a harmonic framework which does not apply. Further, the description will tend to befog the underlying bases for comprehensibility and coherence which Boulez and other twentieth-century composers have established. (See Chaper 11 for more on this.)

Transposition: The process of rewriting a melody (or a whole passage) so as to keep the successive relationships the same but making use of a different set of absolute pitches. Or putting it another way, if we play a melody in the key of C and play the same melody in the key of B, we will keep the intervals between pitches the same and the scale degrees the same but these same numbers will now refer to different pitches. For example, *Lassie* begins with a broken tonic triad—the scale degrees 1-3-5, followed by 6, and then a return to the starting tonic 5-4-3-1, again basically outlining the tonic triad. No matter what pitch we begin with, as long as we agree that it is the tonic, thus calling it 1, the subsequent scale degrees will be the same. However, if we name the pitches, instead of the scale degrees, we will find that the two versions of the same tune look different. Thus a transposed melody is both the same (in interval relations) and different (in actual pitches) from its initial statement:

Lassie:	1-	3-	5-	6-	5-	4-	3-	1
C:	C-	E-	G-	A-	G-	F-	E-	C
B:	B-	D♯-	F♯-	G♯-	F♯-	E-	D♯-	B
F:	F-	A-	C-	D-	C-	B♭-	A-	F

Scale degrees (key of C):

1 3 5 6 5 4   3 1 1   2 5 5   3 1 1 3 5 6 5 4   3 1 1   2 5 5 1   5 6 (7) 1 2 3 4 5 6 7 1

Pitch material reordered:

Tonic Dominant

Scale degrees (key of B):

1 3   5 6 5 4   3 1 1   2 5 5   3 1 1 3 5 6 5 4   3 1 1   2 5 5 1   5 6 (7) 1 2 3 4 5 6 7 1

Tonic   Dominant

If one were actually to write this melody in B major, the sharps would be assimilated into the key signature as shown here:

EXERCISE 5.1
Major and Minor; Full and
Half Cadences
(Side 8)

This exercise has a somewhat different purpose from Exercise 4.1. The earlier exercise was intended as an initial step toward your discovery of structure. This exercise, coming after you have had some experience with musical organization (return, sectional and continuous structure, and harmony), is intended simply to give you practice in hearing two rather specific aspects of harmony: (1) major and minor modes, and (2) phrases which end either on the tonic (full cadence) or on the dominant (half cadence).

Major and Minor

In Chapter 3 (p. 111 and Ancillary Reading) we briefly discussed the difference between the major and minor modes. You may remember that the essential difference between the two modes lies in the third degree of the scale: While the third degree is a *major* third above the tonic (two whole steps) in the major mode, it is a *minor* third above the tonic (a whole step plus a half step) in the minor mode. Or, putting it more simply, the third degree of the scale is a half step closer to the tonic in the minor mode than it is in the major mode. The tonic *triad,* which involves this third degree, is therefore also different in major and minor. The Ancillary Reading sections for Chapter 3 and for this chapter show the various forms of minor scales as well as the resultant triads.

Tonic triad in C major   Tonic triad in C minor

The following exercises (Examples 5.21 to 5.26) will give you some practice in distinguishing between pieces in the major and minor modes. While pieces in major and minor do indeed sound different, no rules can be given for acquiring the ability to distinguish between them; we might compare the problem to finding rules for distinguishing between red and pink. In fact, the difference between major and minor is like a change in the color of a tonality, for it is not a change in the key, or of the tonal center itself. (The effect of the major mode is sometimes associated with "happy" in contrast to the minor mode, which may be heard as "sad.") Learning to distinguish between colors or between modes comes basically from experience and practice. In the case of the modes, it is useful to be able to *hear* the difference (particularly as a source of contrast within a piece). Naming that difference is simply a way of focusing your attention on it.

Listen to each example and determine whether the piece is in the major or minor mode, or whether it changes from one to the other during its course. (Correct Answers can be found on p. 188.)

Example	Major	Minor	Major → Minor	Minor → Major
5.21				
5.22				
5.23				
5.24				
5.25				
5.26				

Full and Half Cadences

In this group of examples (Examples 5.27 to 5.32) you are asked to discriminate between phrases which end on the tonic (I)—a full cadence—and phrases which end on the dominant (V)—a half cadence. The significant factor in this perception is the feeling of stability or completion in the full cadence in contrast with that of incompletion or of being left suspended in the half cadence. You should go back and refer to the discussion of the Mozart sonata theme in Chapter 3 where this distinction was illustrated through melodic aspects alone. However, melody and harmony are inextricably interrelated in tonal music; thus the sense of incompleteness of an antecedent phrase usually results from the absence of the tonic in both melody and harmony at the cadence, while the consequent phrase ends solidly on the tonic.[3]

---

[3] But see also the discussion of *Lassie* in Chapter 3.

Guitarists know about the two chords I and V, usually either in D major (D = I, A = V) or A major (A = I, E = V). A song like *Clementine,* for example, uses only these two chords: Beginning on the tonic, reaching the dominant on "Clemen-TINE," staying there until

V

"for-GOT-ten," then to V and back to I at the end. In general, it is

I

important to remember that while a piece need not begin with the tonic harmony it almost always ends with it.

Listen to each of the examples and determine if the excerpt ends on the tonic (full cadence) or on the dominant (half cadence). (Correct Answers can be found on page 189.)

Example	Tonic (I)	Dominant (V)
5.27		
5.28		
5.29		
5.30		
5.31		
5.32		

CORRECT ANSWERS

Example	Composer, title, date	Major	Minor	Major → Minor	Minor → Major
5.21			X		
5.22	Mozart, *Sonata for Piano in A,* K. 331, first movement, 1781–1783	X			
5.23	Mozart, *Sonata for Piano in A,* K. 331, first movement, 1781–1783		X		
5.24	Beethoven, *Violin Concerto,* Op. 61, first movement, 1806			X	
5.25	Schumann, *Album for the Young,* "The Wild Horseman," 1848				X
5.26	Schubert, *Die Schöne Müllerin,* "Tränenregen" ("Rain of Tears"), 1823			X	

CORRECT ANSWERS

Example	Composer, title, date	Tonic (I)	Dominant (V)
5.27	Brahms, *Variations on a Theme by Haydn,* Op. 56a, 1873	X[a]	
5.28	Haydn, *Symphony 104,* first movement, 1795		X[a]
5.29	Beethoven, *Septet,* Op. 20, third movement, 1800	X	
5.30	M. Reynolds, *Little Boxes* (sung by Pete Seeger), 1962		X
5.31	Bach, *Suite in B Minor,* minuet, c. 1740		X[a]
5.32	Schubert, *Die Schöne Müllerin,* "Der Muller und der Bach" ("The Miller and the Brook"), 1823	X	

[a] Phrases do not end on the first beat of the measure.

DEMONSTRATION 5.3
Harmony: Structural
Functions
(Side 8)

We will now turn to a Haydn minuet (Example 5.33) in order to show how harmony serves various structural functions. The written material requires very close reading, and even more important, the analysis demands that you listen very closely to the music. You should go back and play the examples a number of times. The score is printed on the following pages, and will aid you in the discussion.

Example	Composer, title	Date
5.33	Haydn, *Symphony 100,* third movement, minuet	1794
5.34	*a* section of minuet	
5.35	*a'* section	
5.36	*b* section	
5.37	*b* section (measures 17–35)	
5.38	*b* section with artificially imposed return	
5.39	*b* section with return as Haydn wrote it	

The overall structure can be diagramed as follows: *a   a'*‖:*b* + *a"*:‖ It is essentially an expanded version of the structure heard in the Mozart *Eine kleine Nachtmusik* minuet (Example 4.10). In this Haydn minuet,

Example 5.33 HAYDN, *Symphony 100,* third movement (minuet)

of Phrase 1); in *b* this same chord has become a tonic, and we speak of being *in* the dominant key. We have modulated from G to D (cf. Example 5.15), and Phase 1 is our "tonal no-man's-land."

It is important to notice, here, that it is the close relationship between the *feeling* projected by a passage and its intended structural function within the piece that makes the organic musical process work effectively. That is, both *feeling* and *function* result from Haydn's ingenious use of harmonic, textural, and motivic means. For example, the brief passage we have called Phase 1 creates a feeling of instability or flux. The same musical means also make the passage function as a moment of contrast and development within the organic process of the piece as a whole. Haydn is expanding the previous tonal universe, moving out and beyond the harmonic limits of the original key. In Phases 2 and 3 the feeling of flux gives way to one of directed tension (Phase 2), and then to a feeling of momentary rest (Phase 3). In turn, Phase 2 plays the role of a waiting passage "setting up" the move to a new tonal area, while Phase 3 functions to affirm the tonal broadening directly implied by the previous Phase 2. Phase 4 is perhaps most intriguing as Haydn uses his skill to create ambiguity in both feeling and function. Is this a preparation for return or confirmation of a new key area?

We have hinted that in Phase 4 the new key is not quite solidly established; there is still a certain restlessness—both in rhythm and in key. (Are we *on* the dominant or *in* the dominant?) In any case the dominant (key or chord) must resolve ultimately to the original tonic. Indeed, the return could take place at this point. Listen to how the *b* section would sound if *a* did return after Phase 4 of the *b* section (Example 5.38). Then listen to what Haydn actually does (Example 5.39). What is the difference?

In our artificial return the structural rhythm is speeded up: *b* is shortened and is not allowed to unwind itself gradually. Haydn, in contrast, slips back into *a* through a highly chromatic, unstable passage which even at its end generates a rather fuzzy "waiting passage," Phase 5. Thus, Haydn has composed a kind of musical joke by seeming, albeit somewhat ambiguously, to prepare us for a return at the end of Phase 4 of *b* and then diverting this expectation with the sliding, modulatory, delaying passage which eases back to the tonic key and to the return of the thematic statement of *a*. Our feelings about the return itself are also different in Examples 5.38 and 5.39. The abrupt juxtaposition of *b* and *a* in Example 5.38 simply puts us down into the stability of *a*'s statement; in Example 5.39 the clarity and stability of key, phrase structure, texture, and rhythm in *a″* constitute not only a return to familiar material but a return to the comfort of stability after a period of feeling "Where am I? Where am I going?" In short, Haydn provides us with a more dramatic contrast than exists if we bypass Phase 5.

Listen now to the whole minuet (Example 5.33). You will notice that *a* returns with still further changes in instrumentation and with the addition of a coda. Comparing it with the minuet from Mozart's *Eine kleine Nachtmusik* (Example 4.10), you will notice that this Haydn minuet has a considerably more dramatic effect. While the *b* section of the Mozart remained fixed harmonically and only hinted at a contrast in key area, this minuet, in its considerably lengthened *b* section, introduces modulation into a new key, establishes it (although we have some doubts in retrospect), and then wends its way back to the original key. Thus, the Haydn minuet is more dramatic; as you become aware of its details you respond to its greater variety of emotions over a longer period, but still this is variety on a small scale.

DEMONSTRATION 5.4
The Twelve-Bar Blues
(Side 9)

What I think about that makes the blues really good is when a fellow writes a blues and then writes it with a feeling, with great harmony, and there are so many true words in the blues, of things that have happened to so many people, and that's why it makes the feeling in the blues.[5]

J. D. SHORT

Now that you have had some experience with harmony, both on the level of the individual chord and in larger dimensions, you can listen with new insight to the following group of pieces, all of which are based on a chord progression involving basically only the I (tonic), IV (subdominant), and V (dominant) chords.

Example	Composer, title	Date
5.40	J. Yancey, *How Long Blues*	1943
5.41	J. Wood, *Mean Old Bedbug Blues* (sung by Bessie Smith)	1927
5.42	B. Holiday, *Fine and Mellow*	1939
5.43	L. Armstrong, *Muggles*	1928
5.44	C. Parker, *Relaxin' at Camarillo*	1947
5.45	King and Josea, *Be Careful with a Fool* (sung by J. Winter)	1969

[5] J. D. Short, as quoted in Samuel Charters, *The Poetry of the Blues* (New York: Avon Books, 1963), p. 17.

In *How Long Blues* (Example 5.40) you hear a series of variations on a theme. The pianist was improvising, and thus there was no fixed number of variations. When this recording was made in 1943, the three-minute 78 rpm record would have been the sole determinant of the number of variations. The theme on which the pianist improvised is the following basic harmonic progression.[6]

$$| \ \text{I} \ | \ \text{I}^7 \ | \ \text{IV} \ | \ \text{IV} \ | \ \text{I} \ | \ \text{V} \ | \ \text{I} \ | \ \text{I} \ |$$

The pianist, with his left hand, plays a simple bass accompaniment outlining the basic triads; over this accompaniment he plays with his right hand a free melodic improvisation.

The basic blues progression, however, is a twelve-bar progression, much more common than the eight bars of *How Long Blues.* The next five examples are all twelve-bar blues, spanning a period of about 50 years. You will hear vocal and instrumental blues, slow and fast blues, music of different styles and periods. At the same time you should gain a feeling for the intimate relationship between harmony and phrase structure in tonal music.

Listen to Example 5.41, which is sung by Bessie Smith, one of the great singers in the early history of jazz. If you analyze the melody, you will hear that each phrase is four measures long and that three phrases (one for each line of text) constitute a stanza or chorus. There are twelve bars in all—thus the "twelve-bar blues." Generally in vocal blues, as in these, the singer ends the phrase at the beginning of the third measure, leaving almost two full measures for the instrumentalists to fill in. The phrases relate to each other in both text and melody as *a a' b:*

---

[6] In this progression $\text{I}^7 = \text{V}^7$ of IV, or V^7/IV. That is, adding the flatted seventh degree of the scale to the tonic chord (I) transforms the function of the chord into the dominant (V^7) of the IV chord:

See also Example 5.14 (*Voices of Spring*), where the same progression is used by Strauss to get from one key area to another and from the first to the second themes.

a   Bedbugs as big as a jackass will bite you and stand and grin,   [instrumental]
      I   **I**   **I**   **I**

a' Bedbugs as big as a jackass will bite you and stand and grin;   [instrumental]
      IV   **IV**   **I**   **I**

b   We'll trick all those bedbugs 'fore them turn around and bite you again.[7]   [instrumental]
      V   **V**   **I**   **I**

This constitutes only the first verse, or stanza; there are three stanzas, but the last is only eight bars long. Listen to the example again, this time concentrating on the harmonic underpinning, or chord progression. Notice that although the text and melody are essentially the same in the first two phrases (*a* and *a'*), the harmony is different. You will feel the changes as the second phrase (*a'*) begins. The progression of the twelve-bar blues can be represented in its essential form as follows:

       a   *a'*   *b*

I	**I**	**I**	**I**	**IV**	**IV**	**I**	**I**	**V**	**V**	**I**	**I**	**V**[8]
1	2	3	4	5	6	7	8	9	10	11	12	

Can you hear the difference between the IV → I progression in *a'* and the V → I progression in *b*? It is the V chord that gives the final phrase in each stanza not only its conclusiveness but also its fresh quality (which always coincides with the fresh words of the *b* text). To hear this harmonic progression clearly, listen to the piece several times and concentrate on the instrumental accompaniment. Finally, listen to the piece once again, focusing on what is most important—the singer herself.

In Billie Holiday's blues (Example 5.42), recorded 12 years later than *Mean Old Bedbug Blues,* the fundamental twelve-bar blues pattern is the same, but there are slight differences (in addition to those resulting from the more advanced recording techniques). We hear first a four-measure introduction on tonic harmony played by the saxophones, which first repeat a one-measure motive, then compress it, and then restore it to its original form. Billie Holiday comes in after the muted trumpet, singing:

---

[7] *Mean Old Bedbug Blues,* lyrics and music by Jack Wood. © Copyright 1927 by Jack Wood. © Copyright renewed by Jack Wood.

[8] The V at the end leads into the next chorus.

a   My man don't love me, treats me oh so mean;   [instrumental]
       I   **IV**   **I**   **I**

a'   My man he don't love me, treats me awful mean;   [instrumental]
    IV   **IV**   **I**   **I**

b   He's the lowest man that I've ever seen.[9]   [instrumental]
      V   **V**   **I IV**   **I**

Listen closely to the harmony, which is essentially as follows:

	a				*a'*				*b*		
I	**IV**	**I**	**I⁷**	**IV**	**IV**	**I**	**I**	**V**	**V**	**I IV**	**I**
1	2	3	4	5	6	7	8	9	10	11	12

How does this harmony compare with that in Bessie Smith's blues? With the exceptions of measures 2 and 11, the chords are the same. Although you probably cannot identify all the chords in this piece, you should be able to hear how the basic progression and its subtle variations relate to the organization of the text into lines and stanzas. There are three stanzas in this excerpt. Listen several times, comparing Billie Holiday's blues with Bessie Smith's more prototypical version.

Now listen to Louis Armstrong's *Muggles* (Example 5.43). In this instrumental blues, the musicians take the fundamental twelve-bar blues progression as the basis for extended improvisation. There are five variations on a theme here, the theme being not a melody but the basic blues harmonic progression. In a live performance the players might have continued to improvise on the blues progression for a half hour or more.

Muggles begins with solo piano, not playing a theme but rather improvising on the tacitly understood blues progression. The pianist, Earl Hines, plays around with the chords and their rhythmic placement in an interesting way. Then a soloist on trombone, clarinet, and trumpet (Louis Armstrong) each, in turn, plays a chorus; Armstrong plays two and surpasses by far the trombone and clarinet. Notice how Armstrong enters in the last two bars of the clarinet solo with an excitingly syncopated ascent, as the orchestra goes into double time behind him with sustained chords. Armstrong reiterates the tonic note, jumping up and down the octave and subtly varying the syncopated patterns.

---

[9] Copyright Edward B. Marks Music Corporation. Used by permission.

In improvisation creative musicians play around even with the given harmonic material (the constant), so the blues progression is still more varied in this example than it was in the two previous ones. Nevertheless, the piece still retains its essential I → IV → I → V → I progression. Listen to how beautifully Louis Armstrong plays with the larger structural rhythm. Although he never loses sight of the twelve-bar phrase rhythm, always coming out right, he freely weaves his way between and around both the metric and the harmonic down-beats—the returns to the tonic in measures 3 and 7, the motion to IV in measure 5, and the return to I in measure 11. The actual harmonic progression of *Muggles* is roughly:[10]

a				a'				b			
I	II^7 V^7	I	I^7	IV	IV (minor)	I	I V$^{\flat 9}$/II	II^7	II^7 V^7	I IV	I V
1	2	3	4	5	6	7	8	9	10	11	12

Those of you who have had some experience playing the twelve-bar blues might like to compare the progression in Example 5.43 with the essential blues progression given for Example 5.41. Even if you cannot hear each individual chord change, listen very carefully, and try to follow the fundamental progression in the twelve-bar structure: to IV (bar 5) in the second phrase, back to I in bar 7, to V in bars 9 and 10, and once again back to I in bars 11 and 12.

Nineteen years later (a big time span in jazz history), Charlie "Bird" Parker recorded his own "line," or "head," based on the blues progression. This highly syncopated melody, played in unison by the group after a piano introduction, recurs at the end of the piece (Example 5.44). After this beginning there are improvised solos by alto saxophone (Parker) and tenor saxophone (two choruses each); the excerpt ends at that point. This is the style of jazz called *bebop,* and the harmony is still more varied than in the previous examples.

Finally, listen to Example 5.45, *Be Careful with a Fool,* a rock blues. Notice how the accompaniment plays a slow four-beat measure, with each of the beats divided into a faster triplet rhythmic pattern:

---

[10] Roughly because there are slight variants from chorus to chorus. For a further explanation of seventh and ninth chords, see the Ancillary Reading at the end of this chapter.

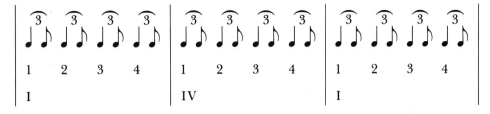

The harmonic progression is simpler than in the last two examples, closer, in fact, to the earlier blues. And as in the earlier vocal blues, there is an instrumental fill-in between the singer's phrases. The rock style, however, though retaining the shell of the old twelve-bar blues, has a very different mood.

Listen again to all six pieces (Examples 5.40 through 5.45). They should have:

1. Given you some lively practice in hearing the workings of the I, IV, and V chords.
2. Focused your attention on the role of harmony as a fundamental skeletal framework.
3. Pointed up the distinction between the larger design of a work (in this case a harmonic progression and a rhythmic structure) and its details, which, even though they constantly change, are always related to that larger design.
4. Demonstrated how a framework such as the blues progression can become so internalized—such a natural way of thinking—that it liberates rather than limits the musicians' imagination.
5. Shown you a variety of jazz styles over a 50-year period.

While these aspects of musical composition may be more obvious in relation to the twelve-bar blues, they are equally relevant to many of the other pieces which we have discussed. Indeed, one of your principal goals should be to hear the relation between the larger design of a piece and its details—to discover that the larger design both contains and is realized by its details. Perhaps this kind of awareness is even one definition of perceptive listening.

Your experience with the twelve-bar blues should help you to realize that other procedures (the simple *a b + a'* phrase form, or the minuet and the sonata forms discussed in Chapter 6) can also be a natural way of thinking for composers who have truly internalized the fundamental relations of these procedures. The whole question of limits and freedom of expression, which has become such a large part of our harmonic considerations, will be one of the principal issues returned to in the concluding chapters.

Example	Composer, title	Date
5.46	Mozart, *Serenade in C Minor,* K. 388, fourth movement	1782

With these thoughts in mind, turn now to a performance of the final movement of Mozart's *Serenade in C Minor* for two oboes, two clarinets, two horns, and two bassoons (Example 5.46). Similar to the pieces based on the twelve-bar blues, this movement is also a theme and variations. The structure of the theme is the familiar $\|:a:\|:b + a':\|$ (16 bars in length). The design of the theme differs from that of the twelve-bar blues in that it includes a clearly defined middle section (*b*) and a return (*a'*). In addition, each of the two large sections is repeated, so that there are 32 bars from the start to the finish of each variation. The general harmonic motion is

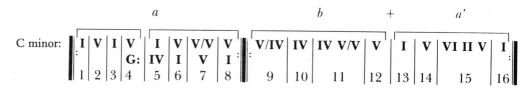

Variations on a theme

In the Mozart serenade, with the exception of the second variation, the harmonic foundation is not created by underlying sustained chords (such as those in *Muggles*), around and within which the melody instruments improvise. Here the harmony is created primarily by the individual melody lines of each instrument. Indeed, this is a significant factor in differentiating the improvised examples from this composed work.

Nevertheless, as in the blues, the I, IV, and V harmony again predominates. Notice that the first phrase establishes the tonic (just I and V), while the second phrase moves strongly to the key area of the dominant (a small-scale modulation). In the *b* section the harmony continues to move on, now sequentially—first, to an emphasis on IV in C minor, and then to V which prepares the return. The *a'* section, unlike *a*, ends with a clear, full cadence on the tonic.

Thus the larger harmonic movement, like the chord-to-chord progressions, travels within the network of closely related fifths. This is, then, a nice example of the point made earlier (p. 180); namely, that harmonic movement on the detail level is reflected again in the harmonic movement of the larger design.

In this movement, the theme and each of the first four variations in the movement all follow exactly the same harmonic progression as well as the same phrase structure. (The fifth and final variations are in major.) While you may not (and need not) follow the chord-to-chord progression, you should be able, as in the blues, to hear the general harmonic movement and its relationship to the phrase structure: The movement from I to V in *a*, the shifting harmony in *b*, and the return to stability in the final phrase, *a'*. Mozart creates marvelous contrasts in character and sound from one variation to the next by changes in instrumentation, rhythm, and texture; but he does so within the limits of his own initial design.

Once again limitations seem to liberate the imagination—as if to say, "How many ways can one find to create anew the same simple set of relationships?" The structure becomes a kind of Phoenix, reborn with each new variation.

ANCILLARY READING

The Basic Triads
The four types of triads are as follows:

In the course of time, additional thirds were added to the basic triads, creating sevenths, ninths, elevenths, and so forth:

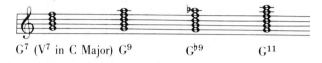

Triads can be built on each scale degree within a key. The following are the basic triads in C major:

The triads on I, IV, and V are major; II, III, and VI are minor; and VII is **diminished.**

Below are the basic triads in C minor.[11] The triads on V and VI are major; I and IV are minor; II and VII are diminished; and III is augmented.

Inversion

---

[11] The harmonic minor scale is derived from the practical use of these triads, particularly I, IV, V; see Chapter 3, p. 132.

There are numerous possible arrangements of the notes of a chord. Here are four examples of a C-major triad. In the second example the root (C) is heavily "doubled." In the third, the triad is played in *first inversion,* that is, with the third of the chord rather than the root in the bass. (See Example 3.20, with its deceptive cadence to a first inversion tonic chord in Zerlina's phrase extension.) In the fourth example, the chord is in the *second inversion.* This chord is often referred to as a *six-four chord* because the upper two notes are a sixth and a fourth above the lowest, rather than a third and fifth as they are in a **root-position** triad.

Cadences

In the traditional study of harmony, chords are written in four parts. Various cadences are illustrated below in the traditional manner.

Full (perfect, authentic)
cadence   Half cadence   Plagal cadence   Deceptive cadence

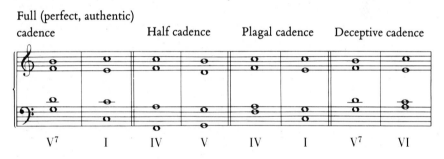

V⁷   I   IV   V   IV   I   V⁷   VI

ADDITIONAL MATERIALS

As in the Additional Materials for Chapter 2, we suggest that you look back over some of the earlier examples, now from the point of view of their harmonic interest.

> Mozart, *The Magic Flute,* aria (Example 3.13)
> Schoenberg, *Herzegewächse* (Example 3.14)

In Chapter 3 these two examples were paired as illustrations of "vocal melodies which span a larger range" but also as representing "quite different ways of relating pitch and time." We also hinted that Schoenberg has a different idea about arranging pitches—a different notion of "comprehensibility." From your study of harmony you can now make this "different notion" more explicit. In fact, the Mozart melody, while certainly including large leaps and an enormous range, still remains solidly in one key. Actually, the soprano is often singing the pitches of the I, IV, or V chords, sometimes stretching them out over an octave or more, which accounts for the large range and the leaps. The Schoenberg song, in contrast, is not only chromatic but is so to the extent that no tonal center is established at all. The chords in the accompaniment are not triads but rather sonorities made up of intervals other than, or in addition to, thirds and fifths. Thus, the functional harmony on which we usually depend for our sense of direction and orientation is not applicable here. And still, if you try to listen to the song on *its* terms instead of listening in terms of previous stylistic expectations, you will hear a structure defined by clear phrases marked by caesuras and repeated pitch-shapes characterized by a large leap followed by a slow descent. Starting with these musical gestures, you may find this so-called atonal music beginning to take shape and to become comprehensible. But you can only enter into this search for coherence once you realize that the conventions of functional harmony are not going to be the key. It's a little like listening to French and hoping it will turn into English. But just as you can use the internalized knowledge of your own language to help you understand an unfamiliar one, so your deepening knowledge of aspects of familiar music that you may not have been aware of before will help you to discover the means of comprehensibility which Schoenberg's music shares with this older music.

Schoenberg, *Six Little Piano Pieces,* Op. 19, no. 4 (Example 4.21)

In Chapter 4 this brief piano piece by Schoenberg was used to illustrate the continuous development of a germinal motive. This is a good example of music that is not tonal (no tonal center and no tonic or dominant functions as such) but where the means of organization are not entirely unfamiliar. Notice, for example, that the ending of the first phrase is marked by a slowing of the tempo and by a fuller texture— the melody line is only now accompanied by chords in the bass. The chords reappear in the next phrase, and at the cadence you will hear, if you listen carefully, that the melodic motive is much the same as at the first cadence—a rising, three-note figure. Finally, the third phrase begins with exactly the same pitches as the first phrase but now transformed by a different rhythm. But perhaps more "hearable" is the strong punctuation at the end by the two chords in the bass followed by a single note in the melody which together seem to achieve resolution—arrival. In the terms set up by the piece, then, each small section has a *structural* function even though these are not dependent on the *harmonic* functions associated with tonality. The first phrase sets forth the motivic material; the second phrase develops this material rhythmically and elaborates its sonorities; the third phrase further transforms the initial motivic material rhythmically and uses the bass chords so as to form a conclusion—an ending. Described in these terms, the structure of the piece and the means Schoenberg uses to create this structure sound quite familiar—an increase in texture and sonority at the cadences, rhythmic transformation of motives (as in the *b* section of the Haydn *Minuet*), and the use of textural punctuation to set up an ending. But in the Schoenberg piece everything is much more compressed; you need to be very attentive to all the details or the piece is gone before you "tune in." In Chapter 11 you will hear another short piano piece, Babbitt's *Minute Waltz,* where the composer also uses means other than functional harmony to develop coherence. There we will discuss in more detail these new and systematic ways of relating pitches to one another.

Wagner, *Tristan and Isolde,* "Love-Death" (Example 3.24)

This is another wonderful example of chromatic harmony, still within a basically tonal framework. Unlike the examples just discussed where chromaticism is so complete as to obliterate tonal functions, Wagner uses chromaticism so as to keep the listener in touch with key centers but often without actually stating their tonics. Thus, for example, you hear extended dominant harmonies heading toward a specific tonic resolution (a waiting passage), but the resolution never arrives. Instead, Wagner shifts away from the expected tonic to set up a different one. In this way the tonal center is continuously shifting, but nonetheless the music depends on tonal functions for its effect—precisely the effect which the example initially illustrated, that is, continuous organization. Heading toward a tonal goal but then veering off to suggest another, Wagner keeps the music moving onward, increasing in tension and excitement almost from the beginning of one act of the opera to its conclusion.

Sourwood Mountain (Example 1.19)
Verdi, *La Traviata* (Example 1.20)
Rossini, *William Tell,* overture (Example 2.15)
M. Reynolds, *Little Boxes* (sung by Pete Seeger) (Example 4.14)
S. Reese, *Which Side Are You On?* (sung by Pete Seeger) (Example 4.19)

All of the above examples are good ones for practicing your skills in hearing I and V chords. In fact, they all use predominantly just these two chords. *Sourwood Mountain,* for instance, hardly moves from its one sound—a single chord—and this single chord is the tonic. The whole song is sung over the repeated tonic chord—another example of "harmonic stasis" but quite different from either the Wagner or Beethoven examples heard earlier (Examples 5.8 and 5.9). In the Verdi aria, the first two phrases are harmonized by only I and V. The next two phrases, a kind of middle section, move away from the tonic momentarily but set up the return with a clear V again. The last phrase is again harmonized with I and V, ending with a full cadence on the tonic. The *William Tell* overture also begins with just I and V harmonies. Then moving away briefly to a different key and to the minor mode, Rossini makes a waiting passage on the dominant that almost caricatures the notion of a waiting passage as it sets up the return. *Little Boxes* and the refrain of *Which Side Are You On?* are both harmonized by just I and V. Listen to them again and see if you can hear the chord changes.

Haydn, *Symphony 8,* first movement (Example 1.5)

Finally, it is interesting to compare Haydn's early *Symphony 8* (Example 1.5) (1761) with his later *Symphony 100* (Example 5.33) (1794). The excerpt from *Symphony 8* is the beginning of the first movement; the excerpt from *Symphony 100* is the third movement, a minuet. Notice that the *Symphony 8* movement begins with two phrases, both of which end on the tonic chord, while the *Symphony 100* movement begins with an antecedent-consequent phrase relationship—the first phrase ending on the dominant, the second on the tonic—creating a sense of closure or of complete statement. The *Symphony 8* excerpt continues with movement between dominant and tonic—a unison phrase outlines the V chord, then the little flute motive outlines the tonic and then two motives which end first on V, then on I. This is the segment printed on p. 7, and it is the first statement section of a movement in sonata form (see Chapter 6). The differences in harmonic structure between it and the minuet movement discussed in this chapter are important to the broader differences between these two ways of organizing music. Listen to the *Symphony 8* excerpt and compare its harmonic structure with that of the *Symphony 100* excerpt—both make use of only I and V in their first sections, but their relations to one another are quite different in each work. It will be interesting to return to this comparison when you study the minuet and the sonata forms in Chapter 6.

For additional jazz examples, you might listen to some of the following blues to supplement those presented on the recordings:

King Oliver, *Dippermouth Blues,* 1923 (Epic)
Louis Armstrong, *West End Blues,* 1928 (Columbia)
Lester Young, Charlie Christian, *Ad-Lib Blues,* 1940 (Jazz Archives)
Sonny Rollins, *Blue Seven,* 1956 (Prestige)
Miles Davis, *Walkin',* 1961 (Columbia)
Roy Eldridge and Earl Hines, *Blues for Old "N's",* 1965 (Xanadu)
Jim Hall, *Two's Blues* (a blues in minor), 1975 (CTI)
Branford Marsalis, *Royal Garden Blues,* 1986 (Columbia)

Finally, a fascinatingly instructive illustration of the interrelationships among harmony, structure, and jazz improvisation can be seen in the jazz version by Al Cohn of *America the Beautiful,* 1976 (Xanadu). (See Example 2.14.)

PART THREE

*Structure:
Form
and
Function*

CHAPTER 6

Piet Mondrian, *Composition in Red, Blue and Yellow*, 1937–1942

Sectional Organization

Byzantine Mosaic, Ravenna, Italy

In Chapters 6 and 7 we finally bring together the various aspects of music which have, of necessity, been discussed separately throughout the book. We are at the moment promised in the Introduction, when you should be able to perceive the effects of the various aspects of music "not as isolated factors but as parts of an inseparable whole, combining and influencing one another to generate the events, motion, and process of a unique work." In this chapter we will be observing the varying roles or functions of certain passages as these interrelate to create particular kinds of musical design or "forms."

First, we must distinguish between the immediate experience of a work and those abstract concepts called *musical forms*. Forms (such as the minuet, sonata form, and rondo) represent a generalization from many works that share, in some sense, the same structure.

On the one hand, you can directly experience a musical work as a series of events—we mean, now, events on a larger scale. You might first sense such events in terms of passages of stability, moving away, tension, culmination, and so forth; and then later in terms of structural function, such as statement of a theme, digression, development, return, or ending. This series of events, when completed, constitutes the form. And, depending on their inner relationships, you can move from the particular experience of these events to a more generalized experience, recognizing the totality as a minuet, a **sonata form,** a rondo, a theme and variations, or some other structure.

On the other hand, you can begin, as we do in Demonstration 6.1, with the generalization—the abstract schema of a form. In doing so, you will be anticipating the order of events. The strength of this vantage point is that you can focus on the *differences* among a group of works (that which makes each of them unique) in the light of the very general organization which they all share. In concentrating on their uniqueness, you can then listen with fascination (as we did in choosing the examples) as each piece unfolds, revealing some of the myriad possibilities that composers have found in realizing a single, basically simple structure. These differences may stem from the particular germinal materials, the personal choices of the composer at the moment, or the specific musical style. (The examples in Demonstration 6.1 span a period of 138 years.)

At first, you may feel more informed and comfortable with the second approach. But as you gain experience in listening to various forms, you may find yourself taking both approaches simultaneously—responding to the unique events of each piece as they happen but also enjoying the process as a particular experience within a more general framework.

Remember, however, that what we think of now as "classical forms" were labeled (and their "rules" codified) only after the fact—that is, after the works themselves already existed. The term *sonata form,* for example, was first used in the 1840s—well after Beethoven's death. The composers who wrote in the "classical forms" were not

> following a recognized pattern but rather were giving their music the shape which the scale of their work, in terms of the materials available to them, seemed to demand. . . . What we call musical form is the design that results from the musical impulse itself, a design of a temporal and in no way predetermined nature.[1]

You may note that in dealing with *sectional forms*—specifically, the minuet and sonata form—we concentrate on music written after the middle of the eighteenth century. Sectional forms became more prevalent after 1750 because of a number of stylistic factors, the most significant being the emergence of tonality as a fundamental syntactical force. Our purpose here is not to survey sectional forms (by looking at all types from all periods), but rather to consider carefully the general characteristics of two forms and, through these more specific considerations, to extend your musical perception.

Central to the expansion and increased complexity which you will find in these works are the possibilities engendered by transformation. The ability to hear development of a germinal idea through various kinds of transformations is therefore crucial to the appreciation of these larger works. It is for this reason that we have returned repeatedly to the notion of transformation. Beginning with the transformations created by changing sound environments (Chapter 1), we then considered melodic transformation by fragmentation and sequence in the discussion of the Berg aria (Example 3.3) and the theme from the Mozart *Piano Sonata* (Example 3.5). In the section which followed, "Motivic Development," we specifically anticipated the importance of transformation by looking carefully at a very simple instance of melodic transformation in *Mary Had a Little Lamb,* and then at considerably

---

[1] Roger Sessions, *Questions About Music* (Cambridge: Harvard University Press, 1970), p. 37.

more sophisticated examples by Haydn, Beethoven, and Schubert. In Chapter 5 you saw (and heard) how the function of a single chord could be transformed as a result of its harmonic context. To develop your awareness and perception of these processes of transformation is a major goal of the book. In these last chapters this growing awareness will help you to participate more fully and more appropriately in these large-scale compositions. This chapter and the next should serve, then, as a culmination of your work thus far and also help you to make sense of where you have been as well as how far you have come.

DEMONSTRATION 6.1
The Minuet and the Scherzo
(Sides 9–10)

On the most general level, the pieces in Demonstration 6.1 (all of which are in triple meter) can be described as shown here:

A	B	A'
Minuet	Trio	Minuet (*da capo*)[2]
$\|:a:\|:b + a':\|$	$\|:c:\|:d + c':\|$	$a\ b + a'$

In Chapter 4 you became familiar with the internal organization of each of the three large sections just diagramed: The minuet, the trio, and the return to the minuet. Here we are concerned not with a new musical design but rather with the possibilities of extending this design into a larger work and the remarkably varied ways in which this extension can be realized.

The sections are indicated on the record, although not exactly at their beginning, so that you can experience these structural events yourself. In a few examples, because of the lack of recording "time-space," the trio and minuet **da capo** have not been included.

Each composer has played with the possibilities inherent in this general schema. Notice particularly the following:

1. The nature of the return to *a'*. Is there a "waiting passage" or not? Is the return varied?
2. The "development" of thematic material. Where does it occur, or does it?
3. The nature of the contrast between *a* and *b*.

---

[2] *Da capo* (D.C., literally, "from the head") is an indication to the performers to go back to the beginning and play the first part of the piece over again. It is most often found at the end of the trio section, indicating a replaying of the minuet ("Minuet *da capo*"), usually without repeats.

4. The nature of the contrast between the minuet (or A section) and the trio (or B section).
5. The addition or lack of a coda.
6. The proportions of the whole, and the parts to the whole.
7. The nature of the thematic material itself and how it influences the realization of the overall structure.

As you listen to this collection of works you should discover a richer significance in the simple notion of statement-contrast-return (set forth in Chapter 4) and the influence that stylistic change can have on it.

The Minuet

Example	Composer, title	Date
6.1	Mozart, *Eine kleine Nachtmusik*, K. 525, minuet	1787
6.2	Haydn, *Symphony 99*, minuet	1793

You are already familiar with Examples 6.1 and 6.2. The minuet from Mozart's *Eine kleine Nachtmusik* (Example 6.1) presents the minuet

The minuet: an 18th-century royal ballroom scene

Example 6.1 MOZART, *Eine kleine Nachtmusik*

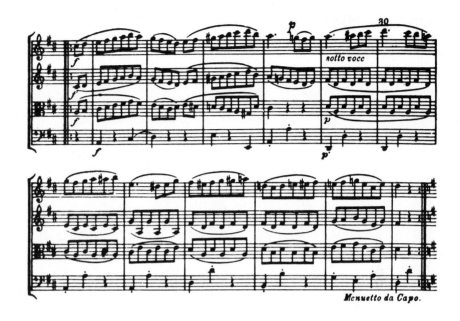

Menuetto da Capo.

structure in its irreducible form. On first hearing, the *a* section sounds like one long, continuous, eight-measure phrase. Closer listening, however, will reveal its antecedent-consequent phrase structure, concealed by the increased rhythmic activity in the fourth bar. There are, in fact, two phrases here, as determined by both harmonic and melodic means: The movement to the dominant at the end of the first phrase (fourth bar) to create a half cadence, and the repetition of the first part of the melody at the beginning of the consequent phrase (bars five and six). Of additional interest in this deceptively simple piece is the effect of duple meter against the basic three in the consequent phrase.

The brief *b* section provides contrast in almost every dimension—in dynamics (softer), texture (thinner as the bass drops out), and harmony (moving away from the tonic it touches on the "relative minor"). For melodic material Mozart uses in *b* the little figure from the fourth bar of *a* (♩ | ♪♪♪♪♪♩ |), which served there to conceal the articulation between phrases. In what ways does the trio contrast with the minuet?

In Example 6.2, from Haydn's *Symphony 99,* the proportions of the movement are considerably expanded. You may remember that in studying the Haydn symphony movement in Chapter 1 (Example 1.29), we noted that *a* itself included three sections, each with a different

Wolfgang Amadeus
Mozart, 1789

Minuet (A)

a   *b*   +   *a'*

Trio (B)

c   *d*   +   *c'*

Minuet *da capo* (A')

a   *b*   +   *a'*

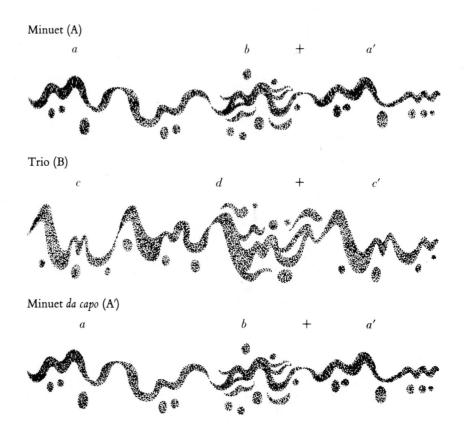

function: A *statement,* consisting of antecedent and consequent phrases; an *extension* and *elaboration* of this material, generated by a more active texture; and a *closing* section. In *b* the contrast (indeed, the basis for calling it a new section) is created by *development* of the initial thematic material. Haydn transforms the germinal musical idea. He inverts it (the melody goes up now rather than down), fragments it, and embeds it in a more active texture and a less stable harmony.

The return is prepared for by the gradual emergence of the opening material. Imitative statements of the initial motive evolve into a complete statement of the original theme with its rhythmic unison texture. Can you next hear how the change in *a'* creates a sense of greater finality? What seemed in the *a* section an elaboration or exploration of implications becomes in *a'* their resolution.

The trio contrasts with the minuet in its more lyrical character, softer dynamics, reduced orchestral forces, and smaller structural dimensions. But can you hear how it is directly related to the minuet? The trio follows the same general structure as the minuet, but a brief transition section is added before the *da capo* in order to effect the modulation from the distant key of the trio to the original key of the minuet.

Two Scherzos

Example	Composer, title	Date
6.3	Beethoven, *Quartet,* Op. 18, no. 1, scherzo	1799
6.4	Schubert, *Quintet in C,* Op. 163, scherzo (without trio and scherzo *da capo*)	1828

The third movement of a symphony or quartet changes in Beethoven's hands from a minuet to a scherzo. While the "form" remains, the character of the scherzo takes this movement even further away from its elegant courtly origins. Notice the following in Example 6.3:

1. The extreme brevity of *a* and, to a lesser degree, of *b*.
2. The greater expansion that takes place in *a'*.
3. In the trio, the almost unrecognizable return in *c'*.
4. The lack of repetition of *d* + *c'*, which stems from the varied nature of *c'*.

How does the nature of the thematic material in the trio influence the effect of return in *c'*? At what point in the process do you finally feel the stability usually associated with return?

Example 6.4, taken from the Schubert *Quintet in C,* is the longest of all the movements heard so far. Unlike Example 6.3, this scherzo also has an expanded *a* section, and all the sections (*a*, *b*, and *a'*) are nearly equal in length.

Notice that the opening material is already considerably elaborated in *a*: The harmony becomes more complex, contrasting material is introduced, and the section ends with a codetta. The *b* section introduces not only further development of the opening material of *a*, but also a new melody (though one that seems to derive from *a* material). The *b* section leads into *a'* with a prolonged waiting passage. This passage was included as Example 2.24 where it was used to illustrate syncopation.

You can hear now how the rhythmic agitation, along with the harmony and the repeated melodic figure, help to generate a waiting passage—a preparation for return that is followed by the return itself. Note how your increased ability to perceive harmonic stability and instability furthers your ability to respond to the evolving structure of a work as well as to its overall effect. (Note that *a'* ends with a brief codetta.) In this performance *b* + *a'* is not repeated.

While the music you have heard in these first four examples spans a period of only 41 years, from 1787 to 1828, its variety in the light of our point of departure, the minuet from Mozart's *Eine kleine Nacht-musik,* is remarkable. The changes can perhaps best be summarized by noting the proportions of stable melodic statements to unstable elaborations, developments, and codas. While the Mozart minuet is composed primarily of melodies—their appearance, disappearance into brief "development," and reappearance—the later works are concerned primarily with realizing the *implications* of briefly stated thematic material through subtle transformations of it. And the thematic material is itself often dramatic and unstable. As a result, the character and purpose of the minuet is dramatically transformed from its original function as music for the royal ballroom. In the works under discussion here, the minuet appears as a stylized dance—which means it embodies features of the social dance (meter and form, for example) but is designed for listening rather than for dancing.

Later "Minuets"

Example	Composer, title	Date
6.5	Mahler, *Symphony 1,* second movement	1888
6.6	Schoenberg, *Suite for Piano,* Op. 25, minuet	1925

The movement by Mahler from his *Symphony 1* (Example 6.5), marked simply *Kräftig bewegt*—"lively, animated"—couples two seemingly disparate musical phenomena: The simple, diatonic tunes of the Austrian village band on the one hand, and a very large orchestra and much expanded (chromatic) harmonic vocabulary on the other. The result is a piece rich in contrasts of sonority and full of "sound effects." Within the structure of A, notice the following:

Austrian village band

1. There are no literal repeats.
2. The *b* section is relatively long in relation to *a* and has greater contrast in harmony,[3] sonority, and texture. Note particularly the increase in textural activity and the thickening of the texture at the climax, followed by a thinning of the texture down to only one group of instruments at the waiting passage before the return of *a'*.
3. *a'* is introduced softly and with a thin texture, followed by a full orchestration of the original theme, which is then varied to create a dramatic coda.

The trio (B) provides contrast in almost every dimension and is freely structured. The return to A includes essentially only the *a'* section with its coda.

In Example 6.6, from his *Suite for Piano,* Schoenberg has adapted the old minuet form to a new harmonic context—chromatic and without a tonal center. What creates stability of thematic statement and instability of development? The traditional structure within the minuet is in many senses maintained: *a* is repeated literally; *b* + *a'*, however, is not (literal repeats are rare in Schoenberg); and only portions of *a*

---

[3] The beginning of the *b* section was used in Chapter 5 (Example 5.13) as an illustration of change of key by juxtaposition: "Mahler states his motive in one key, then immediately begins again with the same motive but in a new key." In context, you hear these means as contributing to the greater contrast of the *b* section.

return exactly in *a'*. The larger structure—minuet-trio-minuet *da capo*—is also maintained.

Note that the sense of dramatic possibility which we saw emerging even in the earlier minuets is developed still further in the last two examples. In particular, the returns are consistently more varied. They generate within the structure exactly the kind of drama—almost in the narrative sense—that is inherent in the attitude which sought a new kind of personal expression in the Romantic period (see Part Four).

DEMONSTRATION 6.2

Sonata Form

(Side 10)

This demonstration differs from Demonstration 6.1 in two ways:

1. While in Demonstration 6.1 we began with an abstract schema—minuet form—in Demonstration 6.2 we begin with events themselves. We concentrate on the varying functions which passages can assume, only later arriving at the generalization—in this case *sonata form*.
2. In Demonstration 6.1 we considered a number of examples written over a relatively long time span and reflecting great diversity in musical style. Here, in contrast, we concentrate primarily on the music of only two composers, Mozart and Beethoven.

The difference in approach in these two demonstrations stems largely from the nature of the sonata form itself, particularly its greater length and complexity. Therefore, instead of using a historical approach, as with the minuet, the emphasis here will be on music from the Classical period. But for contrast, in Demonstration 6.3 and in the Additional Materials we discuss pieces from both the nineteenth and twentieth centuries.

Structural Functions: Means and Effect

Example	Composer, title	Date
6.7	Mozart, *Symphony 40*, K. 550, fourth movement	1788
6.8	Mozart, *Symphony 40*, K. 550, fourth movement	1788

Begin with Examples 6.7 and 6.8; listen to them several times. While they both work with the same material, one of the passages is more stable. Why? Which of the two might be the opening statement of the theme?

Example 6.8 is the initial *statement* of the theme; Example 6.7 is a subsequent **development** of it. The stability of the statement is generated by balanced phrase structure and by the emphasis on tonic and dominant harmony, as well as by the clear (now familiar) structure shown below.

Example 6.8 MOZART, *Symphony 40,* fourth movement (initial statement)

a	+	*a'*		*b*	+	*a'*
‖: antecedent		consequent :‖		‖: digression		consequent :‖

Later in the movement (Example 6.7), Mozart develops this theme, beginning somewhat as he did originally but quickly breaking up the germinal material—dissecting it and in effect keeping the listener guessing by avoiding clear tonality, rhythm, and phrasing. Listen to Examples 6.7 and 6.8 again—now in their proper order—as Examples 6.9 and 6.10.

Example	Composer, title	Date
6.9	Mozart, *Symphony 40,* K. 550, fourth movement, measures 1–32	1788
6.10	Mozart, *Symphony 40,* K. 550, fourth movement, measures 125–205	1788

These two excerpts bring together in one work the kinds of contrast that we have seen in excerpts from individual works and have discussed separately in previous chapters. Using the same motivic material, Mozart changes the initially stable statement into one of dramatically different effect and function.

In his reworking of the theme the harmony is ambiguous; it moves rapidly through a series of tentative key areas. The metric and phrase rhythm are also less regular and less clear, and the balanced phrase structure of the statement gives way to a phrase structure blurred by active, imitative texture. In short, all dimensions are transformed. Your sense of clear sectionality in the initial statement becomes one of continuous and agitated motion in the later development of the opening thematic material.

Evolving Musical Shapes

Examples 6.9 and 6.10 illustrate a basic distinction in the presentation of musical materials. We might describe them as music of *being,* that is, thematic statement (6.9), and music of *becoming,* that is, of development or transition (6.10).

Example	Composer, title	Date
6.11	Beethoven, *Quartet,* Op. 18, no. 1, first movement, measures 101–114	1799
6.12	Beethoven, *Quartet,* Op. 18, no. 1, first movement, measures 101–154	1799
6.13	Beethoven, *Quartet,* Op. 18, no. 1, first movement, measures 115–186	1799

Next listen to Example 6.11 to determine its character and its place in the movement. Actually, this Beethoven excerpt closes off a large section of a work. The static harmony restrains the forceful rhythmic and melodic motives. Over an embellished tonic **pedal**[4] played by the cello, the other instruments play, with rhythmic regularity, a series of V-I progressions followed by scale passages. The effect is one of further extending or elaborating the tonic harmony. This is a *closing section.*

Listen to the excerpt again with its continuation (Example 6.12). Unlike the closing section, this continuation is highly unstable and charged with excitement—modulating and avoiding clear cadences. The whole passage is characterized by a rapid rate of change and a continuous transformation of motivic material. This section is concerned with *development,* or "analysis," in the sense of breaking up and revealing the implications of previously stated material. This continuation constitutes the first half of the *development section* of the movement.

Now listen to the entire development section and its continuation (Example 6.13). Toward the end you have an exciting experience of return to familiar territory—to stable ground—in fact, to the tonic of the piece and to the very opening of the work. This return is anticipated by a lengthy *waiting passage*—an ornamented dominant pedal with a very agitated rhythm. The waiting passage gives way to return through the striking change in rhythmic and textural activity. With the entrance of the melody (return to opening material), the rhythmic motion slows down, the texture becomes less active, and agitation subsides into calm.

---

[4] Known as a *pedal* because in organ works the performer would hold his or her foot on a single bass pedal.

Once again these examples demonstrate the combined use of various musical dimensions—sound, rhythm, motivic manipulation, harmony—to generate the contrasting passages which define and articulate structure. Relationships which initially might have seemed dichotomous (for example, active and inactive texture, sectional and continuous melodic organization, diatonic and chromatic harmony) are now heard as the tools of musical process—the means of creating an ever-evolving, organic, multifaceted whole.

A Complete Movement in Sonata Form

Example	Composer, title	Date
6.14	Mozart, *Quartet in G Major,* K. 387, first movement	1782

Example 6.14 presents the entire first movement of Mozart's *Quartet in G Major,* K. 387. It falls into nine sections, more or less clearly articulated by the kinds of contrasts you have heard in previous examples, but now operating within one movement. Each section has its role—its *function*—in the evolution of the total work. Listen carefully, trying to hear the structural functions of each section. Ask yourself the following questions:

1. Is there a tune or well-defined *thematic statement,* with clear phrasing and stable harmony?
2. Or is the music unstable, fragmented, changing frequently in texture, and harmonically ambiguous or modulating—thus *transitional* or *developmental* in character?
3. Or is the harmonic movement directed toward a certain goal—a *waiting passage?*
4. Or does the music seem to be cadential in some way—a *closing section?*

Listen to the entire movement at least once before reading the analysis which follows. Try to listen on a broader scale. Step back, as it were, and use your increased awareness of musical possibilities to take in and respond to the larger gestures of the music. You should now be able to absorb the details of your molecular analysis into a more intense response to the total design.

The various sections, their respective structural functions, and the relationships among them together constitute what is generally known as *sonata form.*

Section 1 states the *opening* theme. Mozart uses material from this opening prominently throughout the entire movement. The phrasing is clear, the harmony stable within the tonic key—here, G major.

In Section 2 the thematic material is fragmented; there is a change to a more active texture, contrast in textural density, and imitation. The passage is much more continuous and is modulatory in harmony. It finally arrives at a waiting passage in the new key, the dominant, in preparation for the statement of another theme. This is a *transition* section.

Section 3 presents a contrasting melody. What means are used to create a melody different in character from that of the opening theme?

In Section 4 you hear a series of extended cadences always returning, sometimes with delay, to the tonic of this section. This is a *closing* section.

Sections 1–4 together constitute the **exposition** of the movement.

Section 5, a *development* section, is characterized by the greatest rate of change. Motives from the themes of the exposition are manipulated and thrown off balance. We are ushered into this section by a marvelously unsettling transformation of the opening theme. As it proceeds the tone colors of the instruments are exploited, and the texture is varied in both activity and density. The harmony is at first ambiguous, then shifts from one key to another, coming to rest in a passage reminiscent of the closing section of the exposition. But the deceptiveness of this closing is revealed as we move into a waiting passage which prepares for the return of the opening theme and the return to stability.

Sections 6–9 together constitute the **recapitulation;** they parallel Sections 1–4 of the exposition. Thus in Section 6 we have the opening theme; Section 7 parallels Section 2 (the transition); Section 8 parallels Section 3, stating the second, contrasting theme. Finally, Section 9 parallels Section 4, the closing section which completes the movement.[5]

Listen again to the entire movement. Its dramatic evolution is created by the composer's imagination and skill—his command over the musical means we have discussed throughout the book and which you now hear in guises appropriate to making this movement a whole.

---

[5] The term *recapitulation* is somewhat misleading in that this section is not really a summary or recapitulation of what has gone before; yet the term is universally used and so we retain it here.

Exposition

I   Transition   II   Closing

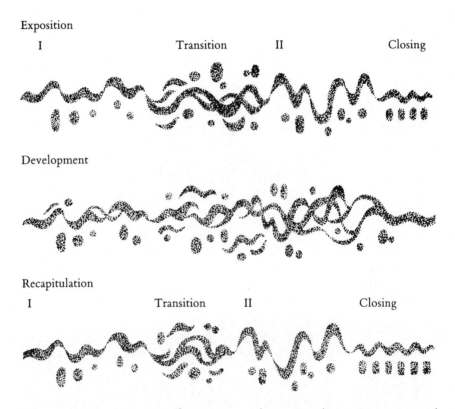

Development

Recapitulation

I   Transition   II   Closing

Listen to Mozart's use of sonority and texture, his contrasting and combining of rhythmic and melodic shapes, and the varieties of harmonic motion.

The generalized structure of the Mozart quartet movement, as well as that of any movement in sonata form, can be outlined as follows. But please remember that this is a generalization, that is, a description of a procedure which represents a number of works in general but may represent no one of them in particular.

Sonata Form

(Introduction—found only in some allegro movements**)**
Slow, exploratory, and wandering in character; modulatory and often tonally ambiguous until just before the end; leads directly into the exposition.

Exposition
1. *Theme Group 1.* One or more themes in the tonic key, characterized by the harmonic stability and generally regular phrasing of thematic statement.

2. *Transition.* Modulating, generally more active in texture, motives broken up and regrouped, more continuous.
3. *Theme Group 2.* One or more themes in another key (primarily the dominant) which usually contrast in character with those of Theme Group 1.
4. *Closing Section.* Cadential in effect; closes off the exposition with emphasis on the new tonic.

Development

5. "Analysis" and exploration of material presented in the exposition, characterized by modulation, tonal ambiguity, melodic material fragmented and in other ways transformed, and a rapid rate of change. This section is more active in texture and more continuous; occasionally a new theme is presented.

Recapitulation

A repetition of the sequence of events in the exposition:

6. *Theme Group 1.*
7. *Transition.*
8. *Theme Group 2.* Now in the tonic of the piece.
9. *Closing Section.*

(Coda)

May take the form of further development of material before ending the piece in an even more final fashion than the closing section.

Two points should be made about the above outline as a generalization:

1. The sonata form (or any musical form) as described in a diagram is a generalization made from a large number of works, each of which is unique—as you have heard in listening to the minuets. A musical form is not a mold like those into which you pour plaster, hoping that each cast will be identical. The generalization is most useful, in fact, not in categorizing or labeling but in perceiving distinctions. Given sufficient time and experience, you can come to hear within a given framework not devices or formal sections but rather organic movement, function—you can respond to the composer's musical gestures.
2. The second point concerns the effect your knowledge of forms has on your expectations. For example, when you listen to the first

movement of a symphony by Mozart, you can with justification anticipate a different series of events from those that will occur when you listen to the third movement: The first movement will almost certainly be in sonata form, while the third will be a minuet.

What are the differences in your expectations for the minuet and sonata-form movements? The sonata form is larger in every sense. More happens. There are two contrasting statement areas; these necessitate a transition between them and often a closing section before the development. The development is the heart of the sonata form. Here the composer reveals to the listener the implications of what may have seemed straightforward, simple melodies in the exposition. The recapitulation, in turn, is not heard as simply a repeat of the exposition—you hear the music now in a new light, having experienced the development, where the potential of the thematic material was explored.

As a result, this **first-movement form,** as it is sometimes called (though not correctly, since it may occur in a second or final movement), is expansive, organic, and dramatic. So much happens in a movement in sonata form: Transformations in both motivic material and in character, conflict, revelations of hidden implications, and so forth.

In the minuet your expectations are different. The experience is of two usually quite separate wholes and a third which repeats the first: minuet-trio-minuet. This is quite different from your experience of dramatic growth in the sonata form. When we consider any of the three parts of the minuet (since we do consider them separately), our sense of proportion is much smaller than it is when we listen to a movement in sonata form. There is but one theme in the *a* section; development of the material of *a*, primarily in the *b* section, is on a considerably smaller scale than what we can expect in the development section of a sonata-form movement; and return will be less dramatic because of the shorter, less revealing excursion.

Put in these terms, however, the comparison is inherently dangerous, since it pits the minuet against the sonata. Each deserves to be heard on its own terms. We must listen to the way each composer realizes or exploits the possibilities of a particular set of formal relationships. Thus, on the one hand, each piece must be heard as a unique series of events. But on the other, these events must be perceived as realizing in some way the set of formal relationships which the piece shares with other works.

We turn in this demonstration to the first movement of Brahms's *Symphony 3* (Example 6.15), written just over 100 years after the Mozart *Quartet in G Major.* This symphonic movement, like the Mozart *Quartet* movement, is in sonata form. However, in listening to it, we ask you to focus on how style, in this case the Romantic style of Brahms, influences the personal way in which a composer realizes, even brings to life in new ways, a structure that is in some respects common to works by many composers writing at different times in the history of music. We touched upon the issue of style in Demonstration 6.1. For example, we observed that in the chronologically later works the dramatic possibilities of the minuet form came to the fore, particularly in the movements by Schubert and Mahler.

The issue of stylistic differences might be thought of in terms of three progressively smaller concentric circles. The largest circle refers to the implicit working assumptions or basic "means of comprehensibility" shared by musicians during a *particular era*—what we usually call the style of a period, be it **Baroque, Classical,** or **Romantic.** The middle circle refers to the particular characteristics of an *individual composer's* style—his or her personal and unique ways of shaping musical materials (rhythm, melody, instrumentation)—still within the general stylistic "belief systems" of the time. Finally, the third, inner circle, refers to the style of an *individual piece*—the implications, for example, of an opening theme as these are realized in contrasts and developments throughout the unfolding of the composition. Much, but not all of your work thus far has been within this inner circle.

In Part Four of the text, "Style and the Historical Context," we will ask you to broaden your vista so as to include the outer circles as well. We do so first, in Chapters 8 through 11, by considering works widely separated in time (and, not surprisingly, also in style) but that share some common human theme—religion, love, dance. Then, in Chapter 12, we focus in on one relatively short period in music history—the 54 years between 1859 and 1913—in order to give you a feel for stylistic change during a time when underlying musical assumptions were in unusual flux. This is the period that we now, in retrospect, think of as the end of the Romantic period and the beginning of the Modern period.

It was also in the midst of this same time (1883) that Brahms composed his *Symphony 3,* and we will return to it during the discussion in Chapter 12. As preparation and a kind of foreshadowing of things to come, we ask that you listen to the movement in the present context of sonata forms while paying particular attention to the influence of style—for instance, the Romantic style of Brahms in comparison with the Classical style of Mozart. Ask yourself, for example, how might the characteristics that you associated with Romanticism in listening to the Schubert and Mahler minuets influence the shaping of a Romantic sonata-form movement?

Example	Composer, title	Date
6.15	Brahms, *Symphony 3,* first movement	1883

Listen just to the opening of the Brahms symphony. Then compare it with the openings of the Mozart symphony and quartet movements discussed in Demonstration 6.2. Think about the character or feeling of each, noticing the striking differences between the opening theme of the Brahms and those of the other opening themes. Sing them. You will notice immediately the wide range, large leaps, and varied, often irregular, rhythm of the Brahms melody—hardly a melody at all, in the Classical sense. It seems to evolve out of itself, each fragment growing out of the previous one by subtle transformation. In contrast to the clearly articulated, balanced phrases of Mozart's opening statements, Brahms creates in this opening one enormously long gesture. You might also try to think back to Brahms's *Trio* for clarinet, cello, and piano (Example 2.26), which we discussed in the context of rhythmic complexity. You may remember that the *Trio* begins with an equally expansive gesture—the opening cello solo.

Perhaps most striking are the differences in Brahms's orchestration and harmony. The "Romantic" character of Brahms's opening depends greatly on his use of a large and varied orchestra and his thick, almost muddy texture within which the tone colors of specific instruments, particularly the horns, are exploited.

Brahms's use of harmony is often coloristic, bringing the concepts of harmony and sonority very close together. For example, between the first two chords there is an interesting change in color: A major tonic triad is followed by a functionally ambiguous chord which includes the tonic note but hints at the minor mode. This chord suggests both tonic and dominant functions by its particular sonority. (These two chords and the third, together with their upper melody line, below, pervade the entire movement.)

As the large gesture continues, major and minor are juxtaposed, along with chords which exploit the "edges" of the tonality. Brahms creates a kind of chromatic harmony composed of chords not strictly within the key but not changing the tonality either—merely enriching and coloring it. The result is a statement of thematic material that is, in comparison with the earlier sonata-form movements, unstable, wandering, and charged.

Given this style of grand gesture, enriched harmony, exploitation of instrumental color, and affective, almost associative character, is the model of the sonata form valid for the Brahms symphony movement? On what level is the generalization possible?

Listen to the rest of the movement. Notice, for example, the second theme (played by clarinets and bassoons), with its contrasting character, prepared for by the transition and a waiting passage. Note the closing passage, which evolves out of the contrasting second theme and then, by harmonic and motivic manipulation, merges into the development. (There is no clear end to the exposition, as in the other movements discussed.)

The development section includes a remarkable transformation of the second theme. Listen to its rapid shifts in key and its more active texture. The recapitulation emerges slowly through hints at the familiar motives, followed by the two opening chords which lead, finally, into the rebirth of the opening gesture. A long coda is added which includes further development and expansion.

The crucial relationships of the sonata form are thus revealed—almost more as essence than actuality in the light of these changes in style. The structure itself seems to have been altered in some ways; proportions are changed, and the continuous aspects of the form—the areas of organic growth—pervade the entire movement. The functions of the sections are clear, but they are rarely delineated by caesuras or cadences. Even clearly articulated phrase structure is rare; melodies are characterized by large gestures coalescing out of fragments.

Indeed, it is the notion of the sonata form as *sectional* which seems to have changed most as we compare this movement with the Mozart quartet movement (Example 6.14). We are carried along by a process of transformation and change already present in the harmony of the opening chords and in the evolving nature of the first theme. This emphasis on continuous growth, together with the associative implications of Brahms's instrumentation, harmony, and melodic-rhythmic design, generates a "Romantic" work. The course of events, like a narrative, continuously changes our perception of those elements which remain constant.

Having analyzed the different structural functions of passages within a sonata-form movement in Demonstration 6.2, you can test your ability to perceive these musical events. As in the demonstration, we focus here on excerpts from instrumental works by Haydn, Mozart, and Beethoven (Examples 6.16 through 6.24). These three composers are the "greats" of the Classical period (c. 1750 to 1827; 1827 being the year of Beethoven's death). It was in the Classical period that the sonata form became a fundamental way of thinking for composers of instrumental music.

Listen to each passage twice. Determine whether it can be characterized as one of the following, and check the corresponding column in the table below.

A. Statement
B. Transitional-development
C. Waiting passage[6]
D. Closing section

Example	A Statement	B Development	C Waiting	D Closing
6.16				
6.17				
6.18				
6.19				
6.20				
6.21				
6.22				
6.23				
6.24				

---

[6] Examples of waiting passages include brief statements of the thematic material into which they lead.

CORRECT ANSWERS

Example	Composer, title, date	A Statement	B Development	C Waiting	D Closing
6.16	Beethoven, *Quartet,* Op. 18, no. 1, second movement, 1799				X
6.17	Beethoven, *Sonata for Violin and Piano,* Op. 30, no. 2, third movement, 1802			X	
6.18	Beethoven, *Quartet,* Op. 18, no. 1, fourth movement, 1799	X			
6.19	Mozart, *Symphony 40,* K. 550, first movement, 1788	X			
6.20	Mozart, *Symphony 40,* K. 550, first movement, 1788		X		
6.21	Beethoven, *Quartet,* Op. 18, no. 1, fourth movement, 1799		X		
6.22	Beethoven, *Quartet,* Op. 18, no. 1, fourth movement, 1799			X	
6.23	Haydn, *Symphony 96,* fourth movement, 1791	X			
6.24	Haydn, *Symphony 96,* fourth movement, 1791		X		

ADDITIONAL MATERIALS

I   Mozart, *Symphony 40,* K. 550, fourth movement, 1788
Haydn, *Symphony 97,* first movement, 1792
Beethoven, *Symphony 4,* Op. 60, first movement, 1806

These three works (and many others are possible) illustrate large, symphonic sonata-form movements. They exemplify some of the diverse possibilities created by these three composers, who wrote in a relatively similar style and within the same structural framework. Listen to each of the movements several times. First, on the immediate level of a series of events, consider the differences among them in overall character. Then, using the general model on pages 231–232, compare the three movements in terms of structure, proportions, and the musical means used to generate these structural relationships. Consider the following questions:

1. Is there an introduction? How does it relate to the exposition? How would the piece sound without it?
2. What are the differences in character of the opening themes and what musical means are used to generate these differences? How are these differences related to the presence or absence of an introduction? Compare the differences in the proportions of these first theme statements.
3. How does the transition emerge out of the statement? What thematic material does it use? Is it immediately evident that you have left the stable statement? When and how does the composer move away from the first theme and key? What is the nature of the arrival at the new theme—is it delayed (the transition prolonged)? Is there a waiting passage, a pause, or a gradual emergence of the new theme? What is the difference in proportions among the transition passages, especially in relation to the first theme group?
4. What is the nature of the contrast between the first and second theme groups in each piece? What means (such as instrumentation, melodic-rhythmic shape, or harmony) are used to generate this contrast? Are there similarities among the works?
5. What about the closing section? What proportion of the exposition does it occupy? Does it include a new (closing) theme? What means does each composer use to establish stability? Is the exposition repeated on your recording?
6. How does the development section begin? Are you aware at once that this is development—that is, is it immediately unstable, modulatory, or ambiguous in harmony? Do you hear manipulation and distortion of thematic material? What material from the exposition

Haydn, from autograph score of *Andante in F Minor,* 1793

is developed in this section? Is new material introduced? What else does the composer do? Are there contrasts in texture and sonority? Is there a climax? Does the development fall into several sections? How does each composer "get back"? Through an extended waiting passage? Through the gradual emergence of stability and theme? At the climax, or after it? What about the length of the development in relation to the exposition and its parts?

7. Does the recapitulation begin exactly like the opening of the exposition? What differences are there between the recapitulation and the exposition?

8. Is there a coda? If so, how does it relate to the rest of the movement in proportions and function? Does it include, for example, further development? Does the movement end climactically or by "playing itself out"?

II   Sessions, *Piano Sonata 2,* first movement, 1946

Bartók, *Sonata for Two Pianos and Percussion,* second movement, 1937

Webern, *Concerto for Nine Instruments,* Op. 24, first movement, 1934

Schoenberg, *Quartet 4,* first movement, 1936

These works, all of them written within the last 55 years, are in the most general sense in sonata form. At the same time, the syntax of tonality operates, to some extent, only in the piece by Bartók. How, then, can we speak of sonata form, which depends for its very definition on tonal relationships? What is left of the form when the key relationships as well as the concepts of harmonic stability and instability associated with tonality are lacking?

Let us consider one of these movements more closely—Sessions's piano sonata. Listen to the movement several times to see if you can discover within it passages of relative stability. (Notice the opening, for example. It is a motive repeated with slight variation, elaborated to lead to a climax and the statement of another motive.) Hearing these passages in terms of their relative stability is only possible, of course, when you can perceive the work on its own terms—without superimposing on it expectations which distort your perception. You will not hear, for example, stability generated by the resolution of dissonance (since resolution implies a triad) or by a dominant-tonic progression establishing a clear tonal center.

Remember, however, that in the works we have studied the stability of statement was generated by other means as well—a melody-

Bartók, from autograph score of *String Quartet 5,* 1934

(*gliss. il trillo*)

and-accompaniment texture or a more palpable melodic shape and rhythmic motives which together define a theme. Less stable sections were characterized not only by instability of key but also by a more active texture, conflicts in accent and rhythm, melodic fragmentation, and, in general, a more rapid rate of change. Conclusion was generated often by harmonic stasis but also by a braking action which slowed down the rate of events, reiterating rather than generating something new. From these characteristics we were able to perceive the function of a passage, and we described the particular set of relationships among these functions as sonata form.

In Sessions's sonata we hear the stability of statement generated by most of those attributes which we have associated with thematic statement in music of the past *except* that of tonal stability. Similarly, we hear transition, a contrasting second theme, and a closing passage. Development follows the exposition, leading then to a varied recapitulation of the opening material.

In the Brahms movement, we described the relationships of sonata form "almost more as essence"—and so it is with these twentieth-century pieces. Within styles which are radically different from the styles of the works studied earlier, the idea of sonata form is still operative. Consider the works suggested here simply as a group sharing a common organizing principle. As you listen to them, you should become aware of (1) the essential nature of the sonata form and its great flexibility as an organizing principle and (2) the basic differences in style among these contemporaneous works, particularly as they influence the organization itself.

With these considerations we are to some extent anticipating Part Four, in which we will focus on aspects of style at various moments in history.

CHAPTER 7

Vincent Van Gogh, *Starry Night,* 1889

Continuous Organization

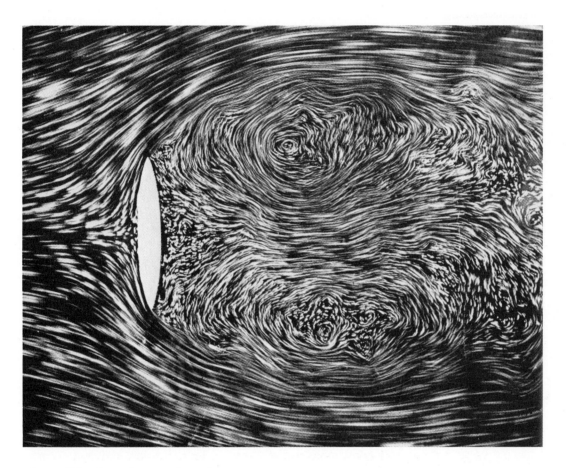

Flow of fluid passing an obstacle

Throughout this book we have emphasized the distinction between sectional and continuous organization as representing two distinct approaches to musical design. We first confronted the distinction on a rather small scale. In Chapter 3, for example, we differentiated between sectional melodies and continuous melodies. We noted that a prototypical tune in our culture tended to be a sectional one (like *Lassie*). Sectional tunes were characterized as having clear phrase structure and clearly articulated, often predictable, moments of arrival. Continuous melodies, in contrast, were different from our intuitive model of a tune especially in that they seemed, at least on first hearing, to go on and on, to be almost "serpentine" in their continuous "unwinding." The Vivaldi *Concerto Grosso* (Example 3.1) and the opening of the Liszt *Faust Symphony* (Example 3.2) were examples of continuous melodies.

In Demonstration 4.1, we focused on the contrast between sectional and continuous organization in larger-scaled structures. The minuet from Mozart's *Eine kleine Nachtmusik* (Example 4.10) was the initial illustration of a sectional piece, while a Chopin *Prelude* (Example 4.11) illustrated a continuous piece. We returned to the same Mozart minuet in Chapter 6 to begin the discussion of two basically sectional "forms," the minuet and the sonata form. We pointed out that sectional pieces are those which more easily lend themselves to schematic representation exactly because they fall into clearly defined sections to which we can give names. The discussion of sonata form, however, made it clear that sectional structures may include areas which are themselves more continuous than sectional. Indeed, it is the contrast between the more clearly sectional passages (statements) and the more continuous passages (development and transition) which contributes greatly to the variety and drama of the sonata form. And, interestingly, these more continuous sections are also apt to be more active in texture. Active texture will often create a more ongoing piece or section of a piece because the separate, independently moving strands tend to overlap.

But continuous organization is certainly not always generated by textural activity. The Chopin *Prelude* that you heard in Chapter 4 is quite inactive in texture, and yet it is fundamentally continuous—it does not fall into clearly distinguishable sections and thus defies schematic representation. In this chapter we will concentrate on the various factors that create continuousness and the ways in which continuous structure is organized. What, for example, does create this sense of ongoing movement in the Chopin *Prelude* you heard earlier? Go back

244

and listen to Example 4.11 again. Your growing awareness of harmonic stability and instability will help you to account for its continuous onward movement. While there are "pauses" in the flow of sound, these cadences are never full cadences (on the tonic); they do not create stable points of arrival. The harmonic instability coupled with the continuous outpouring of notes propels you forward without stop. The piece seems to be a single, cumulative gesture, not only because of its brevity but also because of the tight unity of motivic and harmonic material. Notice how each impulse grows motivically out of the previous one—expanding or compressing it—to generate an improvisatory, impetuous character by the flexibility of pulse and rhythm. It is interesting to note Chopin's final "statement": two chords, V to I. Yet, because of the particular positioning of these last chords, the piece does not seem to come to a full stop. Still caught up in the continuous flow of the music, we listen on until the sound dies away.

Thinking back, then, over the pieces you have listened to and the various aspects of music they have illustrated, it becomes clear that the contrast between sectional and continuous organization encompasses nearly all of these aspects—texture, rhythm, melodic design, motivic development, and differences in formal structure as well. With this in mind, listen now to several pieces which are all continuous but in different ways and for different reasons. You might use them to review and refresh your listening skills as you shift your attention from one aspect of the music to another. As you listen, ask yourself: What, in each excerpt, creates its particular onward movement? What sorts of inner relations give each its particular coherence?

Example	Composer, title	Date
7.1	J. Farmer, *Fair Phyllis*	1599
7.2	Vivaldi, *The Four Seasons,* "Winter"	1725
7.3	Haydn, *The Seasons,* "Summer"	1801
7.4	Debussy, *Pelléas and Mélisande,* Act IV, sc. 4	1902

You will notice that the four examples span a period of more than 300 years and that the pieces are ordered chronologically. Thus, as in previous chapters, you will want to pay attention to stylistic differences as you move through these three centuries of music.

John Farmer's *Fair Phyllis* (Example 7.1) is a late sixteenth-century **madrigal**—a secular work for voices based on a text in the "mother tongue" (rather than Latin). Like many English madrigals, the text is a jolly one and somewhat bawdy, but still more "polite" than many. The text concerns a shepherd who is looking for his fair love, Phyllis, and includes the words:

> Up and down he wandered
> Whilst she was missing,
> When he found her,
> Oh then they fell a-kissing.

Farmer creates a **catch** in both the music and the words by running the last line of the text above, around again to the first line. The piece thus "runs around" continuously both in words and music while the men and women sing the words "up and down" in quick imitation as if chasing one another in a game of "catch." Notice, too, Farmer's use of *word painting* as the pitch goes "up and down" along with the words.

In the excerpt from the fourth movement of *The Four Seasons* (Example 7.2), Vivaldi expresses his impression of winter. Notice, for

Madrigal singers (sixteenth-century German print)

example, the "harsh" sonority of the opening section and later the rushing, downward-tumbling figures played by the violin, reminding the listener perhaps of blustering wind and snow. These imitations of nature in sound (somewhat like the "word painting" in Farmer's madrigal) are organized musically around sequential repetitions of just a few figures. Each figure creates the musical material—the pattern—for the various sections of the piece. Thus the piece is clearly partitioned into large sections, but within sections the music goes on continuously through sequential repetition of the particular figure. For example, the first "figure" is simply a single repeated chord played by the whole string orchestra. Notice that the repeated chord changes regularly every eight beats, the change creating a higher-level structural rhythm corresponding to the rate of harmonic change. The next section is marked by the introduction of the solo violin and a new *melodic* figure which is again repeated sequentially. And once again the length of the figure establishes the structural rhythm within the section. Each statement of the figure marks off a structural unit of time.

As the piece continues, Vivaldi builds up a kind of mosaic of pieces (sections), each heralded by the introduction of a new figure and each made up, in turn, of mosaic-like repetitions of this single, small figure. While the underlying pulse is always clearly present, rhythmic vitality is created by changes in the length of the sequential unit, the rate of the notes within the figures themselves, together with the changing length of the larger units of the mosaic—the sections. In this way Vivaldi creates a boldly hierarchic structure with each element delineated but then grouped together to form the next larger level of structure—notes are grouped into figures, figures are grouped into sequences, sequences are grouped into sections, and sections are grouped together to form the still larger divisions of the whole piece (notice that the excerpt ends with a return to earlier material). Continuousness, then, is contained by the boundaries of this structural hierarchy.

Haydn also composed a piece depicting the changing seasons. In this excerpt (Example 7.3) we find him in the middle of a summer storm which gradually fades away, ending with the sun breaking through the clouds. Haydn marvelously portrays the change by gradually moving from imitative, texturally active, chromatic, and rhythmically agitated music to music which is texturally less and less active, more diatonic, and rhythmically straightforward. Following a cadence on the tonic and a pause, Haydn captures the sense of calm with a simple melody and accompaniment. The striking change occurs as the

Moorish arch
The elaborate figuration is contained by the broader architectural outlines . . . the excerpt ends with a return to earlier material.

structure becomes sectional rather than continuous; the violins play and the tenor sings clearly articulated phrases, which characterize sectional organization. Thus the passage not only depicts the gradual dissipation of a summer storm but also the contrast between continuously organized music and sectionally organized music. Or, the contrast in musical means in fact *creates* the changes in pictorial and dramatic associations suggested by the text:

CHORUS: Furiously rages the storm.
        Heaven help us!
        The broad heavens are aflame.
        Woe to us wretches!
        Peal on peal crashes the heavy thunder.
        The earth totters, shaken
        to the depths of the sea.

TENOR: The dark clouds scatter,
       the rage of the storm is stilled.

In the excerpt from his opera *Pelléas and Mélisande* (Example 7.4), Debussy creates continuousness in a manner quite different from any of the other composers included in this group. We hear one voice at a time singing over a quiet, usually minimal accompaniment with a thin, almost fragile texture. The vocal lines are rhythmically more like speaking than like what we think of as a song. Compare them, for example, to the clearly articulated phrases of the song at the end of the Haydn excerpt (Example 7.3) or to the duet from Mozart's *Don*

Detail of Spanish gold and silk brocade
An intricately woven, animated fabric.

Giovanni (Example 3.20). Certainly there are pauses—breaks in the flow of sound which at times give the lovers a breathless quality. But we move through these pregnant silences which carry the music dramatically onward rather than stopping it. Harmonically, Debussy

Debussy, from autograph score of *Pelléas and Mélisande*, 1892–1902

combines pitches to create sonorities that are tonally ambiguous and ephemeral, and this too contributes significantly to the sense of continuous movement. This same excerpt is discussed again in Chapter 12, where we compare this love scene to one from Wagner's *Tristan and Isolde.* You may want to look ahead to that passage for further comments (see p. 414). Listen to the excerpt again, now following the text below. Notice especially the extraordinary way that Debussy captures the mood and feelings of this climactic moment in the opera when the two secret lovers meet in the forest for the last time:

PELLÉAS: Ma pauvre Mélisande! J'aurais presque peur de te toucher. Tu es encore hors d'haleine comme un oiseau pourchassé. C'est pour moi que tu fais tout cela? J'entends battre ton coeur comme si c'était le mien. Viens ici, plus près de moi.

MÉLISANDE: Pourquoi riez-vous?

PELLÉAS: Je ne ris pas; ou bien je ris de joie sans le savoir . . . Il y aurait plutôt de quoi pleurer.

MÉLISANDE: Nous sommes venus ici il y a bien longtemps. Je me rappelle . . .

PELLÉAS: Oui . . . il y a de longs mois. Alors, je ne savais pas. Sais-tu pourquoi je t'ai demandé de venir ce soir?

MÉLISANDE: Non.

PELLÉAS: C'est peut-être la dernière fois que je te vois. Il faut que je m'en aille pour toujours.

MÉLISANDE: Pourquoi dis-tu toujours que tu t'en vas?

PELLÉAS: Je dois te dire ce que tu sais déjà? Tu ne sais pas ce que je vais te dire?

MÉLISANDE: Mais non, mais non; je ne sais rien.

PELLÉAS: Tu ne sais pas pourquoi il faut que je m'éloigne? Tu ne sais pas que c'est parce que . . .

PELLÉAS: Poor Mélisande! I'm almost afraid to touch you. You're still out of breath like a hunted bird. Was it for me you did all that? I hear your heart beating as if it were my own. Come closer to me.

MÉLISANDE: Why do you laugh?

PELLÉAS: I'm not laughing; or perhaps I'm laughing for joy, without knowing it. There's really more reason to cry.

MÉLISANDE: We came here a long time ago. I remember . . .

PELLÉAS: Yes . . . months ago. I didn't know then. Do you know why I asked you to come this evening?

MÉLISANDE: No.

PELLÉAS: It's perhaps the last time I shall see you. I must go away for ever.

MÉLISANDE: Why do you always say you are going away?

PELLÉAS: Must I tell you what you already know? Don't you know what I'm going to say?

MÉLISANDE: No, no, I don't.

PELLÉAS: You don't know why I have to go away? You don't know that it's because . . .

(kissing her suddenly)

. . . je t'aime.   . . . I love you.

MÉLISANDE: Je t'aime aussi.   MÉLISANDE: I love you, too.

DEMONSTRATION 7.2
The Fugue
(Sides 11–12)

In Chapter 6 we dealt with two sectional forms, the minuet and sonata form, which are perhaps unusual in recurring through several centuries; yet each instance of these forms brings them to life in a unique and particular way. In Demonstration 7.1 you heard pieces which had a number of things in common—they were all continuous rather than sectional in their organization, they all were associated with a story or an impression of nature, and all but one were written for voices. But unlike the examples in Chapter 6, they were all quite different in their form. How, you might ask, could there be a "form" that composers might use to organize extended compositions which are continuous? The **fugue** is just such a form; but exactly because it is more continuous than sectional, the working out of the fugal process varies considerably from one example to another. Like sectional forms, any one fugue is always the result of its particular germinal motives, as well as the general stylistic characteristics common to the time in which it was written and to the style of the particular composer. But the differences among fugues go beyond this; in fact, the only part of the fugue really common to all of them is the opening procedure. Listen, for example, to the opening of the C-sharp major fugue from the *Well-Tempered Clavier* (Example 7.5) by Bach.[1]

Example	Composer, title	Date
7.5	Bach, *Well-Tempered Clavier,* Book I, fugue no. 3 in C-sharp major, opening	1722
7.6	Bach, *Well-Tempered Clavier,* Book I, fugue no. 3 in C-sharp major, complete	1722

The fugue begins with a single unaccompanied melodic line called the **subject.** You will quickly discover that the entire fugue is concerned with it—a continuous exploration of its implications and possibilities. After the statement of the subject, the opening continues with the

---

[1] The *Well-Tempered Clavier,* Books I and II (two sets of preludes and fugues in all 24 major and minor keys), was written for the harpsichord or clavichord (the term *clavier* referred to stringed keyboard instruments). "Well-tempered" refers to a system of tuning which divides the octave into 12 equidistant tones, thus allowing for performance in all keys.

entrance in "imitation" of the two other participants, the middle and lower voices, which complete the texture. Notice that each voice enters with a complete statement of the subject. When the middle voice enters, however, the top voice continues on with a related melody, called the **countersubject,** which is played "against" the subject. As the third voice enters, the two higher voices continue; the texture grows progressively thicker and more complex. This opening portion of the fugue which introduces all the participants, each stating the subject, is called the *exposition.* It may be diagrammed as shown here:

Example 7.5 BACH, *Well-Tempered Clavier,* Book I, Fugue no. 3 in C-sharp major, (exposition)

H:	Subject	Countersubject	Free material
	M:	Subject	Countersubject
		L:	Subject

Example 7.6 BACH, *Well-Tempered Clavier,* Book I, Fugue no. 3 in C-sharp major (complete)

H: _____

M: _____   Episode 1   _____   Episode 2

L: _____

     (Sequential)   (Subject emerges out of episode)   (Modulates, shifts to minor mode)

     Episode 4   _____   Episode 5

     (Head of subject in sequence)   (Subject sneaks in)   (Extended sequence—ending with waiting passage)

You have already heard a number of fugal expositions in previous demonstrations, for example, in Example 1.11, from the Bach *Suite in B Minor,* and Example 1.31, from the Handel *Concerto Grosso,* Op. 6, no. 2, where we discussed the procedure in terms of its texture and the embedding of a motive in "new sound environments." In Chapter 2 you heard the opening of a Mozart string quartet movement which we discussed in the context of "rhythmic complexity," pointing out that its active texture went together, in this case, with a slow-moving, nonactive subject. In Chapter 5 we used the exposition of the Bach fugue in B minor from his *Well-Tempered Clavier* to illustrate chromaticism. Finally, in Demonstration 7.1, the excerpt from Haydn's *The Seasons* begins with a fugal exposition.

To use the same word, *exposition,* to describe both the opening phase of the fugue and the first large section of the sonata form seems hardly appropriate. And in fact, a comparison of these two types of exposition will reveal some of the striking differences between the two approaches to musical design. You may want to consider these differences as you go on listening to the C-sharp major fugue.

Listen to the whole fugue now (Example 7.6). Following the diagram that begins on page 252 and continues below will help you pay attention to the contrast between moments when the subject is

---

Episode 3

(Minor mode,
texture
thins)

(Sequential,
modulating)

(Subject rather submerged,
minor mode, extended to
cadence with less
active texture)

Episode 6

present and when it is not. Notice, for example, that after the exposition the piece continues with a passage that does not include the subject. These phases of the fugue, in which the subject does not appear in its entirety, are called **episodes.** The term conveys a sense of their freer, more continuous character. It is in the episodes of the fugue that Bach creates the greatest structural contrast. To do so, he uses the following compositional means:

1. The three voices are more equal in importance, since the fugue subject does not predominate.
2. The subject itself loses its integrity through fragmentation and other subtle transformations, such as the inversion of a melodic figure.
3. The harmony shifts in tonal center, often through the use of sequential passages.
4. The normative rhythmic unit (the length of the fugue subject) is disrupted.

This contrast between phases in which the subject is present and those in which it is not is crucial to the inner motion of the fugue. As the subject becomes submerged in the intricacies of the episodes, one feels a sense of instability and tension. The reappearance of the subject in turn creates a renewed stability in the otherwise continuous flow of the piece.

As you listen to the fugue, notice that in spite of these contrasts, the fugue seems a homogeneous whole; when the second voice and the countersubject have entered, all the material of the piece has been introduced. How different this procedure is from sonata form, with its clearly differentiated areas and dramatic contrasts! Your listening process must also be different: To expect from a fugue the kind of contrast that one finds in sonata form—contrasts in theme, character, texture, rate of events, and often instrumentation—could blind the listener to its pleasures. In listening to the fugue, you can become fascinated not only with the appearance and disappearance of the subject, but also with the subtle changes in texture and sonority. Enjoy the relative degrees of motion in the various strands of the texture and the changes in sonority that result from different voices playing the subject and from the surrounding activity.

The score of this fugue is printed on pages 255–258. However well (or poorly) you read music, you will be interested in following the music as you listen to the entire fugue. The episodes and reentries of the subject and countersubject are indicated in the music.

Example 7.6 BACH, *Well-Tempered Clavier,* Book I, Fugue no. 3 in C-sharp major

Continuous Organization

Episode 5

Waiting passage (dominant pedal = x)

In a certain sense the fugue is player's rather than listener's music; the player, with the music before him or her, is extremely aware of the texture and its component lines. Yet in a work which may at first sound much the same all the way through—which is, indeed, monothematic (and might even be termed *monochromatic*)—the listener too can come to hear the subtle changes within its homogeneous, continuous structure—to perceive the art in the midst of artifice.

Example	Composer, title	Date
7.7	Handel, *Messiah,* "And with His stripes we are healed"	1742
7.8	Telemann, *Trio Sonata in D Minor,* fourth movement	1740
7.9	Beethoven, *Symphony 7,* Op. 92, second movement	1811–1812
7.10	Hindemith, *Mathis der Maler* (symphony)	1934

In the next group of examples you will hear two more fugues from the Baroque period by composers who were contemporaries of Bach, and fugatos from a Beethoven symphony and a twentieth-century symphony. The fugue was at its height during the Baroque period. Essentially a procedure rather than a fixed form like the minuet in the Classical period, the fugue could assume a variety of characters in both vocal and instrumental music. Handel, Bach's contemporary, wrote a fugue in his oratorio *Messiah* on the words "And with His stripes we are healed" (Example 7.7). The wide leap on "His stripes" (i.e., his lacerations) contrasts with the **melisma** (many tones on one syllable) on "healed"—both are examples of Handel's word painting. The voices enter successively from highest to lowest—sopranos, altos, tenors, and basses.

Another contemporary of Bach, not nearly as well known today yet quite famous in the eighteenth century, is Georg Phillip Telemann. In fact, when the important position of Cantor (director of music) at St. Thomas's Church in Leipzig became vacant in 1722, Telemann was the first choice, over Bach, of the Church authorities. Only when Telemann declined the position was Bach chosen for the post the following year. Example 7.8 is the last movement of the *Trio Sonata* by Telemann for flute, oboe, and basso continuo (the second movement of which you heard previously, Example 2.18), and it is a fugue. Since this is only a three-voiced fugue, and each of the instruments has a

Detail from *Ecce Homo* by Pedro de Mena
"And with His stripes we are healed."

distinctive timbre, you should be able to follow the course of the fugue very clearly. The three parts (basso continuo actually includes cello and harpsichord) enter in the order flute, oboe, and basso continuo. After a short episode, we hear a statement of the subject in the major mode by the flute followed by a cadence which marks the end of the first large section of the fugue. Notice that unlike Bach in the C-sharp major fugue, Telemann marks off boundaries which contain the otherwise continuous motion. The next large section begins with an episode followed by statements of the subject by oboe and then flute, separated by an episode which is again marked by a cadence. Finally, in the last section we hear statements by continuo and flute in close imitation, called **stretto**—that is, the flute begins its statement before the continuo has completed its statement. A brief *ritardando,* a rather surprising unison passage (in the midst of all this activity), and a cadential passage complete this short, spirited fugue.

Example 7.9 is a **fugato,** that is, a long fugal section, often climactic in effect, in a larger composition, as opposed to a fugue as an independent movement. Here Beethoven uses the theme of a theme-and-variations movement as a fugue subject, and uses the cumulative aspect of the fugal exposition to build to a climax. The passage begins softly in the strings with the subject (♩ ♫ | ♩ ♪) combined with a countermelody in faster-moving notes. After all the strings have entered, the winds enter quickly in succession with a crescendo leading to a thunderous *fortissimo* statement of the subject and countermelody by the entire orchestra, constituting another variation.

The practice of fugal writing continued into the twentieth century. Hindemith, somewhat analogously to Beethoven, wrote a fugato in the first movement of his symphony derived from his opera *Mathis der Maler* ("Matthias the Painter") (Example 7.10). Like earlier classical symphonies, this first movement is in sonata form. But unlike the Beethoven excerpt, Hindemith's fugato occurs in the development section: Near the beginning he uses the second theme from the exposition, where it had a more lyrical, romantic character, as a more angular fugue subject. How do you know this is not a nineteenth-century piece?

While this chapter has been concerned with continuously organized music, the examples themselves should make it clear that "continuous" and "sectional" represent the extremes of a continuum rather than a simple dichotomy. That is, any particular piece might be described as more or less continuous or sectional, each one falling somewhere along this continuum. More important, as we have suggested earlier, pieces which are, say, primarily sectional in their organization will most likely include significant contrasting passages which are themselves continuous. Indeed, such passages will then take on a particular *functional* significance (as transition, development, dramatic climax, etc.) within the context of an otherwise clearly sectional structure. In a similar way, pieces which are primarily continuous will include passages that clearly delimit sections; within these sections, though, the music is continuous. For example, we noted that Vivaldi, in the "Winter" excerpt from *The Four Seasons,* created a hierarchy of mosaics with the musical "content" of these mosaics made up of continuously related sequences and groups of sequences. The fugue, while at first seemingly continuous in its general procedure, was found to fall into phases (if not sections) characterized by the statement of the fugue subject in one voice or another in contrast to episodes where motives from the subject were treated more freely. Furthermore, each of the fugues you heard differed in their relations between subject statements and episodes—depending on the length of the fugue subject itself, the number of voices involved, and the proportion of time devoted to statements of the subject in contrast to the manipulation of subject motives in the episodes. Finally, in the Telemann fugue we found that, somewhat like Vivaldi, the larger architectural design was defined by periodic cadences which bound together into sections the continuousness of fugal imitation and freer episodes.

But the distinction is perhaps most important as it contributes to the art of listening. We pointed out earlier that an awareness of the differences between the two approaches to musical design in fact involves nearly all the aspects of music which we have discussed throughout the book. Thus, growing more sensitive to this general contrast between two ways of shaping music and hence of *listening to music* means, at the same time, growing more appreciative of the many dimensions of music and multiplicity of ways composers can interrelate them. In the end, then, this thread which we have woven through all the sections of the book is perhaps as much a way of unifying *its* concerns as it is a way of helping you toward the art of listening.

ADDITIONAL MATERIALS

One aspect of our initial distinction between sectional and continuous organization remains to be clarified. We indicated that works described as continuous in organization "defy schematic representation"; that is, they cannot be meaningfully described in terms of some combination of letters (A, B, *a*, *b*, etc.). What, then, can be said of the fugue? Is it not a "form"?

Listen to the following pieces, all of which are fugues. Think about the concept *fugue* as a generalization applicable to these works, compared with the concept *sonata form* as a generalization applicable to the works discussed in Chapter 6.

> Bach, *Cantata 21,* final chorus, 1714
> Mozart, *Requiem,* Kyrie, K. 626, 1791
> Beethoven, *String Quartet,* Op. 133 (*Grosse Fuge*), 1825–1826 (Example 5.17)
> Liszt, *Faust Symphony,* "Mephistopheles" (fugue exposition only), 1854–1857
> Brahms, *Variations and Fugue on a Theme by Handel,* fugue, 1861
> Bartók, *Music for Strings, Percussion, and Celesta,* first movement, 1936
> Hindemith, *Ludus Tonalis,* first fugue, 1942

While we emphasized in Chapter 6 that the sonata form is an abstraction which each piece realizes uniquely, the design nevertheless does describe the whole work. It includes a basic *ordering* of functional relationships: exposition (statement, transition, statement, closing), development, recapitulation, coda.

Whatever the common attributes of fugues, however, their continuous nature precludes (except in the exposition) such a generalized ordering of events. The course or design of each fugue is unique. Tovey makes the distinction clear in his definition of fugue: "Fugue is a texture the rules of which do not suffice to determine the shape of the composition as a whole."[2]

For example, notice that in the fugue from Bach's *Cantata 21* the subject is nearly always present, one statement following immediately upon another. Only once before the freer coda do we find an episode. In this piece a normative structural rhythm is established by the length of the subject and is maintained almost throughout. How different from Bach's fugue no. 3 in C-sharp major (discussed in Demonstration 7.2), in which the play between subject statements and episodes is an ever-present source of structural tension! In the fugue from the cantata, the omnipresence of the subject itself transfers our attention to the tone color of the particular voice or instrument playing it, the contrasts in density and complexity of texture, and the fashion in which each subject statement emerges out of the total sound fabric.

While the different effects of the two Bach fugues stem primarily from the spectacular use of chorus and orchestra (with prominent trumpets) in the cantata, as opposed to the solo harpsichord or piano used in the C-sharp major fugue, the particular ordering of events in each fugue is also a contributing factor. Certainly the cantata fugue seems, in our continuum of sectional-continuous organization, much nearer the sectional pole, while the C-sharp major fugue seems much more continuous.

In listening to the other fugues listed above, notice the following aspects: (1) the relative proportions of subject statements and episodes; (2) the character of the subject itself and how this influences other events in the fugue; (3) the effect of harmonic style (for example,

---

[2] Donald Tovey, *The Forms of Music* (New York: New American Library, Meridian Books, 1957), p. 36.

whether the piece is tonal or not); (4) consistency of texture and textural contrasts (in density, complexity, and activity); and (5) the importance of thematic material other than the subject and, indeed, whether more than one subject is developed.

PART FOUR

Style and the Historical Context

Introduction:
Listening to History

On several occasions in the course of this book we have asked you to think about questions of musical style, but usually within the context of some particular aspect of music. In Demonstration 1.1, "The Variety of Sound," for example, we asked questions concerning different "sound worlds," uses of the orchestra—even different uses of music in varying social contexts. Each of these characteristic aspects of a piece, in fact, helps to define its particular style. In Chapter 2 we made a quick sweep through music history, considering the varying uses of rhythmic complexity in works written over a period of 400 years. In Chapter 3 we drew attention to your intuitive "model of a sensible tune," contrasting this with melodies that seemed to derive from a different set of norms for melody making. This was another way of pointing to differences in style. Chapter 5 included not only a discussion and illustrations of possibilities other than functional harmony—that is, differing *harmonic* styles—but also contrasting examples of the twelve-bar blues, showing stylistic change within a single structure. This idea was carried further in the historical trip through the minuet and sonata forms in Chapter 6. Finally, in Chapter 7 we illustrated stylistic differences within continuously organized music generally and within fugues specifically. But in none of these excursions did we deal directly with how the words *style* and *history* relate to a given work or composer or how various styles interact within one musical era. It is to these more specific historical questions that we now turn.

Style, as we shall use the term, refers to the collection of musical attributes that characterizes the music of a particular composer or era. A composer's style is, in fact, his or her set of implicit norms, assumptions, and unique characteristics; it is this which allows you to say, even when you turn on the radio in the middle of a work, "Ah, Bach!" or "That's Brahms!" How do you know?

But we are not concerned here merely with identification, which can become a game substituting for, or at least interfering with, the experience of the unique work in its totality. Rather we are concerned with a kind of flexibility in listening, at times approaching virtuosity, which allows you to shift your focus—to move freely from one period of music to another, perceiving as configurations and events those which are appropriate to the piece in question. In short, we are concerned with your ability to involve yourself with the work on its own terms.

We have emphasized throughout the text that in experiencing music, the context will define the particulars and the particulars generate the context. And as you moved from one musical dimension to another, the notion of context itself—for example, your sense of what the important features of a piece were as well as how they interrelated—changed. In the chapters that follow we introduce a range of historical and stylistic contexts, each suggesting alternative possibilities composers have found for shaping the fundamental materials of music. Listening to music *on its own terms,* then, assumes on the part of you, the listener, both the ability to perceive the various possibilities we have discussed in previous chapters together with an awareness of the particular manner in which a composer manipulates and plays with these possibilities. Expanding and using this new awareness will give you a sense of music history that you can use in a practical way to enhance your everyday listening experience.

How can we characterize the set of perspectives we are about to explore? Imagine a map on which historical time is plotted against various musical elements of the sort we have already considered: melody, rhythm, texture, and so forth.

Our method in the preceding chapters has mainly been to extract *horizontal* slices out of the terrain represented by this map. That is, we have compared music of diverse periods and cultures with respect to a particular dimension (melody, texture, etc.) of music. In the section that follows, we will explore a complementary approach to this by considering *vertical* slices of the map. Rather than considering a single dimension of music individually, we will discuss the ways in which particular musical features interact during a particular "slice" of time. This merging and integration of musical dimensions during a given period in history, or within the work of an individual composer, is another way of describing *style.*

How do individual styles emerge and change? These are not simple questions, and they cannot be approached simply by altering the way we slice the map of the musical terrain. We must consider a number of other issues: What is the role or social function of music in different cultures? How do musicians themselves view artistic expression in different cultures or periods? What instruments, vocal techniques, or other music "technologies" are available for making and organizing sound in a particular era? Who performs music in a particular culture? Who listens to it?

Recall your reactions to two of the earliest examples in Chapter 1, Haydn's *Symphony 8* and Mahler's *Symphony 1*. (Examples 1.5 and 1.6). When we originally discussed the differences between these pieces, we made two observations: (1) that the Mahler piece used many *more* instruments than the Haydn, and (2) that Mahler used a larger *variety* of instruments. Why did these composers choose such different means while ostensibly writing for the same medium (the *orchestra*) and in the same genre (the *symphony*)? Was Haydn simply a less imaginative composer than Mahler? Was he making a capricious or willful choice to restrict the size of his orchestra? Or, conversely, was Mahler's orchestration excessive or overly grandiose?

We cannot answer these questions without knowing some of the circumstances of these composers' careers and the larger social contexts in which they practiced their art. In other words, we need to place these composers in their respective historical contexts. Haydn, for example, had little or no choice about the instrumentation of his *Symphony 8*. The work was composed for Prince Paul Anton Esterházy, a minor aristocrat who employed Haydn and also a limited staff of performing musicians. Haydn's instrumentation reflects both the small size of this staff orchestra and the kinds of instruments represented in the group. Moreover, the symphony in question was meant to be performed in one of the palace chambers, as an after-dinner entertainment for the prince and his guests.

As for the instruments used in the symphony by Mahler, some of them didn't even exist in Haydn's time. Furthermore, by the 1880s, when Mahler wrote his *Symphony 1,* symphonies were not being written as "after-dinner amusements" to be performed in private rooms. Most major cities had large, publicly supported orchestras that performed in concert halls accommodating a thousand or more people. Not only had performance situations evolved into something quite different physically, but even the generally accepted meaning of the terms "orchestra" and "symphony" had changed considerably since Haydn's time, and large orchestrations such as Mahler employed in his *Symphony 1* were considered artistically ambitious but not excessive.

Considerations of this kind illustrate how knowledge of historical circumstance can heighten your understanding of particular pieces. In the following sections, we will explore a series of comparisons similar to those observed between the Haydn and Mahler symphonies. The juxtaposition of pieces—alike in some of their dimensions, but radically different in style—will dramatize the relation between musical expression and historical-cultural context. But your engagement with these new issues depends on your skills in using the listening approaches introduced in the previous sections. Thus, the first stage in discussing cultural contexts will be to draw the lines of basic musical kinship and contrast between the works being compared. Only then can you begin to appreciate the significance of the social-historical situations that underlie these relationships.

We are asking you, then, to experiment once again with different contexts in which to regard great musical achievements. Along the way you should remember Stravinsky's hopeful admonition: That while we cannot expect to explain away the unique "dialectic of music" with words, we may continually broaden and refine our frames of reference, bringing more knowledge and skill to the art of listening.

In keeping with the spirit of the text, we approach the study of history and style as we have other aspects of music—through your direct listening experience. To do so, we have chosen works in these demonstrations that, in most instances, are immediately striking in their stylistic differences but are so in different ways and for different reasons. For example, Chapters 8 and 12 are organized chronologically while the three middle chapters—Chapter 9, 10, and 11—weave in and out of chronological time. Further, in Chapter 8, we begin—not

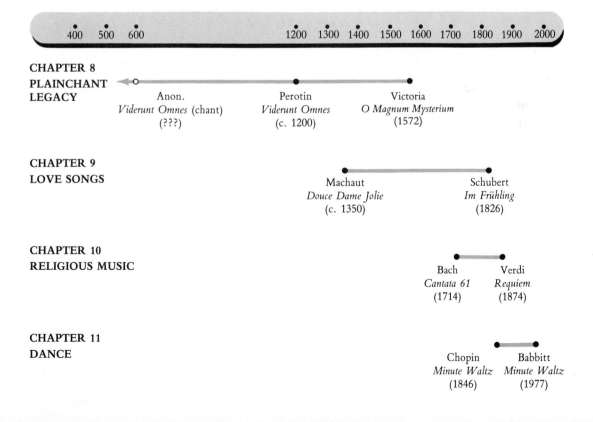

surprisingly—with the chronologically earliest of our examples, and the examples in this chapter span the longest time period—roughly 800 years in all. In contrast, Chapter 12, which brings us up almost to the present, covers the shortest period of time—just 50 years. In Chapter 13 we present a final overview of all the examples you will have heard, placing them in the order in which they were written so you can view them in their chronological context.

Chapters 9, 10, and 11 include pairs of examples that are starkly contrasting in style and in time of composition, but so chosen because, in each case, they share some common human theme that has engaged the interest of composers throughout history—love, religion, dance. With each succeeding chapter, the pairs close in on historical distance in two ways: The historical distance *between* pairs becomes less—500 years, 160 years, 130 years—while at the same time their dates of composition come closer and closer to our own time (the most recent composed in 1977). Interestingly enough, though, this gradual *historical* convergence does not result in *stylistic* convergence; indeed, pieces in the last pair, separated by the least time, may well sound the most divergent stylistically. In contrast, you will probably find that the examples in Chapter 8 sound the most similar to one another, even though their dates of composition cover the longest time span. (Of course, given the remoteness of those times, we tend to gloss over differences that may have been experienced by the original participants as quite radical.)

This question of nonparallelism between chronological distance and stylistic distance is an intriguing one, which we pursue in Chapter 12. Here, we consider in some depth the rather dramatic stylistic changes that occurred in the music composed during a relatively short period in history—the 55 years bridging the turn of the twentieth century, 1859–1913.

By approaching history and style in this way we hope to give you a sense of music history in practice: On one hand, an immediate feel for the questions and puzzles that continue to intrigue historians; and, on the other, at least an inkling of the ways in which composers' past musical experiences—their own personal and internalized music histories—can play a very active role in the compositional process.

You may wonder, as you work your way through these examples, why we have not included any from the so-called Classical period. This historical lacuna results from our unique approach and its emphasis on your own direct experience. Music of the Classical period is the most familiar to you, partly because it has been emphasized throughout the earlier chapters, and partly because this is the music that is most often performed and recorded. As a result, this music has become a kind of reference literature: An experiential point of comparison in relation to which the music composed both before and after is not only heard, but often *judged* (recall our discussion of your "model of a sensible tune" [Chapter 3], and later the tacit assumption of tonality as basic to your sense of musical coherence [Chapter 5]). And since our purpose in Part Four is to bring you closer to questions of stylistic contrast and change, we focus your attention precisely on music that is less familiar. This serves to heighten your awareness of differences in stylistic norms—what Schoenberg has called the "means of comprehensibility"—which composers in differing times and places have taken as *their* frames of reference.

In learning to approach these few works in this fashion—with more appropriate "ears," so to speak—you will find it easier and more rewarding in the future when you approach other, less familiar works for the first time in live or recorded performances. While you cannot expect to put yourself into a thirteenth-century cathedral to listen to the latest composition by the composer Perotin, or even an eighteenth-century church to experience a work that Bach has just completed for a special occasion, you *can* develop a sense for where the musical action is in a piece, where to focus your attention, and, in general, what to expect as well as what *not* to expect.

As in all of your work, we encourage you to listen actively and questioningly to each example:

> What creates contrast—particularly between stability and instability, tension and repose?
> What musical means are used to create structural boundaries—of phrases, of whole sections?
> How is time organized?
> How is detail related to large design?
> What, in turn, was the social and cultural environment during these varied moments in time and place?
> Who, at the time of composition, was listening to the music you are hearing now?
> Where and why did people listen?
> What were the composers' working conditions, who were their colleagues, what were the social and musical rewards, the freedoms, the constraints?

While we will try to guide your listening toward these questions, often proposing answers, a personal and practical feel for music history will only result from your developing sense of how composers variously shape musical materials to create expressiveness and coherence.

CHAPTER 8

A page from a Medieval illuminated music manuscript

Plainchant and Its Legacy: Medieval and Renaissance Polyphony

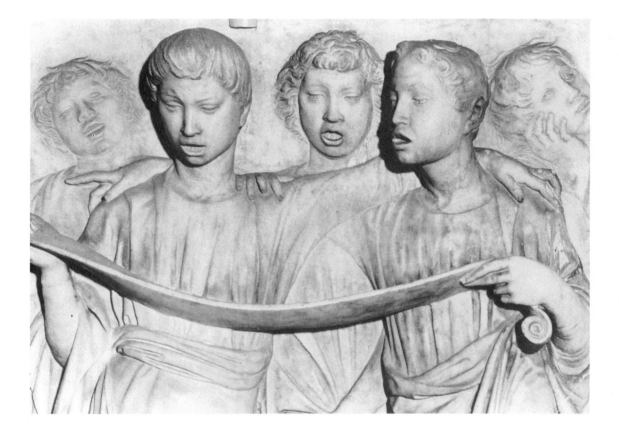

Luca Della Robbia (1399–1482) bas-relief: choristers

In speaking of music history and the historical context, we have implicitly been referring only to the history of Western music. And, indeed, our discussion in the chapters that follow will be confined largely to that tradition. However, to remind you that there are other musical traditions and to set our study of Western music history into the larger context of world music, we begin with two examples from very different musical traditions: one a religious chant from an Eastern religious tradition; the other a religious chant from the very beginnings of our own Western European tradition.

Listen now to these two examples: the first from a Tibetan Buddhist ceremony; the second from the vast repertory of Christian plainchant. The text for Example 8.2 is provided below.

Example	Composer, title	Date
8.1	*Khyabjug*, Tibetan Buddhist chant ("Invitation to the Diety")	Unknown
8.2	*Viderunt Omnes* ("All Have Seen")	Unknown

Viderunt omnes fines terrae salutare Dei nostri: jubilate Deo omnis terra. Notum fecit Dominus salutare suum: ante conspectum gentium revelavit justitiam suam.

All the ends of the earth have seen the salvation of our God. All the earth shall rejoice in God. The Lord has made known his salvation: Before the face of all the peoples He has revealed His righteousness.

The Buddhist example (Example 8.1) probably seems much further from your notion of singing than the plainchant. The pitch register is unusually low, the tone quality rough, almost growl-like, and the singers seem unconcerned about moving together from one pitch to another. The monks, especially the lead singer, seem at times to be clearing their throats, and in fact their singing is directed in part toward helping them attain a certain physical state, one appropriate to their meditation on the sacred words they are chanting. The example of plainchant (Gregorian chant) may, on first listening, seem more familiar; but it may be as difficult for us to understand the *experience* of singing plainchant for the Christian monk as it is for us to appreciate how the Buddhist monk experiences the singing of Tibetan chant. Both the plainchant and the Tibetan chant were sung by clerics and lay monks in performing rituals of their respective religions. This is not music intended for the passive enjoyment of an audience. It is music directed inward rather than outward, its primary aim always being to enhance the sacred texts for the participants—the officiating monks or priests and the assembled worshipers.

PLAINCHANT

Turning now directly to the beginnings of Western musical tradition, recall that you have already encountered examples of plainchant (more commonly called Gregorian chant) in the first three chapters. The sound of plainchant was probably somewhat familiar to you even then. Plainchant has often been used in film and television scores to help create the ambience of the Medieval era. Most of the plainchant repertory is, however, far older than the Middle Ages, dating back to the earliest period of Christianity and before. Understanding its original purpose is a crucial step toward listening artfully to all of early music, since the repertory of plainchant spawned many of the most significant developments in Western music.

Plainchant is religious music, the sung portion of the liturgy of the Catholic church. As such, it is one of many ancient traditions in which sacred texts are sung as a form of prayer, that is, as a part of religious ritual. Other examples of religious chant are the Vedic chant of India, Jewish chant, and the chanting of the Koran.

One of the problems we face in listening to plainchant today is the deceptively simple nature of its texture. Plainchant consists of a single, unaccompanied melodic strand; it is monophonic. However, to the medieval singer of chant, or the initiated listener, this single strand might not have been simple at all. The different sound qualities of different vowels, the pacing of the breathing according to the phrases of the text, the perception of resonance within the body and within the performing space—any or all of these could have been experienced

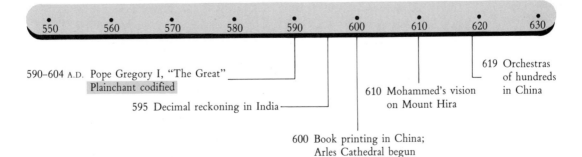

| 550 | 560 | 570 | 580 | 590 | 600 | 610 | 620 | 630 |

590–604 A.D. Pope Gregory I, "The Great"
Plainchant codified

595 Decimal reckoning in India

600 Book printing in China;
Arles Cathedral begun

610 Mohammed's vision
on Mount Hira

619 Orchestras
of hundreds
in China

as different "dimensions of music." Thus, for the monks, chant may have presented as many separable dimensions as we perceive in pieces of more explicitly complex texture.

As we pointed out in Chapter 2, the rhythm of plainchant melodies is ametrical: In both *Veni Creator Spiritus* (Example 2.5) and *Viderunt Omnes* (Example 1.3) there is a gentle sense of pulse; however, there is no regular grouping of the pulse, nor are there regularly recurring accents so as to generate a sense of metrical hierarchy such as we illustrated in the lecture-demonstration (Chapter 2). The rhythm of plainchant is based primarily on the rhythmic patterns and sentence structure of the Latin religious texts and not on a fixed pattern of accents and regular beats. There are, of course, accented notes in the chant melody, but they occur irregularly and somewhat unpredictably. The phrase lengths in plainchant comfortably accommodate the natural rhythms of breathing, and the melodic line rises and falls similarly to the inflections of spoken language. In short, plainchant is a kind of heightened speech, a musical enrichment of the religious text being presented.

You will notice that syllables of texts in the plainchant example are often set to single notes; that is, one pitch per syllable. This kind of text setting is called, for obvious reasons, syllabic. However, some of the vowel sounds in our example are sung not to a single pitch, but to a succession of pitches. The melodic figures that result from this temporal elongation of a vowel are known as melismas, and this kind of text setting is known as *melismatic.*

Viderunt Omnes is a complete melody, but it is very different from most of the melodies you heard in Chapter 3. This is only partly because of its ametrical rhythmic organization. There are also important differences in the choice of pitches and in the way the pitches relate to one another to form the melody.

In Chapter 3 (pp. 108–111), we discussed various modes and their particular orderings of whole steps and half steps as these are derived from the pitch material of a piece. We went on to say that the composition of tonal music makes use of two principal modes, called major and minor. These modes have dominated Western compositional practice from the seventeenth to twentieth centuries, the period of tonal music. Since you have probably heard far more tonal (major/minor) music than any other kind, you are most familiar with music that depends on these two modes for its underlying melodic coherence. But the melodies of plainchant, a much earlier music, move in orbits other than our familiar major or minor; from these melodies the so-called Church Modes are derived (see Chapter 3). Incorporating particular successions of whole steps and half steps different from those that characterize the major and minor modes, each of these medieval modes also implied particular and characteristic melodic patterns and tones of stability and instability. For example, the notion of dominants and "leading tones" moving toward tonic "goals" was not characteristic of the medieval modal system. These differences in pitch organization and function, coupled with the nonmetric basis of the rhythm of plainchant, help to explain why chant sounds so different from the music of the tonal period.

Plainchant and Notation

For many centuries plainchant was performed without the aid of any kind of musical notation. The monks performing the plainchant were "specialists" who partially memorized and partially improvised a repertory of melodies, transmitting these traditions to succeeding generations orally.

Though the monks did not initially perform from musical notation, they did have written versions of the plainchant texts, the copying of sacred texts being the most important job of medieval monk-scribes. These texts were copied into large volumes known as liturgical books. The creation of even a few copies of such books involved the work of many people working thousands of hours. With books of this kind open before them on massive wooden stands, the monks would scan the lines of text while they sang, each syllable and word helping them to recollect the appropriate music. Thus, it was the text and its place within the service that stimulated their performance of the music.

When musical notation made its first tentative appearance in Europe, sometime around the ninth century, it may not have been considered as revolutionary an advance as we might think in retrospect. It first appeared as annotations to already existing liturgical books in the form of signs added above the words. These signs, called **neumes**, acted as graphic mnemonic devices. Why a written notation became necessary when the repertory had been transmitted orally for so many centuries is not precisely known. However, scholars today believe that music notation arose at least partly in a continuing effort by the Roman Catholic church to unify and regularize the various oral traditions that had emerged throughout England, France, and Italy. As one writer says, it was "in the interest of a transcendent ideal of clarity and normativity."[1]

---

[1] Leo Trietler, "Reading and Singing: On the Genesis of Occidental Music-writing," *Early Music History 4,* 1984.

Three stages in the development of notation
Neumes (top); one-line notation (center); four-line notation (bottom).

Unlike modern notation, early medieval notation did not capture precisely the pitches and rhythms of the music, but rather suggested, very generally, the direction of melodic lines. It was initially of use only to those who had some previous knowledge of the melodies associated with the texts they were reading. Often, single notational signs were used to indicate melismas, which, as you will remember, are musical figures of several pitches on a single vowel. This use of a single sign to stand for a sung figure, regardless of the number of pitches involved, implies that both singer and scribe took such melodic figures, rather than individual pitches, to be the fundamental musical entity. Contrast this attitude, born of an essentially oral culture, with our modern tendency to think of music as being composed of discrete, individual pitches—or "notes." The tendency to think of notes as the fundamental units is a product of centuries of notated music.

Though we have been emphasizing the importance of its textual basis, the melisma is clearly also a musical event. The progress of the text is temporarily delayed as the musical figure unfolds. The historical importance of this practice cannot be overestimated. The melisma is musical composition in microcosm, since its creation involves decisions having more to do with music than with words.

The Sources of Plainchant

Plainchant was part of Christian religious practice from its beginnings. In fact, the roots of plainchant practice can be traced back before the time of Christ. The chant sung by the early Christians was initially an adaptation of Jewish chant practice, and, in fact, the basic notion of chanting certain parts of the liturgy was itself taken over from the older religion.

The large repertory of music known as plainchant accumulated and was modified over the course of the whole Christian era—a period of almost two millenia. How did these plainchant melodies come into being? There is no simple answer. The question is akin to that of how a spoken language comes to develop a vocabulary and an expanding repertory of usages from generation to generation. This musical repertory, like language, developed communally, the product of thousands of anonymous clerics and monks. Though it was not the result of any particular individual's invention, we can assume that certain members of the monastic communities were assigned the task of dealing with musical matters, and that these monks applied some combination of creation, compilation, and editing in working with the plainchant repertory. From time to time, identifiable individuals instituted reforms or codified the shared body of practice, much as grammarians and lexicographers did for languages.

By the ninth and tenth centuries, the chants of the Christian church were sufficiently notated so that, officially at least, they constituted an unchanging repertory. A knowledge of these plainchant tunes and texts formed part of the education of monks in monasteries all over Europe. This degree of relative uniformity, though, had not always existed. During the first few centuries of the church's existence, the Christian communities were scattered widely throughout Europe, and the performance of the plainchant repertory often differed markedly from place to place. Many, though by no means all, of these local variations disappeared around the end of the sixth century, when an attempt was made to organize the musical items of the liturgy systematically and to collect them into an officially sanctioned repertory. This effort at standardizing church music throughout Europe was carried out during the time of Gregory I (pope from 590 to 604) and is sometimes referred to as the Gregorian reform. (Though it is highly doubtful that Gregory dealt directly with the music of plainchant at all, he has traditionally been associated with its conservation, which led to the use of the term *Gregorian chant* as a synonym for *plainchant*.) The Gregorian reform had two objectives: To make the chant universal and to make it enduring. This attempt to define and stabilize liturgical music

Pope Gregory I

The dove, representing the Holy Spirit, whispers chant melodies to Gregory while he dictates to a scribe.

was in consonance with the general policy of Rome to extend its doctrinal authority throughout the whole of Europe.

EARLY POLYPHONY AND NOTRE DAME

In adopting as its official music a repertory that was exclusively monophonic, the church was not aiming to limit itself to a texture of simple austerity. It is quite possible that virtually *all* music was monophonic before the ninth and tenth centuries. It was only after this that important changes in textural possibilities began to occur. We cannot say with certainty, however, that earlier music was exclusively monophonic because we have only very indirect knowledge about folk music or about any music outside the circle of the church. As central as Christianity was within medieval life, it seems certain that there must also have existed a rich culture of music outside the walls of church and monastery—such as music for dances, festivals, wedding celebrations, and funerals—though not necessarily without clerical involvement. This kind of music making, which is traditionally improvised, was not written down at all during this early period, and so was not preserved. Though notation was available at the time, its invention was clearly directed at preserving the plainchant repertory, and only later did its use extend beyond church music.

We have mentioned "important changes" in the preceding paragraph. What were these changes? Listen to a portion of a piece that was sung for the first time during a Christmas Mass service sometime during the late 1100s or early 1200s. The setting of this original performance was Paris, and specifically, the tiny Île de la Cité in the middle of the Seine, the very heart of the city. It was here during the twelfth and thirteenth centuries that a newly invigorated intellectual culture flourished; the University of Paris was taking shape around an informal nucleus of scholars and students, and one of the first great Gothic cathedrals, Notre Dame de Paris, was in the midst of construction, replacing the older Romanesque church that had existed there. The music you are about to hear (Example 8.3) was created within this cultural milieu and was sung as part of an otherwise traditional monophonic plainchant service.

Example	Composer, title	Date
8.3	Perotin, *Viderunt Omnes* (organum quadruplum, excerpt)	c. 1200

Imagine the impact this sudden expansion into many voices must have had! The contrast during the service between the surrounding plainchant and the Perotin composition must have been enormous. We could compare it with singing first in a modest, relatively small, and spatially contained Romanesque church and then being whisked off to sing in one of the soaring spaces of a Gothic cathedral. (See illustration, p. 285). Obviously, this kind of religious music, so different from plainchant, must have been the result of a vast conceptual change in musical "norms." Among the many characteristics that distinguish the Perotin excerpt from chant, perhaps most noticeable are those having to do with *rhythm* and *texture.* Its rhythm is clearly metric. (We will have more to say about this shortly). The textural difference is perhaps even more significant. The Perotin is not monophonic; instead of one line, there are four. It is an example of *polyphony.*

Pieces like the Perotin played an important role in the rise of

(*Right*) Notre Dame Cathedral in Paris (12th century, Gothic); (*left*) Church at Assisi (10th century, Romanesque).

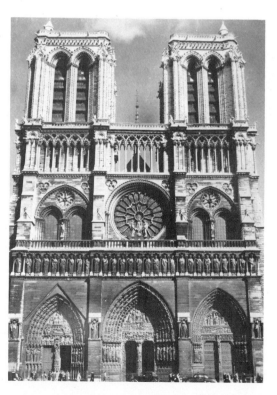

polyphony, marking a decisive and permanent change of direction in the course of Western music. From this period forward, much of the creative attention of musicians would be focused on issues related to the composition of music in several lines or voices.

When or where polyphony first arose cannot be fixed precisely; it seems to have been a phenomenon that gathered impetus slowly and in many different localities. The earliest examples of polyphony predate our Perotin piece by about three centuries, and resulted from a practice known as **organum,** an alternative way of singing plainchant.

Though it is not at all clear how organum singing got started, it is possible to suppose that it was based on the natural phenomenon of singing in octaves, something which commonly occurs when groups of untrained singers attempt to sing the same tune. While one singer in such a group may find a certain register quite comfortable, another may find the pitch range too low or too high and may switch, perhaps unconsciously, to the register an octave above or below. (This occurs almost inevitably whenever men and women or men and boys make

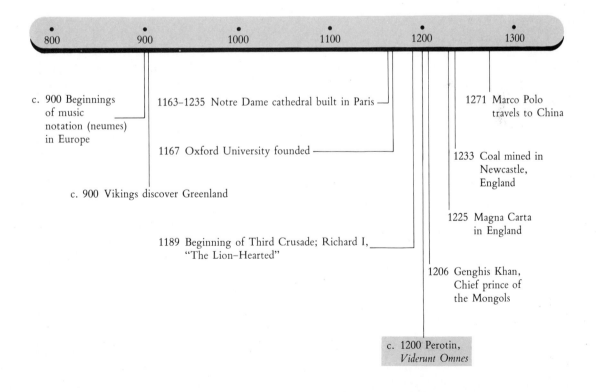

800   900   1000   1100   1200   1300

c. 900 Beginnings of music notation (neumes) in Europe

1163–1235 Notre Dame cathedral built in Paris

1167 Oxford University founded

1271 Marco Polo travels to China

1233 Coal mined in Newcastle, England

c. 900 Vikings discover Greenland

1225 Magna Carta in England

1189 Beginning of Third Crusade; Richard I, "The Lion–Hearted"

1206 Genghis Khan, Chief prince of the Mongols

c. 1200 Perotin, *Viderunt Omnes*

up the group). The result will be that the melody, though being conceived *monophonically* by the singers, will in reality be heard as two parallel strands an octave apart. Though there is no proof that this was the model for organum, it is known that sometime around the ninth century a few monastic communities consciously adopted a way of singing certain portions of the plainchant in a similar, and novel, way; namely, by dividing the voices into two groups. One group sang the official chant tune itself. The other sang a second line that began in unison with the chant but then moved to a position at a constant distance of a fifth, fourth, or an octave from the original line. In this way, they created a kind of nascent polyphony.[2] The newly added line, known as the *vox organalis,* or organal voice, would eventually merge back into the official chant line, and the service would continue monophonically. This earliest kind of polyphony was known as *parallel organum.*

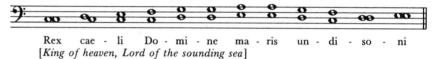

Rex cae - li Do - mi - ne ma - ris un - di - so - ni
[*King of heaven, Lord of the sounding sea*]

Parallel organum can only be called polyphony in the most narrow sense of the word. Since the added voice mostly followed the official chant line slavishly, at a constant interval distance, it could not claim to be a truly independent line, and probably no such claim was made for it. It is more likely that the organal voice was considered merely a respectful ornamentation of the plainchant melody. Eventually, organum developed further "variations," each of which gave more and more rhythmic and melodic independence, and even prominence, to the organal voice. The historical development of varieties of organum corresponds roughly to the way we presented varieties of texture in Chapter 1. There we also moved from unaccompanied melody (Examples 1.12 and 1.13), to unison texture (Examples 1.14 and 1.15), and then to more complex textures. Such a movement from the simple to the complex, while true enough for organum, cannot be taken as a norm for *all* of music history; there are perhaps just as many contrary examples of simplifying trends gradually replacing what were perceived as overly complex kinds of musical expression.

---

[2] You heard a similar procedure in the Bulgarian folk song in Chapter 1, Example 1.17. However, intervals created by the several lines in that example produced seconds or sevenths—that is, more intense dissonances than fourths or fifths.

Cathedral at Rheims (interior)

. . . one of the soaring spaces of a Gothic cathedral.

All of these changes reached a period of especially stable expression around the end of the twelfth and the beginning of the thirteenth centuries, with the emergence of the repertory known as Notre Dame organum. The Perotin piece you just heard is part of that repertory, so different in sound from both plainchant and the earlier kinds of organum. Notre Dame organum was a product of the same culture that produced new works of architectural ingenuity with the building of the Gothic cathedrals, and also contributed significantly to shaping the novel idea of a university. It was in this active and intellectually vibrant cultural context that the natural creativity of artists and crafts-men was allowed to flourish in the service of the church. This period was later called the **Gothic** era. Though its more intense cultural ac-tivity distinguishes it from the Romanesque period which preceded it, the Gothic can be seen as bringing to fruition trends that had already been set in motion during the tenth and eleventh centuries. (The music of the Romanesque and Gothic periods is considered, along with fourteenth-century music, as part of an even longer stretch of time, the Medieval period.)

The less anonymous quality of Gothic art and life is exemplified in our example of music from Notre Dame as well. For one thing, we know the name of its composer, Perotin. For another, we know Perotin had a predecessor at Notre Dame whose name was Leonin. However, all that is known about these two musicians are their names, the fact that they were associated in some way with the cathedral community of Notre Dame, and that they were said to have composed the bulk of the repertory of Notre Dame polyphony. Despite the skimpiness of our information about them, Perotin and Leonin emerge as the first figures whose careers seem connected directly with the creation of new music. As such, they are the first true composers in the history of Western music.

The Perotin piece is written for four voices, a rare occurrence in this period, since most Notre Dame polyphony is two-voiced, including all of Leonin's music. (By the sixteenth century, a texture of four voices in polyphony would be commonplace.) In listening, however, you more than likely perceived this texture not as four individual lines, but as two distinct layers, each layer differentiated with respect to rhythm. The lower layer seems to describe a single line comprising a series of notes of very long duration. The pitches in this lower layer are so elongated that they sound like a series of drones. Each time a "drone" pitch changes, you have the feeling that an important event has occurred in the piece.

But perhaps it was the upper layer which claimed most of your attention. This layer is made up of several voices (of course three in number, since there are four lines in all), voices which move mostly in rhythmic unison. While the lower layer seems static, the upper one is very lively rhythmically. It generates not only a regular pulse, but regularly occurring accents. In other words, its rhythm is metric. Why might Perotin have decided in this polyphonic portion of the Mass service to abandon the traditional nonmetric rhythm of plainchant so as to create a metrically organized piece? Perhaps partly for practical reasons, because of new considerations presented by the nature of polyphony. Musicians like Perotin had to think about the kinds of intervals produced by simultaneously sounding lines, since, even in this early period, the possible intervals were classified as relatively consonant or dissonant. (To refresh your understanding of the terms *consonance* and *dissonance*, see Chapter 5, p. 183.)

There is a clear duple meter in the Perotin piece, but it would be more precise to call it compound duple:

♩.   ♩.

1   2

♩ ♩ ♩ ♩

♫♪ ♫♪

1 2 3   4 5 6

♩ ♩ ♩.

1   2

The pattern that results from the subdivision of each beat into long-short, long-short predominates here. During the Gothic period meter was generated through the use of patterns like these exclusively. Six rhythmic groupings of these typical compound-duple patterns were established and referred to as the **rhythmic modes.** (Perhaps you are familiar with similar patterns as they apply to "meter" in poetry—as in iambic, trochaic, etc.) The Perotin piece is organized according to these rhythmic modes.

The advent of the rhythmic modes brought about an advance in notation as well, so-called modal notation, which, unlike plainchant notation, was able to render rhythms as well as pitches. To listeners of today, the rigid adherence of the music and the text to these schemes seems to produce a sing-song quality. There is no reason to assume, however, that listeners in the thirteenth century would have experienced it that way.

You may have been wondering why this Perotin piece, *Viderunt Omnes,* shares its name with the plainchant melody with which this chapter began, or how the piece qualifies as "organum" when it seems so utterly removed from plainchant performance of any kind. What precisely can the connection be between such different-sounding music? The answer lies in the lower layer of the piece, in the succession of dronelike notes. If you were to take the sequence of pitches making up the lower layer and sing them much more quickly, you would discover that they in fact form a melody. This melody turns out to be the very opening section of our original plainchant example, *Viderunt Omnes.* In Perotin's reuse of the plainchant melody, the individual notes of the tune are so drastically elongated that they are no longer recognizable as a coherent melody. Nor is it at all obvious that the original *words* of this section of the plainchant are also present here, since each syllable in the text has been correspondingly lengthened. This explains why the piece may have sounded as if the performers were merely singing a series of meaningless vowel sounds. The upper parts are, in a sense, enormously long melismas. The section you heard (over four minutes of music) covered only the first two words of the chant, "Viderunt omnes."

Earlier kinds of organum had preserved the chant tune in clearly recognizable form, even as the organal voice grew in complexity. The organal voices never obscured the function of the plainchant as the principal element since the added lines were merely ornamentation. But the extreme elaboration of the composed parts in Notre Dame polyphony went far beyond anything done previously. In Perotin's piece the *Viderunt Omnes* chant is not used as a recognizable melody, but rather as a sort of interior scaffolding around which an elaborate, fanciful musical architecture of organal lines was constructed. An elongated plainchant tune used in this way became known as a **tenor.** In this context, the term does not refer to a kind of male singing voice, as it does today, or a particular register, but the preexistent musical line within a medieval polyphonic piece whose notes were "held" as the piece progressed (Latin *tenere,* "to hold"). It was later on in the history of polyphony, when an additional, lower-pitched line (a bass) was added below the tenor that the term took on its more modern connotation of a higher male voice. The use of a preexistent melody in this way, whether derived from plainchant or not, is an example of composition "on a tenor" or, as it was called from the Renaissance onward, composition "on a *cantus firmus*" ("fixed tune").

Composing music based on a tenor, or *cantus firmus*, was the normal procedure in this period and for many centuries beyond. A composer would begin with a tenor, most usually a preexistent melody, and compose a new line to go with it. If the piece was to have more than two lines, each additional line would be written from beginning to end before the next was added. This layering process has been called successive composition. It implied that the medieval composer thought of music linearly; that is, as being composed of individual lines. To the medieval perspective, the act of composition was validated (and valued) precisely because of its link, audible or not, to earlier received tradition. Contrast this attitude to the modern perspective, which places such a premium on total originality, on creating a piece "from scratch." (But see, also, the comments on the continuing role of received tradition, p. 297.)

The Notre Dame repertory was a high point in the early history of polyphony, and Perotin its greatest exponent. Here is what a scholar writing about medieval music had to say about Perotin:

> Never before had musical structures attained such astonishing dimensions. It would seem that, as the nave of Notre Dame neared completion, the cathedral's unprecedented size and magnificence stirred Perotin to fill the vast space with music of equal splendor. For his successful achievement of this goal he well deserves to be remembered as Perotin the Great.[3]

RENAISSANCE POLYPHONY

Though organum composition itself waned and disappeared before the end of the thirteenth century, the possibilities of polyphony continued to excite the creativity of composers and the interest of listeners from the time of Notre Dame onward. If the music of Leonin, Perotin, and their circle represented the first full expression of the possibilities of polyphony, its period of greatest refinement was to be reached some 350 years later during the sixteenth century, the musical period sometimes called the High Renaissance. (We skip across this 350-year period now but will return to it about its midpoint in Chapter 9.)

---

[3] R. H. Hoppin, *Medieval Music* (New York: Norton, 1978), p. 241.

Johannes Ockeghem, great composer of the early Renaissance and director of church music for the King of France in the late 1400s, leading a church choir. Ockeghem is depicted wearing eyeglasses which were invented in the 15th century.

The era of polyphony, in the sense of vocal music making use of several basically independent lines, can be said to end with the sixteenth century. In the more narrow sense, of course, composition in many voices has never ceased to be the dominant texture in Western music, but beginning in the seventeenth century, the multilinear aspect of traditional polyphony gradually yields to the new conceptions of the Baroque period. The first generation of Baroque musicians were much more interested in a kind of texture sometimes known as **homophony,** or what we have described earlier as one kind of inactive texture, where one line predominates as melody, while the other "lines" are really an accompaniment of vertical sonorities, or chords.

The piece you are about to listen to (Example 8.4) was written during the High Renaissance by the Spanish composer Tomàs Luis de Victoria (c. 1548–1611). The piece is representative of the final and most polished form of Renaissance linear polyphony, yet it also contains chordal aspects which foreshadow the new texture of the early Baroque period. The piece was written in Rome and, like Perotin's *Viderunt Omnes,* was intended to be performed in church at Christmas. The original text and translation for Example 8.4 are given below.

Example	Composer, title	Date
8.4	Victoria, *O Magnum Mysterium* ("O Great Mystery")	1572

O magnum mysterium, et admirabile sacramentum, ut animalia viderent
Dominum natum, jacentem in praesepio:
O beata Virgo cujus viscera meruerunt portare Dominum Christum.
Alleluia.

Oh great mystery, and holy wonder, that beasts should behold the newborn Lord lying in the manger:
Oh blessed is the Virgin whose womb was deemed worthy to bear the Lord Christ. Hallelujah!

Notice that the piece begins monophonically but starts expanding almost immediately into a texture of many lines. The first voice presents a slowly unfolding melodic line which sets the seven syllables of the first three words, "O magnum mysterium." This melodic line, presented in the soprano register, descends by a fifth, reiterates the starting pitch, ascends by a half step for two syllables, and then returns to its starting point. If you listen carefully, you will hear that this motive is imitated, though on different pitches, first by the altos, and then by the tenors and basses. You have heard this kind of staggered entry of a single motive through several voices, called *imitation,* in previous examples, such as the Gabrieli *Ricercare* (Example 1.26) and the *Sanctus* from a Mass by Victoria (Example 4.15). Imitative textures such as these were a mainstay of Renaissance polyphonic practice.

Imitation stresses the linear shape of each voice as it enters, but at this late stage of the Renaissance composers are also thinking of the potential of the chosen lines in combination to form pleasing and expressive chordal entities. By the period of the Renaissance, many generations of composers had explored the possibilities of combining lines, and an informal body of compositional conventions had accumulated. (See the example of Machaut in the next chapter.) These conventions reflected general agreement on such things as how best to treat dissonance and consonance, how to produce a smooth imitative texture, and how to create appropriately expressive melodic lines. The result for composers like Victoria, who learned his craft in this atmosphere of compositional consensus, was the creation of a body of music that radiates a quality of smoothness and technical command.

Although *O Magnum Mysterium* employs the linear technique of imitation to bring the voices in, the motive itself has been so designed that, when all four voices have arrived, the combined result is perceived primarily as a chordal texture. This happens just at the point where the important words "Oh great mystery" are restated. As new lines of text are sung, new motives are introduced, but because of the predominance of imitative polyphony the boundaries between the entrances of the motives are smoothed over. As one motive works itself out imitatively, a new one is being introduced in another voice. This creates a basically seamless texture. (Compare this with his later mass based

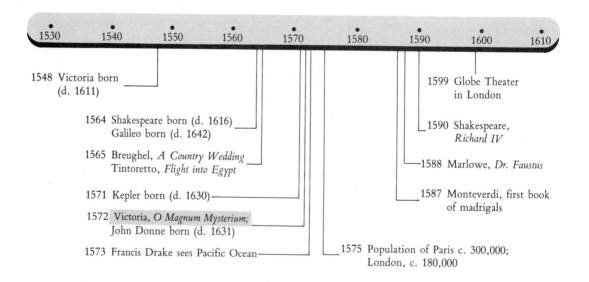

1530 1540 1550 1560 1570 1580 1590 1600 1610

1548 Victoria born
(d. 1611)

1564 Shakespeare born (d. 1616)
Galileo born (d. 1642)

1565 Breughel, *A Country Wedding*
Tintoretto, *Flight into Egypt*

1571 Kepler born (d. 1630)

1572 Victoria, *O Magnum Mysterium*;
John Donne born (d. 1631)

1573 Francis Drake sees Pacific Ocean

1575 Population of Paris c. 300,000;
London, c. 180,000

1599 Globe Theater
in London

1590 Shakespeare,
Richard IV

1588 Marlowe, *Dr. Faustus*

1587 Monteverdi, first book
of madrigals

on this motet, Example 4.15.) At times, the imitative sections give way to chordal sections (in other words, rhythmic unison), but these passages soon flow into another imitative section. There is only one major break in the texture of this piece, corresponding to the one major subdivision in the text, just before the words "O beata Virgo." Notice that after this dramatic pause, Victoria responds musically to the return of the initial exclamation "Oh" by bringing back a reminiscence of the chordal music used near the beginning for the restatement of "Oh great mystery." Thus the piece divides into two parts, the openings of each being subtly but unmistakably related. The piece also has a distinct ending section (a coda) where the meter goes into a dancelike triple meter at the jubilant word "Alleluia" (from the Hebrew *Halleluyah,* "Praise the Lord"). Note that the piece ends with a complete major triad, in contrast to the cadences of the Perotin, which ended in the relatively empty-sounding sonorities of octaves and fifths alone; that is, without the third of the full triad. Notice, too, that this beautiful cadence is extended as Victoria gradually resolves dissonance into consonance moving around the third of the major triad.

The Victoria piece is an example of a **motet,** a genre whose origins in fact go back to the period of the great organum compositions of Notre Dame. But in the Renaissance period, which extends from 1400 to 1600, approximately, the motet became somewhat standardized as a polyphonic setting of a religious text, albeit usually an addition to the liturgy rather than an integral part of it. Renaissance motets, and all Renaissance vocal polyphony, were almost always sung without instrumental accompaniment, a practice known as *a cappella* singing. Motets tended to be sung on special occasions. Some were commissioned by leading citizens for the celebration of important family events or even state occasions; others were composed by musicians attached to some of the larger church centers and cathedrals, or to aristocratic courts that had private chapels.

What about the spaces in which motets of this period would have been performed? The word *cathedral* probably brings to mind a Gothic cathedral, such as Notre Dame or Chartres. But by the 1500s all the artifacts associated with the Gothic, including Notre Dame organum, had long ago gone out of fashion and out of favor. To the people of the Renaissance, the Gothic style was perceived as crudely wrought and lacking in aesthetic grace. One fifteenth-century Italian artist cursed "the man that invented this wretched, Gothic architecture" and decried the "barbarous people" who brought it to Italy!

The Renaissance, graced with such towering artistic figures as Leonardo da Vinci, Michelangelo, Brunelleschi, Botticelli, and Raphael, was a society in which art and ideas were being generated and made available as never before in European history. Technological advances helped this along, the invention of printing above all. But it was also a time of a restless creativity that radiated in all directions, a period which nurtured an unprecedented enthusiasm for the exploration of new worlds and the rediscovery of ones gone by. The artists and thinkers of the period were well aware that their age was an exciting one, that Europe had in fact experienced a "rebirth." The composer and music theorist Tinctoris, writing in 1477, claimed that music written before about 1440 was not "worth hearing." In general, the Renaissance tended to look at the Medieval period with patronizing disdain at best. It was during the Renaissance, in fact, that the term *Medieval* (*Medium Aevum,* or "middle age"), was coined, implying that all the centuries between their own time and that of the ancient Classical world amounted to little more than a fallow period of transition.

In this light, it is understandable that the medieval cathedrals, which overawed worshippers with their angularity, pointed arches, unlit corners, and rough stone, should no longer be prized. The concept of religious architecture had changed as Greek and Roman achievements attained the status of models. The new architecture adapted and integrated the proportions and detailing of Classical buildings, while aiming at designing churches more in conformity with human proportion: The angles of the Gothic were smoothed out, the interior walls more fully decorated with murals and paintings—color and light combining to create an opulent, comfortable atmosphere. The architecture of the Renaissance, with its rounded arches and domes and its carefully controlled symmetries, is impressive but not forbidding.

One might describe the Victoria motet in similar language. A calmly flowing sense of movement; gently curving lines that sometimes run in parallel and at other times diverge; a rich and warm vocal blend—all these are combined with a smooth technical assurance by a composer aware of the highly developed critical faculty of his audience. Centuries of development of the polyphonic art enabled composers like Victoria to clothe the sacred text in ways that accommodated the audience's desire to be surrounded by beautiful objects.

It is ironic that the Cathedral of Notre Dame in Paris should be precisely the kind of structure that Renaissance critics maligned, for without the pathbreaking compositional activities that were supported there during Perotin's day, Renaissance polyphony might not have reached the level of refinement and technical poise that it did. The Renaissance/Medieval aesthetic dichotomy dramatizes how much the collective taste of a changed society can color judgments about good and bad art.

To illustrate this point, we will ask you, as an experiment, to reconsider the Perotin *Viderunt Omnes* from the point of view of a hypothetical sixteenth-century Italian critic. (This, of course, is doubly hypothetical, as there is no way a Renaissance person could have heard this music. It was only in the nineteenth century that earlier music began to be revived and performed, as in concerts today.) Keeping in mind that you, as a "Renaissance listener," would have the characteristic sound and text-setting procedures of the Victoria motet as a measuring stick, the first thing you would probably object to in listening to Perotin would be that the text is essentially absent; the voices seem to be merely vocalizing on vowel sounds. Secondly, the mood of the piece would be objectionable. For sacred music, the piece is too jumpy, too strongly accented, and too fast. It lacks the gravity and serenity of an appropriately slow tempo. Moreover, the melodic patterns would seem repetitive, the phrases far too clipped. And you would also find disturbing the tremendous dichotomy between the fast-moving upper parts and the infinitely slower bottom part. You would wonder why the composer would be using four voices but keeping the upper three circling about each other basically in the same register. Recall that, in the Victoria motet, also for four voices, each voice had its own distinct register; each contributed its own color to the total blend.

Next, you would likely be struck by the occasionally sharp dissonances of the harmony (for instance, at the end of "omnes"). The Victoria motet has a predominance of consonant harmony with judiciously placed dissonances. You might also judge the harmonic rhythm—the change from one vertical sonority to another—to be too quick, as abrupt in its movements as the rhythm. In general, you would be unhappy with the prevalence of rhythmic unison and the consequent lack of long stretches unified by carefully calculated imitative passages, such as the one that opens the Victoria motet. You would find the voice quality of the Notre Dame piece to be surprisingly earthy and full-throated (that is, if our recordings reasonably reflect the performance practices of the respective periods). You would probably be much relieved to return to the more ethereal and homogeneous sound of sixteenth-century polyphony.

To cap our hypothetical exercise, we can entertain the idea that you, as a Gothic time traveler, would, in turn, find much to complain

Orlando di Lasso leading musicians at the court of the Duke of Bavaria, c. 1570. (Lasso is seated in front of the flutist playing a keyboard instrument.) Notice the differences between this late Renaissance aristocrats' band and Ockeghem's church music group of a century earlier (p. 290).

about in Victoria's motet. Since both *Viderunt Omnes* and *O Magnum Mysterium* are intended for Christmas celebrations, it is possible that you might see the joy of that celebration of the birth of Christ more clearly expressed in the bouncy, yet powerful, movements of the music of your own time. You might conversely find the Victoria motet somewhat pallid, inappropriately grave and serene.

One final point. The compositional technique of using a tenor or *cantus firmus* continues in one form or another right up to the late Baroque (in the music of Bach, for example), though such techniques had become much rarer by that time. In the Victoria motet, all the lines are composed freely—that is, they do not derive from plainchant or any other earlier source. It is interesting to note, however, that Victoria later borrowed a small "slice" of the texture of *O Magnum Mysterium* in order to incorporate it in a polyphonic mass (Example 4.15). These sorts of transfers of material, often by one composer of another composer's music, were part of the tradition and spirit of musical composition until roughly the Classical period. But the practice of reworking existing music in new ways or embedding it into new contexts continues, even today.

In the most general sense, music making inevitably includes absorbing a received tradition so as to refashion it or reexplore its possibilities. In the previous chapters of this book, you listened to a number of examples where composers explicitly borrowed from the music of others: Beethoven's transformations of *God Save the King* in the form of piano variations, for instance; different versions of *I Got Rhythm;* or the two very different performances of what is essentially the same piece, Scott Joplin's *Maple Leaf Rag.* In the demonstration of the twelve-bar blues, you heard how a conventionalized chord scheme supported a variety of texts and different kinds of expression.

Similarly, the minuets and scherzos in Chapter 6 illustrated how composers used a single general organizing principle to shape very different kinds of pieces in quite different styles. In each, the composer "thinks" and hears within the framework of a similar design; and yet each work is unique in the ways in which this design is musically realized. It is in this sense that history as past, personal experience becomes part of the present, everyday life of the composer at work.

CHAPTER 9

Procession to the Garden, woodcut c. 1492

Music and Poetry:
Two Love Songs

Solitary Romantic

We begin our paired examples with two love songs separated by almost 500 years in their dates of composition—a period of time that saw enormous changes in nearly all aspects of life as well as in the world of music. The first song, *Douce dame jolie* ("Sweet and lovely lady"), by Guillaume de Machaut, was composed in about 1350, near midpoint between the works of Perotin and Victoria that you have just studied. Franz Schubert composed our second example, *Im Frühling* ("In Spring") in 1826, more than 250 years after the Victoria motet. Comparing the 800-year span covered by the examples in Chapter 8 with the period from 1572 to 1826, one cannot help but be struck by the remarkable and immediately evident changes in musical style that occurred during this 250-year period. Indeed, during this time you will recognize the emergence of much of the music with which you are most familiar: the music of the Baroque period (Bach and Vivaldi) and also the Classical period (Beethoven, Mozart, and Haydn). Schubert, composing in the early Romantic nineteenth century, carries into his work, as we shall see, the living legacy of this fecund musical past.

Example	Composer, title	Date
9.1	Machaut, *Douce dame jolie* ("Sweet and Lovely Lady")	c. 1350
9.2	Schubert, *Im Frühling* ("In Spring")	1826

Of all the varieties of musical activity in which men and women have been involved through the ages, the singing of songs is perhaps the most universal. The marriage of poetry and music may be nearly as old as language itself, and no known culture is without it. Music without words can have its own kind of poetic eloquence, while poetry can be said to be inherently musical. In a way, music and poetry "interpret" one another. The division of a poem into large sections and also into smaller units—single lines, pairs, and then groups of lines—is very much like structure in music. Both deal not only with expression of mood or emotion, but with the creation of form. Finally, both music and poetry generate rhythm, most often the kind of rhythm in which accentuations are organized into regular patterns—in other words, meter.

As for the subject matter of song, perhaps no other has been as eternally fresh a source of inspiration as that of love. We have chosen these songs because they share, in some measure, a particular point of view about love. Poets in both the fourteenth and the nineteenth centuries dealt with the themes of love lost, love unrequited, or love unattainable. In Schubert's time, these themes formed a set of attitudes which can collectively be called "romantic love," just as Romanticism was the dominant artistic movement during the nineteenth century. Machaut's song reflects similar themes which may be seen as part of the "courtly love" tradition, a type of poetry which had first appeared long before the fourteenth century. We will have more to say about this poetic tradition shortly.

Recall that in Chapter 3 you listened to a diverse group of melodies ranging from an aria from Berg's *Wozzeck* to a theme from a Mozart piano sonata to *Lassie;* and you listened closely to another song by Schubert, *Frühlingstraum* (Example 3.7). Some were more prototypically tunelike than others, satisfying your intuitive sense of what a melody is. Now, as you listen to our two songs, following the texts and their translations below, consider the following question: Which of the two settings seem most closely to express its text and which comes closer to your intuitive sense of what a love song should be?

Example 9.1 MACHAUT, *Douce dame jolie* ("Sweet and Lovely Lady")[1]

Douce dame jolie,	Sweet and lovely lady,
Pour Dieu ne pensés mie	For heaven's sake ne'er think
Que nulle ait signourie	That one other than you
Seur moy fors vous seulement.	Holds sway over me.
Qu'adés sans tricherie	Devoid of any falsehood
Chierie	Have I kept you dear
Vous ay et humblement	And served you humbly
Tous les jours de ma vie	Every day of my life—
Servie	And all this without untoward thought.
Sans vilein pensement.	Alas, still must I beg hope and succor.
Helas! et je mendie	You who are my joy,
D'esperance et d'aie;	If pity move you, then,
Dont ma joie est fenie,	Sweet and lovely lady,
Se pité ne vous en prent.	For heaven's sake ne'er think
Douce dame jolie,	That one other than you
Pour Dieu ne pensés mie	Holds sway over me.
Que nulle ait signourie	
Seur moy fors vous seulement.	

---

[1] Translation by Robert Green.

Douce dame jolie,
Pour Dieu ne pensés mie
Que nulle ait signourie
Seur moy fors vous seulement.
Mais vo douce maistrie
Maistrie
Mon cuer si durement
Qu'elle le contralie
Et lie
En amours tellement
Qu'il n'a de riens envie
Fors d'estre en vo baillie;
Et se ne li ottrie
Vos cuers nul aligement.
Douce dame jolie,
Pour Dieu ne pensés mie
Que nulle ait signourie
Seur moy fors vous seulement.

Douce dame jolie,
Pour Dieu ne pensés mie
Que nulle ait signourie
Seur moy fors vous seulement.
Et quant ma maladie
Garie
Ne sera nullement
Sans vous, douce anemie,
Qui lie
Estes de mon tourment,
A jointes mains deprie
Vo cuer, puis qu'il m'oublie,
Que temprement m'ocie,
Car trop langui longuement.
Douce dame jolie,
Pour Dieu ne pensés mie
Que nulle ait signourie
Seur moy fors vous seulement.

Puis que la douce rousee
D'umblesse ne wet florir
Pités, tant que meuree
Soit mercis que tant desir,
Je ne puis avoir duree,
Car en moy s'est engendree,

Sweet and lovely lady,
For heaven's sake ne'er think
That one other than you
Holds sway over me.
Yet does your sweet power
Exert itself so harshly
Upon my heart,
Which it ties and ties
So into love
That, this heart, it seeks no other desire
Than to be a part of what you own.
And still your own heart
Grants mine no respite.
Sweet and lovely lady,
For heaven's sake ne'er think
That one other than you
Holds sway over me.

Sweet and lovely lady,
For heaven's sake ne'er think
That one other than you
Holds sway over me.
And as this illness
Will no wise be
Healed
Other than by you, sweet foe,
Who take pleasure
In my distress;
So with both hands clasped do I beg
Your heart, which has forgotten me,
To kill me with godspeed,
For too long have I now been languishing.
Sweet and lovely lady,
For heaven's sake ne'er think
That one other than you
Holds sway over me.

Because pity does not wish
To see the sweet dew of humility
Come to flower until such time
As mercy has matured as much as desire,
I cannot long endure;
For in me has been born

Par un amoureus desir,	Through beloved desire
Une ardeur desmesuree	A love that knows no measure
Qu'Amours, par son doulz plaisir,	And which Love, by its sweet pleasure
Et ma dame desiree,	And my lady so much desired—
Par sa biauté coulouree,	For her beauty, colored
De grace y ont fait venir.	By grave, love brought forth.
Mais puis qu'einsi leur agree,	Thus as it so does please them both
Je weil humblement souffrir	Humbly will I suffer
Leur voloir jusqu'au morir.	This wish of theirs until I die.

Example 9.2 SCHUBERT, *Im Frühling* ("In Spring")[2]

Still sitz' ich an des Hügels Hang,	Quietly I sit on the side of the hill;
Der Himmel ist so klar,	the sky is so clear;
Das Lüftchen spielt im grünen Tal,	the breeze plays in the green valley
Wo ich beim ersten Frühlingsstrahl	where I in the first light of spring
Einst, ach, so glücklich war;	once was so happy;
Wo ich an ihrer Seite ging	where I walked at her side,
So traulich und so nah,	so intimate and so near,
Und tief im dunklen Felsenquell	and deep in the dark rock-spring
Den schönen Himmel blau und hell,	saw the beautiful heaven, blue and bright,
Und sie im Himmel sah.	and saw her in that heaven.
Sieh', wie der bunte Frühling schon	See how the colorful spring already
Aus Knosp' und Blüte blickt!	looks out of the buds and blossoms!
Nicht alle Blüten sind mir gleich,	Not all the flowers are the same to me,
Am liebsten pflück' ich von dem Zweig,	I like best to pick from the branch
Von welchem sie gepflückt!	from which she picked!
Denn alles ist wie damals noch,	For all is as it used to be,
Die Blumen, das Gefild;	the flowers, the fields;
Die Sonne scheint nicht minder hell,	the sun shines no less brightly,
Nicht minder freundlich schwimmt im Quell	no less cheerfully floats in the spring
Das blaue Himmelsbild.	the blue image of heaven.
Es wandeln nur sich Will' und Wahn,	Only the will and the fancy change,
Es wechseln Lust und Streit;	pleasure turns to strife;
Vorüber flieht der Liebe Glück,	the happiness of love flees away,
Und nur die Liebe bleibt zurück,	and only love remains behind—
Die Lieb' und ach, das Leid!	love and alas, sorrow!

---

[2] Reprinted, with permission, from Philip L. Miller, *The Ring of Words* (New York: Norton, 1973), p. 275; poem by Ernst Schulze.

O wär' ich doch ein Vöglein nur
    Dort an dem Wiesenhang,
Dann blieb' ich auf den Zweigen hier,
Und säng' ein süsses Lied von ihr
    Den ganzen Sommer lang.

Oh, if I were only a bird
    there on the hillside meadow,
then I would stay in the branches here
and sing a sweet song about her
    all summer long.

In all likelihood you chose the Schubert song over the one by Machaut as best meeting your expectations of what a love song should be. Schubert seems to capture in his music the expressive moods of the text—tenderness, delicacy, sweetness combined with sadness. The song by Machaut, in contrast, may have struck you perhaps as gentle, appropriate to a love song, but considering the nature of the poem, not particularly responsive to the passionate feelings it expresses or to its contrasts in mood. While the question of appropriateness must, of course, be considered in the light of the respective time and place of each composition, consider for a moment some of the striking differences in musical materials and how each composer shapes them.

On first or second hearing, perhaps most noticeable is the repetitiveness of the Machaut on one hand and, on the other, the ever-changing variation of the Schubert. This difference in musical organization clearly influences our sense of the expressiveness of each song:

Guillaume de Machaut composing poetry or music. Illumination from a 14th-century manuscript.

Machaut expresses to us a single mood throughout his song despite the poignant, even passionate changes of expression suggested by the text; Schubert, in response to expressive changes in the poem, makes subtle changes in the music both within phrases and especially from one verse to the next (notice particularly the third stanza).

In fact, Machaut's style could be characterized by its musical limits or constraints: An economy of melodic material that moves primarily in conjunct motion through a small range, a few often-repeated rhythmic figures, no changes in the single-line (monophonic) texture, and clearly defined structural boundaries. Later, you will discover that its interest and its inner expressiveness come from the subtle ways in which Machaut moves within rather predetermined limits—limits not only of this song but of the underlying stylistic norms of his time and place.

In contrast, *Im Frühling* could be characterized by its freedom as Schubert expands on and plays with his initial material: Rich, often chromatic, even elusive harmony; both conjunct and disjunct melodic motion moving through a relatively large range; varied dynamics, rhythm, texture, and sonority, together with structural boundaries that sometimes subtly merge into one another. Interest and expressiveness derive not only from this rich palette of variation, but perhaps paradoxically also from the implicit stylistic norms that help to unify the song and against which Schubert's imagination seems endlessly to play, to elaborate, to go beyond.

But there is more. To understand these different expressions of a common subject, we need to place them in their social and cultural contexts. To do so, we need to look at three moments in time: first, our own, and then the respective eras in which Schubert and Machaut lived. As we have already emphasized, our common conception of what is appropriate or suitable, mediocre or sublime, is formed to a great extent by what we absorb from our immediate cultural environment. For example, music that often accompanies love scenes in movies or on television may help to create an expectation with regard to what music about love should sound like. And, in fact, movie and TV music tends to borrow its norms from the musical language of the Romantic period. This helps explain, in part, why the love music of Machaut, which lies far outside the bounds of Romantic musical style, seems not to communicate its message to the modern listener and thereby to suffer by comparison. In some sense, the Romantic era of Schubert and its musical style is still with us.

And yet, when a fourteenth-century poet-musician, separated from

our own time by half a millenium, seeks to give expression to the
plight of a distressed lover, it is reasonable to expect that he will use
very different musical gestures from those we are used to. To get a feel
for the effect of time on our understanding of earlier forms of expression, let's cross over from the music of a French composer to the language of an English poet who lived at approximately the same time
as Machaut. Here is a passage from one of the greatest works of the
fourteenth century, *The Canterbury Tales* by Geoffrey Chaucer. Chaucer
was born when Machaut was in midcareer. See how much of this
passage you can understand.

> Hir mouth was swete as bragot or the meeth
> Or hord of apples leyd in hey or heeth.
> Winsinge she was as is a joly colt,
> Long as a mast and upright as a bolt.
> A brooch she baar upon hir lowe coler
> As brood as is the bos of a bocler.
> Hir shoes were laced on hir legges hye.
> She was a prymerole, a pigges-nye,
> For any lord to leggen in his bedde,
> Or yet for any good yeman to wedde.

By and large, the language is recognizable as English.[3] Many of the
words are the same as those we use; the grammar and syntax in themselves pose no special obstacle. But much of the vocabulary, not to
mention the spelling, is totally mystifying. Below is Chaucer's text
rendered in modern English.

> Her mouth was sweet as drinks made from honey,
> or as a hoard of apples laid away in hay or heather.
> She was as skittish as a colt,
> tall as a mast, and straight as an arrow.
> On her low collar she wore a brooch
> as broad as the boss of a buckler.
> Her shoes were laced far up her legs.

---

[3] Machaut's fourteenth-century French is, like Chaucer's English, recognizable
as French but characterized by somewhat different vocabulary and spelling. As such,
it is as difficult for a modern French reader to understand as Chaucer for the modern
English reader.

She was a morning glory, she was a daisy,
fit for any lord to lay in his bed,
or yet for any good yeoman to marry.

It is easy to recognize *swete* as "sweet," and to be told that *pigges-nye* is an archaic term for "daisy." But notice the difficulty we have in our "translation" with the notion of the lady's mouth being "as swete as bragot or the meeth." Daisies are still with us, but bragot is not. This forces the translator to use a somewhat awkward and abstract phrase, "drinks made from honey," since he cannot hope to refer to your own experience in recalling the taste of bragot.

Though Chaucer's language seems strange in the light of our expectations of what English should be, it is nonetheless English. It is only the separation of centuries that has rendered it partially unintelligible to us. In a similar way, Machaut's love song, also a product of the fourteenth century, is no less a love song, even though it may be quite distant from our notion of what a love song should be. The translation of the Chaucer poem basically succeeds in eliminating the puzzling aspects presented by the original. The puzzling elements of style in Machaut's *Douce dame jolie,* however, cannot be submitted to a comparable process of translation. Indeed, this difference between language and music with regard to "translatability" across styles points up critical differences between the two as modes of expression.

MACHAUT AND THE FOURTEENTH CENTURY

The fourteenth century in Europe brought with it more critical changes than had occurred at any time since the fall of Rome. The atmosphere of unquestioning Christian faith, which had predominated in Europe for almost a thousand years, was rocked by a series of disastrous events, some natural and others manmade. First, there were the terrible wars of the time, culminating in the so-called Hundred Years War between France and England—a struggle that actually lasted 115 years (1338–1453). These prolonged conflicts drained the resources of both countries, much to the detriment of the artistic and intellectual flowering associated with the Gothic cathedrals. The European continent was visited by successive waves of bubonic plague, known as the Black Death (1348–1350), which wiped out a substantial portion of the population and ravaged existing cultural institutions. Late in the century, the notion that the Pope was God's sole representative on earth was

How he þ Sauiour was mayden marie
And hit his loue floure and fructifie

¶Al þogh his lyfe be queynt þe resemblaunce
Of him hath in me so fressh lyflynesse
Þat to putte othir men in remembraunce
Of his psone I haue heere his lyknesse
Do make to þis ende in sothfastnesse
Þat þei þt haue of him left þought & mynde
By þis peynture may aȝeyn him fynde

¶The ymages þt in þe chirche been
Maken folk þenke on god & on his seyntes
Whan þe ymages þei be holden & seen
Were oft onsyte of hem causith restreyntes
Of þoughtes gode whan a þing depeynt is
Or entaylled if men take of it heede
Thoght of þe lyknesse it wil in hym brede

¶Yit some holden oppynyon and sey
þat none ymages schuld ymakd be
þei erren foule & goon out of þe wey
of trouth haue þei stant sensibilite
Passe ou þt now blessid trinite
vppon my maistres soule mcy haue
ffor him lady eke y mcy I craue

¶More othir þing wolde y fayne speke & touche
Heere in þis booke but ochuch is my dulnesse
ffor þt al voyde and empty is my pouche
þat al my lust is queynt wt heuynesse
And heuy spirit commaundith stilnesse

Portrait of Geoffrey Chaucer. Illuminated manuscript of poem by Thomas Hoccleve, early 15th century.

dealt a serious blow by the emergence of two, and eventually three, rival claimants to the papacy, each succeeding in marshaling a substantial body of political support.

On the more positive side, the works of Aristotle (and of Arab thinkers on whom his philosophy had long exercised an influence) began to enter the West from the highly literate and scientifically more advanced culture of Islam. This provided glimpses of alternative systems of thought. For European culture, whose premises had rested more on faith than on reason or empirical investigation, these alternative world views were both invigorating and disturbing. All these developments contributed to the unsettling of the central position of Christian faith in European society. Accordingly, fourteenth-century artistic expression tended towards the secular and away from the exclusively sacred.

But even more broadly significant was the changing view of the place of art during this period. From about the fourteenth century onward, there was a growing awareness of the artist as individual creator endowed with special gifts, and of art as an endeavor which had intrinsic value. As a result, we know much more about particular artistic figures of this period, since many of them were already widely known and admired in their own time. Machaut is a case in point. Here is part of a lament written upon Machaut's death in 1377 by the poet Eustache

| 1270 | 1280 | 1290 | 1300 | 1310 | 1320 | 1330 | 1340 | 1350 | 1360 | 1370 | 1380 | 1390 | 1400 | 1410 | 1420 |

1305 Giotto does famous frescoes in Padua

1307–1321 Dante, *Divine Comedy*

1327 Aztecs establish Mexico City

c. 1329 Philippe de Vitry, *Ars Nova*

1338 University of Pisa founded; Hundred Years War began

1348–1350 "Black Death" plague, millions die in Europe

1397 Landini dies (b. c. 1325)

1387 Chaucer, *Canterbury Tales*

1377 Machaut dies (b. c. 1300)

1375 Boccaccio dies (b. 1313)

1369 Chaucer, *The Book of the Duchess*

c. 1350 Machaut, *Douce dame jolie*

Deschamps and set to music by F. Andrieu: "Oh master of melody, so rare and fine a talent, oh, Guillaume, earthly god of harmony, which poet can ever take your place? I certainly know of none. Your memory will always be cherished, for throughout France and Artois men bewail the death of Machaut, the noblest bard."

Compare this cultural climate, which can inspire a eulogy to the unique inspiration of an artist, to that surrounding plainchant and early polyphony where the musician was an artisan crafting anonymously in the service of God. From the late thirteenth and into the fourteenth century, a great succession of important artists emerged: poets, writers, painters. Among these were such figures as Dante (1265–1321), Giotto (1267–1337), Boccaccio (1313–1375), Petrarch (1304–1374), and Chaucer (c. 1343–1400). As for music during this period, one figure was commonly regarded as towering above the rest. That figure was Guillaume de Machaut.

Many changes in musical style occurred during this time. Perhaps the most significant was the freeing of rhythm values from the narrow limits set by the earlier rhythmic modes. (Recall the discussion of modal rhythm with respect to Perotin and the twelfth and thirteenth centuries.) The feeling that musical composition had entered a new era was reflected in the term *Ars Nova* (the New Art), a label used by some of Mauchaut's contemporaries to distinguish the music of their generation from that of the Gothic, or *Ars Antiqua*.

Machaut, who was born at the beginning of the fourteenth century and lived well into his seventies, was witness to these events and musical developments. Characteristic of his age, he wrote much more secular music than sacred. While many of his works were stylistically "new" (he composed in several genres and styles), his songs bear a strong temperamental connection with a bygone secular tradition—the courtly art of the twelfth- and thirteenth-century troubadours. The troubadours were aristocratic poet-musicians from Provence in southern France who composed and performed monophonic secular songs. Like the troubadours (and their successors the *trouvères,* who worked in northern France), Machaut was a poet as well as a musician.

The text of *Douce dame jolie,* one of Machaut's own poems, has a thematic connection to these earlier traditions as well. The texts of many of Machaut's songs, like those of the troubadours and trouvères, can be characterized by their constraints—in this case by the constraints inherent in contemporary social conventions. Courtly love as a code of behavior involved fairly rigid prescriptions for how an aristocratic courtier should speak to a lady or fellow courtier and what gestures should accompany that speech. The texts of *Douce dame jolie* and other poems of the time clearly reflect this code of behavior: They deal with an idealized often distant ladylove and an aristocratic admirer who expresses his constant and servile adoration for her along with his constant despair at not being able to approach her. This continuing theme is the characteristic motif of the "courtly love" tradition we referred to earlier.

The art of this poetry was not in creating new "stories" or novel outcomes, but rather, within the limits of the same sentiments, to express the lover's dilemma in subtly different ways so that the subject was always fresh, always touching. And as we have suggested, a similar climate of constrained formality applies to the music as well.

Consider, now, the verses of *Douce dame jolie.* The poem is articulated into three 18-line stanzas. Here is the first stanza of the text once again:

Douce dame jolie,	A
Pour Dieu ne pensés mie	
Que nulle ait signourie	
Seur moy fors vous seulement.	
Qu'adés sans tricherie	B
Chierie	
Vous ay et humblement	
Tous les jours de ma vie	
Servie	
Sans vilein pensement.	
Helas! et je mendie	A'
D'esperance et d'aie;	
Dont ma joie est fenie,	
Se pité ne vous en prent.	
Douce dame jolie,	A
Pour Dieu ne pensés mie	
Que nulle ait signourie	
Seur moy fors vous seulement.	

Notice the formal rhyme scheme that Machaut creates: The poem is almost a variation on "ie" and "ent"—the only endings that occur. However, these two end rhymes are not used in simple alternation but are arranged in a subtle pattern. Using x to stand for lines ending in "ie" and y to indicate those ending in "ent," the following pattern emerges:[4]

$$xxxy \quad xxyxxy \quad xxxy \quad xxxy$$

$$\text{A} \qquad \text{B} \qquad \text{A'} \qquad \text{A}$$

This internal pattern is followed in all other stanzas as well.

Another important organizing principle which applies to the larger design of the whole song and which also contributes to our initial sense of repetitiveness, is the constant recurrence of the first four-line segment (the first quatrain); it forms the boundaries of the stanza, appearing at both the beginning and end of each one. Textually and musically it is treated as a refrain, the same words having been set to the same music. This refrain, labeled A, is an unchanging element appearing regularly in the context of the ever-changing verses labeled A' and B, above. (But, as you will hear, changes in text do not elicit from Machaut changes in their musical setting.) The lines of the refrain state the central theme of the poem: That the beloved alone "holds sway"—rules over the poet's heart. The other lines, the ones that appear but once, elaborate on this recurring theme. Structures of this kind, organized around constantly recurring material, are commonly found in both the music and the poetry of almost every period. Recall the pieces discussed in connection with sectional organization in Chapter 4; for example, the song *Which Side Are You On?* and, indeed, all the instances of rondo form (pp. 150–151).

The structures of the poem—rhyme scheme, number of syllables per line, number of lines per verse—produce a form that is not at all unique to this song and, further, did not originate with Machaut. *Douce dame jolie* is an example of the poetic form known as a **virelai.** The *virelai* was only one such generic poetic form; others were the *ballade* and the *rondeau.* So predictable were these poetic structures during the

---

[4] The third verse is labeled A' because, while the rhyme scheme is the same as in the refrain (A), the words are different.

fourteenth century that they became known as ***formes fixes*** ("fixed forms")—a name that again reflects well our initial sense of a style characterized by its constraints. Machaut wrote poems in all of these forms, setting many of them to music. (French songs from this period are often referred to by the French term *chanson*.)

What about the musical organization of the song, and our hints that within its constraints there is subtle change? The larger musical structure clearly follows the larger organization of the poem with each of the three stanzas bounded at the beginning and end by the music of the refrain (A). Though the poem has a complex internal structure, there are, interestingly, only two different musical sections, A and B, and these are repeated literally in each stanza.

	Music	*Text*
Douce dame jolie, Pour Dieu ne pensés mie Que nulle ait signourie Seur moy fors vous seulement.	A	A
Qu'adés sans tricherie Chierie Vous ay et humblement Tous les jours de ma vie Servie Sans vilein pensement.	B	B
Helas! et je mendie D'esperance et d'aie; Dont ma joie est fenie, Se pité ne vous en prent.	A	A'
Douce dame jolie, Pour Dieu ne pensés mie Que nulle ait signourie Seur moy fors vous seulement.	A	A

You see that while the words are new in the third verse of each stanza, the music, like the rhyme scheme for this verse, is always the same; namely, the music of the refrain. Thus, if we are to look for musical contrast in the song, we must focus on a comparison between A and B: What are their similarities and differences?

To hear them you will need to listen again quite closely. Listen first to just the A section in Example 9.3 (the refrain), following the diagram of A, below:

Example	Composer, title	Date
9.3	Machaut, *Douce dame jolie* (A section only)	c. 1350

A:
  Antecedent
  ⌈ Douce dame jolie,
  ⌊ Pour Dieu ne penses mie

  Consequent
  ⌈ Que nulle ait signourie
  ⌊ Seur moy fors vous seulement.

You should hear the clear and balanced phrase structure indicated in the diagram—two pairs of lines, with the first pair set as an antecedent, the second as its consequent. Futher, the accent structure is also perfectly symmetrical: Within each pair of phrases there are four strong accents, two for each line of text (i.e., for each phrase). Notice, too, that each of the first three phrases (lines 1, 2, and 3) ends with exactly the same cadential figure. The figure stands out because of its syncopated rhythm and its movement around the second degree of the modal scale. Only the last phrase comes to rest on 1.

Listen now to B (Example 9.4) following the diagram below:

Example	Composer, title	Date
9.4	Machaut, *Douce dame jolie* (B section only)	c. 1350

B:
  Antecedent
  ⌈ ⌈ Qu'adés sans tricherie
  ⌊ ⌈ Chierie
     ⌊ Vous ay et humblement

  Consequent
  ⌈ ⌈ Tous lés jours de ma vie
  ⌊ ⌈ Servie
     ⌊ Sans vilein pensement.

Notice that the B section shifts to a higher register, centering on the upper part of the modal scale with all cadences circling around the fifth degree except for the last, which also comes to rest on 1. As in

A, you hear an antecedent-consequent relationship, but within these larger groups there are interesting asymmetries. Each group of *three* lines is set musically so as to form *two* phrases—the first line, and then the next two lines. In turn, there is asymmetry in the accent structure; the single-line phrases (1 and 4) include *two* strong accents, while the two-line phrases (lines 2–3, 5–6) include *three* strong accents. Thus, Machaut creates a more fluid, more expressive feeling in B by shifting register and particularly by introducing a more onward-moving, less foursquare phrase rhythm.

Now go back and listen to the song once more, paying special attention to the subtle contrasts described above. With your increased sensitivity to detail, you will also come closer to the expressiveness of Machaut's style—an expressiveness that depends on the refined moves of the courtier-musician within the accepted social and musical constraints of the time.

You might wonder why, if Machaut was indeed the greatest composer of the fourteenth century, he did not try to overcome the limitations of these traditional formal schemes such as that of the *virelai*. In the first place, Machaut, like all composers of his day and in succeeding centuries, made his living by producing music (and poetry) to the specifications of his courtly or ecclesiastical patrons. He wrote the kind of music and poetry that they liked and were accustomed to (and for which they were paying him). More significantly, originality and innovation in the arts were not in themselves considered particular virtues in this period. Rather, the unchanging nature of the poetic forms, realized in subtly different, ever-changing ways, was probably experienced by composers, poets, and audiences of the time not as rigidity, but as a satisfying balance between constraints and freedom. In this sense, the *formes fixes* were somewhat analogous to the sonnet form. Sonnets by Milton may be very different from one another in tone and *content* and also different from a sonnet by, say, Wordsworth, but *formally* they are the same.

This essential tension between constraints and freedom was also emphasized in our discussion of minuet and sonata forms. Each piece is, on one hand, unique, evolving out of its particular musical ideas; but, on the other hand, each shares with others general structural principles. That tension takes another form in the pulls between tradition and innovation. Exactly where Machaut stands in relation to tradition and innovation cannot simply be summed up by such terms as conservative or progressive. For instance, *Douce dame jolie* reveals a conservative side of Machaut's works; it goes back to an earlier tradition in its monophonic texture. However, this song is representative of only a minority of Machaut's songs, for most of his *chansons* are polyphonic.

In addition to writing songs, however, Machaut wrote in a number of other genres; for example, a polyphonic setting for the Catholic Mass known as *La Messe de Nostre Dame*. It is not only one of the earliest multimovement works by a single composer that we know, it may also be the longest musical work written up to that time. And in the practical sense of music history, Machaut also makes an effective link with the past in this work: four of its six movements are composed on plainchant tenors, as in the moribund tradition of Notre Dame organum. At the same time, what Machaut achieves in the Mass is more innovative than traditional. Though it is essentially an isolated work, both within Machaut's output and in the more secular atmosphere of fourteenth-century life, the *Messe de Nostre Dame* looks forward to the music of the fifteenth and sixteenth centuries, the period of the Renaissance, when the composition of polyphonic masses and motets becomes a central preoccupation of composers. Recall, for example, the sixteenth-century motet of Victoria that you listened to in the previous chapter.

Machaut was also in the *avant garde* in his specific crafting of materials. For example, strange as it may seem to us today, the consistent duple meter of *Douce dame jolie* (stronger beats always subdivided into two) was an innovation of the fourteenth century. Recall from the discussion of Perotin in Chapter 8 that, in the period of organum, the beat was subdivided exclusively in three. Grouping in threes was associated with the idea of perfection not only in music but in many aspects of medieval thought. (The sacred Trinity helped reinforce this general idea during the Middle Ages.) When fourteenth-century composers such as Machaut consciously advocated the granting of equal status to duple meter—"imperfect time," as it was called—they were being revolutionary.

Music in duple meter had certainly been around, but there was as yet no theoretical defenses of its legitimacy. A musical issue was escalated to an ideological one as younger composers, deliberately availing themselves of duple meter with duple subdivision (i.e., simple duple), proudly announced the arrival of the *Ars Nova*—the New Art—and the demise of the *Ars Antiqua*. Listen to Jacob of Liège, a fourteenth-century musician of conservative bent, who argues against these innovations in a musical treatise of the time:

> Should the ancients be considered rude for using perfections [i.e., triple meter], the moderns subtle for using imperfections? . . . If the new art

spoke of the said imperfections only in a speculative way, it would be more tolerable; but not so, for they put imperfection too much into practice.[5]

Finally, let us return to the question of appropriate expression in a love song. Listen to another performance of *Douce dame jolie* (Example 9.5).

Example	Composer, title	Date
9.5	Machaut, *Douce dame jolie*	c. 1350

You are probably surprised by the vibrant, earthy quality of the song in this performance. It sounds more like a sea chanty or a drinking song with its quick tempo and marked accentuation emphasized by the participation of instruments, especially the percussion. The song, as Machaut wrote it, is monophonic, thus a large part of this musical activity must be attributed to the performers on this recording, who chose to double the notated vocal line with instruments (i.e., to play in unison with the voices), to add a drone to the texture, and to *improvise* percussion parts. The result is that our initial notion of the restraint in Machaut's expression of unrequited love is put into some question. Performance, then, can also be a critical factor in the particular expressiveness of a piece. But which performance was considered more appropriate at the time?

The answer is subject to debate. Whether these particular songs were meant to be performed monophonically, as in Example 9.1, or with improvised accompaniment, as in Example 9.5, is a question music historians continue to debate. The addition of instrumental accompaniment can be justified by available evidence: There are pictures from the time showing instrumentalists and singers performing together. But the decision to record *Douce dame jolie* unaccompanied and in a somewhat more lyrical manner is equally defensible on historical grounds. In the absence of explicit directions from the composer himself, no modern musical realization of the score can be definitive. Questions such as these, concerning the contemporary performance of works written long ago, and, indeed, questions concerning the musical expression of unrequited love in times gone by, are not readily an-

---

[5] Oliver Strunk, *Source Readings in Music History* (New York: Norton, 1950), pp. 183–184.

swered. They do, however, give you a flavor of the practical work engaging the interests of music historians in our own time.

SCHUBERT AND EARLY NINETEENTH-CENTURY ROMANTICISM

In moving from Machaut's world to Schubert's, we cross over four major boundaries of music style: between the Middle Ages and the Renaissance; the Renaissance and the Baroque; the Baroque and the Classical; the Classical and the Romantic. As with all these boundaries, those of the Romantic period can only roughly be set by dates, and only somewhat more explicitly by particular composers whose work is thought to embody the Romantic musical style. If we place the height of Romanticism around the middle of the nineteenth century, Schubert, who died in 1828, must surely be considered an "early Romantic" in contrast to those who followed him, such as, Chopin, Wagner, Verdi, Brahms, or Strauss. These later Romantics will be

1760	1770	1780	1790	1800	1810	1820	1830	1840

1797 Schubert born (d. 1828);
Coleridge, *Kubla Khan*

1800 Alessandro Volta made the first electric battery;
Napoleon conquers Italy

1801 Haydn, *The Seasons*;
Jefferson first U.S. president to be inaugurated
in Washington, DC

1804 George Sand born (d. 1876);
First steam locomotive, in Wales

1808 Goethe, *Faust*, Part I;
Beethoven, *Symphony 5*

1809 Mendelssohn born (d. 1847);
Haydn dies (b. 1732)

1810 Chopin born (d. 1849);
Schumann born (d. 1856)

1828 Schubert dies
(b. 1797)

1827 Beethoven dies
(b. 1770)

1826 Schubert,
Im Frühling

1825 Manzoni,
I Promessi Sposi;
Pushkin,
Boris Godunov

1824 Erie Canal
finished

1820 Keats, *Ode to a Nightingale*;
Venus de Milo discovered
on Greek island of Melos

1813 Verdi born (d. 1901);
Wagner born (d. 1883)

treated in the subsequent chapters. But, as if to underscore the futility of circumscribing style by dates, and particularly the Romantic style in music, it is Beethoven, born in 1770, who is often considered the first major "Romantic." When Beethoven died in 1827, Schubert, in an act of homage, served as one of 36 torchbearers in the funeral procession; Schubert himself died at a tragically young age less then two years later. Despite the closeness of the two dates, Schubert represents the next generation stylistically. To set the stage, then, for Schubert's work, let us consider more broadly the Romantic legacy he inherited.

For some of the most influential writers of the time (and certainly for many composers and critics later in the century), Beethoven exemplified musical Romanticism. To get a sense of this Romantic image, consider what E. T. A. Hoffmann, a musician-writer contemporary with Beethoven, had to say in 1813 about the composer's famous *Symphony 5,* from which you heard excerpts in Chapter 3:

> Beethoven's music sets in motion the level of fear, of awe, of horror, of suffering, and wakens just that infinite longing which is the essence of romanticism. . . . Can there be any work of Beethoven's that confirms all this to a higher degree than his indescribably profound, magnificent symphony in C minor? How this wonderful composition, in a climax that climbs on and on, leads the listener imperiously forward into the spirit world of the infinite![6]

Many of the themes of Romanticism thread through Hoffmann's rather lyric comments: "infinite longing," "awe," and the "spirit world of the infinite" are invoked. There is a sense of heroic individualism underlying Hoffmann's description, and Beethoven, who felt himself to be an outsider struggling against fate, was a potent symbol of the Romantic artist-hero. His self-perception of alienation and heroic struggle is powerfully described in a statement written by Beethoven in 1802 but published only after his death:

> For me there can be no relaxation with my fellow-men, no refined conversations, no mutual exchange of ideas. I must live almost alone like one who has been banished, I can mix with society only as much as true necessity demands . . . a little more of that and I would have

---

[6] Strunk, *Source Readings,* pp. 777–778.

Ludwig van Beethoven,
c. 1800

ended my life—it was only *my art* that held me back. Ah, it seemed to me impossible to leave the world until I had brought forth all that I felt was within me. So I endured this wretched existence. . . . Oh fellow men, when at some point you read this, consider then that you have done me an injustice; someone who has had misfortune may console himself to find a similar case to his, who despite all the limitations of Nature nevertheless did everything within his powers to become accepted among worthy artists and men.[7]

Beethoven speaks of irrepressible urges, the overcoming of the obstacles of nature, and the transcendence of a miserable and alienated existence. Contrast this self-image, this radically different way of speaking about composition to that of composers just a generation before Beethoven. For example, compare Beethoven's statement to a more casual statement by Haydn (a composer born 38 years before Beethoven and whose music is the epitome of Classicism) describing his career as court composer to the Austrian Prince Nikolaus Esterházy:

My prince was content with all my works, I received approval, I could, as head of an orchestra, make experiments, observe what created an impression, and what weakened it, thus improving, adding to, cutting away, and running risks. I was set apart from the world, there was nobody in my vicinity to confuse and annoy me in my course, and so I had to become original.[8]

---

[7] Elliot Forbes, ed., *Thayer's Life of Beethoven* (Princeton: Princeton University Press, 1967), pp. 304–305. (At the time, Beethoven was confronting impending deafness.)

[8] Jens Peter Larsen, "Haydn, Joseph," *New Grove Dictionary of Music and Musicians,* 20 vols., ed. Stanley Sadie (London: Macmillan, 1980), VIII, p. 335.

Haydn speaks, almost like a scientist, of experiment and observation in patiently learning the craft of composition. He mentions that he was directly responsible to a prince, who was, in fact, his sole patron for much of his career. Haydn wrote the majority of his music explicitly for the prince's court events, both large-scale and small, and he concerned himself with providing the right music for the occasion rather than with achieving immortality or rank among the "worthy artists" alluded to by Beethoven. Only at the very end of his career did Haydn become fully aware of how widely his music was valued throughout Europe, not only by the patron class but by middle-class "consumers" as well. This new audience was beginning to emerge as a force at the close of Haydn's career and the beginning of Beethoven's. Beethoven, a child of a different era, saw *mankind* in general, rather than a particular aristocratic patron, as the significant audience. A composer could therefore achieve noble rank in the performance of great artistic deeds rather than only through an accident of birth.

These differences in perspective between Haydn, the composer in the service of a single aristocrat, and Beethoven, the composer in the service of mankind and immortal art, are not unique to these two great figures. They represent the changing spirit of an age. Heroism and the metaphysical yearnings associated with the individual artist played an important, but not exclusive, role in the development of Romanticism, along with social revolutions against aristocratic domination in the late eighteenth century. Haydn was 57 years old when the French Revolution took place in 1789; Beethoven was 19. Haydn was an established professional composer during this era of rebellion against aristocratic power. Beethoven was an impressionable teenager, infused with the spirit of individuality, emancipation, and social equality that found expression throughout Europe (and the newly independent America) in the last decades of the eighteenth century.

For music, one of the most important practical consequences of the dramatic societal changes that occurred in the Revolutionary period was the rise of the public concert to a position in which it eventually replaced the aristocratic court concert in importance. As the power and wealth of the aristocracy diminished throughout Europe, a new, relatively large middle-class audience for music emerged and musicians began to rely more and more for economic support on this new group. This social process was gradual, but it was decisive by the time of Beethoven. By then, numerous public concert halls had been built; and it was not unusual for performers and composers to fund their work through ticket sales from concert events—in addition to, or often instead of, fees or salaries from aristocratic patrons.

Composers also earned money through the sale of their compositions to music publishers. Indeed, music publishing had, by the time of Beethoven and Schubert, become a flourishing and highly competitive business. The score, then, had gained an independent status. Its growing specificity (and resistance to tampering) is one enormously significant difference between nineteenth-century musical life and that of the much earlier periods we have discussed up until now.

Just why music publishing could flourish during this time also tells us something else about the musical public in the late eighteenth century and on into the nineteenth. Concertgoers among the upper- and middle-class citizens of Europe were not simply passive music consumers; many people owned instruments and were active amateur performers who played or sang solo and chamber music works at home. These works included some they would also hear in public concerts, but also works written especially for amateur performers. Thus, it was to these amateurs at least as much as to professional musicians that publishers directed their business. As a result, there was a lively, and sometimes quite tense, interaction between composers and publishers: the publishers vying among themselves for the "best sellers"; the composers working to sell their wares and, when successful, to control the accuracy of their publication. This reciprocal relationship between composer, publisher, and public had enormous effects on the working lives of artists and, as we shall see, on Schubert's life in particular.

It is interesting here to think for a moment about the role played in music history by notation—the "fixing" and making permanent of sounds that disappear in time. Consider, for example, the following: The very beginnings of music notation—Medieval monk-scribes copying out chant by hand in the service of the church in its desire to standardize and normalize religious ritual; Machaut writing monophonic melodies to which courtier-musicians apparently felt free to add improvised instrumental accompaniments; and the eighteenth-century industrialization of music printing, making the works of great composers available in every detail to professional musicians as well as to anyone who could play a little and afford to buy the music.

Schubert is the first of the composers whose music you have heard in Part Four whose exact dates of birth and death can be stated definitively: born January 31, 1797; died November 19, 1828, at the age of 31. Despite his tragically short life, the extent and breadth of his work is prodigious. *Im Frühling* is but one of more than 600 songs. He also wrote 9 completed symphonies, over a dozen operas, 15 known string quartets, more than 20 piano sonatas, and many other symphonic, choral, and chamber works—over a thousand works in all. While we cannot, here, give more than a few snapshots of Schubert's life, it seems

Franz Schubert,
c. 1822

appropriate to do so since it is individualism (and this individual in particular) that so epitomizes Romanticism.

Born the son of a schoolmaster, Schubert entered the Imperial Chapel-Royal, a school for choirboys, at the age of 11. In the judge's chair at his entrance examination (and later to serve as his composition teacher) sat Antonio Salieri—the same man whose rivalry with Mozart has gained him such infamy. Holzer, another of Schubert's teachers, said of his student: "Whenever I wanted to teach him anything new, he already knew it. I often simply stared at him in silent astonishment." Upon graduation at 16, Schubert spent several years as an assistant teacher in his father's school. But in 1816 he escaped from his teaching duties to try to make it on his own. From the age of 19, then, until his death just 12 years later, Schubert eked out a living by giving piano lessons and occasional public performances. Publications of his work contributed little; his freedom to compose depended mostly on the help of his friends.

It is this intimate circle of friends that comes most immediately to mind in thinking of Schubert. Some of them were former classmates from the choir school, others poets (who often provided him with texts for his songs) and artists. Lawyers and government officials were also counted among them, members of the rising middle class who in many cases were also amateur musicians. As a group the circle could be characterized as almost self-conscious Romantics, devoted to art and to its power to express personal, intimate feelings associated especially with nature and love. While some of Schubert's works were played in public concerts, his music was heard much more frequently in the

Schubert and his friends at a "Schubert evening." Schubert is seated at the piano with Johann Vogl, the singer, on his right.

homes of these musical friends. The following letter written by his friend, Josef Huber, in 1821, gives us a picture of an evening with Schubert, evenings that came to be called "Schubertiads":

> Last Friday I had excellent entertainment as Franz Schober invited Schubert in the evening and fourteen of his close acquaintances. So a lot of splendid songs by Schubert were sung and played by himself, which lasted until about 10 o'clock in the evening. After that punch was drunk, offered by one of the party, and as it was very good and plentiful the party, in a happy mood anyhow, became even merrier; so it was 3 o'clock in the morning before we parted.[9]

This circle of friends provided Schubert with his primary support—both financial and spiritual, while he tried continually to develop a productive relationship with publishers.[10] A major outlet for published music, as suggested previously, was the growing population of home users who, instead of simply listening to music (as do most record buyers today), became familiar with new music by actually playing it. These music consumers were, in fact, the same kind of people that made up Schubert's circle of friends and yet, perhaps paradoxically, the publishers did not see them as potential buyers of his music. As

[9] Otto Erich Deutsch, *The Schubert Reader,* trans. Eric Blom (New York: Norton, 1947), p. 162.

[10] Schubert also devoted a great deal of energy to launching a career as an opera composer, but failed to do so.

one publisher wrote to Schubert in turning down compositions that he had submitted, the public needed works "which without sacrificing any of your individuality, are not too difficult to grasp." The great *Piano Trio in E-flat* was turned down by another publisher because it was "probably too long." Few of Schubert's large-scale instrumental works were printed during his lifetime. Publishers who did print many of his shorter works—dances and songs—treated him as a promising young composer and accordingly underpaid him for his work. Schubert died a poor man at an age when most people have only just begun, leaving an incomparable legacy of which *Im Frühling* is one small but gemlike example. It was written just two years before his death.

    Let us return, now, to the music of Schubert and to *Im Frühling*. Keeping in mind the almost totally different cultures into which Schubert and Machaut were born, it is not surprising that in comparing our two love songs it was Schubert's freedom in contrast to Machaut's constraints—both musical and emotional—that seemed most to distinguish one from the other. By their very nature, constraints lend themselves more easily to description than the qualities that may contribute to freedom. What, then, can be found in the music itself to account for the feeling of expansiveness, of openness in *Im Frühling*?

    Listen to the song again following the text and diagram below.

Example 9.2 SCHUBERT, *Im Frühling* ("In Spring")

I

A   *Introduction (piano alone)* ⎤   4 bars

B

     Quietly I sit on the side of the hill; the sky is so clear; ⎤   2 bars

     the breeze plays in the green valley where I in the first light of spring once was so happy; ⎤   4 bars

     6 bars

A′

     (piano alone) where I walked at her side, so intimate and so near, ⎤   3 bars

     and deep in the dark rock-spring saw the beautiful heaven, blue and bright, and saw her in that heaven and saw her in that heaven. ⎤   4 bars

     7 bars

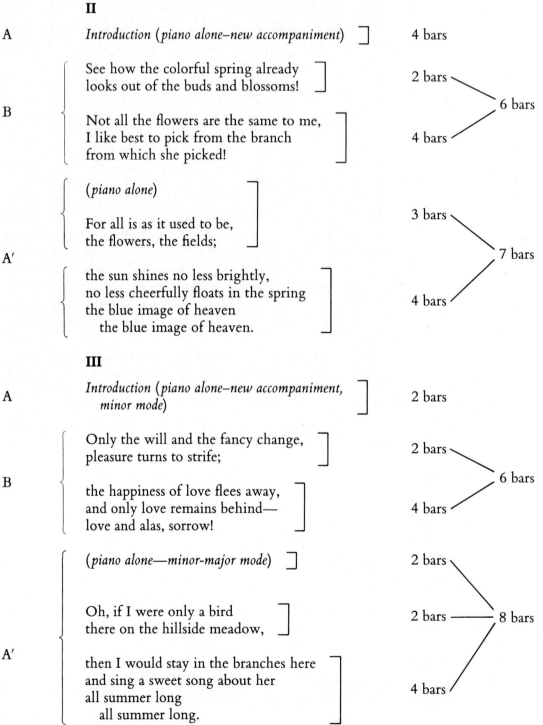

II

A   *Introduction (piano alone–new accompaniment)*   4 bars

B

See how the colorful spring already
looks out of the buds and blossoms!   2 bars

Not all the flowers are the same to me,
I like best to pick from the branch
from which she picked!   4 bars

   6 bars

A′

(piano alone)

For all is as it used to be,
the flowers, the fields;   3 bars

the sun shines no less brightly,
no less cheerfully floats in the spring
the blue image of heaven
     the blue image of heaven.   4 bars

   7 bars

III

A   *Introduction (piano alone–new accompaniment,
     minor mode)*   2 bars

B

Only the will and the fancy change,
pleasure turns to strife;   2 bars

the happiness of love flees away,
and only love remains behind—
love and alas, sorrow!   4 bars

   6 bars

A′

(piano alone—minor-major mode)   2 bars

Oh, if I were only a bird
there on the hillside meadow,   2 bars

then I would stay in the branches here
and sing a sweet song about her
all summer long
     all summer long.   4 bars

   8 bars

Coda ⎧   (*piano alone*)   ⎫

      I sing about her
      all summer long.   3 bars

      (*piano alone*) ⎭

You probably noticed that while the boundaries of the musical structure generally coincide with the boundaries of the three stanzas in the poem, Schubert, unlike Machaut, seems more interested in the poem's intimate expressive content than in its formal structure. Schubert responds in exquisite musical detail to the words of the poem and to the changing moods they express.

Contrasts in the expressiveness of the music are perhaps most immediately noticeable in the changing accompaniment of the piano from one stanza to the next. Unlike the improvised instrumental accompaniment for Machaut's monophonic melody in Example 9.5, the piano accompaniment here is unquestionably written by Schubert as an integral, even essential part of the piece. Schubert composes a new accompaniment for each stanza of the poem. Most striking is the contrasting accompaniment for the third stanza where the speaker, the unrequited lover, is bemoaning his (her) fate: "Love, and alas, sorrow." For this stanza, Schubert moves to the minor mode and, as if imitating the lover's throbbing heart, gives the piano syncopated, sonorous, "throbbing" chords against a continuously moving bass. This accompaniment stops abruptly in the middle of the third stanza. Then, as the mood becomes lighter at the close of the stanza ("Oh, if I were only a bird, there on the hillside meadow"), Schubert brings back the major mode along with the melody heard at the ends of previous stanzas. But even with this return to major, Schubert composes yet another accompaniment, still syncopated as if reminiscent of, affected by, the previous expression of despair.

Freedom is also evident in the phrase structure. In contrast to Machaut's regularly balanced phrase rhythm, Schubert seems to be forever going beyond the expected phrase boundary. But freedom is only possible if there are also limits. Schubert sets up his normative phrase length in the opening piano introduction: Two phrases which, like Machaut's refrain and indeed like many familiar folk songs, is a balanced, antecedent-consequent pair. With the entrance of the voice, the antecedent phrase remains within these normative bounds, but Schubert stretches the consequent phrase, extending it beyond its expected length. In addition, as the lover lapses into past reflection ("where I, in the first light of spring, once was so happy"), the consequent phrase, prolonged, momentarily slips into a minor key area, and only then glides effortlessly back to the original major key and to its tonic.

But Schubert's creative imagination can perhaps best be heard if we compare the opening piano introduction with the return of this same musical material at the end of the first stanza. We have recorded (Example 9.6) just the piano introduction with its clear and balanced phrase structure and then, after a pause, the return to the same material (A′) at the end of the first stanza.

Example	Composer, title	Date
9.6	Schubert, *Im Frühling*, introduction (A); end of stanza 1 (A′)	1826

Notice in the return that the voice (singing "where I walked at her side") gently picks up the melody in the midst of the piano phrase, as if the singer is only then, and quite casually, reminded of the previous melody. Listening to the two passages next to one another, you will easily hear, too, that the initial phrase is not repeated literally. Like the sentiment it expresses, it is prolonged. The consequent phrase is again extended as the singer reaches up and holds, unresolved, the highest note in the song. Then, slowly extending, elaborating (repeating the poet's words but not the music), Schubert resolves the melody, bringing it momentarily to rest as the piano moves on to the next stanza.

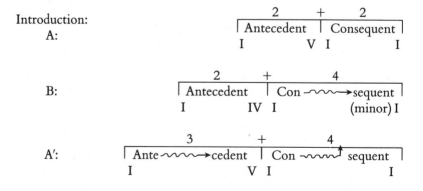

Finally, a word about Schubert's harmony. The harmonic movement is so subtle, even elusive, that it is difficult in analytic description to do it justice here. For example, sometimes Schubert unexpectedly but elegantly makes a harmonic turn toward a new key area and then, almost by sleight of hand, comes back again to where he had been. But, interestingly, even when harmonies move within the primary key of the piece, Schubert uses progressions that revolve around the darker, more subdued areas of the tonality; for example, the subdominant (IV) in contrast to the brighter dominant (V), and especially the minor chords of the major mode such as II and VI. And even when the melody line remains nearly, but never exactly, the same (compare stanzas one and two), Schubert succeeds in varying the harmonic underpinnings, thus breathing new life into what would otherwise have been simple repetition.

But notice that all of this, as it contributes to our sense of freedom and expressiveness, depends on Schubert's, and indeed our own, "received tradition"; that is, on our having internalized the conventions that have accrued from the past, particularly the music of the Baroque and Classical periods. As norms, these stylistic conventions are in many respects still with us—embodied in traditional progressions of tonal harmony, meter, phrase structure, range of textures, and even the Classical forms. Without this backdrop of stylistic norms, the expressiveness of the Romantic period in general, and of *Im Frühling* in particular as an example of that style, would be lost upon us. Schubert takes these norms as "givens" for performers and listeners alike. As a result, in recreating them anew, he can also bend them, playing against them and going beyond them to create the expressive freedom that we quite unanalytically, spontaneously feel, even as we listen to the song for the first time.

CHAPTER 10

Johann Sebastian Bach at the organ

Sacred Music and Dramatic Expression

Guiseppe Verdi at home in his garden

The paired examples in this chapter again interweave chronologically with previous ones: we first loop back to the time just about midway between Victoria's motet (1572) and Schubert's song (1826) to the Baroque period and its greatest master, Johann Sebastian Bach (born March 21, 1685; died July 28, 1750). Then, moving on through the early Romantic period of Schubert, we approach the center of that era in the music of Giuseppe Verdi (born October 10, 1813; died January 27, 1901). Listen now to the two examples.

Example	Composer, title	Date
10.1	J. S. Bach, *Cantata 61, Nun komm der Heiden Heiland* ("Come, Savior of the Nations"), ouverture	1714
10.2	G. Verdi, *Requiem, Dies irae* ("Day of Wrath"), opening	1874

Both of these pieces were composed for special occasions and both are settings of religious texts. The cantata (Example 10.1) was composed by Bach for the Lutheran church service commemorating the first Sunday of Advent on December 2, 1714.[1] The opening words of the text, *Nun komm der Heiden Heiland* ("Come, Savior of the Nations"), reflect the occasion for which the cantata was composed—Advent—which is the season celebrating the coming of the Messiah. The *Requiem* (Example 10.2) was composed by Verdi for a service on May 22, 1874, in Milan commemorating the first anniversary of the death of Alessandro Manzoni, a great writer and political leader. It belongs to the long tradition of musical settings of the Catholic Requiem Mass, the mass for the dead.

Both of these works are unquestionably religious pieces and, as the title of the chapter suggests, both are dramatic. Upon first listening, you may have been surprised that we paired these works as sharing dramatic as well as religious intent. In particular, you may wonder why the Bach composition is considered dramatic at all. To late twentieth-century listeners, the drama in the Bach cantata may seem quite muted and restrained, while the Verdi seems to be about as out-

---

[1] Bach set the same text again, and quite differently, ten years later in Leipzig.

going, demonstratively dramatic, and full of peaks, valleys, contrasts, and brilliant orchestral effects as any piece of music can be. We might put it this way: However it was perceived in its original time and place, from our current perspective, the Bach piece invites association with religious feeling but not with dramatic intensity. The Verdi seems just the opposite—frankly dramatic but not obviously religious in tone.

In this chapter we will try to make the argument that each work is highly dramatic when taken on its own terms, and that each, within its respective cultural setting, is equally religious in its expression. In short, we will try to give you a sense of how the markedly different contexts within which they were composed helped to shape two such different religious pieces: One in north-central Europe, the other in the south; the two separated by exactly 160 years.

Before going very deeply into the music, it will be useful briefly to locate these two examples within the lives of each composer and within the history of the two genres—the cantata and the Requiem Mass.

BACH AND THE CANTATA

The cantata (from the root "to sing," in contrast to sonata, which means "to sound" on instruments) has its roots in early seventeenth-century Italy. The earliest cantatas were almost always secular works, usually for solo voice with harpsichord or lute accompaniment. Later in seventeenth-century Italy, cantatas were composed for several voices and included not only solo arias but also recitatives and instrumental movements. The cantatas composed in Germany during the eighteenth century were quite different from these earlier Italian works. Like *Cantata 61,* they were primarily sacred rather than secular; their texts, usually in German, were written by contemporary poets often deriving their material from the Bible. Further, these sacred cantatas were generally larger in scope than their Italian counterparts. They made use of larger forces—chorus, soloists, and orchestra—and included a number of movements beginning usually with an introduction for chorus and orchestra followed by recitatives, arias, and often a closing chorale.

Bach composed about 300 cantatas of which some 200 are still known. Most of these were written in connection with his regular duties as director of music for the two principal churches of Leipzig: St. Thomas Church and St. Nicholas. He served in this post from 1723 until his death in 1750 at the age of 65. *Nun komm der Heiden Heiland,* however, was composed earlier while Bach was working in Weimar, Germany, in the service of the Duke of Weimar. Bach had moved to Weimar in 1708 at the age of 23 and composed this cantata six years later. While the majority of Bach's cantatas are settings of sacred texts intended for performance during the Lutheran church service, he also composed a number of secular cantatas, usually for some special occasion (for example, the *Coffee Cantata, Peasant Cantata,* and *Wedding Cantata*). Bach's cantatas were, like most music written before and during his lifetime, composed under obligation and many are among his most inspired works. His own deeply felt religious belief infuses this body of works and is the inspiration for its great dramatic range.

VERDI AND THE CATHOLIC REQUIEM MASS

The Requiem has a somewhat longer and more uniform history than the rather free-form cantata. Unlike cantatas, whose texts are not prescribed, all these works share the same text—namely, that of the Catholic Mass for the dead. As a result, the movements of nearly all Requiem Masses follow the same order. The *Dies irae* follows the opening movements, *Requiem aeternam* ("eternal rest") and *Kyrie eleison* ("Lord, have mercy"), and is divided into several parts of which our Verdi excerpt includes the first two—*Dies irae* ("Day of wrath") and *Tuba mirum*

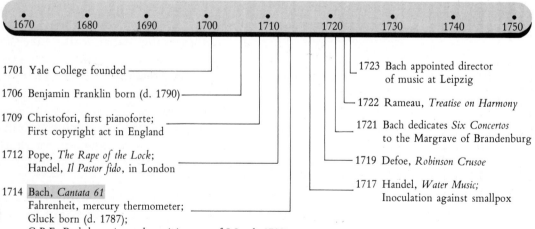

1670 1680 1690 1700 1710 1720 1730 1740 1750

1701 Yale College founded

1706 Benjamin Franklin born (d. 1790)

1709 Christofori, first pianoforte;
First copyright act in England

1712 Pope, *The Rape of the Lock*;
Handel, *Il Pastor fido*, in London

1714 Bach, *Cantata 61*
Fahrenheit, mercury thermometer;
Gluck born (d. 1787);
C.P.E. Bach born (second surviving son of J.S., d. 1788)

1723 Bach appointed director
of music at Leipzig

1722 Rameau, *Treatise on Harmony*

1721 Bach dedicates *Six Concertos*
to the Margrave of Brandenburg

1719 Defoe, *Robinson Crusoe*

1717 Handel, *Water Music;*
Inoculation against smallpox

("The trumpet shall sound"). The earliest surviving setting of the Requiem Mass dates back to Johannes Ockeghem in the late fifteenth century; there are also examples by Lassus (1589), Palestrina (1591), and Victoria, who in 1603 composed a Requiem Mass upon the death of Empress Maria of Spain. Interestingly, it was the dramatic words of *Dies irae* that seem to have inspired the most dramatic music from these and later seventeenth-century composers.

During the eighteenth and nineteenth centuries composers continued to set the text of the Requiem Mass. These later works include the *Requiem* of Mozart, composed in 1791 but left unfinished at Mozart's death, followed by masses of Berlioz (1837), Fauré (1887–1888), and Dvořák (1890). Despite their sacred texts, these later works were not usually intended to be performed as part of an actual church service for the dead but rather in the public concert hall where their much larger orchestral and choral forces found a more fitting cultural and physical space for performance. As you have seen, the composition of religious music had been a primary concern of musicians in earlier times; but by the nineteenth century, composers' interests had swung decisively toward secular rather than sacred music. In this sense, Verdi's

| 1840 | 1850 | 1860 | 1870 | 1880 | 1890 | 1900 |

1861 American Civil War (ended 1865); Italy became a kingdom under Victor Emmanuel II; Dickens, *Great Expectations*

1862 Debussy born (d. 1918); Hugo, *Les Miserables*; Verdi, *La Forza del Destino*

1865 Wagner, *Tristan and Isolde,* first performance in Munich; Lewis Carroll, *Alice in Wonderland*

1866 Dostoevsky, *Crime and Punishment*; Alfred Noble invents dynamite

1870 Tchaikovsky, *Romeo and Juliet*; Huxley, *Theory of Biogenesis*

1883 Wagner dies (b. 1813); Completion of Brooklyn Bridge; Metropolitan Opera House opened in New York

1877 Edison invented phonograph; Henry James, *The Americans*

1876 Bell invented telephone; Brahms, *Symphony 1*

1874 Verdi, *Requiem* Monet, *Impression: Sunrise*; Schoenberg born (d. 1951); Moussorgsky, *Pictures at an Exhibition*

1871 Verdi, *Aida*, in Cairo

Requiem is somewhat an anachronism, comparable perhaps to Machaut's monophonic songs in the midst of the prevailing interest in polyphonic settings of texts.

Verdi had an unusually long creative life spanning a period of nearly 60 years—from 1839, when his first opera was performed, until 1893, when at the age of 80 his last opera, *Falstaff,* had its premiere. The *Requiem,* composed in 1874, belongs then to Verdi's mature middle age. Verdi is best known as an opera composer, and the highly dramatic character of his *Requiem* obviously benefits from his long and very successful career writing in this medium. It will probably not come as a surprise to learn that Bach wrote no operas while Verdi's *Requiem* is one of only a few works he wrote on sacred texts.

The *Requiem* was written in commemoration of the death of a man who was, like Verdi himself, a cultural hero in Italy during the nineteenth century. The work was first performed in Milan at the Church of St. Mark. The soloists were the finest Italian singers, the orchestra numbered 100, the chorus 120. Verdi conducted. This performance was immediately followed by three more in Milan, at the famed La Scala, where, as one writer puts it, "The Mass had arrived at its real home, the opera house."

La Scala opera house, interior, c. 1830

The personal and cultural contexts surrounding the composition and performance of the Bach and Verdi works make a striking contrast which we ask you to keep in mind as we turn to a more careful consideration of the works themselves.

Listen again to the two examples, this time following the texts, below, and considering the way each composer relates text and music.

Example 10.1 BACH, *Cantata 61*

Nun komm der Heiden Heiland,
der Jungfrauen Kind erkannt,
des sich wundert alle Welt.
Gott solch Geburt ihm bestellt.

Der Heiland ist gekommen,
hat unser armes Fleische und Blut an sich
    genommen
und nimmet uns zu Blutsverwandten.
O allerhöchstes Gut,
was hast du nicht an uns getan?
Was tust du nicht noch an den Deinen?
Du kommst und laßt dein Licht
mit vollem Segen scheinen.

Komm, Jesu, komm du deiner Kirche
und gib ein selig neues Jahr!
Befördre deines Namens Ehre,
und segne Kanzel und Alter!
Komm, Jesu.

Siehe, Siehe!
Ich stehe vor der Tür und klopfe an.
So jemand meine stimme hören wird
und die Tür auftun,
zu dem werde ich eingehen
und das Abendmahl mit ihm halten,
und er mit mir.

Öffne dich mein ganzes Herze,
Jesu kömmt und ziehet ein.
Bin ich gleich nur Staub und Erde,
will er mich doch nicht verschmähn,
seine Lust an mir zu sehn,
daß ich seine Wohnung werde.
O wie selig werd' ich sein!

Come, Oh Savior of the Nations,
known as the Virgin's child
who causes all the world to wonder.
God ordained such a birth for him.

The Lord has come,
has assumed this poor flesh and blood of ours
and makes us his blood kin.
Oh Highest Good,
What have you not done for us?
What do you not do daily for those of us who
    are yours?
You come and leave your light
shining with the fullness of grace.

Come Jesus, come to your church
and give us the new year, sanctified by you,
so we might promote the honor of your name,
and bless pulpit and altar.
Come, Jesus.

Look, look!
I stand before the door and knock
so that someone will hear my voice
and open the door.
I will come in and sup with him,
and he with me.

Would that my whole heart were opened
and Jesus would steal within.
I am but dust and clay,
yet he will not scorn me.
He wishes me
for his dwelling place.
O how blessed will I be.

Amen.	Amen.
Komm, du	Come, you
schöne Freudenkrone.	beautiful crown of joy.
Bleib nicht lange!	Wait no longer.
Deine wart' ich mit Verlangen.	It is for you I wait with longing.

Example 10.2 VERDI, *Requiem Mass*

Dies irae, dies illa	Day of wrath, that day will
Solvet saeculum in favila,	dissolve the world in ashes,
Teste David cum Sibylla	as David prophesied with the sibyl.
Quantas tremor est futurus,	How great a terror there will be
Quando Judex est venturus	when the Judge shall come
Cuncta stricte discussurus!	who will thresh everything out thoroughly!
Tuba mirum spargens sonum	The trumpet, scattering a wondrous sound
Per sepulcra regionum,	through the tombs of every land,
Coget omnes ante thronum	will gather all before the throne.
Mors stupebit et Natura,	Death and nature will be stupefied
Cum resurgit creatura.	when creation rises again.
Judicanti responsura.	Answer to the Judge.

Perhaps most immediately striking is the contrast in sheer forces that are participating in the respective works: Verdi uses a large orchestra including many brass and percussion instruments along with a big chorus; the Bach cantata is scored for a small chorus and a small string orchestra with organ.

With this broad sound palette at his command, notice how Verdi graphically depicts his text. The dissolution of the world in ashes is expressed musically with sweeping, rapid scalar passages in the strings, while a trumpet fanfare, supported by a full brass complement in the second section, proclaims the day of judgment. In contrast, Bach's setting, while suggesting contrasts in mood or character, seems, in terms of dramatic intensity, to be pale in relation to the Verdi piece. While the sections of the cantata movement are clearly marked musically, the contrasts in instrumentation, texture, and dynamics are far less extreme, as are the very gestures of the music itself.

BACH AND THE LUTHERAN CHURCH

How then can we propose that the parishioners of Bach's church, listening to *Nun komm der Heiden Heiland* on that first Sunday of Advent in 1714, may have been deeply moved by the dramatic intensity of his work? To answer this question, you will have to listen closely to the opening section of this first movement of the cantata, considering at the same time aspects of the cultural context, factors that were a part of the everyday life of Bach's audience.

Listening again to the opening section (Nun komm der Heiden Heiland), you can hear that there are two distinct kinds of music occurring at the same time. The strings are playing intricate, complex lines and after a few moments the chorus joins in, but only one voice at a time—soprano, alto, tenor, and then bass. Each group, in turn, sings the same phrase but at different pitch levels. Since each melodic phrase in the vocal parts fits rhythmically and harmonically with the instrumental parts, we could assume that the vocal parts were written with the instrumental parts in mind. But, in fact, such is not the case: The melody is the beginning of a Lutheran hymn tune that was not written by Bach at all. Known as a chorale, the melody is an adaptation of the Gregorian chant *Veni Redemptor Gentium;* Martin Luther trans-

St. Thomas Church, Leipzig

lated the Latin text into German early in the sixteenth century. Again we have an example of history, the musical past, playing an active role in the immediate present of a composer's work. Incorporating a melody based on ancient chant into a new work, Bach participated in a long tradition dating back all the way to Perotin. Recall that Perotin used the chant melody *Viderunt Omnes* as a *cantus firmus* (the long, held notes making up the lower layer) around which he composed his organum quadruplum. Once again a tune with a prior history, social context, and meaning is given a new setting and with it new meaning and expressive force.

Introducing a hymn tune was common practice for Bach, particularly a tune that was very well known to his audience. On one hand, the members of the congregation would hear the words and music of hymns that they knew intimately and had sung themselves for much of their lives; but, on the other hand, they would hear them in a new, perhaps startling context. The very familiarity of the tune and the powerful associations of its text, when played off against the instrumental setting, helped to create for Bach's listeners a vividly dramatic experience.

But there is more. Consider just the first few measures of the melody played by the violins. Notice that a single rhythmic motive occurs prominently in this section: long-short-long (♪. ♪ ♩). This rhythm is characteristic of the opening section of a Baroque compositional form that was extremely popular in Bach's time. However, the kind of piece it is associated with is not religious at all. Called a French overture, it is, in fact, the characteristic beginning for an opera or ballet, and we can quite reasonably assume that it was this sort of musical entertainment that the citizens of Bach's time were reminded of when they heard this familiar rhythmic pattern. (This also explains the French spelling, *Ouverture,* in Bach's title.) But to sense fully the drama in this passage as Bach's listeners must have, you also need to know, as they did, that the "dotted rhythm" figure was associated with processions; for example, the stylized entrances of the dance troupe performing at the royal court of the French king, Louis XIV, at Versailles, or indeed, with the majestic arrival of the French monarch, himself. In Bach's cantata, this rhythmic figure is suggestive of a similar meaning. Recall that the *Cantata 61* was written for the first Sunday of Advent, the official beginning of the Lutheran celebration of the coming of the Messiah. So the familiar rhythmic figure that was so often used to herald the arrival of a great monarch was used on this occasion to herald the arrival of the Christian Messiah.

Example 10.1 BACH, *Cantata 61 (Nun komm der Heiden Heiland),* beginning

But there is still more to this loom of cultural connections. It is not only the rhythmic figure of the overture that Bach uses to remind his listeners of the style and substance of the French overture. The French overture, which originated in the second half of the seventeenth century and quickly became popular throughout Europe, also has a characteristic formal structure. It typically begins with a relatively slow, stately section that prominently presents this "dotted rhythm." The second section is characteristically faster and usually has a highly imitative texture. Finally, there is a return to the slower, more stately music at the end of the overture. If you listen, now, to the whole movement, you will hear that this is exactly what happens in the cantata.

A	B	A'
Slow; Duple meter	Fast; Triple meter	Slow; Duple meter
Strings ♩.♪♩	Chorus: Active, Imitative texture	Strings ♩.♪♩
S ___		Chorus
A ___	Strings (doubling voices)	
T ___		
B ___		
"Nun komm. . ."	"des sich wundert. . ."	"Gott solch. . ."

Notice that, like the French overture, Bach's overture to the cantata falls into three sections, and the whole movement can be described as ABA' in form. What musical means does Bach use to mark these structural boundaries, and how do these changes from one section to the next relate to the text? At the boundary between the first and second sections—that is, between sections A and B—Bach creates significant changes in almost every musical dimension: The characteristic long-short-long figure drops out; the instrumental parts suddenly recede in importance, mostly doubling the vocal parts and thus reinforcing the vocal sonority rather than contrasting with it as in section A; the meter shifts from duple in A to triple in B and the tempo becomes faster; and most noticeably, the texture becomes more active and imitative. With all of these musical means Bach helps to convey the meaning of the words in this middle section—the world's wonderment at Christ's birth ("*des sich wundert alle Welt*") and at its significance. At the same time he once more harks back to an earlier tradition as the voices enter in imitation much as they did in the sixteenth-century motet by Victoria. In the third section of the overture, Bach returns

Royal ball at Versailles

to the material of the opening (which somehow sounds still more regal after the more active texture of the middle section), the chorus singing one last phrase of the hymn tune, this time in rhythmic unison.

Finally, we must add one more factor to our cultural weave: The Baroque conception of the depiction of emotions in music. During Bach's time, particular musical gestures were often linked to a specific "affect," a kind of emotional quality or state, such as the dotted rhythm of "regal arrival" in the cantata. But the Baroque conception of emotion did not allow for *gradual* changes in affect. Rather a section of a movement, sometimes even an entire movement, would tend to express a *single* affect throughout. Thus, while there is clear contrast *between* sections in the overture, there is little change *within* each section. Once Bach establishes a texture or a characteristic rhythm, for instance, he maintains it throughout an entire section. This kind of persistence over the course of a section or a work in its entirety is typical not only of this work but of many other late Baroque pieces as well. The text of a vocal piece could, of course, provide the inspiration for the particular emotional quality to be depicted, and, as we have seen in the cantata overture, also suggest musical means to project these emotions.

Such a conception of emotion may seem rigid or stylized now, but it was central to Baroque aesthetics. It contributed to Bach's understanding of musical expression, and it helps to explain the internal coherence of the sections of the overture, as well as the rather abrupt contrasts between these sections. Gradually evolving emotional change expressed musically by gradually evolving changes in dynamics, tempo, or texture was not part of the Baroque conception of music.

Bach, then, was working within a particular context of artistic expression and within a complex texture of social and cultural associations. A familiar hymn tune, sung in German, refers both verbally and musically to the arrival of the Christian Messiah: Arrival is dramatized through associations with the secular French overture, its characteristic rhythmic figure along with its familiar structural organization. The overture, in turn, has powerful associations with the arrival of royalty—the king and his entourage—as embodied in the courtly dance music of the French ballet. For the congregation who heard Bach's cantatas in the church services in Weimar or Leipzig, these startling superimpositions of recognizable but entirely different kinds of music within the opening of *Nun komm der Heiden Heiland* must have produced a breathtaking dramatic effect, a dramatic effect as distinctive and characteristic of Baroque music as the Verdi example is of Romantic music.

VERDI AND MANZONI: ITALIAN ROMANTICISM

Verdi, the composer, and Manzoni, the author, in whose memory the mass was written, represented the most significant and popular artistic trends in Italy during the second half of the nineteenth century. Recalling our earlier discussion of Beethoven and Schubert, it is clear that Romanticism, the name given to these trends, took various forms in different times and places throughout Europe. In Italy, as in northern Europe, Romanticism took its inspiration from the social movements, artistic theories, and the spirit of *heroic individualism* inspired by and associated with the French Revolution. In northern and central Europe—Germany and Austria, in particular—artists were more intrigued, on one hand, with the supernatural, the exotic and remote, and, on the other (like Schubert) with the intimate and subjective along with its feeling of artistic alienation (see, for example, the comments of E. T. A. Hoffmann quoted in Chapter 9, p. 319), In contrast, Italian art, music, and literature in the nineteenth century had closer links to popular nationalistic political events and movements.

During the course of the nineteenth century, Italy was politically transformed from a group of small and culturally diverse political states controlled mostly by foreign powers to a unified nation with a single monarch, Victor Emmanuel II. This political unification had cultural effects as well. For example, at the beginning of the century the citizens of the various states shared no common language; numerous regional dialects were spoken as well as languages of other countries. But by the end of the century, all Italians were speaking the same common Italian that we hear them speaking today. The consolidation of the Italian nation and the patriotic sentiment for Italian nationalism inspired the greatest artists of the country during the latter half of the century. In this environment, political movements and artistic expression complemented one another, both contributing to an intense nationalistic fervor known as the *risorgimento* (literally, "revival").

Verdi perfectly exemplified the nationalist romantic Italian artist. Born in 1813 near a small village, he achieved international fame as an opera composer and traveled often throughout Europe, surpervising performances of his work. By the late 1830s, when Verdi's first operas were composed, the opera had been established as one of the most popular forms of publicly performed music. Opera houses were particularly large and, especially in Italy and France, operas might be received with almost wild public enthusiasm. However, in continued (if self-conscious) solidarity with the "common man," Verdi maintained a residence on a farm near Busseto, close to the place of his birth. In a period of profound national pride, Verdi came to represent the heroic potential of the Italian common man. Even the name *Verdi* became a nationalist slogan, since its letters were an abbreviation of the expression Viva *V*ittorio *E*mmanuel, *R*e *d'I*talia ("Long Live Victor Emmanuel, King of Italy"). The very idea that the entire country might have only one monarch (that is, be politically unified) inspired great patriotic feeling.

For his part, the author Manzoni played an important role in Italian nationalism by writing the novel *I promessi sposi* ("The Betrothed"). In the course of numerous revisions of the novel, he purged it of the parochial regional dialects initially used in the spoken dialogue of the novel, changing all the language of the book to a style of Italian that was coming to be universally spoken throughout the country. For many Italians, Manzoni's novel was the first book they read in the national language shared by all their countrymen. The book was widely associated with the nationalist movement in Italy, and Manzoni, like Verdi, was a patriotic hero.

Thus, the inspiration for Verdi's *Requiem* was not religious conviction and an obligation to a particular church patron (as in the case of Bach), but a tribute to an artistic and political hero. In fact, Verdi

The name *Verdi* became a nationalistic slogan

was not himself particularly religious. (He was known to accompany his wife to church on Sundays, but he would wait outside while she attended, and she referred to him as a "very doubtful believer.") Nonetheless, in a predominantly Catholic country, a Catholic Mass was the appropriate format for commemorating a great political and cultural figure. Still, Verdi's setting of the *Requiem* text is earthy and dramatic, very close in spirit to the emotionally charged operas Verdi wrote throughout his career. As a Viennese music critic described the *Requiem* in 1875: "Mourning and supplication, awe and faith—they speak here in a language more passionate and individual than we are accustomed to hearing in church."[2]

Moreover, while Verdi's *Requiem* is indeed a Catholic Mass, it was conceived as a concert piece. Although the commemorative first performance was given in the Church of St. Mark in Milan, Verdi quickly arranged performances in concert halls and opera houses throughout Europe. The composition's grand orchestral and vocal forces would normally be available only for large public concerts for which ticket sales would cover the substantial costs.

Listen once more to the excerpt from the Verdi *Requiem*. Notice how, consistent with the romantic fervor of the time, Verdi seizes hold of the medieval Latin text, with its powerful, although somewhat primitive imagery, painting a musical portrait of the Last Judgment.

---

[2] William Weaver, *Verdi: A Documentary Study* (London: Thames and Hudson, 1972), p. 232.

Like the Bach overture, the excerpt can be divided into three sections, but the relations among them could hardly be more different. Beginning with four powerful staccato minor chords, swirling strings and the chorus enter to proclaim the Day of Wrath—*Dies irae.* Verdi repeats the opening four chords with an added, syncopated bass drum, and the turbulence continues, the words of the chorus barely distinguishable above the overpowering orchestra. The first section ends with an extended passage in which the energy level, turbulence, and sheer volume gradually dissipate. The storm subsides, the chorus singing a descending sequence as the texture becomes gradually thinner with one voice part after another dropping out. Finally we hear, almost in a whisper, *"quantas tremor"*—"what fear."

The second section emerges out of the first: One trumpet (playing a single note in a characteristically punctuated martial rhythm), then several, first in octaves, then in chords that become richer in harmony, then all the brass, and finally the whole orchestra and chorus. This section gradually reaches the high energy level of the first; but then there is silence. And above a marchlike figure the solo bass voice proclaims, *"mors stupebit"*—"Death is stupefied," as the excerpt ends with a fourfold repetition of the word *mors* ("death").

We move from one emotional peak to another, each section growing out of the other in a gradual flow. How different from the Bach overture where sections were clearly distinct, where there were no transitions but rather abrupt shifts from one texture and expressive quality to another without obvious preparation. Within sections the two works also differ: Consistent with Baroque aesthetics, affect remains constant throughout each section of the Bach overture as does the texture and rhythmic impulse associated with it. In contrast, Verdi's textures and dynamics change dramatically within sections: at times suddenly, interrupting the flow; at other times evolving gradually, building to a climax or slowly fading out. These differences in musical means, and in their resulting structural relations, clearly distinguish Verdi's Romantic style from that of the Baroque exemplified by the Bach cantata.

BACH AND VERDI: A STUDY IN CONTRASTING ARTISTIC CAREERS

Throughout this chapter we have stressed the importance of social, cultural, and personal contexts and commitments as these helped to shape two such different works—both of which, we have argued, are at once sacred and also dramatic. To conclude the chapter, then, we return once more to a comparison of these contexts, this time focusing on the working conditions that influenced the respective careers of these two artists.

Consider, first, the remarkable differences between the opportunities and professional roles available to the two composers. Bach spent his entire musical career as an employee of an aristocrat or of the administrators of a church. His music was written for performance primarily in the church or the court. Verdi, born roughly a century after Bach wrote *Nun komm der Heiden Heiland,* supported himself by teaching music for a short time but spent most of his career composing and, unlike Schubert, successfully supporting himself through the new opportunities provided by the broader relations between artist and public: commissions and fees from widespread and numerous public performances of his operas and the publication of his music.

The difference between the working situations of Bach and Verdi are revealed with particular poignancy in the contract Bach signed in 1723 when he began work in Leipzig:[3]

Whereas the Honorable and Most Wise Council of this Town of Leipzig have engaged me as Cantor of the Thomas-Schule and have desired an undertaking from me in respect to the following points, to wit:

(1) That I shall set the boys a shining example of an honest, retiring manner of life, serve the School industriously, and instruct the boys conscientiously;

(2) Bring the music in both the principal Churches of this town into good estate, to the best of my ability;

(3) Show to the Honorable and Most Wise Council all proper respect and obedience, and protect and further everywhere as best I may its honor and reputation; likewise if a gentleman of the Council desires the boys for a musical occasion unhesitatingly provide him with the same, but otherwise never permit them to go out of town to funerals or weddings without the previous knowledge and consent of the Burgomaster and Honorable Directors of the School currently in office;

(4) Give due obedience to the Honorable Inspectors and Directors

---

[3] *The Bach Reader,* eds. Hans T. David and Arthur Mendel (New York: Norton, 1966), p. 91.

of the School in each and every instruction which the same shall issue in the name of the Honorable and Most Wise Council;

(5) Not take any boys into the School who have not already laid a foundation in music, or are not at least suited to being instructed therein, nor do the same without the previous knowledge and consent of the Honorable Inspectors and Directors;

(6) So that the Churches may not have to be put to unnecessary expense, faithfully instruct the boys not only in vocal but also in instrumental music;

(7) In order to preserve the good order in the Churches, so arrange the music that it shall not last too long, and shall be of such a nature as not to make an operatic impression, but rather incite the listeners to devotion;

(8) Provide the New Church with good scholars;

(9) Treat the boys in a friendly manner and with caution, but, in case they do not wish to obey, chastise them with moderation or report them to the proper place;

(10) Faithfully attend to the instruction in the School and whatever else it befits me to do;

(11) And if I cannot undertake this myself, arrange that it be done by some other capable person without expense to the Honorable and Most Wise Council or to the School;

(12) Not go out of town without the permission of the Honorable Burgomaster currently in office;

(13) Always so far as possible walk with the boys at funerals, as is customary;

(14) And shall not accept or wish to accept any office in the University without the consent of the Honorable and Learned Council;

Now therefore I do hereby undertake and bind myself faithfully to observe all of the said requirements, and on pain of losing my post not to act contrary to them, in witness whereof I have set my hand and seal to this agreement.

JOHANN SEBASTIAN BACH

While Verdi spent his career traveling throughout Europe, conducting and preparing performances of his works, Bach, as you can see (item #12), could not leave Leipzig without first consulting the mayor. This is not surprising considering his very demanding, day-to-day responsibilities as teacher and disciplinarian of the church's music students, together with his responsibilities to write music for a staggering number of church events and to prepare performances for numerous religious services and public events. Notice, by the way, that Bach was explicitly instructed (item #7) not to write music that would "make an operatic impression." While this warning was written after Bach composed the *Cantata 61,* it reflects a general stricture of the time against confusing secular and sacred music. In this light, Bach's superimposition of French operatic music and a German hymn seems all the more daring and dramatic. But despite his lack of mobility and professional freedom, you should not assume that Bach was unknown in his time. As his son, the composer C. P. E. Bach, wrote in 1773, 23 years after his father's death:

> No master of music was apt to pass through this place [Leipzig] without making my father's acquaintance and letting himself be heard by him. The greatness that was my father's in composition, in organ and clavier playing was far too well known for a musician of reputation to let the opportunity slip of making the closer acquaintance of this great man if it was at all possible.[4]

The differences between nineteenth-century Italy and eighteenth-century Germany can be further illuminated by comparing the social *function* of sacred works. For example, the idea of transplanting a religious work from the church service to the public concert hall was clearly unthinkable in Bach's time and place; and yet, it was quite acceptable, even inspired, in Verdi's time. Moreover, given Verdi's sense of public purpose, together with the broadly felt patriotic fervor of the time, it is quite consistent that Verdi's sacred music is addressed *through* the traditional sacred text, and *through* the immediately felt drama of his compositional style, *to* a grand public commemoration and praise of a political-artistic hero of the people.

In reconsidering these differences between the two composers and their times, we may propose an intriguing question that we have touched on before: Was Verdi actually freer from constraints than Bach? Our discussion seems to suggest that the nineteenth-century Italian composer had fewer limitations imposed on his work than his eighteenth-century predecessor. It would be wrong, however, to accept this assumption uncritically. As we have emphasized repeatedly, complex social, cultural, artistic, and other historical forces inevitably shape the work of any composer in any age. And the works of those who

---

[4] *The Bach Reader,* p. 260.

are most influential in any moment in time may themselves become forces that deeply affect their culture. No composer works in a cultural "vacuum." As you have seen, and as we will continue to suggest, every major composer participates in a cultural context that is at once limiting and enabling. Only in the light of such contexts will music be heard as "original" or "old-fashioned," "shocking" or "trivial," "strange" or "readily intelligible." And only by taking such contexts into account can you effectively and appropriately bring into play the full range of listening skills you have developed in the course of this study and of your continuing musical experience.

CHAPTER 11

Promenade Aérienne, a French amusement park, c. 1830

Technology then . . .

Music and Dance:
Two Virtuoso Waltzes

Computer and synthesizer, MIT Electronic Music Studio, 1984
and now . . .

In this chapter we continue our rather serpentine path through music history. Going back 27 years within the Romantic period from the date of Verdi's *Requiem* (1874), you will listen first to Chopin's "Minute Waltz" (1846–1847). Then leaping forward over 100 years from where we left Verdi, you will hear another *Minute Waltz,* written by the contemporary composer Milton Babbitt (1977).

Example	Composer, title	Date
11.1	Chopin, "Minute Waltz," Op. 64, no. 1	1846–1847
11.2	Babbitt, *Minute Waltz,* (or) $\frac{3}{4} \pm \frac{1}{8}$	1977

We have juxtaposed these two pieces partly to point up an apparent paradox that to some degree always confronts you once the historical dimension is integrated into your "listening perspective." Throughout the history section of the text, we have stressed the importance of listening to a work as an expression of a particular stylistic and cultural context. On the other hand, you have heard how composers subtly introduce conventions or gestures associated with other epochs or different musical genres. Thus we enjoy a kind of "hall of mirrors" effect as we listen and orient ourselves in music history.

For example, as Bach composed the cantata for Advent, he brought into his early eighteenth-century workshop a well-known Lutheran hymn from the past and also musical conventions associated with quite a different genre—the seventeenth-century French ballet. Verdi, for his part, uses the text of the ancient and traditional Requiem Mass but sets it in the style of his own nineteenth-century operatic works. In order to appreciate a work fully as you listen to it today, it is important to be sensitive to a whole network of possible musical conventions, both past and present, that a composer may have "in his ear"—this network of musical gestures and idioms is a significant aspect of the raw material he is working with (and also departing from) as he shapes each new and unique composition.

In the case of the two works included here, both composers are working with the conventions associated with the long history of the waltz. Chopin's waltz (Example 11.1) clearly falls within this tradition; Babbitt's waltz (Example 11.2) is more "about" the tradition than within it. Chopin's so-called "Minute Waltz" has been a favorite of pianists for nearly 150 years. Bearing this in mind, Babbitt, when asked along with a number of others to compose a modern waltz, playfully named his waltz after the famous one.[1] In doing so, Babbitt creates a modern-day example of music/historical humor. But, like much humor, in order to "get it" you have to be familiar with the appropriate conventions—in this case the conventional rhythms and gestures of nineteenth-century waltzes. Babbitt playfully embeds these conventions in his own twentieth-century style, and he also plays with the idea of a piece that lasts exactly one minute—which, in fact, Chopin's does not.[2]

Listen to the two waltzes, one after the other. The juxtaposition raises some of the intriguing questions of style and stylistic change suggested earlier: Babbitt's *Minute Waltz,* written only a decade ago, paradoxically sounds less familiar than Chopin's "Minute Waltz," written almost 150 years ago. Further, despite their common names and common ancestry, the differences between them clearly outweigh similarities. But can you say, on first listening, just what it is that makes them so different, or indeed, what they may share? Going further, can you hear what they may share with regard to the musical idioms of dance and, in particular, "waltzness"? Keep these questions in mind as you listen again and as you read the discussion that follows.

THE WALTZ: PAST AND PRESENT

In every culture and in every era music has been composed to be danced. Indeed, it seems entirely natural to associate human physical gestures with musical gestures and similarly to associate music with dancing. In thinking about the association of music and dance, ballet or pop music might most immediately come to mind. But the two examples in this chapter seem to have little in common with either of these. In fact, you will probably agree that the two waltzes paradoxically share one clear quality: It would be difficult to dance to either one of them. Listening to Babbitt's waltz, you will notice that the gestures usually associated with the waltz are only dimly represented and that it is hard to maintain a consistent beat throughout. With Chopin's waltz, the

---

[1] Babbitt's waltz was written as part of "The Waltz Project," organized by the composer Robert Moran, which commissioned 25 waltzes by contemporary composers. The whole set was published in 1978 by C. F. Peters.

[2] The name "Minute Waltz" was given to Chopin's piece some time after he wrote it. Anecdotes suggest that it was because performers tried (unsuccessfully) to play it so rapidly that it would take only one minute.

beat and the waltz gestures are clear enough, but the tempo would make it difficult to dance along. Most music for dance engages our sense of beat and physical gesture, but these two waltzes, while deriving from dance forms, deviate substantially and in interesting ways from the conventions associated with the waltz.

Of course, if a composer merely wished to write successful dance music (clear beat, strong gestures, good tempo, and so forth), there would be no reason to deviate from the conventions. The music of Johann Strauss, Jr., (known as "the Waltz King" and whose music you heard in Chapters 2 and 5), demonstrates much of the expressive range of the waltz as a straightforward dance. You also heard a jazz waltz written by Sonny Rollins (Example 2.12). This highly syncopated example is further from the conventional dance format and therefore raises some of the same questions as the examples in this chapter: Why would a composer or performer create a waltz that was not meant to be danced?

This question was considered, at least implicitly, in the discussion of minuets and scherzos in Chapter 6. Recall the variety of pieces, all of them called "minuet," that you heard in that context. In particular, we pointed out the many ways in which the character and purpose of the minuet was transformed from its original function as a piece to accompany dancing in seventeenth- and eighteenth-century aristocratic European courts. Recall, also, how Stravinsky, in composing his ballet, *Petrouchka,* borrowed Lanner's danceable waltz, transforming it into a new kind of dance by embedding it in new rhythmic and textural contexts (Example 2.27). These transformations again reveal the importance of past music and musical conventions along with the changing preoccupations of composers in different times and places. Similarly, the particular features of the waltz examples in this chapter can serve as clues to the special stylistic characteristics and aesthetic intentions of each of their composers. Even more, they should illuminate some of the general issues that characterize mid-nineteenth-century and late-twentieth-century musical composition.

CHOPIN AND ROMANTIC VIRTUOSITY

Chopin was born in Poland in 1810, just three years before Verdi's birth in Italy. However, the two composers' careers overlapped only briefly. While Verdi lived on into the beginning of the twentieth century, Chopin's short life ended in 1849 at 39—that is, 25 years

Frederic Chopin at the piano

before Verdi composed the *Requiem.* The waltz with which we are concerned here was written when Chopin was 36 years old, 15 years after he had left his native Poland and moved to Paris.

Chopin arrived in Paris in 1831 at a time when the French were still in the first flush of the Revolution of 1830, a brief and colorful *coup d'état* in which workers and shopkeepers had fought at the barricades. Romanticism and its concomitant attack on tradition and authority was in full swing, and dramatic changes in the arts paralleled those in the political realm. By some stroke of great good fortune, the city had become host to an astonishing number of brilliant young writers, artists, and composers. The writer Théophile Gautier later wrote of this period:

What a marvelous time: Walter Scott was then in the flower of his success; one was initiated into the mysteries of Goethe's *Faust,* which as [the essayist] Mme. de Staël said, contained everything. One discovered Shakespeare, and the poems of Lord Byron . . . and *Don Juan* took us to the Orient. . . . All was young, new, exotically colored, intoxicating, and strongly flavored. It turned our heads, it was as if we had entered into a strange new world.[3]

The generation of composers that came into their artistic maturity in the 1830s—including, along with Chopin, Robert Schumann, Felix Mendelssohn, Franz Liszt, and Hector Berlioz—experienced this change of outlook profoundly. They were acutely conscious of the challenges and opportunities of the new artistic movements welling up in all the arts. They also knew one another, maintaining close correspondence, attending the performances of each other's work, and (especially in the case of Liszt and Chopin) engaging in friendly but not always benign competition. Each of these ambitious and talented musicians secured his reputation not only as a composer, but also through some other public activity. Mendelssohn, whose career as a composer began at a very early age, became an important conductor. Schumann became an influential music critic and in this capacity wrote, in reviewing an early work of Chopin's, "Hats off, gentlemen! A genius!" Chopin and Liszt became virtuoso pianists of great repute. Both wrote extensively for the piano, composing extremely difficult pieces that they would perform themselves to great acclaim. The very performance of such demanding works was (and still is) dramatically impressive, and it secured the reputations of both composers as colorful, Romantic artists.

In the Paris of the 1830s, artistic success might have come to Chopin in one of two ways. He might have established himself as a performer in large-scale public concerts, making extensive concert tours and thus supporting himself with ticket sales. Or, he might have gained acceptance into the artistic and aristocratic circles wherein the rich continued to support promising artists of all sorts. While Chopin was initially successful in pursuing a performing career, his health became too fragile to permit extensive concertizing and traveling. In addition, his performance style was too delicately nuanced to project in the largest concert halls. However, his talent as both a performer and composer was ideally suited to the social context of the Parisian salons where, in the homes of wealthy patrons, impressive artistic talents were invited to display their musical virtuosity.

In this post-Revolutionary period, composers were no longer in the service of individual noblemen as Haydn and Bach (in their earlier

---

[3] Théophile Gautier, *A History of Romanticism,* trans. F. C. Sumichrast (New York: Atheneum Society, 1902), p. 19.

Wagner (at left) and Liszt (at the piano) perform at a social gathering in Bayreuth

careers) had been. While many composers continued to depend on financial support from wealthy patrons, this support came in the form of individual commissions and fees for performances and music lessons rather than long-term contracts. In fact, a charismatic artist might contribute indispensably to the luster and status of a patron's social gatherings. Aristocrats would compete for the attention of highly regarded artists as much as the artists would compete for the support of such aristocratic patrons.

Chopin was enormously successful in this environment. As he described it himself in 1833:

> I have found my way into the very best society; I have my place among ambassadors, princes, ministers—I don't know by what miracle it has come about, for I have not pushed myself forward. But today all that

sort of thing is indispensable to me: those circles are supposed to be the fountainhead of good taste. You at once have more talent if you have been heard at the English or Austrian embassies; you at once play better if Princess Vaudemont has patronised you. I can't write "patronises," for the poor old thing died a week ago. . . . She always had a host of little black and white bitches, canaries, parrots, and was the owner of Paris high society's most amusing monkey, which used to bite the other countesses at her parties.[4]

Chopin supported himself in large part by giving piano lessons to the wealthy patrons whom he also entertained at their elaborate parties. At the same time he befriended many of the other artists who frequented these salons. Among these were some of the most influential writers and painters of this mid-Romantic period: The novelists George Sand, Balzac, and Hugo, the German poet Heine, and the painters Ingres and Delacroix.

This social situation encouraged Chopin to compose numerous short but brilliant works for the piano, thus providing himself with material to perform in the salons of his patrons. The waltz and other dance forms were well suited to these occasions. Their familiar rhythms, harmonic structures, and form provided an appropriately simple backdrop against which Chopin could compose new and brilliant pieces. As performer of his own works, these pieces also served him as a medium for displaying his remarkable abilities as a virtuoso pianist. During his all too brief life, Chopin, like Schubert, produced an enormous body of works, many of them short pieces like the "Minute Waltz": 19 waltzes, 58 mazurkas (originally a Polish dance form), 15 polonaises (also based on Polish rhythms), as well as 26 preludes, 27 études ("studies," many of them extremely difficult; professional pianists today are still expected to master them), and a number of other short works such as impromptus (recall also the Schubert *Impromptu,* Example 4.20) and nocturnes. Chopin was, then, primarily a composer of piano works for solo performance. Apart from this he wrote only a few chamber works, two concertos for piano and orchestra, and a handful of songs.

You heard several other brief piano pieces of Chopin in earlier chapters where they illustrated different dimensions of music: Rhythm (Example 2.25), aspects of form, especially continuous organization

---

[4] Arthur Hedley, ed., *Selected Correspondence of Fryderyk Chopin* (London: Heineman, 1962), pp. 114–115.

(Examples 4.4 and 4.11), and chromatic harmony (Example 5.20). In the first of these examples, the *Mazurka*, Op. 17, no. 4, we discussed *rubato* as it relates to virtuoso playing, in particular the rhythmic independence between the melody and accompaniment parts (and correspondingly, the right and left hands of the performer). Listen again now to Chopin's "Minute Waltz." What do you think has made it such a favorite of pianists; what, indeed, makes it such a virtuoso piece?

Chopin's "Minute Waltz"

Perhaps most striking on first or even second hearing is just this sense of sheer virtuosity. Notice that, like his *Mazurka*, Chopin makes the upper and lower parts quite independent of one another. The pianist's right hand, playing the melody, moves in a kind of perpetual motion, roaming extravagantly throughout the upper half of the keyboard. Meanwhile, the pianist's left hand provides the accompaniment, the waltz substructure of the piece. Within the accompaniment you hear the alternation of tonic and dominant harmonies together with the "oom-pah-pah" rhythm associated with the triple-meter waltz. The speed of the melody line and the performance dexterity it demands,

| 1800 | 1810 | 1820 | 1830 | 1840 | 1850 | 1860 | 1870 | 1880 |

1830 Berlioz, *Symphonie fantastique*;
Hugo, *Hernani*

1831 Chopin arrived in Paris;
S.F. Smith wrote words "My Country,
'Tis of thee" to tune of *America*

1833 George Sand, *Lélia*;
Brahms born (d. 1897);
Abolition of slavery in British Empire;
Balzac, *Eugénie Grandet*

1838 Coronation of Queen Victoria

1839 Verdi's first opera,
Oberto, in Milan, La Scala

1842 New York Philharmonic founded;
Gogol, *Dead Souls*, Part I;
Wagner, *Rienzi*, in Dresden

1851 Verdi, *Rigoletto*;
Singer sewing machine;
First edition of *The New York Times*

1849 Chopin dies;
Liszt, *Tasso*, symphonic poem;
Delacroix painted ceiling of the Louvre;
Dickens, *David Copperfield*

1846 Chopin, *Minute Waltz*
Berlioz, *Damnation of Faust*;
Adolphe Sax patents the saxophone;
Declaration of war by U.S. against Mexico

1844 Verdi, *Ernani*;
Mendelssohn, *Violin Concerto*;
Thackeray, *Barry Lyndon*;
Polk elected 11th President of U.S.

George Sand at the age of 60

in contrast to the steady, more slowly moving accompaniment, are among the clearest virtuoso characteristics of the piece.

What makes this perpetual motion of the upper part so effective? Notice that while its rhythm is largely uniform and fast-paced, its contour often changes dramatically. The melody seems to run in place then suddenly sweep up or down rapidly and unpredictably, creating a dizzying "roller-coasterlike" effect. The opening of the waltz reminded Chopin's mistress, the author George Sand (her pseudonym), of a dog chasing its tail. It is the contrast between this circling motion and the more angular up and down contours of the melody that contributes so vividly to its brilliance and wit.

You may also have noticed in your listening that the waltz, as a whole, is in the familiar ABA form, a structure common to many dances and one that Chopin realized anew in many of his other piano pieces. You hear a contrasting, lyrical B section framed by the two more "technical" A sections. On closer listening, you will hear that repetition on this larger dimension of the piece is mirrored on almost every other level of the structure. And yet, the piece remains lively through the interesting moves both within and against this pervasive repetitiveness. For example, on the most detailed level, the opening "tail-chasing" motive is confined to a very small range circling through only four different pitches. This figure is repeated a number of times. But notice that the repetitions of this motive with its four even notes create a duple meter against the prevailing triple-meter accompaniment:

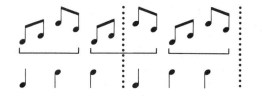

As a result, the regularly recurring accent on the first of every three beats of the accompaniment coincides with different elements of the two-beat melodic figure in each of its repetitions, thus changing the complexion of the figure itself. (You heard a similar effect in Scott Joplin's *Maple Leaf Rag* [Example 2.30], where a three-note figure is played against a duple-meter accompaniment. And, in another similar instance, Stravinsky pits Lanner's waltz against his own compound-duple-meter accompaniment in the excerpt from *Petrouchka* mentioned earlier.)

At a middle level of Chopin's waltz structure, the A sections fall into two somewhat contrasting but balanced subsections, each of which includes nearly literal repetition within it. And on the phrase level of the structure, notice that the flowing running notes of the pianist's right hand group together to form symmetrical phrases that, in turn, group together to form balanced phrase groups with repetitions within them as well. Altogether, then, Chopin's brilliant, rapid passage work is both contained and set off by its symmetrical substructure and by the repetition of minimal thematic material.

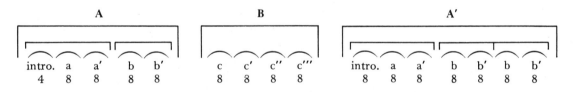

What about the repetitiousness of the left-hand waltz accompaniment? Here, too, Chopin makes slight subtle changes, varying the disposition of the "oom," and the two "pah's":

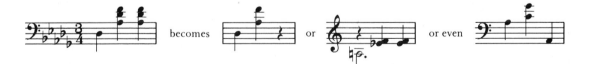

Harmonically, too, the piece includes repetition; it not only remains close to the fundamental tonic and dominant chords, but even stays in just one key throughout. Even the contrasting and more lyrical B section is in the same key. But again, subtle chromatic nuances, especially in the more "romantic" B section, stand out against Chopin's relatively monochromatic harmonic palette here.

Listen once more to the whole piece. Does Chopin vary A when it returns? There is, of course, the trill leading from B back to A—a kind of compressed anticipation of the "tail-chasing" figure which it turns into at the return. But most significantly there is the wonderful leap up to the highest note of the piece just before the end: A small but marvelous touch in this elegant piece.

Imagine the effect of this piece on the audiences who heard the original performances given by Chopin himself during a trip to London in the late 1840s. Listening to the "Minute Waltz," one hears the spirit and the open simplicity of the traditional danced waltz (clear rhythm and harmony, repetitions of a few symmetrical phrases and sections) joined with Chopin's subtle rhythmic complexities and his unique and sparkling style of pianistic virtuosity. The result is a special sense of poise and sophistication that separates this piece from more ordinary waltzes of the time. It is not surprising that the "Minute Waltz" was then and remains still today a favorite of both performers and their audiences.

BABBITT AND TWENTIETH-CENTURY VIRTUOSITY

The American composer Milton Babbitt was born in 1916, only 15 years after Verdi's death, yet the social and musical contexts to which his music belongs seem remarkably far removed from the European Romantic period of either Verdi or Chopin. Even a brief glimpse at Babbitt's life makes a striking contrast to the lives of composers studied earlier.

Babbitt received his early musical training in Jackson, Mississippi, where the conventions of Southern musical education were all but inescapable. As Babbitt himself tells it: "At the time, it was not 'proper' for a young boy in the South to play piano, only the girls did that, so I decided, like other boys my age, to study the violin." Babbitt's exceptional talent was publicly recognized when, as a young boy, he was written up by the local newspaper as a "whiz kid" who had perfect pitch and could add up all his family's grocery bills in his head. Though he intended to continue with the violin, Babbitt became interested in the music of jazz trumpeter and pioneer, Bix Beiderbecke. With Beiderbecke in mind, Babbitt took up the trumpet and later also the clarinet and alto saxophone. Babbitt recalls from those early years that he "played every kind of pop music. I played and arranged with seventeen different bands. I played gigs on Saturday nights when I was ten with

New Orleans musicians who came through Jackson. They thought it was pretty funny to have this kid around."[5]

Babbitt's undergraduate college years were spent at the University of Pennsylvania, where he studied philosophy, especially logic, and at New York University, where he focused more on music. Going to Princeton University for his graduate work, Babbitt studied composition with the eminent American composer, Roger Sessions. The *Minute Waltz* is dedicated to Sessions on the occasion of his eightieth birthday. (You may want to look back at the discussion of Sessions's *Piano Sonata* in Chapter 6 and also read once more his Foreword to this text.) Babbitt joined the Princeton music faculty in 1937 where, as composer and theorist, he continues to be a major figure in the contemporary musical scene.

A striking aspect of this brief story is the new role of the university—in Babbitt's life and, indeed, in the lives of most twentieth-century composers, at least in the United States. In a sense, the university has taken over the role of the royal court in Haydn's day and the salon of wealthy patrons in Chopin's time. For many composers today it is the university that provides the context and support—musical, cultural, financial—for their work. What this dramatic shift means for composers, their music, and their audiences is a complex and intriguing question and, as such, goes beyond what we can adequately deal with here. However, you might want to keep it in mind as we go on to consider the directions music has taken during this second half of the twentieth century.

To appreciate fully the wit and brilliant virtuosity of Babbitt's *Minute Waltz,* it will be important to know something of the methods involved in the pitch organization of the piece and of the origins of these methods. But before going into these issues, some of which are fairly technical, listen to the piece once again. What are your immediate impressions?

On first or even second listening you probably feel, as Gautier had said of the 1830s, "as if you are entering a strange new world." In fact you may wonder why this brief piece belongs to the world of waltzes at all. It is not obviously in triple meter, at least never for long, and there are no straightforward tonic and dominant harmonies artic-

---

[5] Martin Brody and Dennis Miller, "Milton Babbitt: An Appreciation" (unpublished concert program booklet).

ulating "oom-pah" gestures. And yet, on closer listening, shadows of the waltz emerge almost nostalgically. For example, while the piece is certainly not in clear triple meter, you can hear sly allusions to the familiar "oom-pah-pah" accompaniment, especially in the beginning. Moreover, the characteristic "swing" of the waltz lurks behind the rapid virtuoso passages in the upper parts, which seem almost to fly by. But what features contribute to its distinctive style?

As you begin to assimilate the music, you will notice that gestures leap rapidly from one register to another, covering nearly the whole

1963 1964 1965 1966 1967 1968 1969 1970 1971 1972 1973 1974 1975 1976 1977 1978 1979

1968 Assassinations of Rev. Martin
Luther King, Jr.
and Robert F. Kennedy

1969 Vietnam war continues;
"Chicago 8" indicted;
Woodstock Music festival;
Apollo 11 lands on the moon

1970 Roger Sessions, *When Lilacs Last in the Door Yard Bloom'd*

1971 Igor Stravinsky dies

1972 Bobby Fischer wins world chess title

1973 Pablo Picasso dies

1974 President Nixon resigns in "Watergate Affair"

1975 Charlie Chaplin knighted by Queen Elizabeth;
Centennials of Charles Ives
and Arnold Schoenberg celebrated

1976 Mao Tse–Tung dies;
Jimmy Carter elected President of U.S.

1977 Babbitt, *Minute Waltz*
Elvis Presley dies;
SAT scores show steady decline since 1963;
British scientists determine genetic structure of
living organism

1978 First "test tube baby" born in England;
John Belushi in *Animal House*

1979 Three–Mile Island nuclear energy plant disaster;
Shah of Iran deposed; Ayatollah Khomeini returns;
Mother Theresa awarded Nobel Peace Prize;
Margaret Thatcher elected Prime Minister of England

range of the piano in every measure of the piece. In the lowest register, Babbitt plays with the ubiquitous waltz rhythm. But perhaps less obviously, Babbitt has also divided the upper registers of the piano so as to give the middle and uppermost registers a certain degree of individual integrity. If you focus your attention on just one register—say the middle—you can begin to hear it as a single, continuous line. Then shift your focus to the top register, listening for its continuity. In doing so, you may also notice witty allusions to more familiar waltz gestures within these parts, as well. Finally, try to listen for the sparkling movement between these two upper registers of the texture, held down, so to speak, by the more slowly moving bass accompaniment. Babbitt has, in fact, created an ingenious modern version of a many-voiced, active texture—a contemporary transformation of music you heard, for example, in Chapter 1. But here, instead of remaining more or less distinct, the many-note, rapidly moving streams of music seem to tumble over one another, interrupting, intertwining, playing off one another with a rich complexity of rhythms and speed. Babbitt's brief waltz demands the most not only of the pianist's technical and musical skills, but of the listener's virtuosity as well.

In a recent interview, Babbitt spoke forcefully about the different circumstances of contemporary music as compared with that of the past:

> Music changed. It changed significantly and demonstrably some seventy years ago (that's an obvious date). Music changed in a very decisive way, and in ways that created difficulties not only for the listener, but for the performer and above all the composer. It's a different relationship to the whole tradition of music from the one a composer had in 1850. It's ridiculous to pretend "Oh well, this is just a temporary aberration, you're dramatizing your position, and in a hundred years you'll see that it was all really the same." We've lived a half a hundred years already, and it has not been the same.[6]

What is the nature of this "different relationship to the whole tradition of music?" It is perhaps the pluralism of contemporary music, the diversity of autonomous musical values and techniques in our culture that Babbitt refers to when he distinguishes the music of this century from its predecessors. At no point in this century has there

---

[6] Cole Gagne and Tracy Caras, *Soundpieces: Interviews with American Composers* (Methuen, N.J.: Scarecrow, 1982), p. 40.

Milton Babbitt,
c. 1960

been a single dominating compositional style or technique accepted and practiced by all major composers. There are numerous competing aesthetics at work in the music of today, each with its own set of values.

During such an age of artistic pluralism, it is particularly difficult to summarize the major compositional tendencies and achievements. In a sense, the very notion of "compositional achievements" is called into question, for it is often impossible even to compare and evaluate the diverse approaches to making music that coexist in today's musical world. In this regard we should emphasize that the work we have chosen to discuss here represents just one of the many directions that composers have taken in this age of pluralism.

Why have music aesthetics become so dramatically pluralistic in our time? Among the many changes in culture and society that have affected compositional practice, one is surely the move of composers into the academic community, and another, closely related to the first, is the development of sophisticated technology for generating and reproducing sound. As a result of these latter developments, we now have available on records an enormously diverse body of music, including the music of cultures other than our own. You have heard, just in working with this text for instance, a vast range of recorded examples—some from remote cultures (African drumming and Japanese shamisen music), and a wide variety of performances of Western music. Exposure to other musical cultures and music from other epochs contributes to the acceptance of compositional diversity. More than ever before, composers, performers, and audiences are aware of the range of different ways of music making.

Along with sound-reproducing technology, electronic sound-synthesis techniques have profoundly affected the creation of music in our time—first the commercial development of the tape recorder after World War II, and later the development of computers and electronic synthesizers. Much of this latter development was carried out by musicians working together with engineers within the universities leading to wide-ranging implications for composers: Composers can manipulate a wider variety of sounds including, on one hand, sounds found and recorded in the environment—sounds of an automobile engine, a waterfall, or footsteps—and, on the other, sounds generated by electronic synthesizers coupled with computers. Moreover, the tape medium used in conjunction with these sound-generating media provides an opportunity for composers to realize more complex structures with a greater degree of accuracy than human performers can be expected consistently to achieve.

This capacity for the greatest level of accuracy and consistency in performance has strongly attracted Babbitt and others to the electronic medium. As Babbitt proposed in the late 1950s:

> This music (i.e., contemporary music) employs a tonal vocabulary which is more "efficient" than that of the music of the past, or its derivatives . . . and, as a result, the intelligible communication of the work demands increased accuracy from the transmitter (the performer) and activity from the receiver (the listener). Incidentally, it is this circumstance, among many others, that has created the need for purely electronic means of "performance."[7]

You have already heard part of a work of Babbitt's that combines tape with live performance—*Philomel,* composed in 1966 (Example 5.5). The sound world of this music is not only highly original, but it is also very precisely organized, bringing into being a new kind of

---

[7] "Who Cares If You Listen?" in *High Fidelity VIII/2* (February 1958).

musical discourse. In concert performance, the audience listens to an unusual duet: They see and hear the singer performing her part of the composition live while, from speakers positioned on either side of the singer, they hear electronically synthesized music which has been previously taped.

Of course, consistent with the pluralism that characterizes music today, many composers have not been attracted to the electronic medium at all, preferring to write for the traditional complement of instruments in various combinations. But even among those who are using synthetically generated sound, some have put the electronic medium to quite different uses than Babbitt. Of these, the most prevalent emphasis is on the development, for their own sake, of new kinds of sounds and sonorities. This is in contrast to Babbitt's primary interest in the richness and logic of the structural relations among sonorities and rhythms.

Babbitt's Predecessors: Schoenberg and the Development of Twelve-Tone Composition

In Chapter 12 we will once more go back in time; namely, to the period from 1859 to 1913, thus partially filling the temporal gap between the late Romantic period of Verdi and the music of our own time. This period saw dramatic changes not only in the relationships between music and society, but perhaps even more so in the very musical assumptions that composers were taking as "givens." A major figure towards the end of this period was the composer Arnold Schoenberg. We will consider, in Chapter 12, works of some of the composers who were writing just before Schoenberg, as well as a few early works of Schoenberg himself. The discussion here, then, anticipates what is to come in the following chapter, and at the same time it will help you to understand the musical context that still strongly influences Babbitt's work, as well as that of many other composers writing today.

Before going on, you may want to listen once again to several works by Schoenberg that were discussed earlier—*Herzegewächse* (Example 3.14), one of the *Six Little Piano Pieces,* Op. 19 (Example 4.21), and a piece from the *Suite for Piano,* Op. 25 (Example 6.6).

We (and Babbitt) have spoken of the *efficiency* and the *logic* of contemporary music—words that may seem surprising to you as characterizing contemporary musical styles such as Babbitt's. But the appropriateness of these words becomes clear as we examine the link between the music of Babbitt and that of Schoenberg. During the period after World War I, Schoenberg developed a coherent, largely systematic, and original approach to musical structure: What he called the twelve-tone compositional method. While it has not been universally adopted by composers (or even accepted as aesthetically valid by some), this approach to musical structure has strongly affected in one way or another nearly every composer from 1920 to the present.

Since the Second World War no American composer has been a more ardent and persuasive advocate of twelve-tone music than Babbitt. Virtually all of Babbitt's mature music has explored the potentials of the method Schoenberg originated. In fact, the virtuosity of Babbitt's *Minute Waltz* has as much to do with its brilliant exploration of the twelve-tone method as it does with its formidable demands on the performer. Thus, in order to go more deeply into the Babbitt example, we will need to take a close look not only at twelve-tone techniques themselves, but also at the kinds of musical issues that made the development of this new musical idiom seem so urgent.

Schoenberg believed that the development of the twelve-tone method was an historical imperative, a necessary and inevitable outgrowth of the tendencies toward increased chromaticism and progressively freer use of dissonance in the nineteenth century. Some of the principles and issues involved in Schoenberg's new approach to musical structure are summarized below:

1. After initial explorations of chromaticism in which all twelve tones were used—still within the bounds of tonality but pushing this framework to its limits—it seemed necessary to find some new principle to control the organization of the twelve pitches. Schoenberg and his students turned to the notion of controlling the *rate of presentation* of each of the twelve tones. For example, if a melody began with the pitch G♯, that pitch would not be sounded again until all of the remaining eleven were heard. This principle also helped to clarify compositional issues concerning tones that might sound more important or conclusive in a particular context. It was in this regard that Schoenberg called his new approach a "method of composing with twelve tones which are related only with one another."

2. The order of presenting these tones became an important issue for Schoenberg, as well. He began to compose with what he called twelve-tone rows—that is, fixed orderings of the twelve pitches.

Example 11.2A BABBITT, *Minute Waltz* (twelve-tone set)

Notice that each of the twelve pitches is used once and only once. Typically, a single row would be used for an entire movement or piece. The chosen ordering of the twelve tones provided a means for unifying compositions, just as the use of smaller, often chromatic motives and their transformations helped to unify harmonically experimental works of the Romantic period. For example, recall the "twelve-tone" opening theme of Liszt's *Faust Symphony* (Example 5.18): This melody is repeated, as a melody, and its particular harmonic ambiguity helps to shape the character and structure of the first movement of the symphony. However, it does not, as Schoenberg's rows do, actually generate all the melodic and harmonic material of the movement.

3. Schoenberg recognized that the ordering of the twelve tones *per se* was not as important as ordering the *intervals* between the pitches. Thus, he allowed for certain transformations of the original row that would maintain the original *ordering* of intervals between pitches while creating *variety* in the pitches themselves. Take the row in the previous example. If we *transpose* this melody—that is, move each of the notes up (or down) by the same interval—then the relationships among the tones will remain the same in this transformed-row form as in the original form, but the actual pitches will be different:

Example 11.2B BABBITT, *Minute Waltz* (twelve-tone set transposed by six half steps)

Similarly, the original melody can be played backwards, reversing the *order* of the intervals, but not changing them. A backwards presentation of a row is called its *retrograde* form. Finally, the row can be *inverted:* The distances between notes (the intervals) of the original row can be preserved while the *direction* of the intervals is reversed. For example, every major third up in the original row becomes a major third down in the inversion of the row. Here is an inversion of the same row that was transposed in the previous example:

Example 11.2C BABBITT, *Minute Waltz* (twelve-tone set inverted and transposed by six half steps)

Allowing for inversion, transposition, and retrograde forms of the row, 48 forms of any twelve-tone row are possible.

Revisiting Babbitt's *Minute Waltz*

Returning now to Babbitt's brief waltz, you might well ask: How does such an abstract, highly logical system of composition affect what a person actually hears? How can Babbitt relate these techniques to the traditional conventions of the waltz?

To begin with, recall that, despite its complex textures and rhythms, the piece seemed to project a feeling of the characteristic waltz "swing." Closer analysis (and Babbitt's subtitle "$\frac{3}{4} \pm \frac{1}{8}$") tells us that it is his careful compositional logic that helps to generate that waltzlike lilt: Babbitt notates the beginning of the piece in triple meter but as he continues, he adds or subtracts an eighth note from various measures.

Example 11.2 BABBITT, *Minute Waltz (or)* $\frac{3}{4} \pm \frac{1}{8}$, opening

In the end, the whole piece comes out even: exactly 32 triple-meter measures. And if the performer plays at the tempo Babbitt indicates, the waltz takes exactly a minute! By tampering with the meter in this way, Babbitt helps to animate the triple meter and even the "oom-pah-pah" gestures that sneak through the complex texture. In fact, this "robbing" and "paying back" of time is itself an allusion to convention, specifically to the convention of *rubato* playing which is so closely associated with the performance of Chopin's music. Recall our earlier discussion of the Chopin *Mazurka* (Example 2.25) in the section on rhythmic complexity. There, we spoke of a "kind of subtle give-and-take or flexibility with which the performer treats the underlying pulse for purposes of achieving greater expressiveness." In the case of Babbitt's waltz, the composer has, through tight constructions and logical methods, actually written in the *rubato*—the subtle give-and-take of strictly measured time. Babbitt also plays with other fundamental aspects of the waltz, such as the typically simple tonic and dominant harmonies. While the piece includes many triads—the common building blocks of tonal harmony—the relations among these triads are carefully designed to obscure their traditional tonal functions.

What about Babbitt's use of the twelve-tone technique itself? At the outset of the piece, the composer presents four distinct forms of the twelve-tone row, each in its own register.[8] Of course, Babbitt animates these pitches by giving them complex rhythms. Moreover, while row forms remain in their own distinct registers, the flow of melodic strands in this highly active texture cuts across the strict registral boundaries of the rows. This imaginative use of the row forms once more contributes to our immediate experience of the piece, in particular our sense of an active, many-voiced texture. On one hand, you can hear the rapid leaps from one register to another, and, on the other, each register can be heard as maintaining its own integrity and its own structural continuity.

Throughout the short piece, all twelve chromatic notes are presented in full in almost every measure (with occasional "spill-overs" into the next measure) and row forms are completed every four measures. That is, despite the angularity and gestural discontinuity of the piece, its twelve-tone structure is highly regular and balanced. This underlying regularity is a subtle and witty gesture of deference to the typical balanced phrase structure found in Chopin's original "Minute Waltz."

The logic of Babbitt's technique is, then, not just a matter of pure abstraction but, like more traditional compositional means, contributes to the direct experience of a particular coherence and style. The effect

---

[8] All pitches occurring below middle C constitute one line in the lowest register; each octave above middle C is, in turn, treated as a separate register and forms a separate line in the structure.

is somewhat like that of a cubist painting in which familiar objects and forms are represented, but are fragmented, restructured, and seen from several perspectives at the same time (see picture on p. 417). Remember the way Stravinsky incorporated the Lanner waltz into his ballet, *Petrouchka*. In that context, several layers of music are superimposed. In the Babbitt, the complexity of texture and the movement away from tonal harmony is even more fundamental. The many subtle transformations of the waltz structure are one more indication of Babbitt's compositional virtuosity, a fitting match for the performance dexterity demanded by Chopin's virtuoso precedent.

Listen once more to the two waltzes. As you listen, think about the questions we asked at the beginning of this chapter: What makes these two pieces so different and, in turn, what do they share? We have spelled out in words some of the musical qualities and procedures that distinguish them from one another, as well as some that are common to both; but only your own close listening can give these words experiential meaning. While Babbitt's piece may still seem to you like a "strange new world," it embodies, as we have tried to show, a particularly rich and subtle set of connections with music of the past, along with a virtuoso exploration of twentieth-century techniques. As an example of one contemporary style in this age of musical pluralism, it illustrates the challenge of music today: Composers must critically evaluate these new notions, considering their relationship to musical tradition, questioning their clarity, and pursuing the implications of such new systems with rigor and imagination. In turn, audiences are given the opportunity to hear the music of the past in a new light, illuminated by the transformations of its familiar forms in the music of our own time.

CHAPTER 12

Arnold Schoenberg

1859 to 1913:
A Model of Procedure

Igor Stravinsky by Pablo Picasso

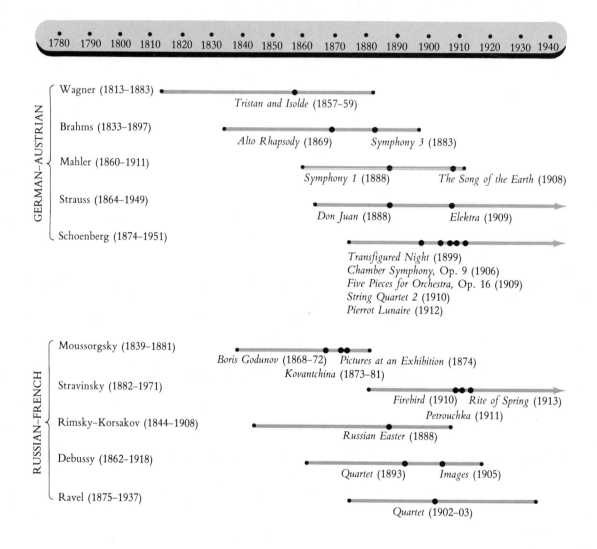

1780 1790 1800 1810 1820 1830 1840 1850 1860 1870 1880 1890 1900 1910 1920 1930 1940

GERMAN–AUSTRIAN

Wagner (1813–1883)
Tristan and Isolde (1857–59)

Brahms (1833–1897)
Alto Rhapsody (1869) *Symphony 3* (1883)

Mahler (1860–1911)
Symphony 1 (1888) *The Song of the Earth* (1908)

Strauss (1864–1949)
Don Juan (1888) *Elektra* (1909)

Schoenberg (1874–1951)
Transfigured Night (1899)
Chamber Symphony, Op. 9 (1906)
Five Pieces for Orchestra, Op. 16 (1909)
String Quartet 2 (1910)
Pierrot Lunaire (1912)

RUSSIAN–FRENCH

Moussorgsky (1839–1881)
Boris Godunov (1868–72) *Pictures at an Exhibition* (1874)
Kovantchina (1873–81)

Stravinsky (1882–1971)
Firebird (1910) *Rite of Spring* (1913)
Petrouchka (1911)

Rimsky-Korsakov (1844–1908)
Russian Easter (1888)

Debussy (1862–1918)
Quartet (1893) *Images* (1905)

Ravel (1875–1937)
Quartet (1902–03)

378

In the previous chapters in Part Four we have asked you to listen closely to just a few pieces widely separated in time and starkly different in musical style. Through these rather intimate snapshots from music history we have tried to give you a feel for historical context along with practice in hearing the kinds of features that distinguish one style from another. But so far (with perhaps the exception of Chapter 8) we have given you little sense of the *evolution* of stylistic change as it has occurred chronologically. We turn our attention now to this aspect of music history. It will be helpful in preparation to look back over the composers and works you heard in Chapter 8 and the pairs of composers whose works followed in Chapters 9, 10, and 11—this time from the view of their respective positions in history. Look again at the overview for Part Four on page 269.

Recalling these examples, it is clear that the four composers in the historical center (Bach, Schubert, Chopin, Verdi) share, each in their own ways, one fundamental characteristic—a dependence on the structures of tonal harmony for both expressiveness and underlying coherence. The composers at the historical extremes (Perotin and Babbitt) differ from the others in this regard.[1] Thus, our examples as a group illustrate at least one critical aspect in the evolution of musical style—the moves into tonality as a basic means of organization around 1600, and the moves out of it some 300 years later.

In this chapter we focus on the brief period that most specifically marks the moves away from tonality or what Schoenberg has called the "dissolution of tonality." We have chosen this half century from 1859 to the outbreak of World War I specifically because it is a time of intense stylistic change. The music composed during this period provides listeners with the opportunity to watch and hear the emergence of new possibilities for creating musical coherence. At the same time, the works of this period demand of listeners an unusual sensitivity to stylistic change if they are to appreciate the diverse musical means composers are finding in their search for greater expressivity.

Our discussion will once again concentrate on just a few significant compositions chosen to illustrate what we take to be the two main trends during this period—one associated with Austria and Germany, the other with Russia and France. Interestingly, the pair of works that you heard in the previous chapter gave you an intimation of these

---

[1] You might glance again at Chapter 5, "Possibilities Other Than Functional Harmony," pp. 161–164.

differences in national "flavor": Chopin—Polish but writing primarily in France; Babbitt—American but strongly influenced by Schoenberg's Austro-German musical origins. Further, in this chapter we will zero in on the music composed during a critical period between these two works—1859–1913—perhaps helping to explain the dramatic stylistic changes that occurred during this time.

These dramatic changes in style will become immediately evident as you listen to brief excerpts from two works that stand as landmarks in the history of music and that also mark the boundaries of our chosen timespan. Both are compositions by men writing in the Austro-German tradition: Wagner's opera *Tristan and Isolde,* completed in 1859 (Example 12.1), and Schoenberg's extraordinary work, *Pierrot lunaire,* composed in 1912 (Example 12.2).

Example	Composer, title	Date
12.1	Wagner, *Tristan and Isolde,* Act II, scene 2	1859
12.2	Schoenberg, *Pierrot lunaire,* "*Mondestrunken*"	1912

What musical features can you point to that can account for the striking differences between these two excerpts? What changes in musical thinking might have been taking place during the time between these two works? Can the Schoenberg work be understood as a "natural outgrowth" of Wagner's music and the music composed during the intervening period? Will the later work be more understandable if we reconstruct that process by tracing its course; that is, by listening carefully to works written during those intervening years?[2]

With these questions in mind listen to two brief excerpts by Russian composers, one written near the beginning of our selected period (Example 12.3), the other at the end (Example 12.4). (You will hear these first four works at greater length later in this chapter.)

---

[2] It has not been possible to include on the records for this chapter all the works that we will discuss, nor in every instance to provide excerpts of ideal length. Those works only mentioned but not recorded here have been marked by asterisks. Excerpts from a number of the works we refer to have already been heard in the context of topics discussed in earlier chapters, and we urge you to go back and listen to those earlier examples. We also urge you to supplement the recorded excerpts with complete recordings of the works discussed. As elsewhere in this book, the discussion that follows will have little meaning if the reader is not also a listener.

Example	Composer, title	Date
12.3	Moussorgsky, *Boris Godunov,* "Coronation Scene"	1868–1872
12.4	Stravinsky, *Le Sacre du printemps,* "Dance of the Adolescents"	1911–1913

Now listen to all four examples again. As you do so, think about how they might best be paired if you use similarity of style as a basis. Is date of composition the critical factor, pairing the two nineteenth-century works and the two twentieth-century works? Or is nationality the critical factor: two Austro-German composers and two Russian composers?

It seems clear that the greatest similarity is to be found between the two Russian examples. What stylistic characteristics do these pieces share? Listen to them again, paying attention to the following features and relations:

1. An insistent sonority (a particular combination of pitches) in each piece pervades the "pitch atmosphere." In Moussorgsky's work the pervasive sonority results from the alternation of two common chords but with a relationship between them that is unusual in tonal music. In Stravinsky's work we repeatedly hear a single chord which, unlike Moussorgsky's pair, is not found in tonal music.
2. A persistent beat—metrically regular in the "Coronation Scene" but much less so in the "Dance of the Adolescents."
3. The elaborate use of instrumental color for its own sake.
4. Movement from one section to another by juxtaposition rather than transition.
5. Folklike melodies that are modal rather than tonal in their pitch organization and which are often repeated with different orchestration but not fundamentally transformed or developed.

The Wagner and Schoenberg examples are less strikingly similar, but still they are more like one another than like either of the Russian pieces. For example, they share the following traits:

1. An emotional effect of charged intensity.
2. The use of short melodic motives as the basic source of unity (rather than the persistent sonorities used by Moussorgsky and Stravinsky).
3. Continuous transformation of these motives through sequence, im-

itation, and other techniques, in contrast to simple repetition of motives in the Russian works.

4. A sense of continuous development including *transitions* rather than *juxtaposition* in moving from one section to another.

5. An active texture with the various parts of the texture competing with one another to be heard.

6. Along with this, an absence of clear phrase structure resulting from the motivic nature of the melodic lines and from overlapping among the various parts of the active texture.

7. A large range in both the instrumental and vocal parts.

8. The absence of a regular pulse as a prominent feature; instead, there is a sense of structural rhythm created by chord changes, the length of motives as they move through sequential repetitions, and by the ebb and flow of intensity.

In pairing these four works we have illustrated the two major and contrasting stylistic trends which emerged during the latter half of the nineteenth and the beginning of the twentieth centuries. While change takes place within these two groups (as the examples themselves demonstrate), the differences which we have observed here remain to distinguish German and Russian music throughout the period. We will continue our discussion, then, by pursuing these two trends individually and then bring them back together to consider them both in the context of the total period from 1859 to 1913.

FROM WAGNER TO SCHOENBERG

As we narrow our discussion to the Austro-German composers, differences (which may appear small in a larger context) emerge even between two composers who were writing contemporaneously. In the case of Brahms and Wagner, these differences became a *cause célèbre*.[3]

Wagner (1813–1883) and Brahms (1833–1897)

Go back and listen to the first movement of Brahms's *Symphony 3* and compare it with the *"Liebestod"* ("Love-Death") from Wagner's *Tristan and Isolde*.

*Brahms, *Symphony 3*, first movement, 1883 (Example 6.15)
*Wagner, *Tristan and Isolde*, "Liebestod," 1857–1859 (Example 3.23)

---

[3] See Donald F. Tovey, *The Forms of Music* (New York: New American Library, Meridian Books, 1957), pp. 128–132; Gerald Abraham, *A Hundred Years of Music*, 4th ed. (London: Duckworth, 1974), pp. 129–132.

Johannes Brahms in his
study

Brahms wrote no operas, Wagner no symphonies. Inherent in
this fact is a fundamental difference in approach. For example, the
Brahms *Symphony 3* falls into the traditional four movements, each of
which in some way embodies a traditional organizing principle (such
as sonata form or ABA). On a more detailed level, you will remember
from our discussion of the Brahms first movement that its structure
was realized through contrasts in the functions of sections: Statements
(generally in one key with a relatively clear melodic shape), transitions
(modulatory and more fragmented melodically), elaborations and development, and cadential passages. In addition, the statement passages
differ in character, providing another kind of contrast. In short, while
Brahms's harmonic, instrumental, and rhythmic means may be different
from, for instance, Beethoven's, you still respond to those structural
functions which generate drama through purely musical means.

Wagner, on the other hand, developed means of organization
which derived, to a large extent, from the drama of his text. In the
"*Liebestod*," for example, we are swept along both musically and dramatically in a process of continuing transformation. Even the traditional
divisions of opera (aria, recitative, and the like) are no longer heard in
this music.[4]

Wagner writes continuous music—he called it "endless melody"—in which there is sequential development of "significant mo-

---

[4] Compare Wagner's use of the text as a basis for musical organization with
Verdi's use of the text in the *Requiem* written just 15 years later.

tives" (each one usually associated with a character or idea) in a complex, often highly active texture characterized by continuous modulation and avoidance of cadences. In addition to the constant shifting and merging of tonal centers, the harmonic implications of chords are often diverted or left unfulfilled. Specifically, the dominant seventh chord (the crux of the tension-building waiting passages of Beethoven and Bach; see Demonstration 5.1) is frequently heard as *stable.* It resolves more ambiguous harmonic movement by momentarily defining or pointing to a specific key. The result is music that is continuously searching and building toward a climax. How different from the carefully contrasted passages, each with its own function, that we hear in Brahms's *Symphony 3!*

Example	Composer, title	Date
12.5	Brahms, *Alto Rhapsody,* Op. 53, excerpt	1869

Listening to the *Alto Rhapsody* (Example 12.5), however, one recognizes that Brahms and Wagner are contemporaneous. Given a text describing an unhappy youth wandering through a desolate, wintry landscape, Brahms explores broader expressive means in his music. In this piece, the harmony, like Wagner's, is more chromatic. Cadences are avoided, and sectionalism is therefore abandoned. The mood is unified; and, in a sense, we are asked to listen in a different way. This is dramatic music, but without the charged intensity of the Wagner excerpt—and with the singer playing a more predominant role.

It is, then, the *genre* rather than the date of composition that brings these two composers stylistically closer together. In Chapter 6 we suggested that traditional forms became more dramatic in the nineteenth century. But set alongside Wagner, Brahms now appears rather closer to tradition in his instrumental works. It is when Brahms turns to music inspired by and expressive of a text that we hear him exploring other musical dimensions.

Mahler (1860–1911)

Example	Composer, title	Date
12.6	Mahler, *The Song of the Earth (Das Lied von der Erde)*, "Autumn Loneliness," excerpt	1908–1909

The Song of the Earth (Example 12.6), a piece for voice and orchestra written 39 years after Brahms's *Alto Rhapsody,* at first sounds almost like a continuation of that piece. The affinity between the two works lies in:

1. Their clear, largely diatonic melody lines, which soar above a relatively thin orchestral texture.
2. The rich harmony of the accompaniments with their elusive cadences.
3. The unchanging, poignant mood of the texts, from which the continuous musical structure of each piece derives.

Mahler, like Brahms, chooses a text that evokes the darker side of nature. It begins thus:

> Autum mists float over an azure sea.
> The grass stands covered with frost.
> One could believe that an artist
> had taken finely powdered jade
> and dusted the petals

The last stanza ends:

> Sunshine of love, will you shine no longer
> to dry my bitter tears?

Gustav Mahler by Auguste Rodin
(The Rodin Museum, Philadelphia)

Paradoxically, Mahler, who considered himself in the Wagner camp, was not fond of Brahms's music: "All I can say of him is that he's a puny little dwarf with a rather narrow chest. . . . It is very seldom he can make anything whatever of his themes, beautiful as they often are. Only Beethoven and Wagner, after all, could do that."[5] (Of course, it should be remembered that Mahler was speaking here primarily of Brahms's symphonies rather than of his dramatic vocal music.)

But despite Mahler's devotion to the music of Wagner, his style differs from Wagner's in that he does not create a "competition" between voice and orchestra. Mahler's orchestra lacks Wagner's thick, active texture in which the instruments merge into a mass of sound; and in Mahler we do not hear Wagner's constant surging toward an even bigger climax.

*Mahler, *Symphony 1,* 1888 (Examples 1.6, 5.13, 6.5)

Listening again to the second movement of the Mahler symphony (Example 6.5), you will hear that similarity of genre need not result in similarity of style. Mahler's *Symphony 1* was written only five years after Brahms's *Symphony 3,* yet the differences between them are striking. Mahler, unlike Brahms, tended to be influenced by extra-musical associations even in his symphonies. For example, his *Symphony 1* is subtitled "The Titan." Many of his later symphonies also have programmatic associations, and often a text and voice are introduced even in symphonic works. Traditional forms appear in a freer guise; they are greatly expanded and do not have the same sense of classical tradition which pervades the symphonies of Brahms. Notice particularly:

1. The large orchestra and extensive use of horns, trumpets, and even woodwinds at the top of their ranges.
2. The very active texture, which is yet so transparent that you seem to be able to hear through it, with each instrumental color standing out clearly.
3. The folklike and strongly diatonic melodies contrasted with more chromatic, almost Wagnerian melodies.
4. The strong pulse, often emphasized by tympani.

---

[5] Letter to his wife, written June 23, 1904; quoted in Irving Kolodin, ed., *The Composer as Listener* (New York: Collier, 1958), p. 51.

The jubilant mood of this movement is created in part by Mahler's virtuoso ability to toss these contrasting melodies through the orchestra, combining them, fragmenting them, and opposing them with abandon. Mahler himself described this process in terms of his use of

> *themes*—clear and *plastic,* so that they are distinctly recognizable in every transformation and further unfolding; then a working out, full of variety, and, above all, gripping because of the *development* of the inner idea and also because of the *genuine opposition* of the motifs placed in contrast to each other.[6]

Richard Strauss (1864–1949)

*Richard Strauss, *Don Juan,* 1888–1889

Mahler described Richard Strauss as a "literary man." Indeed, the majority of Strauss's works are programmatic in some sense. In the same year that Mahler wrote his *Symphony 1,* Strauss composed a tone poem—an orchestral work in one movement inspired by the poem *Don Juan* by the Hungarian poet Nikolaus Lenau. The character of the Don "on a gallant hunt for womanly perfection" is immediately portrayed in the music by its huge melodic range (so different from Mahler's folklike melodies), its martial rhythmic patterns, the use of brass in a characteristic fanfare manner, and the massive orchestra and thick texture out of which melodies and instruments seem to compete for individual existence.

As the piece progresses, notice how themes of strongly contrasting character rapidly succeed one another (for example, a momentary dance melody, the Don's theme, and eventually a "feminine" solo violin melody). The structure is generated largely by *extramusical* events and characters with which particular themes, instruments, and rhythms are associated. The music is more chromatic than Mahler's, full of contrast and yet nonsectional in the classical sense. We hear it freely evolving through the transformation, juxtaposition, and intertwining of thematic material.

We turn now to an opera by Strauss, *Elektra.* Listen to Elektra's soliloquy on the death of her murdered father, Agamemnon.

---

[6] Gustav Mahler, *Briefe,* 191, quoted in William A. Austin, *Music in the Twentieth Century* (New York: Norton, 1966), p. 129.

Richard Strauss

*R. Strauss, *Elektra*, Act I, excerpt, 1906–1908

STRAUSS, *Elektra*[7]

Allein! Weh, ganz allein. Der Vater fort,
hinabgescheucht in seine kalten Klüfte . . .
Agamemnon! Agamemnon!
Wo bist du, Vater? hast du nicht die
  Kraft,
dein Angesicht herauf zu mir zu
  schleppen?
Es ist die Stunde, unsre Stunde ist's,
die Stunde, wo sie dich geschlachtet haben,
dein Weib und der mit ihr in einem Bette,

Alone! Alas, all alone! Father is gone,
shoveled down into his cold grave . . .
Agamemnon! Agamemnon!
Where are you, Father? Have you not the
  strength
to drag yourself up before me where I can see
  your face?
It is the hour—our hour it is—
The hour in which they butchered you,
your wife and he who butchered would sleep
  with her in one bed,

---

[7] Translation by David Bain.

in deinem königlichen Bette schläft.
Sie schlugen dich im Bade tot, dein Blut
rann über deine Augen, und das Bad
dampfte von deinem Blut. Da nahm er dich,
der Feige, bei den Schultern, zerrte dich
hinaus aus dem Gemach, den Kopf voraus,
die Beine schleifend hinterher; dein Auge,
das starre, offne, sah herein ins
   Haus.
So kommst du wieder, setzest Fuss vor Fuss,
und stehst auf einmal da, die beiden Augen
weit offen, und ein königlicher
   Reif
von Purpur ist um deine Stirn, der speist sich
aus des Hauptes offner Wunde.
Agamemnon! Vater!
Ich will dich sehn, lass mich heute nicht allein!
Nur so wie gestern, wie ein Schatten dort
im Mauerwinkel zeig dich deinem Kind!

in your royal bed.
They struck at you in your bath, your blood
ran over your eyes, and the bath
steamed with your blood. Then the coward,
he took you by the shoulders, tugged you
head first from the chamber,
your legs trailing behind; your eyes,
that open stare, looking back in the
   house.
So come you again, set foot over foot,
and stand there suddenly, both eyes
wide open, and around your brow a kingly
   circlet
of purple that nourishes itself
from the open wounds on your head.
Agamemnon! Father!
I want to see you, do not leave me alone today!
But, as you did yesterday, show yourself,
like a shadow there in the angle of the wall,
   show yourself to your child.

In *Elektra,* written some 20 years after *Don Juan,* note how Strauss, like Brahms, pushes his musical vocabulary to its extremes in the service of his text. At the same time notice how Strauss contrasts the expanded possibilities of chromaticism with the more traditional conventions of tonal harmony as a means for expressing the text. For example, the aria begins with a low, ominous "rumble" in the orchestra, followed by repetitions of a jagged, chromatic motive as Elektra quietly sings, "Alone. Alas, all alone." But with the words "into his cold grave," the vocal line falls and the chromatic harmony clears. Settling down to the familiar directed tension of the dominant seventh, the sustained chord resolves in a full cadence to a minor triad as Elektra, outlining the triad, sings her father's name, "Agamemnon, Agamemnon." With this gradual emergence of traditional tonal functions, Strauss creates a sense of stability to express Elektra's tender feelings for her father and for the past. Then, as Elektra tells the story of her father's murder in all its gory detail, her melodic line becomes more chromatic and more disjunct, with large leaps and a range that puts the most extreme demands on her voice. After reaching a climax on the words "fed from the open wounds of your head," Elektra once more invokes her father's name singing a varied version of the minor triad motive. With this, the mood becomes quieter—the texture becomes more transparent, the harmony more tonal. Elektra sings, "Don't leave me alone today! ... show yourself to your child." And on the word "child" Strauss helps to express a return to the simplicity of the past by again returning to clear tonal functions. The passage ends with a full cadence now in the more open major mode.

Stylistically and expressively the contrast between Strauss and Mahler is striking—particularly in their differing uses of chromaticism, orchestration, and melodic line. Imagine Mahler choosing the intensity of the grief-stricken Elektra as a subject for his music!

Schoenberg (1874–1951)

We approach the last phase of our study of Austro-German works up to World War I by taking a close look at the works of Arnold Schoenberg between the years 1899 and 1912. In doing so we focus on the style of a single composer, a move which might seem to make issues of stylistic change less problematic. However, the transformations in Schoenberg's own style during this period of 13 years is in fact quite remarkable. His essays and letters poignantly describe his personal struggle for what he considered a search for "necessary" new means of expression; but the works themselves are at least equally revealing.[8]

*Schoenberg, *Transfigured Night,* 1899

Schoenberg's *Transfigured Night* was written almost ten years before *Elektra* and goes back still further to Wagner for its musical ancestry. The long climaxes, thick, turbulent texture, chromatic harmony, motivic manipulation, unified mood, and even the motives themselves are particularly reminiscent of *Tristan and Isolde.* A jury that reviewed the piece for possible performance declared: "It sounds as if one had smeared over the still moist Tristan score."[9]

Example	Composer, title	Date
12.7	Schoenberg, *Chamber Symphony 1 in E Major,* Op. 9, first movement	1906

---

[8] See especially Schoenberg's essay, "Composition with Twelve Tones," in Arnold Schoenberg, *Style and Idea,* trans. Leo Black, ed. Leonard Stein (Berkeley: University of California Press, 1975), p. 217.

[9] The Vienna *Tonkünstlerverein* jury (which refused performance of the work); in Sam Morgenstern, ed., *Composers on Music* (New York: Pantheon, 1956), p. 377.

Self-portrait by Arnold
Schoenberg

(Used by permission of
Belmont Music Publishers,
Los Angeles, CA 90049)

Chamber Symphony 1 (Example 12.7), written seven years after
Transfigured Night, is scored for 15 solo instruments. The charged atmosphere, reminiscent of the earlier work, requires the utmost from
each instrument in the unique ensemble. The two pieces are also similar
in their extensive use of a few motives—rather than clear, palpable
melodies—and in their constant manipulation of them. The music is
continuously developmental. In the following extract Schoenberg dis-
cusses the composition of this work.

> There was at hand from the start a sufficient amount of motival forms
> and their derivatives, rather too much than too little. The task, therefore,
> was to retard the progress of development in order to enable the average
> good listener to keep in mind what preceded so as to understand the
> consequences. To keep within bounds and to balance a theme whose
> character, tempo, expression, harmonic progression, and motival contents
> displayed a centrifugal tendency: this was here the task.[10]

---

[10] Schoenberg, "Heart and Brain," in *Style and Idea,* pp. 60, 61.

The striking difference between this work and *Transfigured Night* is the curious mixture of new and old found in the later work. In the chamber symphony, tonality is still operative; notice, for instance, the title which includes the key (E major) and, at the end of the brief introductory passage, the full cadence in that key. But tonality is clearly on shaky ground in this work, almost as if it were fighting for its survival under an attack of extreme chromaticism. Coupled with this erosion of tonal functions is the brilliantly active texture in which angular, even jagged motives overlap, interrupt, and intrude on one another.

Rhythm depends on the length of motives, pace of attack, and harmonic change rather than on pulse or meter, which are often submerged. The ascending chain of fourths in the horn near the beginning of the piece is used as a basis for new chord formations built on the interval of the fourth rather than the third. The use of solo instruments creates a complex but transparent texture, which becomes increasingly significant in Schoenberg's music.

The dramatic intensity of the piece lies not in a program but in more purely musical processes; for example, the transformations of a few motives, the movement from solo statement to increasing textural density and activity, and the dissolution to solo statement again. The strangely anguished quality of the piece seems to lie partly in its struggle with past means of comprehensibility—with past assumptions which are being pushed to their limits. What emerges is music that is simultaneously decadent and explosive!

Example	Composer, title	Date
12.8	Schoenberg, *Five Pieces for Orchestra,* Op. 16, no. 1	1909

Three years later, Schoenberg had created a new musical world, a world that has had its effect on every subsequent composer (Example 12.8). This "new" music was characterized by its extreme brevity, and its sense of condensed action. Schoenberg says of the works of this period:

The first compositions in this new style were written by me around 1908 and, soon afterwards, by my pupils Anton von Webern and Alban Berg. From the very beginning such compositions differed from all preceding music, not only harmonically but also melodically, thematically and motivally. But the foremost characteristics of these pieces *in statu nascendi* were their extreme expressiveness and their extraordinary brevity. At that time, neither I nor my pupils were conscious of the reasons for these features. Later I discovered that our sense of form was right when it forced us to counterbalance extreme emotionality with extraordinary shortness. Thus, subconsciously, consequences were drawn from an innovation which, like every innovation, destroys while it produces. New colorful harmony was offered; but much was lost.[11]

With this work we hear a new kind of music: Schoenberg seems to have freed himself from the limiting conventions of tonality with which he was so evidently struggling in the chamber symphony. Schoenberg ascribes the difference to the "emancipation of the dissonance":

> The term *emancipation of the dissonance* refers to its comprehensibility, which is considered equivalent to the consonance's comprehensibility. A style based on this premise treats dissonances like consonances and renounces a tonal center. By avoiding the establishment of a key, modulation is excluded, since modulation means leaving an established tonality and establishing *another* tonality.[12]

But with tonality "renounced" and with it the framework within which melody and harmony had been understood, what is left for the listener to attend to in making sense of this music? Most immediately evident is the critical importance of germinal motives. For it is through close attention to particular germinal materials—melodic, rhythmic, textural—as they are developed and transformed that the inner logic of this music can be heard to unfold. Schoenberg himself says in an essay entitled "My Evolution":

> Coherence in classic compositions is based—broadly speaking—on the unifying qualities of such structural factors as rhythms, motifs, phrases, and the constant reference of all melodic and harmonic features to the center of gravitation—the tonic. Renouncement of the unifying power of the tonic still leaves the other factors in operation.[13]

Indeed, as suggested in our discussion of Babbitt's *Minute Waltz,* learning to understand this "new" music may lead us to hear the most

---

[11] Schoenberg, "Composition with Twelve Tones," in *Style and Idea*, p. 217.
[12] Ibid.
[13] In *Style and Idea*, p. 87.

familiar music in new ways. For instance, in our discussions of earlier music, we often emphasized the importance of singular germinal "ideas" and their transformations as a central factor in following the structural evolution of a work. (See, for example, the discussion of the theme from the Mozart *Sonata in A* and the *Symphony 5* of Beethoven in Chapter 3). But there is an important difference: Because we have so thoroughly internalized the conventions associated with tonality and also metric rhythm, we can casually follow the general ebb and flow of pieces without specifically attending to the details of motivic development which give a great work its unique quality. But with these conventions no longer present, it becomes a *necessity* to give our attention to the unique material of each piece. It is as if each work in this style creates anew, through its particular germinal melodic, rhythmic, and textural materials, the context within which it is to be understood. As with the inner logic of poetry, Schoenberg's orchestra piece develops out of itself as each transformation leads inevitably to the next.

Consider a poem by T. S. Eliot written during the same period. Notice particularly the opening, "germinal" phrase, "Let us go," as it undergoes transformations in rhythm and meaning. Notice, too, the shifts in meaning of the word *go* as well as the word *streets*.

The Love Song of J. Alfred Prufrock[14]

Let us go then, you and I,
When the evening is spread out against the sky
Like a patient etherised upon a table;
Let us go, through certain half-deserted streets,
The muttering retreats
Of restless nights in one-night cheap hotels
And sawdust restaurants with oyster-shells:
Streets that follow like a tedious argument
Of insidious intent
To lead you to an overwhelming question . . .
Oh, do not ask, "What is it?"
Let us go and make our visit.

---

[14] From *Collected Poems 1909–1962* by T. S. Eliot, copyright 1936 by Harcourt Brace Jovanovich, Inc.; copyright © 1963, 1964 by T. S. Eliot. Reprinted by permission of Harcourt Brace Jovanovich, Inc. and Faber and Faber Ltd.

The underscore is ours.

> In the room the women come and <u>go</u>
> Talking of Michelangelo.

Each statement of the opening "motive" changes both in rhythm and in subtle meaning as it is embedded in an ever more explicit context: First, simply, "Let us go"; then more specifically, "through certain half-deserted streets"; and at the end of the stanza, as if in answer to a question not asked—go where?—"go and make our visit." And in the couplet that follows, Eliot moves in still further—"In the room"—to create another context for "go" where, pinned down, it becomes more static then active. At the same time he maintains the rhythm of the original fragment: "Let us go"/. . . "come and go."

Listening again now, carefully, you can hear in Schoenberg's Opus 16, no. 1 terse, melodic fragments that evolve, changing their "meaning" as they are embedded in ever new contexts: sometimes heard against a repeated figure in the bass; sometimes in the midst of an array of slightly varied, interconnected motivic shapes and instrumental colors. While Schoenberg has written the piece for large orchestral forces, he treats his orchestra almost like a group of solo instruments. And as in the chamber symphony, the clarity of solo playing allows highly intricate detail to emerge. The overall effect is one of great energy and vitality. The work seems alive and fresh rather than decadent, self-contained rather than seeking to escape from the bounds of tradition.

*Schoenberg, *Quartet 2 in F-Sharp Minor,* third movement, 1910

In this composition Schoenberg introduces the voice into the string quartet. He writes:

> . . . it seemed at first impossible to compose pieces of complicated organization or of great length. A little later I discovered how to construct larger forms by following a text or poem. The differences in size and shape of its parts and the change in character and mood were mirrored in the shape and size of the composition, in its dynamics and tempo, figuration and accentuation, instrumentation and orchestration. Thus the parts were differentiated as clearly as they had formerly been by the tonal and structural functions of harmony.[15]

The third movement from the *Quartet 2* is somewhat reminiscent of *Elektra* in the great demands made on the singer, the wide range,

---

[15] Schoenberg, "Composition with Twelve Tones," pp. 217, 218.

the very disjunct melody, and the quest for climaxes. But unlike Strauss, Schoenberg uses a limited number of instruments. He exploits their possibilities in new ways, creating a texture which is relatively thin and transparent but rich in coloristic effect. Throughout we hear Schoenberg reaching for the extremes to create an effect of intense emotional expression.

Example	Composer, title	Date
12.9	Schoenberg, *Pierrot lunaire*, *"Mondestrunken"*	1912

We conclude our study of German and Austrian music by returning to one of the works you heard at the beginning of this chapter. In *Pierrot lunaire* (Example 12.9), one of the masterpieces of the twentieth century, Schoenberg brings together in the most concentrated form all the aspects of his music that we have heard emerging in his earlier works. The bizarre, almost frightening atmosphere of the text (by the Belgian poet Albert Giraud) is reflected in every detail of the music. Combining singing and speaking (*sprechstimme*), the singer penetrates the atmosphere, portraying the madness of a moonstruck clown.

Example 12.9 SCHOENBERG, *Mondestrunken* ("Moondrunk")

Den Wein, den man mit Augen trinkt,
Giesst Nachts der Mond in Wogen nieder,
Und eine Springflut überschwemmt
Den stillen Horizont.

The wine that one drinks with his eyes
Pours in waves from the moon at nightfall,
And like a spring flood overwhelms
the motionless rim of the horizon.

Gelüste, schauerlich und süss,
Durchschwimmen ohne Zahl die
   Fluten!
Den Wein, den man mit Augen trinkt,
Giesst Nachts der Mond in Wogen nieder.

Desires, shivering and sweet,
Are swimming without number through the
   flood waters!
The wine that one drinks with his eyes
Pours in waves from the moon at nightfall.

Der Dichter, den die Andacht treibt,
Berauscht sich an dem heilgen Tranke,
Den Himmel wendet er verzückt
Das Haupt und taumelnd saugt und schlürft er
Den Wein, den man mit Augen trinkt.

The poet, driven by his ardor,
Grown drunken with the holy drink—
To heaven he rapturously lifts
His head, and reeling, slips and swallows
The wine that one drinks with his eyes.

The music unfolds with an intense, tight logic. Scored for only five players and eight instruments (piano, flute and piccolo, clarinet and bass clarinet, violin and viola, and cello), the song develops with an extreme concentration of detail out of initial motives which the composer transforms to reflect the text.

Notice, for example, the "waves" in the first stanza created by a sequentially repeated motive played transparently by the flute, violin *pizzicato,* and the upper register of the piano. The motive "pours in waves from the moon at nightfall." This passage is in immediate contrast to the thick, active texture of the third stanza where the cello enters and the motive moves within the predominant sound of percussive low piano chords: "The poet, driven by his ardor."

Historically, perhaps the most remarkable aspect of this piece is that in it Schoenberg, incorporating many of the characteristics of his earlier style (so clearly reminiscent of the Austro-German composers of the late nineteenth century), has spawned something entirely new. Schoenberg's stylistic change over this period of 13 years includes both what he termed the "dissolution of tonality" and the creation of fresh bases for organizing pitch. The full implications of these new means of organization were realized only in the years following 1914, as we discussed in Chapter 11. The particular means which Schoenberg found are inextricably bound with the stylistic characteristics of the Austro-German tradition—as will become even clearer when we consider the quite different style of Stravinsky and his predecessors. You may find it interesting now to go back to the first Wagner examples and listen to them in the light of your awareness of later developments in German and Austrian music.

FROM MOUSSORGSKY TO STRAVINSKY

In our earlier discussion we noticed a rather striking similarity between the two Russian composers who delimit our time period: Moussorgsky (1839–1881) and Stravinsky (1882–1971). Indeed, there seemed to be more in common between them than between the two Austro-German composers. Their similarities suggest a clear stylistic tradition in the Russian music of this period.

The fact that the similarity between the two Russian works is more striking than that between the German works (*Tristan and Isolde* and *Pierrot lunaire*) tells us something about the stylistic traditions of each country. We might say that the "surface," or the "face," of German music changed radically during these 50 years, while certain less immediately accessible characteristics (such as structural process) remained to define the tradition. In Russian music the surface remains recognizable, and it is this more obvious quality that is crucial in defining the style.

Another body of music, that of France, relates closely to the Russian music of this period. There was a great cultural affinity between Russia and France during the late nineteenth century. Members of the Russian aristocracy spoke French as a second language. The intellectual, artistic, and social elite traveled frequently between the two countries (Debussy, for example, worked for some months in Moscow in his early years). Both Russian and French intellectuals shared a certain revolutionary spirit. This relationship comes alive in the novels of Tolstoi, Dostoevski, and Turgenev and in the plays of Chekhov.

A Characteristic Surface

Musically, this affinity is immediately evident. Listen again to the following excerpts spanning a period from 1873 to 1913.

> Moussorgsky, *Khovantchina,* prelude, 1872–1880 (Example 3.21)
> Debussy, *Rondes de printemps,* 1905–1909 (Example 1.7)
> Ravel, *Daphnis and Chloé,* 1909–1912 (Example 2.2)
> Stravinsky, *Le Sacre du printemps,* Introduction, 1911–1913 (Example 4.23)

Notice that each of these examples initially occurred in different contexts illustrating quite different musical characteristics: the Moussorgsky prelude illustrated unpredictable phrase structure approaching continuous melody; Debussy's *Rondes de printemps* showed the use of the orchestra to create a "kind of kaleidoscope of sounds"; with the Ravel excerpt in the chapter on rhythm it was "difficult to find an underlying pulse;" and the Stravinsky was described as "static and in motion at the same time" in our discussion of sectional and continuous musical organization. These various qualities, in fact, include the spectrum of stylistic affinities among Russian and French works of this period. Listen now to one additional example that seems to epitomize the characteristic surface of this music—Example 12.10, Debussy's *Images.*

Example	Composer, title	Date
12.10	Debussy, *Images,* "Iberia"; "*Parfums de la nuit*" ("Perfumes of the night")	1905–1908

What, then, contributes to the characteristic sound of all these works? They are rhythmically amorphous, haunted by the changing

Modest Moussorgsky by Il'ya Yefimovich Repin
(Sovfoto, New York)

color of solo instruments (particularly winds) set against a mobile background texture that is often shimmering and nebulous. We are drawn into a world in which the play of sounds itself is the prime source of pleasure. Although differences will emerge as we study the period and the individual works of Russian and French composers, these qualities persist. They make it possible to speak of a Russian-French tradition.

Russia: Nationalism and Folk Song

Our approach to this music will be somewhat different from that used in examining the music of Germany and Austria. Instead of treating the period strictly chronologically, we will focus on its recurring common threads. We will make a series of temporal sweeps rather than temporal steps—first within Russian and then within French music.

Listen once again to the following excerpts from Russian works heard previously. As you listen, ask yourself what musical features—melody, harmony, texture, orchestration—contribute to their peculiarly Russian "flavor."

Moussorgsky, *Khovantchina,* prelude, 1872–1980 (Example 3.21)
Stravinsky, *Firebird Suite,* finale, 1909–1910 (Example 1.10)
Stravinsky, *Petrouchka,* Part I, 1910–1911 (Examples 2.27 and 4.7)
Moussorgsky/Ravel, *Pictures at an Exhibition,* 1874/1922 (Example 1.16)

To these we add another work associated with Russian nationalism of the late nineteenth century, Rimsky-Korsakov's *Russian Easter Overture* (Example 12.11)

Example	Composer, title	Date
12.11	Rimsky-Korsakov, *Russian Easter Overture*	1888

In these examples a new element appears—a pervasive sense of Russia. Nationalism was a powerful factor guiding and inspiring a group of Russian composers known as the Mighty Five—Moussorgsky, Borodin, Rimsky-Korsakov, Cui, and Balakirev.[16] Seeking out Russian history, myth, and folk song, they tried to free themselves from foreign (especially German) influence to create a music that was truly Russian. Their aggressive, almost violent anti-German feelings were expressed by Moussorgsky in the following remarks, written to two young women requesting information about German songs:

> Of the German things sing the ones you like, because it's better for you to make the choice *accidentally,* than for me—at a distance: *accidentally,* for I am very doubtful about German vocal music in particular. German men and women sing like roosters, imagining that the more their mouths gape and the longer they hold their notes, the more feeling they show. To speak harshly, *Kartoffel, Kirschensuppe, Milch* and *Tchernickensuppe* do not have an especially good influence on the power of feeling and particularly on artistic feeling, and for my taste the Germans, moving from their leather fried in pork-fat to the seven-hour operas of Wagner, offer nothing attractive for me.[17]

---

[16] Recall that in Italy, around the same time, Verdi was participating in the strong spirit of nationalism that had arisen there.

[17] Letter to Alexandra and Nadezhda Purgeld, written June 20, 1870 in Petrograd; in Jay Leyda and Sergei Bertensson, eds. and trans., *The Musorgsky Reader* (New York: Da Capo, 1970), p. 138.

The Mighty Five used Russian folk melodies or composed folklike melodies extensively. Cesar Cui describes the attributes of the Russian folk song as follows:

> One of the principal elements in the structure of Russian song is the complete freedom of rhythm, carried to the point of caprice. Not only may the musical phrase be composed of an unequal number of measures, but even in the same song the rhythm of the measures may change several times. These changing rhythms are, above all, *right,* since they are supremely expressive. At the same time, they utterly exclude the impression of banality and monotony which sometimes results from the prolonged use of a uniform and over-worked rhythm.
>
> But their very variety is such that an unpracticed ear does not grasp certain Russian songs clearly, as long as the musical phrases are not divided and established into precise measures. Another notable fact is . . . that very often, the theme is not constructed on the current European scale, but on old Greek modes, the origin of church music. . . . The use of the Greek modes . . . has the further advantage of a great diversity because, in Greek music, the position of steps varies with each mode, while in European music it is fixed.
>
> The Russian folk song imperiously demands an original harmonization and a very special art of modulation. First, it is rare to come on a song the melody of which can be treated entirely in one of the two modes, major or minor; most often, even if it spans but a few measures, it passes from the minor to its relative major and vice versa.
>
> It also happens that the harmony of a single chord remains stationary throughout an entire song, which lends it an overall quality of vague melancholy, a complexion of deliberate monotony.
>
> Russian folk tunes are ordinarily confined within a very restricted note-span, only rarely exceeding the interval of a fifth or sixth. . . . The theme is always short; some are limited to two measures, but these measures are repeated as many times as the scope of the text demands.[18]

Cui's comments are a wonderful example of style analysis and, as such, quite accurately describe the unique qualities of the melodies you heard in the previous examples. In Rimsky-Korsakov's *Russian Easter Overture,* for example, as Cui suggests, the "musical phrases" of the opening melody are "not divided and established into precise measures." Indeed, the three short phrases of this melody include seven,

---

[18] Cesar Cui, from *La Musique en Russie,* quoted in Morgenstern, *Composers on Music,* pp. 220–225.

five, and nine beats, respectively. Further, as in Russian folk tunes, this melody is "confined within a very restricted note-span." How different from the melodies of Strauss or Schoenberg with their large leaps and wide range!

All of these works are characterized by a process of organization that also stems from the use of folk song. Sectional in the large sense, they proceed from one part to another by juxtaposition rather than by transition. Within parts we hear clear smaller sections. These sections are often created by the repetition of whole, continuous melodies which are varied largely by orchestration and texture rather than by transformation or motivic elaboration. Notice in this regard that the *Russian Easter Overture* (Example 12.11) clearly divides into the following sections:

1. Opening melody played in unison.
2. Interlude (plucked strings).
3. Repetition of opening melody reorchestrated and accompanied.
4. Improvisatory violin solo played over a sustained chord in the orchestra.
5. New tune (with characteristics similar to the first); accompanied cello solo.
6. Flute interlude.

After a brief pause, sections 1 through 6 are then repeated with slight variations, mostly in instrumentation. The excerpt, then, is sectional both in its division into two larger sections as well as in the smaller divisions within the larger sections.

One of the crucial differences between Russian and German compositions of this period lies precisely in the concept of development. In the German music we noticed an emphasis on what we called "organic growth": The manipulation of a motivic germ to create passages of varying structural functions, climax, dissolution, and so forth. In Russian music, melodies tend to remain intact. Development then consists of exploiting a variety of coloristic and textural possibilities while melodic and harmonic relationships remain relatively constant within any one section.

On the other hand, the fluid and elusive structure of the melodies themselves, as described by Cui, generates a kind of mobility within stasis. For example, the *Khovantchina* melody, especially the ordering of its various phrases, is difficult to remember. The wandering quality of this melody contributes to the prelude's sense of mobility in spite of the many repetitions. (It would be useful to go back and read again the analysis of this melody in Chapter 3.)

Perhaps most important to the sense of contained mobility of these pieces is their remarkable richness of texture and, even more striking, the use of strange and wonderful instrumental colors. Listen to these works again, and pay particular attention to how the composers change the character of a melody or a chord by altering its instrumentation or its sonorous surroundings. But the emphasis on color and texture in Russian music is not confined to works for large orchestra. In Moussorgsky's *Pictures at an Exhibition* (Example 12.12), which he wrote originally for piano, the sound possibilities of the piano alone are exploited in dramatic ways. Listen to two "pictures" from this work:

Example	Composer, title	Date
12.12	Moussorgsky, *Pictures at an Exhibition,* "Ballet of the Unhatched Chicks"; "The Marketplace at Limoges"	1874

How does Moussorgsky make the piano sound at one moment like chicks, at another like a marketplace, and in other "pictures" (not recorded here) like an oxcart, an old witch, and even the great gate of Kiev? This wonderfully imaginative use of the instrument for creating "sound pictures" results from the following:

1. Exploiting the suggestiveness of the various registers of the piano (high and low).
2. Using at times a small, pinched range and at other times a large, sweeping range.
3. Contrasting all kinds of textures—thick chords, unison, thin linear textures.
4. Demanding *legato, staccato,* or sometimes an almost percusssive touch.
5. Using rhythm to imitate, at times almost to mimic, the movement of what is being depicted—for example, two Jews, or children playing.
6. Using particular combinations of tones (chords) that do not operate functionally but, like the rhythm, imitate, evoking images of people or things.

What about the harmonic framework in the works we have been discussing? Interestingly, harmony is tied very closely to color and

Project for the City Gate of Kiev by Victor Hartmann (*Pictures at an Exhibition*)

Bronze Clock in the Form of Baba Yaga's Hut by Victor Hartmann (*Pictures at an Exhibition*)

sonority. For example, a particular combination of tones (a chord) may be used to imitate the sound of an object (bells or chicks) or to evoke an image (dancing adolescents). Or chords may be used as the sonorous framework for a whole section of a piece as in the "Coronation Scene" from *Boris Godunov* (Example 12.13). There, two chords move only by alternating with one another. Each is in itself a familiar combination of tones, but juxtaposed they create a particular ambience that neither implies a particular tonal center nor creates harmonic direction or even tonal ambiguity. Harmonically the passage is static, animated only rhythmically and texturally. In the "Dance of the Adolescents" from *Le Sacre du printemps* (Example 12.14), a particular sonority is also used to create a sonorous framework that contains rhythmic, textural, and motivic motion within it. Chords, then, become a part of the dimension of color. They are sensuous entities to be embellished and enjoyed rather than elements in a network of interrelated tonal functions.

Compare the use of harmony in these works with its use in works where functional harmony is still operative, such as Strauss's *Elektra* or even Schoenberg's *Chamber Symphony*. The situations are almost opposite. In the German works, we still hear directed motion created by the framework of tonality; harmonic tension, resolution, and goals are at least implied if not always immediately achieved.

Listen once more, now, to the two Russian works written at either end of our half century of music. As you listen, make your own list of the stylistic traits they share, as well as those that distinguish the later work from the earlier one.

Example	Composer, title	Date
12.13	Moussorgsky, *Boris Godunov,* "Coronation Scene," excerpt	1868–1872
12.14	Stravinsky, *Le Sacre du printemps,* "Dance of the Adolescents"	1911–1913

How does your list compare with ours at the beginning of this chapter (p. 381)? Do you understand the two works differently now that you hear them in the context of their Russian compatriots? Does Stravinsky's *Sacre,* written 45 years after Moussorgsky's *Boris,* make more sense to you now that you are somewhat familiar with its evolution and its ancestry in the Russian nationalism that characterized the music of this time? We shall return to these questions at the end of this chapter.

We have attributed the special quality of Russian music in part to the nationalistic loyalties of its composers. But to the folklike melodies and the harmonic and structural characteristics which follow from them must be added a particular kind of originality, stemming perhaps from the fact that all but one of the Mighty Five were amateurs who had had little formal musical training. Moussorgsky in particular was proud of being a self-taught composer. Undoubtedly this was a crucial factor in his own peculiarly original style. All of Moussorgsky's music is in some way motivated by extramusical considerations (he wrote no symphonies, no chamber music, and no sonata forms). Yet how different his music is from that of Mahler, Strauss, or Wagner! The following comments written in a letter to a friend express Moussorgsky's attitude toward academic music and learned musicians:

In one [music school] Z . . and T . ., in their professional, antimusical togas, stuff the heads of their students with various abominations and infect them in advance. The poor pupils see before them not human beings but two fixed pillars to which are nailed some silly scrawls said to contain the laws of music . . . . Being raised to the rank of a doctor of music—*a cobbler in an academic fool's cap*—he [Z . .] is not so childish as to base his opinions and advice on esthetics and musical logic—oh no! He has learned the rules and uses this as a smallpox antitoxin to inoculate against free learning anyone who longs to study art.[19]

Moussorgsky was often criticized for his lack of "technique." Of this he says:

Why do I, *do not tell me,* when I listen to our musical brethren, seldom hear a vital idea, but mostly stuff from a school-room bench—technique and musical ABC's? . . . Maybe I'm afraid of technique, because I'm poor at it? However, there are some who will stand up for me in art. . . .

Leave aside the boundaries of art—I believe in them only very relatively, because *boundaries of art* in the religion of the artist, means *standing still* . . . . I've taken up the cross and with lifted head, bravely and happily, I shall go forth against *all sorts of things,* towards bright, strong and righteous aims, towards a genuine art that loves man, lives his joys, his grief and his sufferings.[20]

Finally here is what Debussy writes about Moussorgsky:

He is unique and will remain so because his art is spontaneous and free from arid formulas. Never has a more refined sensibility been conveyed by such simple means; it is like the art of an enquiring savage discovering music step by step through his emotions. Nor is there ever a question of any particular form; at all events the form is so varied that by no possibility whatsoever can it be related to any established, one might say official, form since it depends on and is made up of successive, minute touches mysteriously linked together by means of an instinctive clairvoyance.[21]

France: Debussy (1862–1918) and Ravel (1875–1937)

These comments provide a convenient link to the French music of this period. Debussy's admiration and sympathy for Moussorgsky's music is reflected in his own music—perhaps not so much by "influence"

---

[19] Letter to Mili Balakirev, written April 28, 1862, in the village of Volok; in Leyda and Bertensson, p. 44.

[20] Letter to Vladimir Stasov, written July 13, 1872, in Petrograd; in Leyda and Bertensson, pp. 192–194.

[21] Claude Debussy, *Monsieur Croche the Dilettante Hater* (London: N. Douglas, 1927), p. 35.

(although he knew the Russian's music well) as by "elective affinity." The importance given to color and texture and the immersion in direct, sensuous sound relationships, together with the organizing processes we have observed, identify the fundamental similarity between Russian and French music. Let us consider this similarity, as well as the differences between the two bodies of music more carefully now.

Only some of the works discussed here are included on your records. Those not recorded are commonly available in music libraries, and excerpts from some you have heard before. The complete Debussy *Prélude, "Brouillards"* ("Fog") is included on the records (Example 12.15). These works span the period from Debussy's *Rondes de printemps* (1905–1909) to Ravel's orchestration of Moussorgsky's *Pictures at an Exhibition* (1922).

Debussy, *Rondes de printemps,* 1905–1909 (Example 1.7)

Debussy, *Images,* "*Iberia*"; "*Parfums de la nuit*," 1905–1908 (Example 12.10)

*Ravel, *Rapsodie espagnole,* "*Prélude à la nuit*," 1907–1908

Ravel, Orchestration of Moussorgsky's *Pictures at an Exhibition,* 1922 (Example 1.16)

Example	Composer, title	Date
12.15	Debussy, *Préludes,* Book II, no. 1, "*Brouillards*" ("Fog")	1910–1913

As in the Russian works, we hear again music characterized by a kind of animated, ebullient stasis. The means of animation, however, are different, more subtle, and perhaps more refined—perfume rather than a coronation or a great gate. In "*Parfums de la nuit*" from *Images* (Example 12.10) the stasis is quite literal—a single note is sustained while melodic fragments hover above and below it. We relish the sound of each instrument (often a solo woodwind) as it appears and disappears. The melodic fragments are wispy (in contrast to the folk melodies of Russian music), defined neither by clear tonal relationships nor by phrase structure. Rhythmically, events take place extremely slowly. Pulse seems nonexistent, and we are encouraged to surround ourselves with the sonorities without concern for their extension in time. Contrast and movement are created by the introduction of new sounds (new chords, a thicker or more active texture, different instruments). But instead of a juxtaposition of events as in Russian music, there is a merging of one sound into the next.

Harmonically, this music does not obstruct or negate tonality (as does the music of Wagner and Schoenberg). Instead, it seems to absorb it, replacing it with a chordal sonority which is often repeated up or down a series of whole steps. Unlike Moussorgsky's, Debussy's chordal sonorities are sometimes nontriadic combinations of pitches. Thus they are less defined—more amorphous.

In Ravel's *Rapsodie espagnole,* "*Prélude à la nuit,*" a single *melodic* motive generates the sense of stasis. The varieties of sounds it acquires seem endless. The varieties of *surroundings* it assumes give the listener full opportunity to revel in sensory delight. It is like watching the reflection of a branch in rippling water. It never moves but is moving all the time; motion is contained within the limits of its confining shape.

In his piano prelude, appropriately titled "Fog," we hear Debussy exploiting the sonorous qualities of a single instrument. Like Moussorgsky in *Pictures at an Exhibition,* Debussy seems able to work magic in creating unique piano sounds. While his purposes are also pictorial, Debussy makes more of sounds for their own sake; their associations are somehow more private.

Claude Debussy

The pianist Paul Jacobs says this about the piece:

Edward T. Cone, in his book *Musical Form and Musical Performance,* cites this prelude as a work without a "frame," a work whose very outlines are blurred (*brouillés*). Even the tonality is murky: although the left hand plays a seemingly diatonic melody in chords on the white keys, the right hand "fogs" the tonal center by filling in the other chromatic pitches on the black keys. Through the haze one can barely perceive the wisps of melody.[22]

In all these works we have little feeling of directed motion. Instead of a German walking tour punctuated by arrival at certain destinations, our experience is one of sitting quietly, deeply absorbing a single vista. Debussy wrote of his *Images:*

The music of this piece has this about it: it is elusive, and consequently cannot be handled like a robust symphony which walks on all fours (sometimes on threes, but walks nevertheless).

   Besides, I am more and more convinced that music is not, in essence, a thing which can be cast into a traditional and fixed form. It is made up of colors and rhythms.[23]

Finally, listen to Ravel's orchestration of Moussorgsky's *Pictures at an Exhibition.* (The work is the result of a fascinating intertwining of personalities and media. An exhibition of watercolors and drawings of architecture by Victor Hartmann, Moussorgsky's friend [see pictures, p. 404], inspired a set of pieces for the piano; Ravel, inspired in turn by these pieces, composed an orchestral version.)

   As you listen to it, consider why Ravel was drawn to the possibilities of orchestrating this work. In what ways does the orchestration change the effect? Do you think Ravel has improved it? Which piece do you like better? Which more effectively evokes the intended images? Does Ravel's style intrude on Moussorgsky's?

   *Ravel, String Quartet in F Major, 1902–1903, second movement

Example	Composer, title	Date
12.16	Debussy, *Quartet in G Minor,* second movement	1893

[22] Paul Jacobs, record jacket notes for Debussy, *Preludes for Piano, Books I and II,* performed by Paul Jacobs (Nonesuch 7303).
[23] Letter to Jacques Durand, September 3, 1907; quoted in Morgenstern, p. 329.

Debussy and Ravel each wrote one string quartet. Both are rather early works, Debussy's dating from his thirty-first year. It is difficult to describe Debussy's *Quartet in G Minor* adequately in the terms we have been using. Listen to the second movement (Example 12.16), for example, marked scherzo (*assez vif et bien rythmé*). Its relationship to traditional scherzos is tenuous though revealing. In form the movement can be described as ABA', but this fact seems unimportant in the light of its unique inner processes.

Harmonically the movement could again be described as static—one bass note is maintained throughout a large part of the A section. Yet it seems inappropriate to describe the harmony negatively as "without motion." In the context of tonal harmony the implications of the term *static* (as used in Demonstration 5.1) are quite different; harmony plays a different role in that style, where syntax is largely defined or generated by harmonic functions.

Listening to this movement, we perceive the bass note as a *dynamic* element: A constant against which all the events of the piece take place but which (like any background) is itself affected by them. For example, there is a passage near the middle of the A section (*b* in the *a b + a'* structure within A) in which the bass note is not played. This is a moment of tension—of climax; resolution occurs with the return of the bass note. Another point of tension occurs at the end of A, when the cello, carrier of the constant, takes up the predominant melody and goes on to form a transition to the B section.

Equally "static" is the melody: A single two-measure figure which is also repeated almost continuously throughout the A section. But like the bass, it is not heard as unchanging. It does, in fact, move about. In the beginning it is played by the viola. The violin takes it up in the second half (*a'*), and finally it is given to the cello. But more important, its surroundings vary so much that it is only after listening analytically that we realize it remains literally unchanged for long stretches.

Coming now to the surface of the Debussy work, we focus on what is more immediately perceived—the sparkling *pizzicato* upper strings. Moving through a large range, they enliven the piece by creating marvelous rhythmic shifts from the prevailing three-beat to two-beat groups, teasing the regularity of the repeated motive, the beat, and the phrase grouping. Toward the middle (*b*) of the first section, the *pizzicato* "component" takes over. The sparkling surface seems to absorb the rest at this moment of tension. The two constants (bass note and motive) cease, and we are left suspended, to return to an altered norm in which the sound fabric is tipped over—the motive appearing on top, the *pizzicato* underneath.

To describe this as *a b + a'* is certainly correct, but does this place the work in the tradition of eighteenth- and nineteenth-century German composition? Does it significantly contribute to an understanding of its style? How does form function in this work? This last question is a crucial one in our consideration of stylistic character.

What of the B section, whose themes (related to A) are elusive enough to make it difficult to say whether they are one or several? What of the passages which we hear as "waiting," but not so much because of their dominant harmonic implications as because of their thinner texture and relative cessation of activity? What *does* articulate structure in this work? What means does Debussy use to create stability, tension, and climax? Is there a sense of directed motion?

These are some of the questions that must be answered if we are to define or describe the style of this music. Debussy warned against this kind of analysis, however, in a letter to a musician who had tried to describe his harmonic style:

> Think of all the inexpert hands that will utilize your study without discrimination, for the sole purpose of annihilating those charming butterflies which are already somewhat crumpled by your analysis.[24]

Listen now to the Ravel quartet (not recorded here) written ten years later. Compare the second movement (marked, similarly to Debussy's *assez vif—très rythmé*) with that in Debussy's quartet. Notice that the ABA' structure is much more clearly articulated. The B section is much slower and has a distinctly contrasting character. The return of A is prepared for by a long passage where the motives of A appear in fragmentary fashion, finally emerging full-blown in the return (A'). The return here is closer to the original A section than it is in the Debussy movement.

Harmonically Ravel depends more on functional chord relationships. We hear, for example, clear tonic-dominant and tonic-subdominant progressions. The melodies are more diatonic (although they have modal aspects, like the lowered seventh degree in the otherwise A-minor opening melody). There is a stronger sense of pulse and a clearer articulation of the phrase rhythm in Ravel's work. The

---

[24] Letter to René Lenormand; quoted in Austin, p. 19.

feeling of static structure is not a pervasive one. While color and texture are certainly a source of variety and contrast, they seem to reinforce the other structural elements rather than to be themselves the means of structural articulation.

For all these reasons Ravel is often said to be more in the "Classical tradition" than Debussy. But what does this mean in the light of Ravel's use of that characteristic French shimmer, his cascading of sounds and rhythms in the final movement of the quartet, his own way of "teasing" functional harmony, which makes that harmonic framework really quite different from what it is in the hands of Brahms or Strauss?

Opera: Wagner and Debussy

Let us leave these questions and turn for a moment first to opera and then to another group of pieces which unites Russian and French forces, namely, music of the ballet.

Debussy wrote one opera, *Pelléas and Mélisande,* using Maeterlinck's symbolist play as his literary source (Example 12.18). Like *Tristan and Isolde,* this is essentially a love story, but at no point does it approach

Wagner's *Tristan und Isolde* (Photograph taken at first performance, 1865)

A scene from the New York City Opera production of *Pelléas et Mélisande*
(Photo by Beth Bergman)

the heavy, hyperemotional atmosphere characteristic of Wagner's opera
(Example 12.17). Even at the moment of greatest emotional intensity—
when Pelléas and Mélisande finally declare their love for one another—
the atmosphere is one of understatement, of a tender, quiet, make-
believe world of unreal children. Compare this scene, which you heard
in Chapter 7 and return to briefly here, with an excerpt from the
lengthy and passionate scene in which Tristan and Isolde first meet as
lovers (they still have two more hours to consummate their love).[25]

Example	Composer, title	Date
12.17	Wagner, *Tristan and Isolde,* Act II, scene 2	1857–1859
12.18	Debussy, *Pelléas and Mélisande,* Act IV, scene 4	1902

[25] It is also interesting to compare these two musical expressions of love with the
expressions of *unrequited* love in the songs by Machaut and Schubert that you heard
earlier. The comparisons among all four works make vividly clear the important influence of cultural context not only on a composer's musical style but also on the
attitudes and feelings associated with romantic love.

These two moments seem to epitomize the differences between German and French styles during the half century of music with which we have been concerned here. They differ in nearly every dimension that you have studied—melody, harmony, rhythm, texture, orchestration, and expressive quality.

As you listen, notice, for example, the difference in the relationship between the voices and the orchestra. In the Debussy opera the orchestra rarely impinges on the vocal line. With the Wagner work, in stark contrast, we hear both singers, at the extremes of the range and volume of their voices, matched in both dimensions by the orchestra.

In *Pelléas,* Debussy's orchestra is again often static, sustaining one sonority while the voice hovers above it in recitativelike song. Once more, in contrast, we hear in this moment from *Tristan,* Wagner's characteristic motives moving sequentially and continually toward ever increasing climaxes. Active texture is combined with highly chromatic harmony, still dependent on tonal functions for its sense of directed tension, but tension that gains in intensity as Wagner withholds or delays implicit harmonic goals. We feel little sense of this directed tension, avoided cadences, or ambiguous chromaticism in Debussy's music. Instead, tension is created coloristically—by instrumentation, range, contrasts in density of texture, increase in rhythmic motion. Notice particularly the beautiful moment when Pelléas says, "Je t'aime," and Mélisande answers, after a breath of silence, "Je t'aime aussi," on one unaccompanied note. We are gently led into a world that seems ephemeral, refined, dreamy, and sensuous. How different from Wagner's tempestuous love scene.

And yet, if you place these two moments into the context of, say, the span of Western music from Perotin to Babbitt, the differences in style seem to blur: both are clearly identifiable as late-nineteenth, early-twentieth-century works. When viewed from the limited perspective of a brief half century of music, stylistic differences stand out as if magnified; placed in the broader context of some 700 years of music, these differences in style become, instead, similarities. Listen once more to these two excerpts, keeping in mind this broader perspective. What are the similarities that mark them both as belonging to roughly the same time in music history?

Ballet: Stravinsky (1882–1971)

Turning finally to the ballet, we come once again to Stravinsky, in whom our rather rapid sweeps through Russia and France converge. Stravinsky's three early ballets were commissioned by Sergei Diaghilev, whose Ballets Russes had its first season in Paris in 1909. This company was a vital force in Parisian artistic life for 20 years. Diaghilev, the director, Fokine, his choreographer, and Nijinsky, his principal male dancer, all played a part in the inception and realization of Stravinsky's early ballets. (Diaghilev also commissioned Ravel's *Daphnis and Chloé,* as well as other works by Debussy, Stravinsky, Satie, and Prokofiev.)

Firebird Suite, Introduction, "Dance of King Kastchei," finale, 1909–1910 (Example 1.10)
Petrouchka, Part I, Part III, 1910–1911 (Examples 2.27, 4.7)
Le Sacre du printemps, Introduction, "Dance of the Adolescents," 1913 (Examples 1.1, 4.23, 12.14)

These three ballets are all based on Russian folklore. Listen carefully to the excerpts listed above (some of which you have heard before), noting particularly the changes in style between the earlier and the later works, the reflections of earlier Russian composers (Stravinsky had studied with Rimsky-Korsakov), and the effect of Stravinsky's wider international musical experiences.

Stravinsky wrote *Firebird* in Paris, working closely with Fokine. He gave Fokine the music bit by bit as he wrote it and attended all the rehearsals of the company. The effect of this close association is hard to estimate, but surely the very special character of the work derives in some measure from the immediacy and excitement of performance and from the interactions between choreographer, dancers, and composer.

In *Firebird* and *Petrouchka* we hear the beginnings of the style that came to fruition in *Le Sacre du printemps.* In all three works we hear the sectionalism of the earlier Russian composers, the use of folk song, the strong pulse, and the coloristic use of instruments to activate the "static" harmony. But these characteristics are already becoming transformed in *Firebird.* There is greater variety within the sections, made possible by the materials themselves. The pulse cannot be taken for granted. It is alive, shifting, grouped, and regrouped. Rhythmic patterns are established only to be extended or broken apart, fragmented and put back together; and the folklike melodic fragments are treated similarly.

The orchestra is larger and is used with all the imagination and skill of the earlier Russian and French composers. But Stravinsky adds new sounds (instruments played in unusual ways), along with a new kind of "layered" effect in which instrumental colors are heard inter-

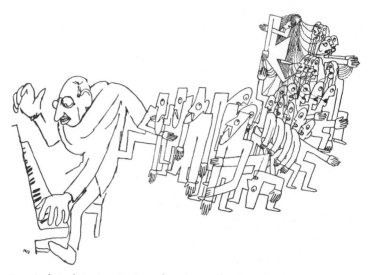

Stravinsky rehearsing *Le Sacre du printemps* by Jean Cocteau
(Permission S.P.A.D.E.M. 1974 by French Reproduction Rights,
Inc.)

twining with one another to create a more complex texture. Harmonically, sections are static, yet tonal implications remain. For instance, we hear a repeated bass figure (**ostinato**) composed of fifths, and also a relatively tonal melody from which the harmonic sonority seems to derive (the opening of Kastchei's dance, for example).

In *Petrouchka* the *ostinato* becomes more important as an organizing, stabilizing factor in an atmosphere in which sonorities have become more complex (less triadic), and the texture thicker and more active. Notice how the *ostinato* functions in the opening of Part I. It is not simply a bass figure, but rather a kind of bubbling sound in which it is difficult to pick out individual instruments or even specific durations. It forms an animated color over which melodic fragments, solo instruments, and rhythms are superimposed like flashes. Often stopping abruptly as if used up, one *ostinato* yields to another, creating strong contrast and sectional articulation. How does Stravinsky's use of a "background" differ from Debussy's in his quartet or in *Iberia*? Why is an *ostinato* rare in the works of Schoenberg?

Melodic repetition also has a new life in *Petrouchka* because the recurrence of a motive is unpredictable and rarely literal. Stravinsky constantly alters the length of the melodic fragment. The static quality of repetition is both there and not there at the same time. The first

Harlequin by Pablo Picasso

bubbling *ostinato* stops suddenly, yielding to a chordal texture—a kind of congealing of the whole sonority—which then becomes the norm to be unpredictably manipulated. One thinks of the painter Matisse and his myriad textures, juxtaposed to form a design in which the viewer continuously discovers new relationships.

In *Le Sacre du printemps* Stravinsky created a work equaled in importance only by *Pierrot lunaire* as a disruption of the musical status quo. The ballet generated an equally new but quite different world of musical possibility. Indeed, the works symbolize the two approaches to music which, in the years that followed, often divided composers into opposing camps. Stravinsky himself was more understanding and appreciative of *Pierrot lunaire* than many of his followers:

> Whatever opinion one may hold about the music of Arnold Schoenberg (to take as an example a composer evolving along lines essentially different from mine, both aesthetically and technically), whose works have frequently given rise to violent reactions or ironic smiles—it is impossible for a self-respecting mind equipped with genuine musical culture not to feel that the composer of *Pierrot lunaire* is fully aware of what he is

doing and that he is not trying to deceive anyone. He adopted the musical system that suited his needs and, within this system, he is perfectly consistent with himself, perfectly coherent.[26]

Yet at the same time Stravinsky viewed the piece from his own vantage point, in terms of his concern with instrumentation and texture, as these create design:

> The instrumental substance of *Pierrot lunaire* impressed me immensely. And by saying "instrumental" I mean not simply instrumentation of this music but the whole contrapuntal and polyphonic structure of this brilliant instrumental masterpiece.[27]

Why is *Le Sacre* considered a revolutionary work? (This was, incidentally, a reaction Stravinsky did not appreciate—"I confess that I am completely insensitive to the prestige of revolution.") Consider the opening. The bassoon plays alone at the top of its range, sounding to some listeners marvelously new and strange, while sounding to others badly distorted. The melody, based on a Lithuanian folk song, is characteristically repetitive—a small collection of pitches varied by a completely flexible rhythm. As instruments are added, they combine to form sonorities that are no longer triadic but are the result of layers of fragmented melody superimposed—held together and made comprehensible—either by an *ostinato* or by the flashes of repeated melody. Juxtaposition of textures and melodic fragments still characterizes the structural motion. But now the juxtaposition is more abrupt, episodes are shorter, and motives appear, disappear, reappear unpredictably—recognizable but often in new garb.

In the "Dance of the Adolescents" the unique sound is created by Stravinsky's superimposing two functionally unrelated triadic chords. It is as if he had compressed Moussorgsky's juxtaposed chords into one sound which is neither of them. The unifying sonority is all-pervasive here—more so than in Stravinsky's earlier work because the sound itself seizes and haunts the listener. We feel a strong pulse. But the beats are grouped so irregularly (through sudden accents) that they form not a background but an active ingredient in the compositional

---

[26] Igor Stravinsky, *Poetics of Music* (New York: Random House, Vintage Books, 1956), p. 14.

[27] Igor Stravinsky and Robert Craft, *Conversations with Igor Stravinsky* (Garden City, N.Y.: Doubleday, 1959), p. 79.

fabric—a vital force in the effect of earthy sensuousness. Stravinsky said of the work: "I saw in imagination a solemn pagan rite: sage elders, seated in a circle, watching a young girl dance herself to death. They were sacrificing her to propitiate the god of Spring."

While the composer breaks up the sonority in various ways to create, at times, a linear *ostinato,* the sonority seems never to disappear. And to it he adds such a variety of elements that it is small wonder that the piece left its first-night audience reeling—from the flashes of coloristic sound, fragments of folklike tunes, instruments playing at the extremes of their ranges, rhythms clashing and abruptly shifting. Can you imagine the dance itself? Certainly it was far different from the toe dancing, arabesques, and tutus of nineteenth-century ballet.

Pagan rites, the unusual Nijinsky dancing in Paris, while the moonstruck Pierrot sang in Vienna and Berlin! Go back now and listen to *Pierrot lunaire* with its concentration of detail; its thin, polyphonic texture; and its brief, closed, organic forms in which development means evolution of a seminal motive. How different from Stravinsky's static structure, within which melodic fragments and fixed sonority undulate and revolve, but somehow create, in themselves, definition and limits. And how very different in mood!

Lévi-Strauss, an anthropologist writing about the social implications of Schoenberg's "new" music, talks of the changed relationship between composer and listener:

> [Schoenberg's music may] succeed in bridging the traditional gap between listener and composer and—by depriving the former of the possibility of referring unconsciously to a general system—will at the same time oblige him, if he is to understand the music he hears, to reproduce the individual act of creation on his own account. Through the power of an ever new, internal logic, each work will rouse the listener from his state of passivity and make him share in its impulse, so that there will no longer be a difference of kind, but only of degree between inventing music and listening to it.[28]

And Stravinsky, himself, says this of his own creative process:

> The creator's function is to sift the elements he receives from her [imagination or fantasy], for human activity must impose limits upon itself.

---

[28] Claude Lévi-Strauss, *The Raw and the Cooked* (New York: Harper & Row, 1969), p. 26.

The more art is controlled, limited, worked over, the more it is free. . . .
My freedom thus consists in my moving about within the narrow frame
that I have assigned myself for each one of my undertakings. I shall go
even farther: my freedom will be so much the greater and more meaningful the more narrowly I limit my field of action and the more I
surround myself with obstacles. Whatever diminishes constraint diminishes strength. The more constraints one imposes, the more one frees
one's self of the chains that shackle the spirit.[29]

As you stand back now and consider the period from 1859 to
1913—from Wagner and Moussorgsky to Schoenberg and Stravinsky—in the larger context of all the music you have heard in Part
Four, you could view stylistic change in terms of the changing notions
of limits and freedom. In a crucial sense, composers' styles are defined
by the personal and often unconscious limits they impose on possibility
and within which they find the freedom to express what is relevant to
them.

Historically, too, you can watch and listen to the ebb and flow
of this relationship between freedom and limits. Wagner and Moussorgsky, for example, living by and espousing expansive freedom, each
in a different way; Schoenberg and Stravinsky, each searching for his
own limits to contain and at the same time intensify expressiveness.

Think back over the stylistic comparisons you have heard. We
have emphasized throughout that to view a work historically is to
grasp in it the interplay of tradition and innovation: To listen with an
expanded awareness of historical context while at the same time remaining sensitive to the processes through which each work uniquely
unfolds.

ANCILLARY READING

Abraham, Gerald, *A Hundred Years of Music,* 4th ed., London: Duckworth,
1974.
Austin, William A., *Music in the 20th Century,* New York: Norton, 1966.
Boretz, Benjamin, and Cone, Edward T., *Perspectives on Schoenberg and Stravinsky,* New York: Norton, 1972.
Debussy, Claude, *Monsieur Croche the Dilettante Hater,* London: N. Douglas,
1927.
Del Mar, Norman, *Richard Strauss,* 3 vols., Ithaca: Cornell University Press,
1986.

------

[29] Stravinsky, *Poetics of Music,* pp. 66, 68.

Hanslick, E., *The Beautiful in Music,* New York: Da Capo, 1974. A contemporary discussion of the Brahms-Wagner argument, heavily weighted toward Brahms.

Leyda, Jay, and Sergei Bertensson, eds. and trans., *The Musorgsky Reader,* New York: Da Capo, 1970.

Lockspeiser, Edward, *Debussy,* New York: Pellegrini & Cudahy, 1951.

Mahler, Alma, *Gustave Mahler: Memories and Letters,* 3d ed., Mitchell and Martner, Seattle: University of Washington Press, 1968. A rather personal account of the composer's life and work, by his wife.

Mellers, Wilfred, *Man and His Music: Romanticism and the Twentieth Century,* New York: Schocken Books, 1969. A good overview of the period from the mid-nineteenth to the mid-twentieth century; available in paperback.

Newlin, Dika, *Bruckner, Mahler and Schoenberg,* rev. ed., New York: Norton, 1978.

Orenstein, Arbie, *Ravel: Man and Musician,* New York: Columbia University Press, 1975.

Rimsky-Korsakov, N. A., *My Musical Life,* New York: Knopf, 1942.

Schoenberg, Arnold, *Style and Idea,* ed. Leonard Stein, Berkeley: University of California Press, 1985.

Slonimsky, Nicholas, *Music Since 1900,* 4th ed., New York: Scribner, 1971.

Stein, J. M., *Richard Wagner and the Synthesis of the Arts,* Detroit: Wayne University Press, 1960.

Stravinsky, Igor, *Poetics of Music,* New York: Random House (Vintage Books), 1956.

Stravinsky, Igor, and Robert Craft, *Conversations with Igor Stravinsky,* Garden City, N.Y.: Doubleday, 1959.

Stravinsky, Igor, and Robert Craft, *Dialogues and a Diary,* Garden City, N.Y.: Doubleday, 1963.

Stravinsky, Igor, and Robert Craft, *Expositions and Developments,* Garden City, N.Y.: Doubleday, 1962.

Stravinsky, Igor, and Robert Craft, *Memories and Commentaries,* London: Faber, 1960.

Stuckenschmidt, H. H., *Arnold Schoenberg,* trans. E. T. Roberts and H. Searle, New York: Schirmer, 1978. A biography by a close friend of the composer.

Wagner, Richard, *My Life,* trans. A. Gray, New York: Cambridge University Press, 1983.

White, Eric W., *Stravinsky: The Composer and His Works,* 2nd ed., Berkeley: University of California Press, 1980.

CHAPTER 13

Aphrodite, Greek, 2d century B.C.

A Chronological Outline

Head of Woman, Picasso, 20th century A.D.

A T THIS POINT WE SUGGEST you go back and reread the introduction to Part Four: Style and the Historical Context. This will help put into focus the work you have done in Chapters 8 through 12. In this final chapter we give you a skeletal outline of the history of Western music through all the examples cited in the text. We have saved this outline for the last in keeping with the fundamental approach of the book; namely, that your *experience* of music should precede the discussion and acquisition of facts *about* music. To this end, we have put all the examples you have heard thus far (as well as those referred to but not recorded) into their chronological order. In addition, we have provided brief comments on each historical period and suggested some further readings.

As you work your way through this chapter, you have the opportunity to review the music you have studied. While examples were initially grouped with others that shared either common or clearly contrasting compositional features (rhythmic, textural, harmonic, etc.), they were often quite distant in their places and times of composition and even sometimes in their cultural contexts. In this chapter you can reconsider (and, at best, listen once again to) these same examples now grouped in proximity with others composed at roughly the same time and thus sharing common stylistic characteristics. These multiple views of the same works should help you gain a more meaningful sense of the pieces themselves, as well as a richer feel for musical styles and how they evolved.

But from a purely historical perspective, this chapter has certain clear limitations. For example, since the pieces in Chapters 1 through 12 were chosen with other purposes in mind, it follows that they may not be the most "representative" works; that is, they may not give an adequate picture of the period (were this even possible within our limited time and space and without superficiality). To overcome this limitation, we suggest other works you might listen to and additional readings in order to help you get a more complete sense of each period. The detailed discussion of style change during the half century between 1859 and 1913 presented in Chapter 12 might serve as a model for a detailed study of other periods.

Suggested Reading

The general histories of music listed below are all highly recommended for their comprehensive coverage, though, as their titles suggest, they differ somewhat in their approach.

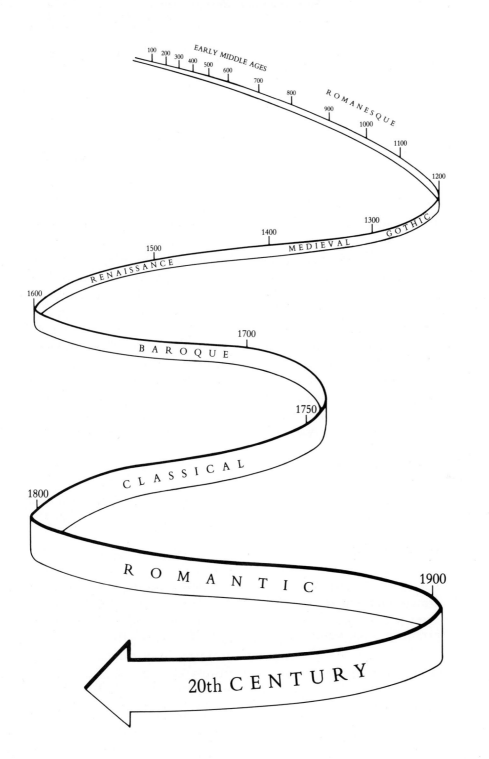

EARLY MIDDLE AGES

100 200 300 400 500 600 700 800 900 1000 1100 1200

ROMANESQUE

1300 1400 1500 1600 1700 1750 1800 1900

GOTHIC

MEDIEVAL

RENAISSANCE

BAROQUE

CLASSICAL

ROMANTIC

20th CENTURY

Crocker, Richard L. *A History of Musical Style.* New York: McGraw-Hill, 1966.

Grout, Donald. *A History of Western Music,* 3d ed. New York: Norton, 1980.

Lang, Paul Henry. *Music in Western Civilization.* New York: Norton, 1941.

Rosentiel, Leonie, ed. *Schirmer History of Music.* New York, 1982.

ANTIQUITY

Though much visual art and literature survives from Classical antiquity, we know very little about the music of ancient Greece and Rome. About a dozen fragments of Greek music have been discovered, but the notation is so sketchy it is difficult to know how the music actually may have sounded. (No Roman examples seem to have survived.) We have learned a certain amount about the music of this time from writings by contemporary theorists like Pythagoras and Ptolemy and philosophers like Plato and Aristotle, as well as from Greek vase paintings and Roman frescoes. For example, the music was primarily monophonic, improvised, vocal, and associated with dramatic performances or dance. The most obvious indebtedness of the West to ancient Greek music is in the mode names (see page 131), adopted by medieval theorists based on their readings of Greek treatises.

Suggested Reading

Sachs, Curt. *The Rise of Music in the Ancient World, East and West.* New York: Norton, 1943.

MEDIEVAL: c. 400 to c. 1400

The Medieval period (from the Latin *Medi* + *aevum*—"middle age") spans the era from the fall of the Roman Empire through the fourteenth century. It is sometimes divided into the Early Middle Ages (400 to 1100) and Later Middle Ages (1100 to 1400), or the Romanesque and Gothic periods. As with ancient Greek and Roman music, there are far fewer extant sources for music history than the surviving sources for medieval art and literature, particularly music from the Early Middle Ages.

Date	Composer, title	Source
unknown	*Veni Creator Spiritus* (plainchant)	2.5
unknown	*Viderunt Omnes* (plainchant)	1.3, 8.2
unknown	*Offertory* (chant from the Christmastide midnight mass)	3.22
c. 1200	Perotin, *Viderunt Omnes* (organum quadruplum)	8.3
c. 1350	Machaut, *Douce dame jolie*	9.1

Of the five pieces presented in earlier chapters, all are sacred but one; three of these sacred works are plainchant, and the fourth (Perotin) is based on a chant excerpt. The chant examples illustrated unaccompanied melody (monophony); in discussing the Perotin piece, we showed how church composers used chant to create a richer, more complex texture (polyphony). As we saw in Chapter 8, plainchant (and its even less extant secular counterpart, the music of the troubadours and *trouvères*) prevailed in the earlier period as polyphonic music began to develop. Parallel with this development, composers emerged from anonymity. Among the more famous were Leonin and Perotin in Paris around the year 1200, and Guillaume de Machaut and Francesco Landini in the fourteenth century.

Machaut was both a poet and musician who was in the service of the highest nobility of Luxembourg and France. His work earned the attention of a number of popes. As you learned in Chapter 9, Machaut's *Douce dame jolie* is representative of the "courtly love" tradition, and, like the chant examples, is monophonic—though the majority of Machaut's music is, in fact, polyphonic. Francesco Landini (c. 1325–1397) was, like Machaut, also a poet as well as a composer. A blind organist, he worked in Florence, Italy, writing mostly pieces called *ballate,* for two or three voices.

Most medieval music (these five examples are no exception) is *modal* (e.g., Dorian, Phrygian—see the Ancillary Reading to Chapter 3) rather than *tonal* (major-minor); one does not feel the strong pull of dominant to tonic movement as in functional harmony (see Chapter 5). Also, most of the music that has come down to us (in manuscript only, of course) is sacred vocal music. Idiomatic instrumental music develops at a later date.

Suggested Listening

Anonymous, Gregorian chant, *The Play of Daniel* (a liturgical drama)

Adam de la Halle, *Le Jeu de Robin et Marion,* c. 1285 (a musical play)

Leonin, *Viderunt Omnes,* c. 1180

Perotin, *Sederunt Principes,* c. 1200

Machaut, Mass and secular works, c. 1350

Landini, secular works, late fourteenth century

Suggested Reading

Hoppin, Richard H. *Medieval Music.* New York: Norton, 1978; accompanied by an *Anthology of Medieval Music.*

Reese, Gustave. *Music in the Middle Ages.* New York: Norton, 1940.

Seay, Albert. *Music in the Medieval World.* New York: Norton, 1965.

RENAISSANCE: c. 1400 to c. 1600

The Renaissance—literally, a "rebirth," and a new era as those at the time saw it—went for its inspiration back past the "Dark Ages" (as they considered the Middle Ages) to the glories of the Classical civilizations of Greece and Rome. At the same time, with the development of humanism, life and culture became increasingly secularized. The Renaissance was a period of great expansion in every area—geographical, economic, scientific, and cultural. The arts flourished at the many courts throughout Europe. Though the impetus for the Renaissance came from Italy, most of the greatest music of the period was the product of Franco-Flemish composers who traveled throughout Europe. The sense of the age as being new and important is well illustrated by the following statement, made in 1477 by the Flemish theorist and composer Johannes Tinctoris: "There does not exist a single piece of music, not composed within the last forty years, that is regarded by the learned as worth hearing."[1]

---

[1] *Liber de Arti Contrapunti,* as quoted in Friedrich Blume, *Renaissance and Baroque Music* (New York: Norton, 1967), p. 15.

Date	Composer, title	Source
?	Anonymous, *Bransle de Poitou*	2.16
1572	Victoria, *O Magnum Mysterium*	8.4
c. 1580	Gabrieli, *Ricercare*	1.26
1592	Victoria, *Missa O Magnum Mysterium,* Sanctus	4.15
1594	Morley, *Ho! Who Comes Here?*	1.36
1599	J. Farmer, *Fair Phyllis*	7.1
c. 1608	Gibbons, *Fantasia a 4*	Ch. 1 AM[2]
c. 1608	Gibbons, *Fantasia a 2*	1.23
1611	Gesualdo, *Dolcissima mia vita*	5.4

All but three of the Renaissance excerpts listed here served earlier to illustrate either aspects of texture (active) or continuous organization. And as you have learned, polyphony (active texture) tends to generate continuous organization. Our nine examples hardly give a complete picture of Renaissance music: all are from the High or Late Renaissance, none is from the fifteenth century, two are by Gibbons, and three are from the early seventeenth century (the late Renaissance in Elizabethan England). In the discussion of the Victoria motet in Chapter 8, your attention was directed to the elegant polyphony, permeated by imitation and with the combining of parts "to form pleasing and expressive chordal entities." These aspects of texture and continuous organization apply to all these pieces, with individual differences. The more chromatic, almost acerbic harmony of the Gesualdo madrigal, conveying the text of "love or death," may be considered as a very late example of Renaissance polyphony, what some consider "mannerist" in style.

In addition, five of the nine pieces are performed *a cappella,* that is, by voices alone. On occasion, instruments might also have been played along with the vocal parts, and, sometimes, pieces which were originally vocal were performed only by instruments. Even in pieces that are clearly nonvocal, composers did not specify instrumentation. (Recall also our discussion of the earlier song by Machaut.) The Gabrieli *Ricercare,* also without specific instrumentation, is performed in the recorded example on modern brass instruments; the *Bransle de Poitou*

---

[2] "AM" refers to Additional Materials. "Ch. 1 AM" indicates that the excerpt originally was given in the Additional Materials section of Chapter 1. This form of abbreviation is used throughout this chapter.

(2.16) and the Gibbons pieces, on the other hand, are played by recorders or viols, common instruments in the Renaissance. To gain a better sense of the rich diversity of this period, listen to some works from the following list.

Suggested Listening

> Dunstable, *Veni Sancte Spiritus, O rosa bella*
> Dufay, secular works, *Missa Se le face ay pale*
> Ockeghem, secular works, *Missa Prolationum, Missa Fors seulement*
> Obrecht, *Parce Domine* (motet), *Missa Fortuna desperata*
> Isaac, *Innsbruck ich muss dich lassen, Quis dabit capiti meo aquam*
> Josquin des Prez, secular works, *Missa Pange lingua,* motets
> Praetorius, dances from *Terpsichore*
> Willaert, madrigals, instrumental *ricercare*
> Palestrina, *Missa Papae Marcelli, Stabat Mater* (motet)
> Lassus, secular works, *Missa Puisque j'ay perdu, Tristis est anima mea* (motet)
> Madrigals of Gesualdo, Marenzio, Monteverdi, Morley, Weelkes, and Wilbye
> Instrumental pieces, including variations, for lute, organ, and virginals
> Byrd, motets

Suggested Reading

> Blume, Friedrich. *Renaissance and Baroque Music.* New York: Norton, 1967.
> Brown, Howard M. *Music in the Renaissance.* Englewood Cliffs, N.J.: Prentice-Hall, 1976.
> Reese, Gustave. *Music in the Renaissance.* New York: Norton, 1959. An exhaustive, scholarly study of the period; almost more of a bibliographical reference work than a readable survey of Renaissance music.
> Strunk, Oliver. *Source Readings in Music History.* New York: Norton, 1950, pp. 193–359.

BAROQUE: c. 1600 to c. 1750

The Baroque period may be said to extend from about the beginning of the seventeenth century until the death of Johann Sebastian Bach in 1750. As with all eras, the beginning and ending dates are conveniences rather than precise moments of historical change. Aspects of the new Baroque style began to emerge before 1600, as was pointed out in the discussion of Victoria's *O Magnum Mysterium* composed in 1572. At the other end of the period younger composers began to move away from the Baroque style during Bach's lifetime; in fact, to the extent that he was known beyond his own local region, he was considered as a rather old-fashioned composer. Also, within this century and a half—the period from Monteverdi through Bach—there were so many significant changes and developments that historians have some difficulty defining the period as one era.

The examples from the Baroque period you have heard previously are, once more, hardly a representative sample. About half are by a single, late Baroque composer, Johann Sebastian Bach (1685–1750), and thus the generalizations we can make will apply primarily to late-Baroque music. For a fuller appreciation of Baroque style, listen to works by the seventeenth- and eighteenth-century composers cited in Suggested Listening.

As can be seen in the list of excerpts that follows, most of the Baroque examples that you have heard illustrated varieties of texture (Chapter 1) and aspects of continuous organization (Chapters 3, 4, and 7). Indeed, a description of late Baroque music would focus on these musical dimensions. Many of the examples illustrate late Baroque polyphony, in which the independence of all the parts that characterizes music of earlier periods yielded somewhat to a polarity between the outer voices. The lowest part (the **basso continuo,** played by a bass instrument and a keyboard instrument playing chords) was combined contrapuntally with the top part within the context of functional harmony, which was now clearly established.

Bach, from autograph score of *Clavierbüchlein vor Wilhelm Friedemann Bach,* 1720

Date	Composer, title	Source
1686	Lully, *Armide*, overture	Ch. 1 AM
1689	Purcell, *Dido and Aeneas*, "Dido's Lament"	Ch. 4 AM
1690	Jacchini, *Sonata with Two Trumpets*	2.17
c. 1712	Vivaldi, *Concerto Grosso*, Op. 3, no. 11	1.32
c. 1712	Vivaldi, *Concerto Grosso*, Op. 3, no. 6	3.1
c. 1712	Vivaldi, *Concerto Grosso*, Op. 3, no. 7	4.6
1714	Bach, *Cantata 61*	10.1
c. 1715	Bach, *Cantata 31*	1.38, 2.19
1720	Bach, *Partita 2 for Unaccompanied Violin*	1.13, 3.15
c. 1720	Bach, *Concerto in E Major for Violin and Orchestra*	4.3
c. 1721	Bach, *Brandenberg Concerto 5*	5.10, Ch. 3 AM
1722	Bach, *Well-Tempered Clavier*, Book I, prelude no. 2 in C minor, fugue no. 24 in B minor, fugue no. 3 in C-sharp major	4.2, 5.16, Ch. 3 AM, 7.6
1723	Bach, *Two-Part Invention in F Major*, no. 8	4.16
c. 1723	Bach, *St. John Passion*	1.28, 1.41
1724	Rameau, *Suite in E*	4.17
1725	Vivaldi, *The Four Seasons*	7.2
1729	Bach, *St. Matthew Passion*	1.18, 3.23
1735–1740	Bach, *Concerto in D Minor for Harpsichord and Orchestra*	1.2, 1.15, Ch. 2 AM
1739	Handel, *Concerto Grosso*, Op. 6, no. 2	1.31, Ch. 3 AM
1740	Telemann, *Trio Sonata in D Minor*	2.18, 7.8
c. 1740	Bach, *Suite in B Minor*	1.11, 5.31
1742	Handel, *Messiah*	7.7

The first movement of Bach's *Cantata 61* (Example 10.1) highlighted a discussion of "sacred music and dramatic expression." While the cantata is clearly representative of late Baroque style, you have also heard how Bach, looking back over several centuries, integrated other musical styles into his own; that is, he used a Lutheran chorale melody from the sixteenth century (which in turn came out of medieval plainchant), as well as aspects of the seventeenth-century French overture.

The Bach two-part invention (1723, Example 4.16) illustrated continuous organization—the polyphonic interrelationship of the two parts generating a nonperiodic structure in which caesuras (and "predictable" phrase lengths) occurred infrequently. This kind of "spinning out" or unraveling of the rhythmic and melodic movement can be heard in most of the pieces listed on p. 432. The effect of continuous unraveling is heightened by the prominent use of sequence, which functions rhythmically, melodically, and harmonically in building up the structure. One also feels a very strong pulse, but one which is not always grouped into higher-level metrical units.

You also may have noticed how many instrumental works there were among the excerpts—many more than in the earlier periods. In the Baroque period instrumental music developed at a rapid pace. In fact, many of the instrumental genres still in existence today (such as the sonata, concerto, and overture) originated then. Toward the end of the seventeenth century, major-minor tonality became established, and it enabled composers to create more extended structures without relying on a text. This development helped instrumental music to flourish. Within this new harmonic framework chromaticism was used as a basis for harmonic contrast and, with it, a means for heightened expression.

Suggested Listening

J. S. Bach, *Cantata 78,* "Jesu der du meine Seele"; *B Minor Mass; Brandenburg Concerto 5; English Suite No. 3; Toccata and Fugue in D Minor; Violin Concerto 2 in E Major*
Carissimi, *Jephtha* (oratorio)
Corelli, *Concerto Grosso,* Op. 6, no. 8 ("Christmas Concerto")
F. Couperin, *Suites* for harpsichord
Frescobaldi, *Toccatas* for organ
Handel, *Julius Caesar* (opera); *Messiah* (oratorio); *Concerto,* Op. 6, no. 12
Lully, *Alceste* (opera)
Monteverdi, *Orfeo* (opera)
Purcell, *Dido and Aeneas* (opera)
Rameau, *Les Indes Galantes* (opera-ballet); *Castor et Pollux*
D. Scarlatti, *Sonatas* for harpsichord

Suggested Reading

Bukofzer, Manfred. *Music in the Baroque Era.* New York: Norton, 1947.
Grout, Donald. *A Short History of Opera.* 2d ed. New York: Columbia University Press, 1965, pp. 1–215.

Milner, A. *The Musical Esthetic of the Baroque.* Cambridge: Oxford University Press, 1960.

Newman, William S. *The Sonata in the Baroque Era.* 4th ed. New York: Norton, 1983.

Palisca, Claude, V. *Baroque Music.* 2d ed. Englewood Cliffs, N.J.: Prentice-Hall, 1981.

Strunk, Oliver. *Source Readings in Music History.* New York: Norton, 1950, pp. 363–615.

CLASSICAL: c. 1750 to c. 1827

As with all periods, the dates defining the Classical period are almost impossible to fix. The era is generally marked off by the dates of the deaths of two composers: Bach in 1750 at one end and Beethoven in 1827 at the other. Furthermore, the very term *classical* is used in many different, and sometimes conflicting ways. Art historians, for example, refer to the art of fifth-century B.C. Greece as "Classical." Looked at another way, aspects of the Classical style in music roughly parallel styles called Neoclassical in other arts. These once again (as in the Renaissance, for instance) were inspired by the art works of ancient Greece and Rome. To some, Classical style in the arts generally is characterized by the predominance of form over content, reason over emotion, manner over matter. Music, however, transcended these formal restrictions through the works of three great composers, Haydn, Mozart, and Beethoven, all born within a 40-year period. In the works of these three composers the more typical characteristics of the style are so fully integrated and expanded as to create music of intense personal expressiveness and meaning.

Date	Composer, title	Source
c. 1761	Haydn, *Symphony 8*	1.5, Ch. 1 AM, Ch. 5 AM
1781–1783	Mozart, *Sonata for Piano in A,* K. 331	3.5, 5.22, 5.23
1781–1782	Mozart, *Variations on "Ah, vous dirai-je, maman,"* K. 265	4.13
1781–1783	Mozart, *Sonata for Piano in F,* K. 332	Ch. 4 AM
1782	Mozart, *Quartet in G Major,* K. 387	2.20, 6.14
1782	Mozart, *Serenade in C Minor,* K. 388	5.46
1783	Mozart, *Duo for Violin and Viola,* K. 424	1.24
1783	Mozart, *Concerto for Horn and Orchestra, no. 2,* K. 417	4.1

Date	Composer, title	Source
1787	Haydn, *Symphony 88*	2.1
1787	Mozart, *Eine kleine Nachtmusik,* K. 525	Ch. 3 AM, 4.10, 6.1
1787	Mozart, *Don Giovanni*	3.20
1788	Mozart, *Symphony 39,* K. 543	Ch. 3 AM
1788	Mozart, *Symphony 40,* K. 550	6.7–6.10, 6.19, 6.20, Ch. 6 AM
1790	Haydn, *Trio in G,* "Rondo all' Ongarese"	4.18
1791	Mozart, *The Magic Flute*	3.13, Ch. 5 AM
1791	Haydn, *Symphony 96*	4.5, 6.23, 6.24
1791	Mozart, *German Dance,* K. 605, no. 1	Ch. 4 AM
1792	Haydn, *Symphony 97*	Ch. 6 AM
1793	Haydn, *Symphony 99*	1.29, 6.2, Ch. 3 AM
1794	Haydn, *Symphony 100*	5.33
1795	Haydn, *Symphony 104*	3.8, 5.28
1796	Haydn, *Concerto for Trumpet and Orchestra*	1.21
1797	Haydn, *String Quartet,* Op. 76, no. 5	2.23
1798	Beethoven, *Trio,* Op. 11	Ch. 1 AM
1799	Beethoven, *Quartet,* Op. 18, no. 1	6.3, 6.11–6.13, 6.15, 6.18, 6.21, 6.22
1800	Beethoven, *Septet,* Op. 20	5.29
1801	Haydn, *The Seasons*	1.42, 7.3
1802	Beethoven, *Sonata for Violin and Piano,* Op. 30, no. 2	6.17
1803	Beethoven, *Symphony 3,* Op. 55	1.43, 5.9, Ch. 1 AM
1804	Beethoven, *Variations on "God Save the King"*	2.21
1806	Beethoven, *String Quartet,* Op. 59, no. 3	1.33
1806	Beethoven, *Symphony 4,* Op. 60	Ch. 6 AM
1806	Beethoven, *Violin Concerto,* Op. 61	5.24
1808	Beethoven, *Sonata for Cello and Piano,* Op. 69	2.22
1808	Beethoven, *Symphony 5,* Op. 67	3.9, Ch. 3 AM
1811–1812	Beethoven, *Symphony 7,* Op. 92	7.9
1824	Beethoven, *Symphony 9,* Op. 125	1.9, Ch. 2 AM
1825–1826	Beethoven, *String Quartet,* Op. 133 ("*Grosse Fuge*")	5.17
1826	Beethoven, *String Quartet,* Op. 131	Ch. 3 AM

A glance at the long list of Classical period pieces shows that the examples occur in almost every Demonstration and Exercise. They reveal the great diversity of the style—diversity in almost every dimension of music. In a sense, this variety—this freedom—demands the containment of the forms as we have found in Classical period music; but at the same time the wealth of possibilities makes these more rigorous structures come alive as process. Recall, for example, how our explanations of fundamental musical procedures, as well as of sectional and continuous organization, were necessary to a full appreciation of sonata form in Chapter 6.

There are several other reasons why the music of the Classical period is so well represented in the text:

1. Music of this period, sometimes called the "common practice" period, is the music with which we are most familiar. Just as it makes up the largest collection of examples here, it also constitutes the mainstay of current concert programming.
2. The compositional means that generate coherence in Classical period music continue with us as underlying principles in much of the contemporary popular and folk music we hear everyday, for example, the functional harmony of tonality, rhythm organized in metric hierarchies, clear and balanced phrase structure, inactive rather than active textures. Thus, while surface and style may be noticeably different, within them we still take these traditional "means of comprehensibility" as our musical norms—our "model of a sensible tune."

Beethoven, from autograph score of *Sonata for the Pianoforte in E major,* Op. 109, 1820

3. The robustness and clarity of these prototypical compositional means, together with the wealth of possibilities for varying and developing them, make it possible to isolate, describe, and demonstrate the facets of music that contribute to structure and expressiveness in a wide range of musical styles.

4. But all of these reasons also contribute to a paradoxical situation to which we have alluded before: Exactly because we are so comfortable with this "common practice" in all its various manifestations, we may fail to appreciate the unique qualities of a particular work, satisfying ourselves with merely listening to the style it shares with a vast body of other music. It is for this reason that we have gone deeply into a number of Classical period works, helping you to distinguish between what Schoenberg calls "style and idea," where "style" refers to generalizable features, and "idea" refers to the unique unfolding of musical material in a particular piece.

Moving back now to examples in the book, in Chapter 1 we discussed aspects of the Classical orchestra and its function in articulating musical events. Then in Chapter 3, a Mozart aria (1787, Example 3.20) illustrated balanced, clear phrase structure, and a Haydn symphony movement (1795, Example 3.8) aspects of motivic transformation; in Chapter 4 a Mozart minuet (1787, Example 4.10) served as a model of sectional organization. The discussion of functional harmony (the foundation on which nearly all aspects of the style rest) also drew numerous examples from the Classical period.

Demonstration 6.1 set forth the notion of listening in terms of a structural norm—in this case a schema derived from the Classical minuet. Perhaps the fundamental tenet of Classical style is this establishment of norms (and consequently expectations). Deviations from the norm become highly significant. The integrity of the theme is violated in development, the predominant melody-and-accompaniment texture yields to polyphony at crucial points in the structure, harmonic stability is broken by modulation, and even metrical regularity is upset by syncopation. The term *balance* becomes important here, as composers succeeded in integrating and coordinating all facets of music into a balanced, unified style. If you reconsider Chapters 5 and 6 now, the essentials of Classical style should become clear.

Suggested Listening

The pieces mentioned above would constitute an excellent listening list for this period. Missing, however, are some works by lesser masters.

If time permits, it would be especially instructive to listen to works by composers other than the three greats in the list above—two sons of Bach, Johann Christian and Carl Phillipp Emanuel, Haydn's gifted brother Michael, as well as Antonio Salieri, Muzio Clementi, Luigi Boccherini, and Giovanni Paisiello, to name only a few of the many good composers in this fertile period.

Suggested Reading

Grout, Donald. *A Short History of Opera.* 2d ed. New York: Columbia University Press, 1965, pp. 215–314.

Newman, William S. *The Sonata in the Classic Era.* 3d ed. New York: Norton, 1983.

Pauly, Reinhard G. *Music in the Classic Period.* 2d ed. Englewood Cliffs, N.J.: Prentice-Hall, 1973.

Ratner, Leonard G. *Classic Music: Expression, Form, and Style.* New York: Schirmer, 1980.

Rosen, Charles. *The Classical Style: Haydn, Mozart, Beethoven.* New York: Norton, 1972.

Strunk, Oliver. *Source Readings in Music History.* New York: Norton, 1950, pp. 619–740.

ROMANTIC: c. 1827 to c. 1900

In the nineteenth century music occupied a unique position. According to the writer-composer E. T. A. Hoffmann, music was *the* romantic art; and the critic Walter Pater wrote that "all art constantly aspires toward the condition of music." A period which witnessed an increasing interrelationship among the arts and among artists themselves, the nineteenth century saw music push toward extremes in all its dimensions—dynamics, length (or brevity), and emotional expression, to mention only the most obvious. It is also a regrettable fact that music of the Romantic and Classical periods together provides the bulk of the standard concert repertory—regrettable certainly not because this music is inferior to that of any other period, but because in our time, for the first time in history, music of living composers makes up only a small part of concert programs.

Music of the Romantic period has been well covered in the historical section: three specific pieces and composers are spotlighted in Chapters 9, 10, and 11, and the second half of the period treated in detail in Chapter 12, where 8 of the 19 composers on the following list are discussed. And we have covered a wide geographical range in Part Four: Schubert in Vienna in the 1820s, Chopin in Paris in the 1830s, then in the second half of the century, Verdi in Italy, Wagner and Brahms in Germany, Debussy in France, and Moussorgsky and Rimsky-Korsakov in Russia.

Date	Composer, title	Source
1819	Weber, *Invitation to the Dance*	5.7
1823	Schubert, *Ländler,* Op. 171, no. 4	4.12
1823	Schubert, songs from *Die schöne Müllerin*	Ch. 3 AM, 5.26, 5.32
1826	Schubert, *Im Frühling*	9.1
1827	Schubert, *Frühlingstraum*	3.7
1827	Schubert, *Impromptu,* Op. 90, no. 2	4.20
1828	Schubert, *Quintet in C,* Op. 163	2.24, 5.12, 6.4
1829	Rossini, *William Tell,* overture	2.15
1832	Chopin, *Étude,* Op. 10, no. 3	5.20
1832–1833	Chopin, *Mazurka,* Op. 17, no. 4	2.25
1838	Chopin, *Prelude,* Op. 28, no. 18	4.4, 4.11
1846–1847	Chopin, Op. 64, no. 1, "Minute Waltz"	11.1
1848	Schumann, *Album for the Young,* "The Wild Horseman"	5.25
1853	Verdi, *La Traviata*	1.20
1854–1857	Liszt, *Faust Symphony*	3.2, 5.18
1854	Wagner, *Das Rheingold,* prelude	5.8
1855	Bizet, *Symphony in C*	4.9
1857–1859	Wagner, *Tristan and Isolde*	3.24, Ch. 4 AM, Ch. 5 AM, 12.1, 12.17
1868–1872	Moussorgsky, *Boris Godunov*	12.3, 12.13
1869	Brahms, *Alto Rhapsody,* Op. 53	12.5
1872	Bizet, *L'Arlésienne,* Suite 2	1.39
1873	Brahms, *Variations on a Theme by Haydn,* Op. 56a	5.27
1874–1881	Moussorgsky, *Khovantchina*	Ch. 1 AM, 3.21, Ch. 12
1874	Moussorgsky, *Pictures at an Exhibition*	1.16, Ch. 2 AM, 12.12
1874	Verdi, *Requiem*	10.2
1876	Tchaikovsky, *Marche slave*	2.10
1877–1878	Tchaikovsky, *Symphony 4*	5.15
1883	J. Strauss, *Voices of Spring*	5.14
1883	Brahms, *Symphony 3*	6.15
1888	Mahler, *Symphony 1*	1.6, 5.13, 6.5, Ch. 12

(continued)

Date	Composer, title	Source
1888	Rimsky-Korsakov, *Russian Easter Overture*	12.11
1888	Sousa, *Semper Fidelis*	1.8, 2.13
1888–1889	R. Strauss, *Don Juan*	Ch. 12
1889	J. Strauss, *Emperor Waltz*	2.9
1891	Brahms, *Trio for Piano, Cello, and Clarinet,* Op. 114	2.26
1893	Debussy, *String Quartet*	12.16
1897	Sousa, *Stars and Stripes Forever*	2.7
1898	R. Strauss, *Ein Heldenleben*	3.11
1899	Schoenberg, *Transfigured Night*	Ch. 12

In the nineteenth century, color in harmony and instrumentation becomes a significant end in itself. (See, for example, Mahler, *Symphony 1,* Example 6.5, or Liszt, *Faust Symphony,* Example 3.2, or Moussorgsky, *Boris Godunov,* Example 12.13; and on the use of the orchestra in this respect, see Chapter 1.) The piano, which had recently undergone a number of technological improvements, was also exploited for its coloristic possibilities. (See the discussion of Moussorgsky's *Pictures* in Chapter 12.) Pianists (Chopin, Liszt) and violinists (Paganini) displayed their virtuosity as "superstars" of the day. And the orchestra grew in size with the addition of more and different brass and winds (English horn, trombones, the valved horn and trumpet), harp, and many more percussion instruments.

In Chapter 5, in Demonstration 6.1 ("The Minuet and the Scherzo"), and in the discussion of the first movement of Brahms's *Symphony 3* (Demonstration 6.3) as well as in Chapters 11 and 12, we gained a sense of the increasing chromaticism in harmony and the changes in structural procedure that characterize the music of the Romantic period. But one more significant difference between this music and that of earlier periods should be mentioned.

Before the nineteenth century, composers often borrowed freely from preexisting musical scores—either their own works or the works of others. (See for example, the discussion of Perotin in Chapter 8, or Bach in Chapter 10.) As a result, the style in these earlier periods is more generalized; there is a kind of community of composers and compositions within which the "beacons" of each era stand out. With Romanticism, the "art of the ego," individuality becomes increasingly important, and a composition almost self-consciously tends to take on the particular stamp of its composer.

Suggested Listening

Berlioz, *Symphonie fantastique*

Brahms, *Symphony 3; Concerto 2 for Piano and Orchestra;* songs; *Clarinet Quintet; String Sextet 1*

Chopin, piano music

Dvǒràk, *String Quartet in F,* Op. 96, "The American"; "Dumky" trio

Liszt, piano music; *Faust Symphony*

Mahler, *Symphony 1*

Mendelssohn, overture and incidental music to Shakespeare's *A Midsummer Night's Dream*

Moussorgsky, *Boris Godunov; Pictures at an Exhibition*

Puccini, *La Bohème* (opera)

Schubert, songs; *Great C Major Symphony; Piano Sonata in A*

Schumann, songs; *Concerto for Piano and Orchestra*

R. Strauss, *Till Eulenspiegel* (tone poem)

Tchaikovsky, *Symphony 4*

Verdi, *La Traviata* (opera)

Wagner, *Tristan and Isolde* (opera)

Suggested Reading

Abraham, Gerald. *A Hundred Years of Music.* 4th ed. London: Duckworth, 1974.

Einstein, Alfred. *Music in the Romantic Era.* New York: Norton, 1947.

Grout, Donald. *A Short History of Opera.* 2d ed. New York: Columbia University Press, 1965, pp. 315–493.

Longyear, Rey M. *Nineteenth Century Romanticism.* 2d ed. Englewood Cliffs, N.J.: Prentice-Hall, 1973.

Plantinga, Leon. *Romantic Music.* New York: Norton, 1984.

Strunk, Oliver. *Source Readings in Music History.* New York: Norton, 1950, pp. 743–902.

TWENTIETH CENTURY

The Romantic and Modern periods overlap. In a sense the twentieth century in music does not really begin until about 1910, and the characteristics of Romanticism linger on in music written far into the century. In fact, the label "New Romanticism" has been applied to a variety of works being written today—many of which borrow frankly from the musical styles and sensibilities of the late nineteenth century.

In the first decades of the century, however, avant-garde composers were self-consciously concerned with freeing themselves from the shackles of Romanticism; and the term *new music* became significant, as it had, for example, at the turn of the fourteenth and seventeenth centuries.

The first 13 years of the twentieth century and all of the composers represented in the chronology up to 1913, except for Webern, are discussed at some length in Chapter 12. But what has happened since then? It is nearly impossible to give a cursory account of the music which developed after this date—partly because it has been a period of intensive experimentation along with a proliferation of styles, but mostly (and perhaps refreshingly) because we have very little historical perspective from which to view the immediate past.

Date	Composer, title	Source
1899	S. Joplin, *Maple Leaf Rag* (played by S. Joplin, 1916)	2.30
1902	Debussy, *Pelléas and Mélisande*	7.4, 12.18
1902–1903	Ravel, *String Quartet in F Major*	Ch. 12
1903–1905	Debussy, *La Mer*	Ch. 1 AM
1905–1909	Debussy, *Rondes de printemps*	1.7
1906	Schoenberg, *Chamber Symphony 1 in E Minor,* Op. 9	12.7
1906–1908	R. Strauss, *Elektra*	Ch. 12
1905–1908	Debussy, *Iberia,* "Parfums de la nuit"	12.10
1907–1908	Ravel, *Rapsodie espagnole,* "Prélude à la nuit"	Ch. 12
1908–1909	Mahler, *Das Lied von der Erde* ("The Song of the Earth")	12.6
1909	Schoenberg, *Five Pieces for Orchestra,* Op. 16, no. 1	12.8
1909–1912	Ravel, *Daphnis and Chloé*	2.2
1909–1910	Stravinsky, *Firebird Suite*	1.10, Ch. 1 AM, Ch. 12
1910	Schoenberg, *Quartet 2 in F-Sharp Minor*	Ch. 12
1910–1913	Debussy, *Préludes,* Book II, no. 1	12.15
1910–1911	Stravinsky, *Petrouchka*	2.27, 4.7
1911	Schoenberg, *Herzegewächse*	3.14, Ch. 5 AM
1911	Schoenberg, *Six Little Piano Pieces,* Op. 19	4.21, Ch. 5 AM
1912	Schoenberg, *Pierrot lunaire*	Ch. 3 AM, 12.2, 12.9

Date	Composer, title	Source
1913	Webern, *Five Pieces for Orchestra,* Op. 10, no. 2	2.29, 4.8
1913	Stravinsky, *Le Sacre du printemps*	1.1, 4.23, Ch. 1 AM, Ch. 2 AM, 12.4, 12.14
1914	Stravinsky, *Four Études for Orchestra*	1.30
1922	Hindemith, *Kleine Kammermusik,* Op. 24, no. 2	2.8
1922	Berg, *Wozzeck*	3.3
1922–1923	Stravinsky, *Octet for Wind Instruments*	2.6, 3.12
1923	Milhaud, *La Création du monde*	1.37
1925	Schoenberg, *Suite for Piano,* Op. 25	6.6
1927	J. Wood, *Mean Old Bedbug Blues* (sung by Bessie Smith)	5.41
1928	L. Armstrong, *Muggles*	5.43
1930	Gershwin, *I Got Rhythm*	3.6, 3.16
1932	S. Reese, *Which Side Are You On?*	4.19
1934	Hindemith, *Mathis der Maler*	1.34, 1.35, 7.10
1934	Webern, *Concerto for Nine Instruments*	Ch. 6 AM
1936	Varèse, *Density 21.5*	1.12
1936	Schoenberg, *Quartet 4*	Ch. 6 AM
1937	Bartók, *Sonata for Two Pianos and Percussion*	2.28, Ch. 6 AM
1938	Gordon, Roberts, and Kaufman, *Me, Myself and I* (sung by Billie Holiday)	1.25
1938	S. Joplin, *Maple Leaf Rag* (played by Jelly Roll Morton)	2.31
1939	B. Holiday, *Fine and Mellow*	5.42
1943	J. Yancey, *How Long Blues*	5.40
1946	Sessions, *Piano Sonata 2*	Ch. 6 AM
1947	C. Parker, *Relaxin' at Camarillo*	5.44
1948	C. Parker, *Steeplechase*	3.17
1952	Boulez, *Le Marteau sans maitre*	5.5
1956	S. Rollins, *Valse Hot*	2.12
1960	J. Lewis, *Django* (played by the Modern Jazz Quartet)	4.22
1962	M. Reynolds, *Little Boxes* (sung by Pete Seeger)	4.14, 5.30
1964	Babbitt, *Philomel*	1.22
1967	W. Shorter, *Pinocchio* (with Miles Davis)	5.19

(continued)

Date	Composer, title	Source
1969	King and Josea, *Be Careful with a Fool* (sung by Johnny Winter)	5.45
1976	Ward, *America the Beautiful* (played by the Al Cohn Quartet)	2.14
1977	Babbitt, *Minute Waltz*	11.2

We will not attempt, then, to survey all the music written since 1913; the discussion of Babbitt's *Minute Waltz* (1977) gave you some sense of the twentieth-century musical and cultural context. You can gain a more complete view of twentieth-century music by reading some of the books listed in the Suggested Reading for the period or, even better, by listening to music written during the last 75 years. For, after all, it is the works composed during this period that make up its musical history. We will, however, comment further on some of the experimentation that has occurred since 1945. Our goal is to provide you with both a larger framework for the pieces included in previous chapters and a fuller but still only a partial sequel to the period from 1859 to 1913, discussed in Chapter 12.

The two contrasting trends described in that chapter—music of Austro-Germany and music of Russia and France—continued to provoke stylistic (and sometimes personal) differences well into the twentieth century. Schoenberg in Germany—along with his students, Webern and Berg—found followers among composers both in Europe and, like Babbitt and others, in America. Stravinsky in France became the hero and moving spirit in the opposing camp. Interestingly, both composers lived the last years of their lives in the United States.

The kinds of musical experimentation that have occurred since 1945 are in many ways a spin-off from the expansion of possibilities found in the music of Schoenberg and Stravinsky. We will focus on three areas: experimentation with new sound sources, experimentation with various kinds of structural constraints, and experimentation with procedures of "chance." The categories are not mutually exclusive. Indeed, while any one of these concerns may be a focal point for a composer, the interrelationships among these factors often define the particular differences among specific works.

The challenge of new sound or new sound sources brings with it, for example, the search for limits—for ordering principles. But the kinds of limits a composer chooses—his or her means of defining order, may also generate new sounds. (See, for example, the discussion of the blues in Demonstration 5.4 and the discussion of the music of Schoenberg and Babbitt in Chapter 11.) And even experimentation with chance, which has led to *aleatoric* music (from *alea,* "dice," and by extension, "chance"), can bring forth not only innovative sound combinations but also new structure.

In the earlier works of Stravinsky and Schoenberg we already hear the expansion of sound possibilities as well as new kinds of structure. Stravinsky emphasized the use of sonorities—a particular collection of pitches sounding together—which he extended in time and animated through rhythmic, textural, and instrumental transformations. (Listen, for example, to *Le Sacre du printemps,* "Rondes printanières," or to the "Dance of the Adolescents" in Example 12.14 or the *Firebird Suite,* Example 1.10.) In later experimental music, sound became something to be made and molded almost as a thing in itself, not just the medium for projecting pitch or rhythmic structures. Edgar Varèse in his *Ionization* (1931) used percussion instruments including sirens, chains, anvils, and a whip as the material for a tightly organized work which was highly influential. Examples of later experimentation with sound can be heard in Example 1.22, *Philomel,* by Milton Babbitt (1964), and Example 5.5, *Le Marteau sans Maître,* by Pierre Boulez (1952–1954). Both works feature a very difficult soprano part with an accompaniment rich in colorful sounds, electronically generated in the Babbitt work. John Cage, who might be described as writing music which is philosophy (music which comments on music) has said, "As contemporary music goes on changing in the way I am changing it, what will be done is to more and more completely liberate sounds."[3]

For Schoenberg, sound as a generalized quality was more closely integrated with sound in its most specific sense—pitch. The development of his new compositional methods focused in large part on the realization of a new system of pitch relations. Indeed, it was the orderings of pitch relationships conceived of as a set of linear intervals—a row—that, more as a by-product, generated new sounds in his music. Out of his early, highly chromatic music emerged not only the "emancipation of the dissonance" (see Chapters 11 and 12) but also Schoenberg's compositional procedure, the twelve-tone technique, or as he preferred to call it, "composition with twelve notes related only to one another." Schoenberg added, "Personally, it is on the word *com-*

---

[3] John Cage, *Silence* (Middletown, Conn.: Wesleyan University Press, 1961), p. 161.

Cassiopeia

Reproduction of autograph manuscript of the composition *Cassiopeia,* George Cacioppo. (From *Notations,* by John Cage, editor. Copyright © 1969 by John Cage. All rights reserved. Reprinted by permission of Something Else Press.)

position that I place the emphasis. Unfortunately, most would-be followers of this method do something removed from the idea of composing music."[4] We discussed this idea of "serializing" pitches in Chapter 11—establishing an initial ordering of the twelve pitches, which then became the normative "pitch set" for an entire work. From this possibility grew procedures for "totally ordering" other aspects of music, such as rhythm or timbre.

But the bases for so organizing the various dimensions or parameters of music—timbre, rhythm, pitch—have varied greatly among recent composers. Some composers have used varieties of arithmetic or statistical manipulations as a basis for determining the succession of events—permuting and interrelating numerical series, for example. At the opposite extreme, some composers have allowed chance to make their decisions. They have tried tossing coins, using random number

---

[4] As quoted in J. Rufer, *Composition with Twelve Notes,* trans. Humphrey Searle (London: Barrie and Rockliff, 1965), p. 2.

tables, or even, in the case of John Cage, using the *I Ching,* the classic Chinese Book of Changes, to predetermine events in various dimensions. Xenakis has combined chance and determinacy by using the kinetic theory of gases, for example, to control the density and structure of his "clouds" of sound.

The development of electronic means for generating sound (the various kinds of synthesizers, some coupled with computers) encouraged composers to play with sounds (and silence) almost as if the sounds were as tangible and as material as the tape on which they were recorded.

The most dramatic recent developments in electronic music derive from the development of new computer sound synthesis technology. Much of this technology began to emerge from Bell Laboratories in the 1950s, though it didn't have a substantial effect on the musical scene for about a decade—that is, until the first computer music studios were up and running.

All computer sound synthesis is based on the principles that sound (which is no more or less than a fluctuation of pressure in the air) can be represented numerically, and that computer programs can be written to generate numerical representations of any and all sounds. Armed with these principles, musicians and scientists investigated a variety of questions; for example:

1. How many numbers must be generated to accurately represent a second of sound (40,000 is now often considered the standard)?
2. How are numerical representations of sound turned into the electrical signals which actually drive audio speakers—that is, produce the sounds themselves?
3. Perhaps most importantly, assuming that we can represent any sound through a series of numbers generated by a computer, what kinds of sounds do we want to create? What makes a sound acoustically interesting or pleasing?

This final question has received an extraordinary amount of attention during the last quarter century, and a wide variety of sound-synthesizing techniques have been explored, among them additive synthesis, frequency modulation, waveshaping, and linear prediction.[5]

---

[5] A good introduction to several of these sound-processing methods will be found in "The Computer as a Musical Instrument," by Max V. Mathews and John R. Pierce, in *Scientific American,* February 1987, pp. 126–133.

Just as importantly, a wide variety of new synthesizers have appeared recently, and a new technology, MIDI (musical instrument digital interface), has allowed for communication between synthesizers, microcomputers, and other digital devices for altering sounds. Through the use of MIDI, complex sounds can be generated relatively quickly and with much less expensive equipment than that available in the earlier days of electronic sound synthesis. At the same time, major research centers in computer music (such as those at MIT, Stanford, and the Centre Pompidou in Paris) are bringing forth unprecedented and increasingly rich methods for generating sound electronically. New developments in (and applications of) computer music technology are currently developing at a breathtaking pace.

Most systems are "interactive"—that is, composers can type in their instructions to the computer, listen to the results, and then immediately make any changes they want. These possibilities have also expanded the field of psychoacoustics—the development of theoretical *descriptions* of sounds which account for the *perception* of sounds as our minds make sense of them.

Still other composers have developed theoretical systems sufficiently generalized to enable them to program a computer to "compose" pieces. Using complex and powerful computer languages, composers can describe structural relations of a composition. The descriptions are in terms of computer procedures which when computed generate the sound events (pitch-duration-timbre) which meet the composer's structural specifications.

Some of the most compelling works in this medium have involved computer simulations of human speech (for example, Paul Lansky's "Six Fantasies on a Poem of Thomas Campion" [1979]) or combinations of computer-generated music recorded on tape played together with various instruments or voice performed live (for example, Babbitt's *Philomel* heard earlier, and the numerous "Synchronisms" for tape and various instrumental ensembles by Mario Davidovsky).

Finally, with the development of powerful and versatile personal computers, along with sophisticated music "software," more composers are taking advantage of these as tools for their creative work. A whole range of synthesizers are now available that can easily be "interfaced" with these computers. These, together with the recent possibilities for "digitalizing" the recorded sounds of traditional instruments and voices, have made the home "computer music studio" very much a reality. And, in the area of popular music, many performing groups—especially rock groups—are using synthesizers as instruments to augment their live and recorded performances.

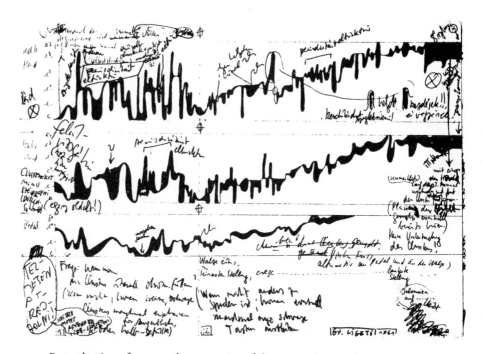

Reproduction of autograph manuscript of the composition *Volumina,* György Ligeti, 1961. (Copyright © 1967 by Henry Litolff. Reprint permission granted by C. F. Peters Corporation.)

Experimentation has also led to new kinds of music notation—computer-programming languages, languages which describe acoustical phenomena, or even a language of inches of prerecorded tape. In other less conventional notations and instructions to performers, the performer is free to improvise around a few indicated pitches, a graphic design (see pp. 446, 449), or some preexisting bit of music (see, for example, Stockhausen's *Hymnen*).

But one should not confuse a technique or a sound surface with the composition itself. For example, Stravinsky, in his later works, used serial techniques as Schoenberg and his students did, but he still maintained his personal rhythmic and textural "gesture" (see, for example, Stravinsky's *Movements for Piano and Orchestra,* 1960, and *Threni,* 1958). Aaron Copland, who was influenced both by his years of study in France and by his American heritage, incorporated the twelve-tone approach with quite different effect, for example, in his *Piano Fantasy* (1957).

In similar fashion, the use of electronically generated sounds can be a vehicle—a medium—for pieces as different from each other as the composers themselves. Composers and performers use their instruments—electronic or otherwise—only as a means. Their composition, design, and expressive gesture depend ultimately upon their intent, their creative imagination, and their skill as musicians—that is, upon their artistic choices.

The last 20 years have seen a change in the general attitude among composers. While the time up to the mid-1960s was marked by "schools" to which young composers were drawn or to which they expressed antagonism, more recently these "isms" have tended to fade. Composers strive to find their own "voice," taking what they like from the past and present and melding it with their own sense of structural constraints as these shape their creative expression.

Our jazz examples have their own history. They span more than half a century, from Scott Joplin's performance of his own *Maple Leaf Rag* in 1916 to Al Cohn's *America the Beautiful* in 1976. Since jazz is an improvisational art, its history is allied with that of recording techniques. We have a body of recordings rather than a body of manuscripts or printed music; we have no trace of the earliest jazz, before 1916.

Joplin's *Maple Leaf Rag* (Example 2.30) was recorded on a piano roll the year before his death (and probably when he was past his prime as a performer). Our next examples are from 1927 (Bessie Smith) and 1928 (Louis Armstrong), when electrical recording was in its infancy. Obviously the sound leaves much to be desired in terms of fidelity. Furthermore, until the development of tape, recorded pieces were restricted in length to three minutes; we thus have no idea of what a live, inspired jazz performance at that time was really like. While both are blues, Louis Armstrong's piece exemplifies late New Orleans style. The blues have followed a parallel but independent course with jazz, which continuously nourishes itself on the blues.

Bessie Smith's *Mean Old Bedbug Blues* (Example 5.41) illustrates a type of blues characterized as classic blues, as differentiated from country blues, which were freer and rougher, and rarely recorded in the 1920s. Bessie Smith was the most popular (she was known as the "Empress of the Blues") of a number of women blues singers who performed in theaters before almost exclusively black audiences.

Louis Armstrong's *Muggles* (Example 5.43), while also a blues, represents a final stage of development of New Orleans style. New Orleans, a most cosmopolitan center at the turn of the century, was a focal point in the origins of jazz. After 1917, when Storyville (the red-light district of New Orleans, where many jazz musicians found employment) was closed, some New Orleans musicians moved north to

Chicago, which became a jazz center in the 1920s. The traditional New Orleans jazz ensemble (in later manifestations the style was referred to as "Dixieland") comprised trumpet, clarinet, and trombone plus rhythm section (in this Louis Armstrong example, piano, banjo, and drums). In the very early days jazz musicians often did not know how to read music; they played well-known tunes ("rags" or marches) with occasional solos but primarily together—trumpet leading, clarinet with a countermelody, and trombone on the bass line. The resultant polyphonic ensembles were unique in that they were a product of collective improvisation. Improvisation flourished in "Classical" music in earlier centuries (Bach, Mozart, and Beethoven, for example, were famous improvisers) but usually done by a soloist, not an ensemble. The Louis Armstrong example represents the dissolution of New Orleans style, for instead of a final ensemble with relative equality among trumpet, clarinet, and trombone, the trumpet (played by Louis Armstrong, the leader and "star") completely dominates the final two choruses.

The two Billie Holiday excerpts (1938, 1939) are from the so-called *swing* period—saxophones are now prominent, the double bass plays *pizzicato* on every beat, and the music is more tightly arranged. In addition, recording techniques were much improved. *Me, Myself and I* (Example 1.25), in its duet of singer and tenor sax above a subordinate accompaniment, has an analogue in Bach arias in which a singer and a solo woodwind or violin create a polyphonic texture above a minimal accompaniment.

Two examples from 1945 and 1947 (3.17 and 5.44) featuring Charlie Parker ("Bird") on alto sax are prime examples of *bebop,* the style of jazz which succeeded swing in the early 1940s. Some of its characteristics can be heard in these two examples—highly syncopated piano chords and unsettling drum accents, more chromatic harmonies with a prominent use of the interval of the diminished fifth, and in *Shaw 'Nuff,* a dazzlingly fast tempo requiring virtuosic performance by the soloists.

Sonny Rollins's *Valse Hot* (1956, Example 2.12) is a comparatively rare example of a jazz waltz. Until recently most jazz has been in duple meter (probably a function of the early influence of the New Orleans marching bands), though currently more complex meters are often used.

The last examples reveal further innovations in jazz history. In John Lewis's *Django* (1960, Example 4.25) we have an unusual structure. While most previous jazz either followed the twelve-bar blues format or a 32-bar *a a b a* or *a + a′*, here we have *a a b a′ c* in which the first two *a* segments are 6 bars in length rather than the usual 4 or 8. In Wayne Shorter's *Pinocchio* (1967, Example 5.19), performed by the Miles Davis Quintet, we hear first a highly chromatic theme with alternative phrase lengths of 8 and 10 measures and an almost atonal harmonic background. The theme alternates, like a rondo, with improvisations—no longer, however, on a fixed structure deriving from the theme.

Be Careful with a Fool (1969, Example 5.45) shows the significant blues and jazz influence on rock. More recently there has been a type of "fusion music" seeking a reconciliation of jazz and rock. In Al Cohn's unusual treatment of *America the Beautiful* we hear, among other things, evidence of the recurrent Latin American influence on jazz—in this case the *bossa nova* from Brazil. Another fairly recent development is "free jazz," that is, a kind of collective improvisation (an echo of old New Orleans jazz), often atonal, without a regular periodic structure, and often without a pulse, or in an unusual meter. Limitations of space have prevented the inclusion of some of these recent examples on the records.

In considering the wide range of styles within our own time— including the seemingly great differences between music composed and written down to be played in the concert hall as opposed to mostly improvised jazz—we should bear in mind that the composer (or composer-performer) in searching for personal expression must always make choices. In many ways the nature of these choices defines his or her style, but choosing always involves a struggle between the challenge of possibility and the search for limits. This struggle may seem more poignant today, but as we have tried to demonstrate throughout this book, it seems to be a universal, pervading all aspects of artistic creation: "Well, of course the dialectic of freedom is unfathomable. . . ."[6]

Suggested Listening

Works by composers on the list on pages 442–444 and mentioned in the preceding pages, as well as works by others such as Babbitt, Berger, Berio, Boulez, Britten, Crumb, Dallapiccola, Davidovsky, Davies, Gideon, Kim, Kirchner, Ligeti, Messaien, Perle, Shapey, Shifrin, Weinberg, Weisgall, Wolpe, and many more.

---

[6] Thomas Mann, *Doctor Faustus* (New York: Knopf, 1948), p. 193.

Suggested Reading

Austin, William A. *Music in the 20th Century.* New York: Norton, 1966.

Boretz, Benjamin, and Edward T. Cone, eds. *Perspectives on American Composers.* New York: Norton, 1972.

Boretz, Benjamin, and Edward T. Cone, eds. *Perspectives on Schoenberg and Stravinsky.* New York: Norton, 1972.

Boulez, Pierre. *Boulez on Music Today.* Cambridge, Mass.: Harvard University Press, 1971. A rather technical but very insightful discussion of analytical procedures applicable to many musical periods but especially appropriate to the twentieth century.

Cage, John. *Silence.* Middletown, Conn.: Wesleyan University Press, 1961. Nontechnical, free-flowing comments on music and contemporary life.

Collier, James Lincoln. *The Making of Jazz.* Boston: Houghton-Mifflin, 1978.

Forte, Allen. *The Structure of Atonal Music.* New Haven: Yale University Press, 1973.

Griffiths, Paul. *A Concise History of Avant Garde Music from Debussy to Boulez.* New York, Toronto: Oxford University Press, 1978.

Jones, Le Roi. *Blues People.* New York: Morrow, 1963.

Hahl-Foch, Jelena, ed. *Arnold Schoenberg, Wassily Kandinsky: Letters, Pictures, and Documents.* Translated by John C. Crawford. London: Faber and Faber, 1984.

Henze, Hans Werner. *Music and Politics: Collected Writings, 1953–81.* Translated by Peter Labani. London: Faber and Faber, 1982.

Howe, Hubert. *Electronic Music Synthesis: Concepts, Facilities, Techniques.* New York: Norton, 1975.

Litweiler, John. *The Freedom Principle: Jazz after 1958.* New York: Morrow, 1984.

Mathews, Max V. *The Technique of Computer Music.* Cambridge, Mass.: MIT Press, 1969.

Perle, George. *Serial Composition and Atonality.* 4th ed. Berkeley: University of California Press, 1978.

Peyser, Joan. *Twentieth-Century Music: The Sense Behind the Sound.* New York: Schirmer, 1980.

Reynolds, Roger. *Mind Models: New Forms of Musical Experience.* New York: Praeger, 1975.

Rhodes, Curtis, and John Strong, eds. *The Foundations of Computer Music.* Cambridge, Mass.: MIT Press, 1983.

Rockwell, John. *All American Music: Composition in the Late Twentieth Century.* New York: Knopf, 1983.

Rosen, Charles. *The Musical Languages of Elliot Carter.* Washington, D.C.: Library of Congress, 1984.

Rufer, Josef. *Composition with Twelve Notes.* Translated by Humphrey Searle. London: Barrie and Rockliff, 1965. The most authoritative book on Schoenberg's compositional procedures.

Salzman, Eric. *Twentieth Century Music: An Introduction.* 2d ed. New York: Norton, 1974.

Schwartz, Elliott, and Barney Childs, eds. *Contemporary Composers on Contemporary Music.* New York: Holt, Rinehart & Winston, 1967.

Sessions, Roger. *Questions About Music.* Cambridge, Mass.: Harvard University Press, 1970. A series of lectures concerning current questions on both contemporary music and the music of the past.

Shapiro, N., and N. Hentoff. *Hear Me Talkin to Ya: The Story of Jazz by the Men Who Made It.* New York: Dover, 1966.

Slominsky, Nicholas. *Music Since 1900.* 4th ed. New York: Scribner, 1971.

Stearns, Marshall W. *The Story of Jazz.* London, New York: Oxford University Press, 1958.

Stevens, Halsey. *The Life and Music of Bela Bartok.* 2d ed. New York: Oxford University Press, 1958.

Stravinsky, Igor, and Robert Craft. *Retrospectives and Conclusions.* New York: Knopf, 1969.

Stuckenschmidt, H. H. *Twentieth Century Music.* Translated by Richard Daveson. New York: World University Library, McGraw-Hill, 1969.

Tirro, Frank. *Jazz: A History.* New York: Norton, 1977.

van den Toorn, Peter. *The Music of Stravinsky.* New Haven: Yale University Press, 1983.

Glossary

A cappella   Without instrumental accompaniment.

Accelerando   A gradual increase in tempo.

Antecedent-consequent   Two complementary phrases; in the most limited sense, the phrases begin alike but end differently—the first (antecedent) ending with a half cadence, the second (consequent) ending with a full cadence.

Arco   With the bow—a direction for players of stringed instruments. (Compare with *Pizzicato*.)

Aria   A song of some complexity, usually for one voice, with instrumental accompaniment. It occurs in operas, oratorios, and cantatas.

Arpeggio   A broken chord; the successive sounding of the notes of a chord.

Atonality   Without tonality; that is, without a tonal center; characteristic of much twentieth-century music.

Augmented interval   A major or perfect interval raised by a half step (e.g., C–E♯ is an augmented third; F–B♮ is an augmented fourth; G–D♯ is an augmented fifth).

Augmented triad   A three-note chord which, going up from its root, includes a major third and an augmented fifth, or two major thirds (e.g., C–E–G♯).

Bar line   Musical symbol indicating the regular grouping of beats, or meter.

Baroque   The period in music history encompassing the seventeenth and half of the eighteenth centuries.

Basso continuo   Literally, "continuous bass," the lowest part in a composition of the Baroque era, played by a bass instrument and a keyboard instrument that plays chords.

Bransle, also **Branle**   A popular sixteenth-century dance.

Cadence   The ending of a phrase or longer section (see also *Full cadence; Half cadence*).

Cadenza   An improvisatory solo passage usually occurring near the end of a movement of a concerto where it serves to delay the conclusion and gives the soloist a chance to display technical brilliance.

Caesura   Moment of arrested motion often articulating phrase structure within a piece; a breathing pause.

Canon   A composition in two or more parts in which the melody is imitated exactly and completely by the successively entering voices though not always at the same pitch.

Cantata   Literally, a piece that is sung (*cantare*, Italian, "to sing"), in contrast to *sonata*, a piece that is played (*sonare*, Italian, "to sound"). It is an extended work for chorus and/or solo voices, usually with orchestral accompaniment.

Cantus firmus   A preexistent melody, often plainchant, that serves as the basis of a polyphonic composition.

Catch   English round of the seventeenth and eighteenth centuries. Catches were often based on rather "indecent" texts.

Chorale   A hymn tune of the German Protestant church. Chorale melodies are best known today through their harmonizations by J. S. Bach.

Chorus   (1) A group of singers; (2) refrain; (3) in jazz, a structural unit, e.g., a twelve- or thirty-two-bar section of a piece.

Chromatic   In tonal harmony, use of pitches in addition to those found in a given major or minor scale—therefore, a "mixing of families of pitches."

Chromatic scale   Scale consisting of all twelve pitches available in Western music.

Classical   The period in music history roughly between 1750 and 1827.

Coda   Literally, "tail" (Italian); a passage at the end of a piece or movement that extends the ideas previously presented, bringing the work to a satisfying conclusion.

Codetta   A small coda, often occurring at the end of a section rather than at the end of a complete work.

Concerto   A work in several movements that exploits the contrast between a solo instrument and the full orchestra. A *violin concerto,* for example, is a work for solo violin and orchestra; a *horn concerto* is a work for solo French horn and orchestra.

Concerto grosso   A work in several movements that exploits the contrast between a small group of solo instruments (called the *concertino*) and the full orchestra (called *tutti*).

Conjunct   Refers to melodies in which the movement is predominantly stepwise.

Consonance   In tonal harmony, a classification of intervals such as the octave and the perfect fifth. Also, moments of relatively stable, or even conclusive, harmony.

Counterpoint   Except for some minor differences in emphasis, synonymous with *polyphony.* (See *Polyphonic.*)

Countersubject   A melody designed as a counterpoint to the subject of a fugue; it usually occurs for the first time above or below the second entrance of the subject.

Crescendo   A continuous increase in loudness.

Da capo   Literally, "from the head" or "top" (Italian); an indication to the performer to go back to the beginning.

Deceptive cadence   A cadence that sounds as if it were going to be conclusive, until its final chord, at which point the conclusion is interrupted (and the motion extended), usually by the substitution of the VI chord for I.

Degree   The numbers (1–7) assigned to the pitches of the diatonic scale;

for example, C is the first degree (tonic) of the C-major scale, B is the seventh degree of the C-major scale.

Development   The section of a movement in sonata form between the exposition and the recapitulation in which the musical material from the exposition is developed, that is, "analyzed," broken apart, its potential explored. In a more general sense, the elaboration, manipulation, or transformation of musical material in the course of a composition.

Diatonic   Using almost exclusively the seven whole and half steps of the major and minor scales, as opposed to chromatic.

Diminished interval   A minor or perfect interval lowered by a half step (e.g., C–E$^{\flat\flat}$ is a diminished third; C–G$^{\flat}$ is a diminished fifth).

Diminished triad   A three-note chord which, going up from its root, includes a minor third and a diminished fifth or two minor thirds (e.g., C–E$^{\flat}$–G$^{\flat}$).

Disjunct   Refers to melodies in which the movement is predominantly by leap rather than by step.

Dissonance   In tonal harmony, a classification of intervals such as the major seventh, major second, or diminished fifth. Also, moments of relatively unstable or unresolved harmony.

Dodecaphonic   Twelve tones; used in reference to music written in "twelve-tone technique" (after Schoenberg); or, more generally, serial music.

Dominant   The fifth degree of a diatonic scale; the chord built on that tone.

Double   To play in unison (or at the octave) with another instrument.

Duo   A piece for two instruments.

Episode   In the fugue, a phase in which the subject is absent or is present only in a fragmentary fashion.

Étude   Literally, "a study" (French); a piece written to help the student in developing technique. Some études (e.g., Chopin's) have become concert pieces in their own right.

Exposition   The first large section of a movement in sonata form; the first section of a fugue in which each of the voices enters with a fugue subject.

Fantasy, Fantasia   A composition in which the composer "exercises his fancy"; thus, a work that tends to be freer in structure than one following a conventional form.

Figure   See *Motive.*

Finale   The last movement of an instrumental work written after about 1750, or the concluding section of an operatic act.

First-movement form   See *Sonata form.*

Formes fixes   Literally, "fixed forms"; poetic and consequently musical forms of the fourteenth and fifteenth centuries, in particular, the *rondeau, virelai,* and *ballade.*

Fugato   Usually a fugal exposition occurring in the development section of a movement in sonata form.

Fugue A polyphonic work for two or more voices or instruments built on a subject (theme) that is introduced in imitation and recurs frequently throughout the composition.

Full cadence A phrase ending with a sense of completion—i.e., on the tonic.

Gavotte A French dance originating in the seventeenth century. It is in a moderate to fairly quick tempo and in duple meter (usually $\frac{4}{4}$) and often begins on the third beat of the measure.

Gigue One of the four traditional dance movements in suites written around 1700, usually the last (standard movements being *allemande, courante, sarabande,* and *gigue*). It is characterized by compound meter and dotted rhythm, and frequently by imitative polyphony.

Gothic The later Middle Ages (c. 1100 to c. 1400).

Gregorian chant The liturgical chant of the Roman Catholic church, named after Pope Gregory I (590–604).

Half cadence Unresolved ending of a phrase, usually with dominant harmony.

Harmonic rhythm The rate of change, the rhythm, of the chords in a composition or a part of a composition.

Homophony An inactive texture in which one instrument (or voice) plays a dominant role while the other instruments play a clearly subordinate accompaniment.

Imitation One instrument or voice "imitating" another; that is, successive statements of a motive in different strands of the texture.

Impromptu A title given to a one-movement piece for piano in the early Romantic Period.

Improvisation Spontaneously performed composition usually with reference to some given progression or structure but without reference to written music.

Instrumentation The assignment of specific instruments to play specific parts in a given composition; composers indicate the precise instrumentation in the score.

Interval The distance between two tones.

Invention A term most commonly associated with a set of fifteen keyboard pieces by J. S. Bach that are written in two parts and are highly polyphonic.

Inversion Literally, a change of direction; refers to melodies in which the direction of the successive intervals is reversed. Also, a rearrangement of the notes in a chord so that the root is no longer the lowest.

Key Tonal center or tonality of a piece.

Ländler An Austrian dance in triple meter, forerunner of the waltz.

Leap See *Disjunct.*

Legato The smooth connection of the successive tones of a melody in performance. (Compare with *Staccato.*)

Madrigal   In the sixteenth century, a choral work, usually unaccompanied, with a text which the music follows rather closely. It is often imitative and polyphonic and tends to have a stronger sense of beat than its sacred counterpart, the motet.

Major   See *Mode.*

March   A piece in duple meter with a strongly marked beat.

Mass   The central Roman Catholic religious service and also a musical setting of that service. Its major sections are *Kyrie, Gloria, Credo, Sanctus,* and *Agnus Dei.*

Mazurka   Originally, a Polish folk dance, later a stylized piano piece.

Mbira   African thumb piano.

Measure   The unit formed by the regular grouping of beats, sometimes called a bar, and indicated in the score by bar lines.

Medieval   Literally, the "Middle Ages," between the Classical civilizations of ancient Greece and Rome and the Renaissance—c. 400–c. 1400.

Melisma   Several tones on a single syllable.

Meter   The regular organization of the beats into larger groups.

Metronome   A device to indicate the precise tempo of a piece; invented by Mälzel in 1816.

Minor   See *Mode.*

Minuet   A French dance of peasant origin in triple meter and moderate tempo. It had a great vogue at the court of Louis XIV and continued its existence in the eighteenth century as a stylized dance in instrumental music.

Missa   Latin for *Mass.*

Mode   The specific scalar arrangement of tones within an octave; e.g., Dorian, Phrygian, major, minor, pentatonic.

Modulation   The process of moving from one tonal area to another, change of key.

Monophonic   Unaccompanied melody such as chant.

Motet   A type of choral work, most often with a Latin sacred text, which had a long history in the Middle Ages and the Renaissance.

Motive   A small melodic-rhythmic pattern; smallest meaningful structural unit.

Movement   The various self-contained sections of an extended instrumental composition such as a symphony, sonata, or string quartet.

Neumes   Signs that represent pitch movement in a plainchant melody.

Note   The written symbol for a tone.

Obbligato   An added part; literally, "required," but it sometimes has taken on the opposite meaning.

Octave   An interval of twelve half steps; the octave(s) separates pitches of like names but different register, such as low C–high C.

Opus   Literally, "work" (Latin); a musical composition; Opus 1 would be a composer's first published work.

Organum Term used for the earliest polyphonic music from the ninth century up to the time of Leonin and Perotin (see Chapter 8).

Ostinato A figure repeated persistently, often in the bass, while other elements of the texture change.

Overture A term that most commonly refers to the instrumental music composed as an introduction to an opera, but also may refer to the first movement of a suite or to an entirely independent work (concert overture).

Partita Originally (in the early seventeenth century) a term signifying a set of variations; later the term was also used to mean a suite.

Passion A musical setting of the gospel accounts of the Passion (sufferings and death of Christ). In the seventeenth century it became a highly dramatic work for chorus and orchestra including recitatives, arias, chorales, and instrumental interludes.

Pedal A sustained or repeated tone, most frequently in the bass, and often the dominant of the key.

Pentatonic A mode of five tones, or a melody based on that mode. In non-Western music, a division of the octave into five tones.

Period A melodic-harmonic unit of two complementary phrases, such as antecedent-consequent.

Phrase A structurally significant segment of a melody.

Pitch Frequency, or vibrations per second; the relative highness or lowness of a musical tone.

Pitch-class The set of pitches described by the same letter name (e.g., all F's or all C's are members of the same pitch-class).

Pitch-space The distance between tones as measured along the chromatic scale.

Pizzicato A direction to players of bowed stringed instruments (violin, cello, etc.) to pluck the strings with the fingers.

Polyphony A texture in which instruments or voices move independently of one another and are all of relatively equal importance.

Prelude Originally, an introductory movement in a suite or an introduction to another piece (as in a prelude and fugue). In the nineteenth century the term was used also as a title for individual piano or orchestral pieces.

Quartet Four instruments or voices; see *String quartet*.

Rag A piece in ragtime style, which flourished between about 1890 and 1915.

Range The pitch-space between the highest and lowest tones of a melody or instrument.

Recapitulation The section of a movement in sonata form that follows the development section and parallels the exposition.

Recitative A style of singing imitating and emphasizing the natural inflections of speech in both pitch and rhythm. It occurs in opera, oratorio, cantata, and passion and tends to serve a narrative function; often coupled with an aria.

Refrain Music which recurs regularly at the end of each large section of a work.

Register A particular segment of the range of an instrument or voice (e.g., the lower register of the clarinet in contrast to the upper register).

Renaissance Literally, "rebirth"; refers to the fifteenth and sixteenth centuries, a period of flourishing artistic activity with frequent references to the art of ancient Greece.

Rhapsody A title given by composers in the nineteenth and early twentieth centuries to instrumental works of a somewhat heroic or "rhapsodic" character.

Rhythmic modes Medieval rhythmic system involving the repetition of simple rhythmic patterns in compound duple meter. (See Chapter 8.)

Ricercare A polyphonic instrumental piece, originating in the sixteenth century.

Ritardando A gradual slowing down of tempo.

Romanesque The early Middle Ages (c. 400–c. 1100)

Romantic The period in music history roughly between 1827 and 1900.

Rondo Most often a movement in a larger work (symphony, sonata, or concerto—of which it is often the last movement) characterized by a highly sectional design which includes a recurring refrain alternating with contrasting material. It may be diagramed as ABACADA . . .

Root The fundamental, or generating, tone of a chord.

Root position Refers to the arrangement of the tones of a chord with the root as the lowest.

Round A circular canon.

Rubato Literally, "rob" (Italian); the subtle give-and-take or flexibility with which the performer treats the rate of the underlying pulse.

Sanctus Literally, "holy" (Latin); a section of the Roman Catholic mass.

Sarabande A dance in slow triple meter which was one of the four dances included in suites around 1700.

Scale Literally, "ladder" (Italian); a series of discrete pitches ordered from low to high.

Scherzo Literally, "joke" (Italian); it is a movement in a symphony (or trio, quartet, or other instrumental work) taking the place of the minuet. Although faster in tempo, it is, like the minuet, in triple meter.

Score The notation of a musical composition.

Sequence Repetition of a melodic pattern or figure at successively higher or lower pitch levels within the same strand of the texture.

Shamisen A Japanese lute, used to accompany singers.

Sitar An Indian lute with many strings.

Sonata Derived from the Italian *sonare* ("to sound"); it is a work in several movements for a small number of instruments.

Sonata form A particular structural design found most frequently in the first movement of a sonata, symphony, or string quartet, but also used in the slow movement and the final movement.

Sonority   The sound resulting from a particular combination of instruments, or (in late nineteenth- and twentieth-century music) the sound resulting from a particular combination of pitches.

Staccato   A manner of performance in which notes are played quickly, lightly, and detached from one another. (Compare with *Legato.*)

Stretto   A phase in a fugue in which each of the voices enters with the subject in rapid succession; that is, before the subject has been stated in its entirety.

String quartet   A group of four string instruments—two violins, viola, and cello; also a work in three or four movements for these instruments.

Subdominant   The fourth degree of a diatonic scale and the triad built on that tone; the "underdominant" or 5th *below* the tonic.

Subject   The opening statement in a fugue; that is, the theme of a fugue.

Suite   Before approximately 1750, an instrumental composition consisting of several movements, each of them dancelike and all in the same key. After 1750, a set of movements excerpted from a ballet or opera.

Symphony   Essentially a sonata for orchestra; that is, a work in several movements composed for a relatively large group of instruments.

Syncopation   A temporary displacement or shifting of the expected accent, often confounding the meter.

Tabla   A small Indian drum.

Tamboura   A large Indian lute used to play a drone, that is, a repeated or sustained bass tone or tones.

Tempo   The rate of speed of the underlying pulse.

Tenor   From Latin *tenere,* ("to hold"). In early polyphony the fundamental (or "holding") part carrying the *cantus firmus;* the highest natural male voice or instruments in that range, between baritone and alto.

Theme   The principal musical idea (melody, motive, harmonic progression, sonority, etc.) or subject of a composition.

Theme and variations   An independent work or a movement of a larger work (such as a sonata or symphony) in which a musical idea (theme) is presented and then varied so that some aspects of the theme remain constant while others undergo change. The composition is generally highly sectional and "additive" rather than developmental; each variation is often a self-contained unit.

Timbre   Tone color; the quality of a tone as played by a particular instrument.

Toccata   From the Italian *toccare* ("to touch"); it is a composition for a keyboard instrument characterized by a free style, often with elaborate running passages contrasted with full chords, and occasionally containing fugal sections.

Tone   A sound with regularity of vibration and consequently fixed pitch; also refers to timbre.

Tone poem, Symphonic poem   A nineteenth-century symphonic composition based on an extramusical idea that is either poetic or descriptive.

Tonic   Tonal center; the pitch which functions as the most stable in a collection of pitches within the context of tonal harmony.

Transition   The moving from one stable area of thematic statement to another, usually involving change of key.

Transposition   In the simplest sense, the playing of a melody in a different key.

Triad   A simultaneous sounding of three tones; a chord of only three pitches.

Trio   (1) A work for any three instruments. A *piano trio* is a composition for violin, cello, and piano; a *string trio* is usually a work for violin, viola, and cello; a *horn trio* may be a work for French horn, violin, and piano. (2) In the minuet or scherzo movement of a symphony, sonata, or quartet, the middle section played between the minuet or scherzo proper, and its repetition.

Trio sonata   In the Baroque period, a work for two instruments and basso continuo; usually played by four instruments since the continuo includes a keyboard instrument (e.g., harpsichord) and a bass instrument (e.g., cello).

Tritone   Literally, "three tones"; the interval of three whole steps, either a diminished fifth or augmented fourth, classified traditionally as the most dissonant interval (for example, C–F♯).

Tutti   Literally, "all" (Italian); in a concerto grosso, the full ensemble in contrast to the solo group; also a section of a piece played by the full ensemble.

Unison   Two or more people playing or singing either the same tones or in octaves.

Variation   See *Theme and variations.* In a more general sense variation consists in realizing the implications of any musical material as, for instance, in development.

Virelai   A form of Medieval French poetry and music; one of the *formes fixes.*

Waiting passage   A passage generating tension through elaboration of dominant harmony and usually preceding a thematic statement.

Waltz   A dance in triple meter which may be slow or fast in tempo. It originated in the late eighteenth century in Austria, and stemmed from the Ländler or German dance.

Acknowledgments

We gratefully acknowledge the use of photographs from the following sources:

Chapter 1
2, 3: The Cleveland Museum of Art, gift from various donors by exchange. **8:** European American Music Distributors Corporation. **12:** Courtesy of Professor Stanley Backer and Dr. Stelios Arghyros, Fibers and Polymers Laboratories, MIT. **33:** Marty Yoss. **34:** Johnson, DPI. **35:** Young, DPI.

Chapter 2
38: Wide World Photos. **39:** Philadelphia Museum of Art, Louise and Walter Arensberg Collection. **42:** India Consulate. **46, 47:** European American Music Distributors Corporation. **48:** Peter Schaaf, Courtesy John Gingrich Management, Inc. **54:** The Metropolitan Museum of Art, Museum Excavations, 1922–1923. **57:** Culver. **61, 62:** The New York Public Library Picture Collection. **63:** Del Rosenfield Associates.

Chapter 3
84, 85: Philadelphia Museum of Art, photo by A. J. Wyatt, Staff Photographer. **90:** The Library of Congress, Washington, D.C. (purchased from the composer in 1934 with the help of funds presented by the "Friends of Music of the Library of Congress"). **95:** From "Geometrical Illusions" by Barbara Gillam; illustration by Jerome Kuhl. Copyright © 1980 by Scientific American, Inc. All rights reserved. **101:** Alinari, Art Resource. **103:** Professor I. W. Bailey, Harvard University (from Gyorgy Kepes, *The New Landscape in Art and Science,* by permission of the author). **106:** From *Handbook of Regular Patterns* by Peter S. Stevens, © 1981, Peter S. Stevens. Cambridge, MA: The MIT Press. **107:** Professor Harold E. Edgerton, M.I.T. **113:** Yaeger, DPI. **117:** Grunnitus Studios.

Chapter 4
136: Bojilova, DPI. **137:** The New York Public Library Picture Collection. **140:** Grunnitus Studios. **144:** (left) The Metropolitan Museum of Art, Murch Collection, Gift of Helen Miller Gould, 1910; (right) Peabody Museum, Harvard University, photograph by F. P. Orchard. **149:** The Metropolitan Museum of Art, New York, The Mr. and Mrs. Isaac D. Fletcher Collection, bequest of Isaac D. Fletcher, 1917. **151:** Bill Hedrich, Hedrich-Blessing.

Chapter 5
158: Victor Vasarely, *Oeta.* Number 4 from *Vasarely,* a portfolio of twelve serigraphs, 1959. Serigraph, $21\frac{13}{16} \times 14\frac{1}{2}''$. Collection, The Museum of Modern Art, New York. Gift of Madame Denise Rene. **159:** Philadelphia Museum of Art, Louise and Walter Arensberg Collection. **161:** Consulate General of Japan, New York. **162:** South African Consulate General. **168:** Courtesy, Dr. Owen Griffin, Naval Research Laboratories. **170:** (top) French Embassy Press Information; (bottom) Stock, Boston. **174:** Martin, DPI. **204:** Cindy L. Shauger.

Chapter 6
214: Piet Mondrian, *Composition in Red, Blue, and Yellow,* 1937–42. Oil on canvas, $23\frac{3}{4} \times 21\frac{7}{8}''$. The Sidney and Harriet Janis Collection, Gift to the Museum of Modern

Art, New York. **215:** Scala, EPA. **219:** Bettmann Archive. **220:** European American Music Distributors Corporation. **221:** The New York Public Library Picture Collection. **225:** Dennis Mansell. **239:** The New York Public Library (presented as a gift in 1932 by the Bliss and Herter families). **241:** The Elizabeth Sprague Coolidge Foundation Collection, The Library of Congress, Washington, D.C.

Chapter 7
242: Vincent van Gogh, *The Starry Night,* 1889. Oil on canvas, 29 × 36¼″. Collection, The Museum of Modern Art, New York. Acquired through the Lillie P. Bliss Bequest. **243:** Professor J. C. Hunsaker (from Gyorgy Kepes, *The New Landscape in Art and Science,* by permission of the author). **246:** The New York Public Library Picture Collection. **249:** (top) The Hispanic Society of America; (bottom) The New England Conservatory of Music, Boston, MA (presented by Mr. Eben D. Jordaon). **248:** Ministry of Information and Tourism, Madrid. **260:** Spanish National Tourist Office, New York.

Chapter 8
272: The Pierpont Morgan Library. **273:** Museo di S. Maria del Fiore, Firenze. **280:** Bayer. Staatsbibliothek, München. **282:** (left) Granger Collection; (right) Anderson, Art Resource. **285:** Granger Collection. **290:** Giraudon, Art Resource. **296:** Bayer. Staatsbibliothek, München.

Chapter 9
298: Granger Collection. **299:** © Kleinhempel, Hamburger Kunsthalle. **304:** Granger Collection. **308:** Bettmann Archive. **320:** Bettmann Archive. **323:** Granger Collection. **324:** Bettmann Archive.

Chapter 10
330: Bettmann Archive. **331:** Bettmann Archive. **336:** Scala, Art Resource. **339:** Knudsen, Taurus. **343:** Culver. **346:** Bettmann Archive.

Chapter 11
352: Musée Carnavalet, Bulloz. **353:** Ivan Masser. **357:** Bettmann Archive. **359:** Culver. **362:** Granger Collection. **368:** Harmonia Mundi, USA.

Chapter 12
376: The New York Public Library Picture Collection. **377:** *Igor Stravinsky* by Pablo Picasso. Copyright © S.P.A.D.E.M. Paris, 1974. **383:** Bettmann Archive. **417:** Bildarchiv Foto Marburg, Art Resource.

Chapter 13
422: Granger Collection. **423:** Bildarchiv Foto Marburg, Art Resource. **431:** John Herrick Jackson Music Library, Yale University. **436:** The Gertrude Clarke Whittall Foundation Collection, The Library of Congress, Washington, D.C.

Note: An attempt has been made to obtain permission from all suppliers of photographs used in this edition. Some sources have not been located, but permission will be requested from them upon notification to us of their ownership of the material.

Index of Composers and Works

Index of Subjects